Georges Rouault

Georges

Pierre Courthion

Rouault

Including a catalogue of works

prepared with the collaboration of

Isabelle Rouault

Harry N. Abrams, Inc. *Publishers* New York

Milton S. Fox, Editor

Library of Congress Catalog Card Number: 61-13855

Gravure colorplates printed in France by Draeger Frères, Montrouge
Black-and-white sections printed in Germany by DuMont Presse, Cologne
Bound in Holland by Van Rijmenam, The Hague

To the family of Georges Rouault

and especially to

Madame Georges Rouault and to Isabelle Rouault

who have been unceasingly helpful,

this book is respectfully dedicated

Table of Contents

ILLUSTRATIONS: BLACK-AND-WHITE SECTIONS

Landscape · 1913

List of Colorplates

Introduction

As I stand on the threshold of this work, I hesitate; I feel a certain difficulty in attacking so big a subject. For Rouault—and this will become more and more evident—touched upon all the problems of our time, left few questions unraised. Indeed, his work has overthrown conventional ideas and, by its own expressive, arresting presence, undermined dogmatic systems in art. It cannot be easily analyzed.

As with all attempts to return to the origins of a creative work, we must try to approximate the vision of this artist who, after three centuries of art conceived according to Renaissance poetics, has introduced us to another way of seeing—one that is not corporeal but spiritual. In fact, it is not unlike the profound vision of the Middle Ages, when painted things assumed the importance the artist conferred upon them in his picture, rather than that which is ordinarily theirs.

After Rouault's death, I went to his home in order to become acquainted with the place where he worked. I had often gone there to chat with him and to take notes for the present volume. Then, I would usually find him in the back room, wearing his little, white surgeon's cap and a generously cut dressing gown which he left open. But no one had ever been allowed in his atelier. Now, with his daughter Isabelle for guide, I entered into this retreat that, during his lifetime, had remained inviolate. Unlike most painters' studios, this large room is sunny. The windowpanes had been frosted, but Rouault, nevertheless, kept one pane clear, a small rectangle through which he could see time by the clock in the belfry of the Gare de Lyon and, when he felt like it, could follow the endless coming and going of cars and people in the large semicircular approach to the station.

Nothing had changed since his death. Behind a gray curtain, the canvases were still there, ready for the further work he had planned for them (he used chalk to mark the "corrections" to be made), and his tools of the trade seemed ready for the next work session.

Rouault painted with his canvas or paper laid out flat on a table upon which there were piles of used paint tubes. His son had carved a broad crescent into the table, in order to make his task easier. Rouault tried out his colors on old platters from Metthey's, daubing them first on one side, then on the other—occasionally making some lovely things. He rarely used his palette, however, and mixed his colors on china plates when he didn't squirt the paint directly from the tube onto the canvas.

I was now embarked on a long voyage through time, with an entire life, an entire *œuvre*, to traverse. As a preliminary, I began to examine on the wall the portrait of Rouault that had been painted by his friend Léon Lehmann, a former classmate under Moreau, at the Beaux-Arts. Then I turned to the less known, less emphatic, but much more alive sketch that hung opposite it; one of the best existing likenesses of Rouault. And I recognized in it the painter whose work, in this day of triumphant science, is a reminder of an inner world that eludes both inquiry and appraisal.

1. Birth and Apprenticeship

Georges Rouault was born on the 27th of May, 1871, at 51, rue de la Vilette,[1] near the Buttes-Chaumont, in the Belleville quarter of Paris. It was at the time of the Commune, and government troops from Versailles were bombarding the northern part of the city. A shell (intended, doubtless, for the last Fédérés du Père-Lachaise), having struck a wall of the house just as Marie-Louise Rouault began to feel the first pangs of childbirth, she was carried on an improvised stretcher to the cellar. Here she gave birth to a son, Georges Henri. His grandfather Champdavoine, arriving home under a shower of shells,[2] called out: "Are you all dead?" And the grandmother answered: "No, there's even one more of us."

Although Georges Rouault was reluctant to speak of his mother, he felt unusual affection for her. He told me that he had kept his first composition paper entitled: "A Lady's First White Hair." His father, a Breton from Montfort, in the Île-et-Vilaine *département* was a working cabinetmaker. He had been employed by Pleyel, the piano manufacturer, as finisher and varnisher, and for him, wood was alive. "Oh, these women!" he would exclaim when his wife opened a drawer too brusquely. "They don't realize how they make wood suffer!" He was a great reader of Lamennais, whose accurate understanding of the labor question he admired.

The real "character" of the family, however, the one who seems to have stood out most clearly in Rouault's memory, was his maternal grandfather. Alexandre Champdavoine (Rouault's first entries in the Salon were signed Rouault-Champdavoine) had arrived in Paris at the age of eleven. After working as an errand boy in some sort of legal office, he had been engaged as head of a mail car, and this permitted him to travel. On Sundays, he would walk along the quays of the Seine with his grandson, in search of reproductions of Manet's and Courbet's works, which he pinned on his walls between busts of Racine and Corneille. "I still have a copy of *Orlando Furioso* which he copied in ink from beginning to end, in Philipon de la Madeleine's translation," Rouault said, adding: "Not bad, eh? Nobody would do that today."

Champdavoine lived with his other daughters, Georges' aunts, on the rue de Sévigné, opposite the Carnavalet Museum. "He was an impecunious man," Rouault told me, "but he had great courage. He used to sing a lot of songs and I recall that the druggist's son came to ask his advice about his thesis."[3]

Georges often spent the night with his relatives in the rue de Sévigné, where he had been taken as soon as he was born, during the fighting. Indeed, it was there that he was to make his first drawing, in chalk, on the red tiled kitchen floor. "I started at the age of five, with my grandfather's parrot," he recalled. "But I can't say whether it was out of some physical need, or because it gave the old gentleman pleasure." At this time his aunts were painting Boucher cupids on large porcelain vases, or fans for Duvelleroy. "He'll end up with his head in a noose," they said jokingly of their nephew. "I held my own against them. When they tried to take me visiting, I hid under the bed. They would call in the *concierge*, a big strapping fellow with shoulders like a wrestler. But I kicked him from under the bed, and they couldn't budge me."

All his life, Rouault remembered the scenes of his childhood. At the time he lived there, his "Belleville village" was not yet an *arrondissement* of Paris, and old stud horses were still peacefully pulling a little omnibus that held the record for slowness. But this was the quarter he was born in, a place he identified with his father's trade, and Rouault always spoke of it with feeling, applying to himself the description of "wan child of the suburban districts of toil and pain."

Not wanting to entrust his son's education to Catholics, Alexandre Rouault enrolled him in a Protestant school, but soon withdrew him because of a punishment he considered too severe, and put the boy in a public school. Georges passed his high-school examinations. Then, his grandfather died, following an accident, and the boy was obliged to earn his own living. At the age of fourteen, he was apprenticed to a stained-glass artist.

He worked for Tamoni from 1885 to 1890, then for Hirsch. "At that time," he told me, "we used to eat at old Mme. Noblet's, and sometimes there were cockroaches in the fried potatoes. I was paid ten sous [then about 15 cents] per week. My task consisted of doing just about everything as well as watching the bake-ovens and sorting out little pieces of glass that fell from the windows under repair." Among other things, Hirsch had copied fragments of old windows which Rouault never tired of looking at during his lunch hour, though the rest of the day was passed in "repellent, stupid, modern, mechanical work." But it was paradise to spend "that hour in the midst of copies of parts of works that had been well conceived and created as 'glass mosaics,' and not as paintings on glass, after the fashion of the time, with modeling, relief, and lighting."[4]

> "*Au verre si franc d'aloi*
> *Je me coupai souvent les doights*"[5]

[On the pure and precious glass I often cut my fingers]

14

Thus it was that beautiful colors, "dull or flamboyant reds, golden yellows, ultramarines like those of early antiquity"[6] passed through the "frail, reverent hands" of the young apprentice, and set him to dreaming. He would have liked to work with colors that were as "pure as flame," restore its former splendor to the art of the stained-glass window, instead of being obliged to cater to the taste of his epoch, which aimed at realistic illustration—the *tableau vivant*—in everything, whether tapestry, frescoes, or stained glass. "I dream of the rose window in Chartres that, to my shame and sorrow, I have not seen!" he wrote Suarès, in 1925, "but my eyes have looked upon other radiant windows." And he added, thinking of his great desire to paint, that he was as "unhappy and alone as Moses in search of the Promised Land."[7]

Rouault felt almost intimidated by certain very old glass pieces with which he was entrusted: "At times it seemed to me that I was unworthy of such fine company." As Jacques Maritain tells us, "When he had to go far to deliver a parcel, his employer gave him three sous for the bus. The boy would do his errand on foot, keeping the three sous to buy paints, but in order not to cheat his employer of a single minute, he started out with the bus and ran the rest of the way without stopping, so as to arrive at the same time as the bus."[8]

On Sundays he went to the Louvre. He also enrolled in evening classes and began to draw with enthusiasm. He himself has told of this second, parallel "apprenticeship," that took place in the same ateliers where, before him, Rodin had studied as a young man.

"Tall, thin, and emaciated, I used to cross Paris about six o'clock in the evening, to go to the School of Decorative Arts, in the rue de l'Ecole de Médecine. In an hour and a half I had to go on foot, from the rue Gauthey, near the Porte de Clichy, where I worked, to the rue du Pré-aux-Clercs, where I was living at the time, and then, after a hasty meal, still on the run, to the rue de l'Ecole de Médecine, hoping the doors would still be open, because they closed at half-past seven.

"The time spent and the harsh compulsion were more than compensated for, however, by the great joy it gave me to draw two hours a day, especially once I could work from live models and from the antique, after having left behind me the drawing from engravings."[9]

The students at the evening classes were seated on tiered benches, or in the basement. "The place was infested with rats that occasionally strayed over to the bread crumbs we used for picking out the highlights on our charcoal drawings."[10]

Rouault's first real drawings date from this time. They are studies of the nude, such as everybody makes. But those of this young artist already bear the mark of a strong personality.[11] The authoritative quality of his line reveals a very sure, one might even say, bold talent, for Rouault never had in his drawing the gentle, meandering charm of the type of artist whose aim is to make things that are pretty and agreeable to the eye. This student, for whom art was still the Land of Canaan ("It will be till I die," Rouault used to say), was struck with admiration when he first saw a Forain drawing. "With mere black and white," he said, "Forain awakened in the lad that I was then, a light, an intuition of something rare that, after the stint of carefully made drawings produced during those evening classes, made me take hope again."[12]

At that time Rouault kept very much to himself. At nineteen, he hadn't the leisure of the young men from well-to-do families who collected about the Pigalle Art Theatre. Nor, probably, had he even time to read the first manifesto, published in the review *Art et Critique*, by a young theoretician, only one year his senior, the painter Maurice Denis. This manifesto contained the following short sentence that later became famous: "We must remember that a picture, before it has become a horse on a battlefield, a naked woman, or any other representational subject, is essentially a flat surface covered with colors that are arranged in a certain order." But Maurice Denis was already an ardent adept of Gauguin's and Emile Bernard's kind of stylization, whereas Rouault was still seeking his way. A decisive event was his firm refusal of an offer made by Albert Besnard, an official painter of great renown then, who had asked him to make some stained-glass windows for the Ecole de Pharmacie. Rouault had other ambitions: he wanted to express himself, to paint in complete freedom. It was, in fact, for this reason that he had in the first place chosen the trade that brought him closest to the painter's art.

On December 3, 1890, young Rouault enrolled at the Ecole des Beaux-Arts, where his first *patron*, or teacher, was Elie Delaunay,[13] a painter with Classical and Renaissance leanings, who had painted the *Plague of Rome*, a picture that I recall having seen in the Luxembourg Museum. Rouault said of him: "He was a *patron* who didn't like very much to see us paint, with the result that our little sheets of paper remained on our easels the entire week. Finally, we grew tired of sitting perched up on high stools, doing nothing, or just dozing a bit, so we left."[14]

Soon Delaunay, who was very ill, disappeared from the scene. He "had himself replaced by another professor, or by a titular *chef d'atelier*, as, for instance, Gérôme, a handsome man with imposing white hair and the manner of a former cavalry officer, who was usually to be seen with his friend Frémiet, the sculptor."[15]

On September 5, 1891, the students learned that Elie Delaunay had died.[16] Before his death, he had requested his fellow members of the Institute to name Gustave Moreau as his successor.

16

1   Georges Rouault

2 Alexandre Rouault, the artist's father.
   Pencil sketch, June 1899

3 Marie-Louise Rouault, née Champdavoine.
   Pencil sketch, May 1899

4 Rouault's father. Pen drawing by Léon
   Lehmann, about 1905

5   Rouault at the age of four. Portrait on
    porcelain, by his aunt, Henriette
    Champdavoine

6   Rouault's mother, about 1912

7 The Atelier Gustave Moreau, about 1895

1. Georges Rouault
2. Albert Marquet
3. Henri Matisse
4. René Piot
5. Simon Bussy
6. Paul Baignères
7. Henri Evenepoel
8. Milcendeau
9. Antonin Bourbon
10. Léon Bonhomme

8   Portrait of Gustave Moreau.
Lithograph from "Souvenirs Intimes," 1926

9   "Salomé," by Gustave Moreau. Musée Gustave Moreau,
Paris

10   "The Council of the Rats," by Gustave Moreau.
Watercolor sketch for La Fontaine's "Fables". Musée
Gustave Moreau, Paris

21

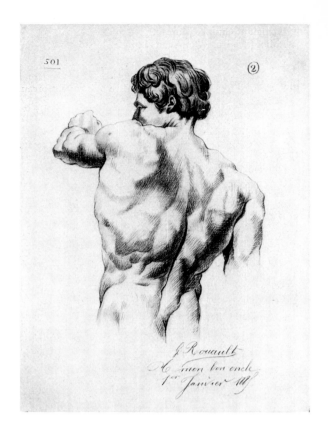

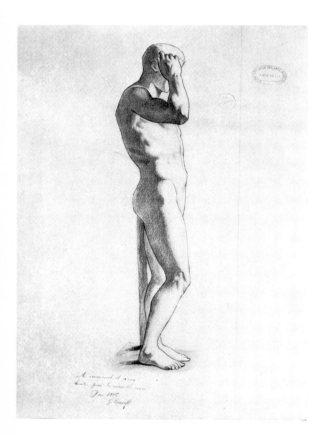

11   Drawing. École Nationale des Arts Décoratifs, Paris

12   Drawing, 1885. École Nationale des Arts Décoratifs, Paris

13   Drawing, 1886. École Nationale des Arts Décoratifs, Paris

14 Portrait of Huysmans. Lithograph from "Souvenirs Intimes," 1926

15 Portrait of Léon Bloy. Lithograph from "Souvenirs Intimes," 1926

16 Portrait of André Suarès. Lithograph from "Souvenirs Intimes," 1926

23

17 Rouault, his wife, and three of their children, Isabelle, Michel, and Geneviève. Versailles, 1914

18 Rouault, about 1930

19 Portrait of Ambroise Vollard, 1925.
    Drawing in India ink

20   Rouault, 1943

21   Rouault with his grandsons, Patrick,
Frédéric, and JeanYves. Paris, March 1943

22   Rouault. Paris, March 1943

23 Profile of Rouault. Ink drawing
   by his daughter Isabelle

24 Rouault and his daughter Isabelle. Paris, 1951

25 Rouault and his grandson Olivier.
   Piazza San Marco, Venice, 1948

26 Rouault in Venice, 1948

27   Rouault's hands

28   Rouault in his studio. July 1953

29 Rouault in his studio. July 1953

30 Rouault in his studio. July 1953

31 On a Seine embankment: Rouault, his daughter Geneviève,
    his son-in-law Dr. Nouaille, and his grandson Olivier

32   Rouault and his grandson Olivier on the quay. Paris, 1955

33   Rouault and his daughter Agnès in the park at Sceaux, 1955

34   Rouault visiting with his son Michel and two of his grandchildren,
Marie-Hélène and Olivier. Châtellerault, 1953

35   Rouault. Paris, 1955

36 Rouault. Paris, 1955

2. Gustave Moreau: Inspiration and Guide

Gustave Moreau's nomination by the administrative council of the Beaux-Arts became official in 1892.[1] He was sixty-six years old at the time, having been born in Paris (at 7, rue des Saints-Pères) on April 6, 1826. His father was an architect and he himself had been a pupil of the architect Picot while studying at the Beaux-Arts, where he failed the Prix de Rome examination. He had been particularly influenced by the work of Théodore Chassériau, to whose untimely end he alluded in a disturbing, academic painting, *Death and the Young Man*, 1865, in which his talent is hidden under a cheap finish.

Having made his painter's tour with Delaunay and Degas in Italy, Moreau entered the 1852 Salon with a *Pietà* that the Goncourt brothers, just beginning their careers as art critics, had remarked upon in *L'Eclair*. In the 1864 Salon, his *Oedipus and the Sphinx* had made a strong impression, and people saw in it the work of a painter who, with one bound, had returned to the great myths of antiquity that had been neglected since Millet and Courbet. Thus Castagnary, who defended realism, called this painting an "archaic daub," "a step backward." Then—and we should not forget this—"just as the 'slice-of-life' epoch began, Moreau had produced what he himself called a 'piece-of-nature.' Long before the Symbolists, he revolted against all that was prosaic and matter of fact. Not that he rejected reality, or was himself lost in the clouds . . . his lyricism was based on factual data."[2] Manet was greatly attracted by him, in fact, but objected that "he takes us back to what is incomprehensible, when what we want is for everything to be understood."[3]

Gustave Moreau arrived just in time to enrich with his highly colored vision the current poetic atmosphere, which was one of sensation and sensuality, characteristic of the movement we call Symbolism. His name was associated with the name of Odilon Redon as that of master to pupil, and his theories delighted the

33

enthusiasts of *Salammbô*, and the *Poèmes antiques*, who also read Edouard Schuré's books and the *Revue wagnérienne* (1885–86).

"Interest in the past, in addition to the popularity of archaeology, had brought with it the dangerous charm of historic revival."[4] Jeweled arts—precious stones and metals—being the style at the time, Moreau's art, in which "the cold gleam of jewels contrasts with the pathos of the sentiments expressed,"[5] also conformed to this style.

In 1876, he could still be seen, with Degas and Clémenceau, behind the scenes at the Opéra; he was also a habitué of Princess Mathilde's salon. Then, one fine day, after an exhibition at Goupil's (1886) of a series of watercolors and gouaches based on La Fontaine's *Fables*, he withdrew from society into the ivory tower of a private house in the Notre-Dame-de-Lorette quarter, to live the life of a bachelor, or lay monk, with his aged mother who was both blind and deaf but whom he adored. From her, apparently, was derived his entire conception of the female sex. When Moreau was elected to the Institut de France in 1889, Degas remarked that Gustave Moreau was "a hermit who knew the schedules of trains."[6] (Degas, it will be recalled, left a little portrait of Moreau showing him—an enemy of any delineation of his person—in an uneasy pose, leaning on the back of a chair with a somewhat haunted look.) In any case, Moreau was a man who suffered from "an unbridled imagination and a sense of criticism that amounted almost to a mania." In other words, he had all the qualities required to make an extraordinary professor. And the fact is that his influence, at the time when Rouault worked under him, made itself felt in all the ateliers, even to the esoteric Nabi and Rosicrucian groups which, at that epoch, were inspired by the prophetic declarations of Sérusier and Sâr Péladan. Alluding, doubtless, to *Trophées*, the poems by Herédia (1893), Jean Lorrain even went so far as to say that the writers and poets were also "enamored of slender Salomes dripping with jewels, and Muses carrying cadaverous, decapitated heads."[7]

When J.-K. Huysmans wrote of Moreau he outdid himself. In his most elaborate manner, he had spoken, in *Certains* (1889), of Moreau's "goddesses astride sea-horses, streaking the dying clouds with the lapis lazuli of their wings," and of his "tiaraed feminine idols, standing on thrones, the steps of which were submerged under wondrous flowers." To Huysmans, Gustave Moreau seems to have been a soul exhausted by the solitary ideas and secret thoughts of a woman "withdrawn into herself, muttering the sacramental words of obscure prayers, or insidious incitements to sacrilege and debauchery."[8] It is certain, in any case, that in what he himself called his "Cyclopean gynaeceum," Moreau envisioned woman in a sublimation that "partook of Messalina and the imperial prostitute,"[9] for he was a strong mixture—unconscious, of course—of faith and perversity. And yet, "this subtle Byzantine mind was not a sickly flower of the modern neurosis that marked the end of an artistic endeavor approaching its exhaustion."[10] Through reaction against the excesses of realism, Moreau sought to "lead nature back to its spiritual origins,"[11] and it was in this role that he was to exert a salutary influence. His initiation was not the same, therefore, as that of Schuré, Jean Lahore, or Péladan, but rather that of a sound, healthy art fed by springs of daring and faith.

34

The reader is asked to understand the importance that will be attributed in the present volume to the influence of this artist and teacher who trained, in addition to Rouault, some of the best painters of our time and, himself, stood for all that was brilliant in the history of painting from the close of the Second Empire until the end of the nineteenth century. Should the amount of space devoted to him seem disproportionate in this work, it only reflects my conversations with Rouault, who talked interminably of Moreau—to such an extent, in fact, that it seemed as though he felt his artist's career would not have assumed concrete form without the instruction of this extraordinary teacher.

Moreau conceived his painting according to epic cycles. He needed centaurs and sphinxes and heroes. He was also somewhat affected by the Wagnerian imagination, whose icy mists he mingled with the atmosphere of the Vedas. For Schuré, who was the high priest of initiation into the world of haziness, Moreau's winged monsters seemed to say: "All ye who know the signs and sense the soul of things, enter; enter into the caverns of passion, and ascend, through dream forests and dream lakes, to the snowy heights of pure idea."[12]

But there were also a number of other critics and art historians to sing his praises: Ernest Chesneau, Maxime du Camp, Philippe de Chennevières, as well as Gustave Larroumet, who had been Moreau's sponsor at the Beaux-Arts; they all defended this rather controversial recluse, who "refused to let the majority of his pictures, which he kept retouching, leave his atelier," and who opened his door to no one, "inviting those who were curious to go look at his canvases in private collections."[13]

Moreau was a great talker who shared with his students both his thoughts and the books he was reading. I am unable to say whether he spoke to them of Henri Bergson, a young philosopher of thirty, whose *Essai sur les données immédiates de la conscience* had just appeared; or of *Tête d'Or*, a medieval drama by a twenty-one-year-old poet, Paul Claudel, that had appeared under the imprint of the Librairie de l'Art Indépendant. But he undoubtedly did talk to them of Verlaine, and of Schuré's book *Les Grands Initiés* (1889) which, at the time, satisfied the momentary disquiet of the younger generation; perhaps, too, of Jean Moréas, who had published the Symbolist manifesto,[14] and of the avant garde critics, Gustave Geffroy and Roger-Marx.

In 1892, in the world of painting, there was plenty to talk about. The Sâr Péladan, who would have liked to see Moreau become the "sage of a new ideal of art, a hawker in shining helmet announcing the good news,"[15] opened the first Rosicrucian Salon, in the Durand-Ruel Gallery. There was an exhibition in Paris by Burne-Jones, one of the English Pre-Raphaelites endorsed by Ruskin. Puvis de Chavannes, Gustave Moreau's rival, decorated the Paris Hôtel de Ville in a symbolism that was as bare as Moreau's was richly adorned. "At that time," Rouault said, "Puvis had a stimulating effect on the younger men; then, later, they began to look at the originals of the works he had drawn upon, and they became better acquainted with the early fresco painters."[16] There was also Carrière who, at the age of forty-three, had had his first exhibition. Rouault was moved by Carrière's portrait of poor Lélian, and the paintings that evoked the moment when his "cherished dream of infinite tenderness and kindness" had evaporated, while "the humblest and most moving features of the home became transfigured."[17] But it was, above all, the man himself he admired in Carrière, the man and his generous, open mind. In less idealistic circles, those that formed outside the school, people were talking about Toulouse-Lautrec, who had painted *Au Moulin Rouge*. They also mentioned the name of Pierre Bonnard, a young painter already known in the circles of the *Revue Blanche* (founded one year after the *Mercure de France*), who shared an atelier in the Place Pigalle with Vuillard, Maurice Denis, and Lugné Poë, at the same time that Emile Bernard, Verkade, and Sérusier, the Nabi leader, had settled in Pont-Aven, following Gauguin.

Rouault and his companions were probably talking about all these things when Gustave Moreau received his appointment as *chef d'atelier*. There must also have been a certain amount of discussion at the Beaux-Arts of Odilon Redon's collection of lithographs, *Dans le Rêve*. (With Seurat and Signac, Redon had been one of the founders of the Salon des Indépendants, which was already in its ninth year.) I don't know whether or not Rouault read the reviews put out by the younger generation: *La Pléiade*, *Le Décadent*, *La Vogue*, *Le Symboliste*. On his way to the Beaux-Arts, the people he met were apt to be "solid citizens" such as, for instance, the editor of the *Revue des Deux Mondes*, whom he met frequently. "Because of his pallor," Rouault wrote, "Brunetière looked as though he had come out of the catacombs. Then, walking in the opposite direction on the same Boulevard Saint-Germain, would come that virulent little man, Floquet,[18] who, with the gesture of a bully on vacation, would poke his cane at the ground from time to time, as he headed jauntily for the Chamber of Deputies. As for myself," Rouault added, "I usually made an about-face in the direction of the Poussin and Puget busts that stand on either side of the rue Bonaparte entrance to the Beaux-Arts."[19]

Inside the school, Moreau was "courteously, but categorically, opposed to his colleagues" whose pupils "produced a heavy, lusterless type of painting that lacked vibration."[20] Although he belonged to the group of men "who had been deeply marked by the evil of literary painting, and were no longer able to conceive of forms otherwise than as bearers of intentions and ideas,"[21] he was nevertheless able to perceive the talent of such men as Manet and Degas. (The latter, however, riddled him with darts: "Moreau knows it all," he would say, half in banter, half in admiration, and Moreau would retort by saying of his friend: "Can all the painting of our epoch be summed up in a dancer's ankle?") Being a "genuinely simple" man, Moreau was on friendly terms with his students, so that "he was never called *cher Maître*." Nor was he the least bit narrow-minded or partial in his judgments. He even went so far as to urge his pupils to go and look at Lautrec's work, which was to be seen in a gallery on rue Lafitte. "There's a picture there," he told them, "that looks as if it had been painted with absinthe."[22]

This, then, was the personality of Georges Rouault's instructor at the Beaux-Arts. Every Wednesday and Saturday, Moreau came to do the correcting. He was "first to arrive and last to leave. At times he would be seen in the Cour du Mûrier, or in some corner, sketching away from an antique cast. When he spoke, the newcomers ran after him, begging him: 'Monsieur, please let us have your corrections!'"

In addition to two lithographs, Rouault left the following portrait of Moreau, who had been the first to encourage him: "Small in size, with keen eyes, he was well-groomed, almost a dandy. Some people compared him to a very erudite Latin scholar. . . . And, indeed, a certain spiritual radiance in his delicate features caused him to be termed highbrow—quite erroneously, however—by persons of judgment who, although they had known and associated with him, had occasionally failed miserably to understand him.

"He used to talk frankly and good-naturedly about himself, admitting that he had been a dunce at school and that, at twenty, he had liked some very bad painting, as well as Aubert's music; he had nevertheless had a weakness for Delacroix.

"Today, thirty years later, I could name a Beaux-Arts attendant who remembers perfectly his intelligent face and the friendly questions he used to put to the simplest sort of men. It was always with a smile, the way people still know how to smile in the Île-de-France, in order both to show and to hide the secret emotion one feels at hearing the humblest artisan, workman, or peasant speak with authority about his own work, to even the highest type of intellectual."[23]

"So you like your artist's materials," Moreau said, looking at the sketches Rouault tremblingly showed him on one of his first visits. "Well, well, I wish you luck . . . you'll see, you'll see! . . ." And Rouault continued: "We had the pleasure of having an instructor who dared to say something else besides such remarks as: 'That foot is too small,' or 'Your painted figure is at least eight heads high,' etc. . . ."[24]

Matisse once described the atmosphere of the atelier to me. "The students were divided into several groups: those who were working for official honors and those who worked independently; others, the ones who got discouraged, didn't work much; and lastly, there were those who really worked well, enthusiasts such as Rouault and Maxence. The latter were placed at the back. In the middle were a few independents and, near the door, the rowdies." (While Matisse was telling me this, in 1941, in a restaurant in Lyons, he began to draw on the tablecloth with the tip of his knife, to show the plan of the atelier and the positions of his own and Rouault's easels.)[25]

"It was a curious atelier," he went on, "with one very quiet corner, while in the other there was an incredible hullabaloo organized especially to annoy the others. I, myself, was between the two. Rouault turned his back on Maxence who, already then, in speaking of the Institut de France, said: 'No matter what you do, you can't make your way without it!' Rouault was a pale, thin chap with fiery red hair. He kept an eye on Maxence who, when he began to put the finishing touches on his study, would take great pains with certain details, particularly with the whites of the eyes. This was the moment Rouault had been waiting for. When Maxence was ready to paint his highlights in the eyes, he would begin to jump and stamp and howl, while Maxence, still holding his brush in the air, protested weakly: 'Rouault, you're annoying me!' "[26]

Rouault fairly worshiped Rembrandt, which was well known in the atelier. As a result of this admiration for the painter of *The Flayed Beef*, the following bit of doggerel—a crude jingle about the source of Rouault's pigments and style— was dedicated to him:

> *Monsieur Rouault*
> *Fait sur son tableau*
> *Et avec du jus de pipi*
> *Croit allier Rembrandt à Signorelli*

At that time, Gustave Moreau's atelier was the rival of the Bonnat and Gérôme ateliers. "Generally, the professors remained silent, and Bonnat even looked at his students' canvases with a certain disdain, while Gérôme tried to discourage his by telling them that they were all 'sure to starve to death!' But Moreau took teaching seriously. He talked to his class a lot about the great masters and about their high-mindedness. He also combatted realism and stimulated the imagination of his students."[27]

Matisse entered the atelier in 1895, one year after the Belgian Evenepoel who has left a very vivid account of it in his correspondence. "All his students are his friends," he wrote of Moreau, "and one feels that he is attached to them. When he enters the room he gives a glance at the entire lot of easels before which the students are standing, and always makes some general remark. Then he goes from one to the other, never omitting a single student."[28]

Moreau arrived for corrections in a "skullcap" and "soiled white smock." "Art," he used to say, "can lead to religion—and to real religion, the kind that elevates the soul."[29] He had a horror of publicity; he would not be photographed . . . . He knew all of Wagner's operas by heart."[30]

The monitor for the atelier was a slender, lithe, easy-mannered man named Léon Bonhomme.[31] He wore a well-trimmed beard and reminded one of the seventeenth-century copyists who made those grotesque little paintings known as *bambocciades*. It has sometimes been stated that he influenced Rouault. "This is quite wrong," a former student said, "and we ought to insist on the truth to the contrary."[32] Bonhomme made some paintings in a manner that resembled Rouault's, especially from 1906 on; that is, from the time of Rouault's first "Prostitutes."[33] In fact, these imitations were even alluded to by the press.[34] However, Bonhomme copied Rouault out of admiration, in the same way that he copied Cézanne, Toulouse-Lautrec, and even Leonardo da Vinci.[35] He made his frankly derivative paintings in all honesty, and without material profit. That was his way of being an artist, for he was quite aware that he lacked personality. "I'd rather copy Cézanne than make a bad Léon Bonhomme," he said himself.[36] Rouault, it will be recalled, remained friends to the last with his former fellow student, after

38

whose death an effort was made to exploit his derivative paintings.[37] When he painted his imitations, Bonhomme used to make a bet. "Hand me your watch!" (He would take it and lay it on the table.) "In three minutes, you'll have a Henner." And three minutes later, there was a nude woman, lying on a panther skin.

But now we must discuss Gustave Moreau's teachings, in this atelier he called his "laboratory."[38] When the students brought him indifferent work he called it torpid. "For him, painting was style, matter, arabesque, and imagined transformations of color which, according to him, had to be 'thought about, dreamed about, imagined.' He spurned painters who 'paint with their hands.' 'Learn to like to think a bit,' he said to his students. 'Don't be afraid to sit down on your chair from time to time in the evening, and let yourself go in thought.' "[39]

Contrary to Beaux-Arts rules, which usually followed the "Ingres" method (Ingres had said: "Drawing is the probity of art"), Moreau made his students paint directly. "Come along," he would say, "paint."[40] He might have added, recalling Cézanne's sturdy example: "When you fail at a thing, you start over again."[41] At times he hesitated between the desire to force his own tastes on his students, and his instinctive knowledge of how angry this would make Gérôme, Bonnat, and all the other Bouguereaus. Finally he blurted out: "Yes, we'll exhibit it, nevertheless! We'll show them something else besides Léonides defending Thermopylae, and Aeneas carrying his father, Anchises. . . . Ah! the helmet!..."[42]

"Don't struggle with nature over 'objective truth,' " Moreau used to say, "and don't think you can obtain the same effects that light does."[43] What such a teacher meant to his pupils, the value of what he gave them, as well as his shortcomings, was summed up by Matisse: "Moreau," he said, "did not set us on the right roads, but off the roads. He disturbed our complacency. With him, each one could acquire the techniques that corresponded to his own temperament. It should also be said, however, that he created aspirations in the minds of those young people that did not always correspond to their possibilities. He could be caustic at times. For instance, he said one day, as he was correcting a sketch, 'That drapery is awful, it's made out of a dish towel; it looks like the draperies of certain artists who use bed sheets for draperies'—this was aimed at Puvis de Chavannes—and he sent his student to look at the drapery on an antique cast in the glassed-in courtyard. He said, too (and this was less helpful): 'When you are doing something, try to envisage how Da Vinci would have treated the same subject, and immediately you'll rise above banality.' "[44] This tendency to take refuge in the past angered Cézanne, and once, when Vollard praised Moreau's pedagogical competence, Cézanne is said to have set his glass down so hard that he broke it, protesting that "there were no good teachers."[45]

Although Moreau admired Carpaccio, Botticelli, and the followers of Leonardo, he nevertheless considered it useless to imitate the great masters. Together with Degas and Renoir, he regretted the decrease in painting skill. "We may deplore today," he used to say, "the absence of their remarkable technical perfection. People talk of the masterpieces that young apprentices used to make in the medieval guilds. Suppose they did. Does anybody think that the surroundings, the atmosphere, the way they lived and felt, are the same; or that even those who retire into an ivory tower are able to escape the atmosphere of our century entirely, if they're sensitive?"[46] Here we see that Moreau occasionally indulged in what today we should call "self-analysis."

"Gustave Moreau," Rouault recalled, "would tell us to meet him in the Louvre, in front of the Poussins and Lorrains, at the same time that he believed in the modernists. ('There are moments,' he used to say, 'when you would give your all for a bit of Rembrandt's mud.') He urged us to study certain very pure, very stark primitives, rather than some of the more conventional Raphaels."[47] "Work standing up," he would say, "take the sketches in your hands, and work fast, as though in ten minutes the attendants were going to call out: 'Closing time!' "[48] "At the Louvre, we tried by every possible means to understand the actual substance of the paintings. We would feel the grain of the canvas and examine in detail how the paint was applied: the different objects, the glazes, the transitions from light to shadow. We even used a magnifying glass."[49] How they analyzed, how they studied the works of the great masters! "But don't neglect the others," Moreau used to say, "the works that, although they are not perfect, are very unusual: there is sometimes more to learn from them, for they contain a ferment." "The copies we made were used as the basis for endless discussion. . . . When we left the Museum, outside on the quay the light around the clock tower of Saint-Germain-l'Auxerrois was soft, and more blue than a mild spring sky. We would talk of poetics or of material vision; we walked home toward the Quai Saint-Michel, near Notre-Dame."[50]

"Gustave Moreau took teaching very seriously. He kindled the imagination of his pupils. Among them were some who were working toward the Prix de Rome, and therefore they did everything that was required so that they would be awarded the medal that led to it. He didn't like these students very much, at the same time that he corrected their work. But his preference went to those who worked independently."[51] "Keep on working in your own corner," he would tell them, "you have found what you were looking for, you are yourselves."[52] And Rouault recalled having heard him say, with a slight note of melancholy, "I am the bridge over which certain of you will cross."[53]

In this way Moreau "aroused the minds of his pupils and opened windows for them that gave onto themselves."[54] He was a dissatisfied man who communicated the fire of genius to the young people about him without himself possessing the gift, the instinct, that would have permitted him to make something out of nothing. For he felt obliged to embellish everything."[55] "Let's paint buses," Marquet exclaimed, by way of protest against the excessive symbolism that he felt threatened him. And in spite of everything, as Rouault said, "even though Moreau's dream is of epic and historical painting, he would nevertheless have been happy, in the presence of an unmistakable painterly talent, to see it turn toward the legendary."[56] "At the Indépendants," he would say, "I see whores and pimps in bars, writhing, swimming in vice, cheap wine, and tobacco smoke, in an atmosphere of cynicism."[57] However, this did not keep him from upholding Rouault, who was his favorite pupil, in the latter's efforts to discover a more direct reality,[58] efforts in which Moreau sensed, nevertheless, a certain spirituality. One day, Rouault showed him a picture of two butchers cutting each other's throats (a canvas sometimes inaccurately called *The Workyard*). "I shan't go so far as to say that he congratulated me," Rouault writes, "but he told me, 'You are a painter, whatever you do.'"[59] This *patron* understood intuitively the poetic insight that was beginning to form in his disciple's style. "Rouault attained to poetic heights in pictorial form. Colored pigment was converted into strong spiritual vibrations, and both his pen and pencil drawings were tightly constructed, with firmness and taste. Certain landscapes in watercolors too, in their dreamlike fluidity, possessed really marvelous distinction."[60]

Gustave Moreau, "the little man with the extraordinarily keen, kind, and intelligent eyes," stimulated Rouault. He often talked to him "of Baudelaire, Nerval, Flaubert . . . of Pascal, the recluses of Port-Royal, also of Nicole, of Racine, of Vigny."[61] He wrote to him. He appreciated Rouault's individuality. For "Rouault was not a good student, according to Beaux-Arts standards. He did not work, as the others did, only in order to get through. He saw beyond the pale whites of his model's eyes."[62] One day Moreau said to him: "For those of you who are poor, art must really be deep-rooted; I tremble, especially when, like yourself, they are unable to do anything but assert their own particular vision. My poor boy, I can see you now, with your uncompromising nature, your desperate eagerness, your love of all that is materially rare, your essential qualities; I can see you becoming more and more of a recluse. Art for you is serious, sober and, in its essence, religious. And everything you do will bear this stamp."[63]

But, one might ask, having been created under the guidance of such a teacher, what were Rouault's early works like? "I started," he tells us, "under the influence of Rembrandt, which did not keep me, however, from liking Delacroix." Moreau had advised the young painter to compete for the Prix de Rome on the theme of The Ordeal of Samson, in 1893. Rouault started working for the competition on March 31, when he asked to have an anatomical plaster cast delivered to his little cubicle at the school, along with a plaster head from Trajan's Column.[64] On May 4, the Director of the school sent his candidate's request to the Secrétaire Perpétuel of the Académie des Beaux-Arts. On May 13, Count Henri Delaborde informed the Director that "at its meeting of May 6, the Academy had authorized the painting candidate, Monsieur Rouault, to have brought into his cubicle, plaster casts made from Trajan's Column and the anatomical figure."[65] The preliminary sketches made for this canvas, which is in the Los Angeles County Museum, already show a keen sensitivity. The expression is accurate and the drawing both supple and compact. There is nothing about it, in any case, that would suggest an over-precise craftsmanship à la David! This, for the Beaux-Arts, was almost heresy. "My *Samson*," said Rouault, "with all its servants' and soldiers' mugs looking like those of Jerome Bosch,[66] frightened the jury. One professor even shook his fist at the canvas."

42

The prize was awarded, as expected, to a composition by one Mitrecey which, although it lacked originality, showed academic competence. Rouault's painting was exhibited at the school with those of the other competitors, among whom were Trigoulet, Déchenaud, and Maxence.

On February 6, 1894, Rouault was awarded the second medal in the Concours Fortin, in Ivry (he had already competed the year before, but he got no further than the second stage of the competition). The subject was Coriolanus in the House of Tullius; and there is really great decision in this little painting, quite powerfully done in the style of the Tintoretto school.[67] It contains a purple and an enamel blue that give us a foretaste of what Rouault was to do later.

In July of the same year, Rouault won the first prize in the Concours Chenavard for the work that really marks the starting point of his painting career: *The Child Jesus Among The Doctors*. This canvas is in the Colmar museum, and the preliminary sketch of it belongs to the Hahnloser collection in Winterthur. It has something of the charm of a Leonardo, or, rather, that of a Luini. Through emotional means that emanate both from his material and his touch, and through an undefinable monumental simplicity, the twenty-three-year-old painter transcended the scene, which is represented according to the precepts of the Moreau atelier; and he achieved a striking plastic manifestation of the evidence of Christ. "A twelve-year-old God," Léon Bloy wrote later, "and three hypocrites who, together, are a hundred and eighty. Jesus is telling them the Truth that is Himself, and while He is speaking, we seem to see issuing from each one of these crucifying men the frightening beast that possesses him and that, one day, will devour him."[68] In the background, at the left, angels may be seen, and at the right, through the archway, the Virgin on the public square, looking for her Son.

Rouault won the Prix Chenavard with this picture, but it was not without difficulties. The original verdict gave the award—a windfall of three thousand francs—to a second-rate canvas by one of Gérôme's pupils; but the students protested in a body, and the verdict was set aside. "The reaction in the three painting ateliers was so great," Léon Lehmann recalled, "that the authorities were obliged to capitulate the same day. A specially composed jury drawn from the Institut was constituted, with the result that Rouault won the prize."

The following year Rouault showed *The Child Jesus* at the Salon des Champs-Elysées, with the study of a head and a drawing.[69] The picture was well received. A certain M.-F. Javel, in *L'Art français* of May 13, warned M. Rouault-Champdavoine[70] (which is how Rouault was listed in the catalogue) "of the dangerous influence of his teacher." In *Le Jour*, mention was made of "a curious, mystic piece, with colors that looked like enamels." Over the signature of Serlat, the *Revue Encyclopédique* (May 15) gave a detailed description of this work and its "rare savor." And although in *L'Etendard* of June 18, there was talk of the "terrible shadows" that hid several parts of the canvas, Paul Flat, in *La Revue Bleue*, hailed this first salon piece by Rouault, and praised "the talent with which this young painter has been able to renew his subject."

44

Undoubtedly, the *patron* gave his pupil a helping hand, especially since 1895 was to be Gustave Moreau's great moment. Aesthetically inclined foreigners invented incredible subterfuges in order to see his paintings, for the little that was known through the students of this man, who hid in his home closed to everybody but themselves, excited people's imaginations. Moreau seemed to be a sort of Goethe of painting. "I could hardly believe," Jacques-Emile Blanche wrote, "that this nervous, retiring little man eating at our table, with the look of an obscure country gentleman in Paris for horse-show month, was the alchemist whom a few privileged persons, friends of mine, were helping in his attempts to find the philosophers' stone! On the contrary, there was something provincial about him that made me think of his friend Fromentin's *Dominique*. How little he looked like someone who would produce Fauves!"[71]

After praising Moreau as a talker and "dazzling connoisseur" of Rembrandt and the old masters, "vastly superior in this respect to his inseparable friends, Fromentin and Ricard," Jacques-Emile Blanche continued: "At that time, we were all under the influence of Hérodiades. . . . With regard to the *Jason* in the Ephrussi collection, Puvis de Chavannes and Ary Renan proved to me that nobody since Leonardo could have painted it."[72]

That same year when, more and more, men of opposed sensibilities were rallying to him, Gustave Moreau was described by Jean Lorrain (in his book *Sensations et Souvenirs*) as a painter who was "so sick with his own visions that he introduced into his works the shudder of anguish and despair they induced." He was a "master sorcerer," Lorrain wrote, who cast a spell over his epoch, bewitched his contemporaries, and "contaminated with ideals the skeptical, practical *fin de siècle*." Indeed, the author of *M. de Bougrelon* applies a number of brilliant epithets to the work of this symbolist painter, whose goddess appears with "half-closed eyes, in a robe stiff with jewels . . . above a prostrate, red mass of handsome, freshly slaughtered young men."[73]

Rouault and his companions must have felt that they were at the very center of this moment of fame. They saw the poets of the time attracted as though by a magnet to their instructor's "violently personal impersonality," finding a source of inspiration in these Salomes that to us, today, seem to be spoiled by a certain dilettantism:

> *L'onde douce a lavé les caillots, et le fleuve*
> *L'a fait de marbre pur de la nuque aux talons;*
> *Porte la tête exsangue entre tes mains de veuve,*
> *Laisse gémir le torse au creux des sables blonds . . .*

> [The gentle wave has washed the clots, the river
> Has made it purest marble, from nape to heel;
> Take the bloodless head in your widowed hands,
> Let the moaning torso lie, in the flaxen sands . . .]

46

wrote Henri de Régnier, in a poem entitled *Sur un tableau célèbre (On a Famous Picture)*, which was dedicated to Gustave Moreau, and published in the *Echo de Paris*. On September 15 of that same year appeared Gustave Larroumet's excellent though somewhat academic book. Larroumet was the most authoritative member of the Académie des Beaux-Arts and had been instrumental in Moreau's election to the Institut. The latter's atelier being still closed to visitors, he had been obliged to make the rounds of the Moreau collectors. But he doubtless had the impression that, with Gustave Moreau (he also commended such a painter as Jules Breton), he was taking the plunge into modernism. After having sung the praises of this "complicated, searching" talent, and observed that Moreau "went so far as to entrust his canvases to the master enamelers Grandhomme and Garnier in order that, by means of fire and metal, they might confer upon them a supreme degree of solidity and brilliance," Larroumet concludes: "For the last seven years, the Prix de Rome competitions and the annual Salons show that the influence of Monsieur Gustave Moreau is already great. By their reds and their blues, by their harmonies and oppositions of tone values ... frequently, too, by their searching for dramatic effects, one may quickly recognize those pictures whose creators have been advised by the painter of *Oedipus* and *Orpheus*."[74]

Their reds and their blues! Was this Academician thinking then of Georges Rouault who, in that same year of 1895, was once more working for the Prix de Rome? His subject was The Dead Christ Mourned by the Holy Women.

"This morning," wrote one newspaper,[75] "shortly after the appearance of these lines, the works of the young painters competing this year for the Prix de Rome will be carried out of the little studios in the old building that houses the Ecole des Beaux-Arts, studios that are badly lighted from a single skylight, and open onto the corridor made famous by the many generations of artists who have worked for this prize.

"The canvases will be varnished, framed, then hung in a good light in the gallery overlooking the Seine, on the second floor. During the afternoon, the public will be permitted to examine them and then, three days later, a jury will decide which of the ten candidates deserves to go and spend three years at the Villa Médicis."

The discussion was a heated one. "The foot of the Christ is too big," said Bonnat of Rouault's entry. "Very well," replied Gustave Moreau somewhat paradoxically, "for that reason it should be sent to Rome because, in your own opinion, your candidate will never be able to do anything better than this chromo of his." And, at a suggestion that Rouault be given a second prize, Moreau remained firm: "Rome or nothing" was his answer.

But Bonnat was standing despotic guard, and in the end, his pupil, a young man named Antoine Larée, was awarded the Grand Prix for a painting (which was shown me at the Beaux-Arts) that was absolutely conventional. A melodramatic Christ, with paired mourners, Mary Magdalene in a conventional crouching pose, boggy, funereal colors, all combine to make it look like a Bonnat painted on one of his bad days; whereas Rouault, by renewing the subject, had succeeded in really moving us.

Close examination of this *Dead Christ* (there exists a charcoal sketch of this work which Rouault signed and dated 1897,[76] and which is similar in almost every respect to the picture itself, now hanging in the Grenoble museum) convinces me more than ever that an injustice was committed.[77] Against an oriental-looking landscape, under a kind of portico, Christ is laid out, with his head thrown back and his hands and arms outstretched, surrounded by the four holy women. Saint John is stooping to examine the wound in the right foot (the foot Bonnat disapproved of), which extends into the foreground. The women's faces are painted in the manner of Leonardo.

There is undoubtedly a reminiscence of Moreau in the whole painting, but less than in the two tall canvases which Rouault painted the same year, *Stella Matutina* and *Stella Vespertina*, for Leopold Goldschmidt, an admirer of Moreau's work.[78] These two paintings which, given their large dimensions, were probably done in the rue la Rochefoucauld atelier, remind one, in their contours, of Chassériau, even of Ingres. The allegory of Morning, with arms outstretched toward the dawning day (a bird flies off from under the feet of beautiful Aurora), and that of Evening, with folded arms, gliding along on the crescent moon, would have delighted a man like Ruskin, I believe. But to return to the *Dead Christ:* In my opinion, there is more warmth in it than in the two canvases in the museum of Avallon. Rouault shows here that he is able to subordinate detail to ensemble (the almost Giotto-like line that forms the curve of Mary Magdalene's back has a simplicity about it that his instructor would certainly not have been capable of).

Moreau was very upset by the failure of his favorite pupil. "He was furious, as were all those who were aware of Rouault's worth."[79] We can imagine, too, with what suspicion this *patron* must have been regarded because of his openness of mind. He was "considered to be a dangerous man. At the Institut he said, 'I myself go to the Salon des Indépendants, and I see interesting things there.'" He was opposed to competitions; once these were done away with he would have liked to see the winning student designated on the basis of his year's work. After the defeat of his disciple, he urged Rouault to leave the Beaux-Arts. "What can you do here?" he asked him. "I don't see you working again for the Prix de Rome, struggling for eighty days on end with your subject. Work at home, and for yourself; in reality, you were never able to do anything else, even when you were working for a prize. That sort of thing is too exhausting and fatiguing."[80]

"What makes the Prix de Rome competition so pernicious," Henri Matisse once told me, "is its preparation, which amounts to a veritable apparatus for destroying people's brains. For one student like Rouault, who has a good, hard skull, how many others who, as a result of it, and not having his personality, lose the possibility of becoming normal citizens and remain simply ineffectual artists! Occasionally the ablest of them—those who have won a first prize—succeed in making their way with the help of prominent women. Or, again, the winners of seco nd prizes become drawing instructors. But think how many others drag out burdensome existences in complete obscurity!"

Rouault decided, nevertheless, that he wanted to show his *Dead Christ*, so he sent it to the 1896 Salon,[81] to which he was admitted "only for this work, which it was materially impossible to refuse him. And at that," wrote Paul Flat, "they took pains to hang it between two enormous, ridiculous canvases, of the nondescript variety of paintings that may be seen by the hundreds on the walls of the Salon."[82]

After noting that among the entries those of Moreau's class were not only superior, but more imaginative, Debay praised Rouault's picture and remarked that, apart from the main subject, "all the rest, both garments and landscape, is in shadow; but this is rich shadow in which the dying rays of the sun are extinct garnets, amethysts and emeralds."[83] In *Le Figaro*, Arsène Alexandre paid tribute to the "gustave-moristes" and especially to Rouault; and Roger-Marx reproached the jury for having refused Rouault's landscape painting.[84]

But what of Rouault himself in all this? How did he take this setback? After having shown his *Dead Christ Mourned by the Holy Women* in the Salon, he sold the picture[85] to the Montmartre deputy, Marcel Sembat, and his wife, Georgette Agutte, which encouraged him to continue working and not to be too impressed by the gentlemen of the Institut. "The fact is," he told me, "those people have plaster in their make-up, and I'm made of Breton granite, the kind you break your teeth on. You remember how the Dutch succeeded in salvaging land from the sea? There's something of that in my nature. If I had been a failure, I would have kept at it just the same. I'm hardheaded, with terrible faults."

At this time, a picture dealer with somewhat audacious tastes, Ambroise Vollard, had noticed this young man with the short, blond beard, among those who came to see his first exhibits in the rue Lafitte. "Discreetly and quietly, he used to look, stop for a moment, then leave without saying a word."[86]

About this same time, Rouault made a self-portrait in charcoal. The face is imbued with a serious, dreamy sensitivity and one feels in it a young painter boiling over with sensations, ready to grapple with adversity, to meet life. He is wearing the same little round felt hat that Renoir and the "independent" painters were wearing then, and about his shoulders hangs the hooded cape that we associate with Charles Péguy.[87] This is the Rouault we see in the foreground of the photograph of Gustave Moreau's atelier,[88] the Rouault who, at the Beaux-Arts, was reminded that Ingres had insisted: "Drawing is the probity of art." But he considered, and rightly so, that the instructors in the rue Bonaparte disparaged Ingres, this "willful, unbending Frenchman," by their constant reference to his probity or fidelity. For, say what we will, the man who, in his canvas, *Turkish Bath*, introduced "lovely cadences, harmonious rhythms and delicate, noble proportions into the splendor of form," went beyond mere fidelity.

Meanwhile, after these first appearances at the official Salon, where he received his "baptism of fire" and felt "something of a leper," Rouault next participated in the Rosicrucian Salon, which opened on Monday, March 8, 1897, in the rue

50

de Sèze, at the Galerie Petit.[89] The titles of some of the canvases by other exhibitors were: *Subtility*, *Red Lips*, *Thirst for Gold*, in which the influence of Turner may be noticed. "Mythological-mystical subjects, underpainted, glazed, scratched, scumbled, polished, stylized forms," all constituted the dominating characteristics of Moreau's students, according to *La Revue Blanche*,[90] which defended the Nabis. Rouault's entry in this show, *Descent from the Cross*, was "very well painted."[91]

After the Rosicrucians came the Salon des Champs-Elysées. Rouault was beginning to feel that he had been rejected by the "market places of painting, where flashy but meaningless brushwork takes the place of the amusing, loud-mouthed palaver of fishmongers."[92] At the Salon "only one of his pastels was accepted. True, it was an essential one, in which the poetry of Corot enhanced the majesty of a landscape organized in the manner of Poussin: *The Bathers*."[93] But in the section of drawings and engravings he showed some "majestic dream landscapes"[94] that, in all probability, were the "two magnificent drawings, *Bathers* and *Landscape*," mentioned by Gustave Geffroy.[95]

It was about this same time that Rouault also made a drawing on a favorite theme to which he often returned during his life—the Prodigal Son. This drawing is dated 1897 and is in Dr. Pierre Collart's collection. It shows the episode when the Prodigal "came to himself," as we read it in the Gospel of St. Luke, 15 : 17.

Just here a break may be seen between the works Rouault had done during his school years and those that were to follow. His work acquired a self-assurance that, now for the first time, marked the emergence of a personality. Indeed, the more I look at *Night Landscape*, erroneously called *The Workyard*, 1897 (a large landscape peopled with small figures), the more I sense in it the revelation of a great change taking place. All that Rouault was to become later is already evident in this astonishing work, which evokes scaffoldings in a workers' suburb, seen from a vacant lot. In the left foreground, some butchers are fighting. A man halts a draft horse he is holding by the bridle. A few figures are sketched in, wearing red-and-green striped shirts, while others, armed with scythes, are swarming onto the slope. The whole thing gives the impression of a revolt, a scene from the life of the workers, and over it all lowers a threatening, sooty sky. Sparse, bare grass, mauve-green in color, is visible in the moonlight. It is a powerful painting, the structure of which recalls certain of Théodore Rousseau's[96] canvases, with the tragic sense of Goya and a force that suggests Rembrandt.

Gustave Moreau died of cancer at the age of seventy-two, on April 18, 1898. This painter-professor had set his affairs in order;[97] then, with much difficulty, he dragged himself back to his atelier. He worked up till the last and even refused the various drugs that might have relieved his sufferings. "No Fontainebleau farewells," he said to Henri Rupp, his executor.

And young Rouault probably read the following funeral oration on the death of his teacher in the *Journal des Débats:* "He left us in the same manner that he lived; hiding his life, hiding his work, taking with him the secret of the mysteri-

ous, restless ideal that fled the garish light of exhibitions."[98] More aptly still, Gustave Geffroy, in *Le Journal*, termed Moreau "a complex scholar, dedicated to working existing veins more deeply, to amalgamating in one rare, precious substance the important advances and achievements made by his predecessors in the use of color and line." Thus, having turned away from "the spectacle of nature, he remained himself by adding his own instinctive personality to those of the great masters in whose footsteps he followed."[99]

The time of "broad, intelligent teaching, respectful of budding originality" was a thing of the past! "Moreau closed the cycle of 'the oil painters' and their excited talk. In the atelier, the Fromentin era had begun."[100]

Rouault, for whom Moreau's death was a deep loss, inherited from this extraordinary instructor a feeling for his material and a love of rare substances, rich harmonies, and bold effects. And if, later, he was "to show a scrupulous—indeed, painstaking—respect for the enamel-like limpidity of the precious pigments as they crystallized on his canvases, it was in the rue La Rochfoucauld that he had learned this."[101] "Moreau," Rouault said, "had taught us to discipline our wills without any preconceived method, to respect a certain inner vision. He gave us a taste for the heroic . . . or for an elevated reality."[102] He had been neither the gloomy professor nor the severe, harsh taskmaster who counted mistakes."[103]

Now that he was no longer there to enchant and stimulate, to help both morally and materially, the pupil had a clearer view of his lost teacher. Repelled by the reality of life, Moreau had tended to take refuge in the past.[104] With his "penchant for ideal existences, or for historical epochs that go back into remote legend,"[105] he had communed with "every mystery," "penetrated many an occult ceremony," and "fervently adored the spirit of divinity." All of this, however, without having "felt the need of a divorce between the Prince of Renunciation and Pan, the god of smiles."[106] Perhaps, too, there was something curiously messianic about his mind. "Do you believe in God?" he would ask. "I don't believe only in Him. I believe neither in what I touch nor in what I see. I only believe in what I don't see, and only in what I sense. My brain and my reason seem ephemeral to me and of dubious reality. My inner feeling alone seems to me to be eternal and undeniably certain."[107]

The fact is that Moreau dreaded life as a result of his almost morbid horror of reality, the reality that often keeps an artist from concentrating all his attention on his work, but which is also constantly forcing him to observation of others, and leads to a disbelief in art as a "superior craft" to which only a few rarely privileged persons may be initiated. Already during his lifetime, this artist had prepared the catharsis of his own character. "Take away the furniture! There should be nothing left but pictures! Little by little," wrote Marcel Proust of Moreau, "all the rooms were so cluttered with pictures that there were very few places left in which the man who wanted to dine, entertain friends, or sleep, could take refuge. Little by little, the moments during which he was not invaded by his inner soul, during which he was still the man that he also was, became rarer and

54

rarer. His house had already become almost a museum, his person was now little more than the scene of accomplishment of a lifework."[108]

Thanks to his skilled artisan background and his firm Breton faith, Rouault was sheltered from these temptations of over-refined intellectualism. He had, too, a sense of unity and monumentality, as well as a fundamental humility that stood him in good stead. Leaving behind him the teaching of Moreau, whose atelier he had seen bursting with canvases of all categories and all poetic styles, among which could be recognized the jumbled talents of more than ten painters, he now had to try to find his own way.

Study of a Head · 1900

The Road to Calvary · 1891

Job · 1892

The Ordeal of Samson · 1893

Self-Portrait · 1895

61

First Notation for "Coriolanus in the House of Tullius" · 1894

Coriolanus in the House of Tullius · *1894*

Sketch for "The Child Jesus Among the Doctors" · *1894*

Sketch for "The Child Jesus Among the Doctors" (fragment) · 1894

Stella Matutina · 1895

Daniel Defending Susanna · 1901

68

The Return of the Prodigal Son · 1897

Study: Drawing Tinted with Sepia · about 1895

The Return of the Prodigal Son · 1892

72

Christ and the Disciples at Emmaus · 1899

3. The Search for Self

This was a terrible blow for Rouault. Alone, left to his own devices, he floundered.

We can imagine the situation in which this Beaux-Arts student found himself, conversant as he was with history, mythology, with the great masters of the Louvre. But above all, he missed the close contact with the hermit-like Gustave Moreau. The doors of the official Salon were soon closed to his painting, as also to that of Matisse and Marquet who, like himself, had deserted the Ecole. On the other hand, among the *Revue Blanche* painters, he was considered to be "behind the times, hardly in the movement."[1]

For now, artists began to paint what they saw in the streets—passers-by, the prostitutes, the music halls. This milieu which, thus far, had been the private preserve of Degas, Lautrec, and Seurat—and which, at that moment, another young painter, Picasso, was confronting in his own way—this world had seemed to Rouault to have no place for him. He had felt that it was impossible for him to adapt himself to it and still continue his work:

> *"D'une rive à l'autre*
> *Je ne voyais de refuge qu'à l'ombre de la mort."*[2]

> [From one bank to the other
> The only refuge I saw was in the shadow of death.]

"And yet I didn't cut off my ear," he told me. "I didn't give way to despair as Vincent van Gogh did. When I crossed the Place Pigalle, where I lived, and saw all that human life about me, I always felt that I had lost my bearings. It was like an abyss. My family having left Paris temporarily for Algiers,[3] I was living in complete solitude." In the populous desert constituted by the great city, Rouault

73

felt sick at heart when he returned to his lonely room. Then it was that he began to write.

The "sensitive, encouraging friend" who had guided his footsteps, the man concerning whom Degas used to say with nervous impatience when someone praised him: "Well, I went to his funeral!" was now himself being riddled by the arrows of criticism that, after men die, attack those who have had their moment of fame, and make them pass through what is called their purgatory.

Rouault understood now why Moreau had spoken so highly of poverty which, although he had never known it, would have been a deepening experience for him. Instead of capturing the very substance of life in order to transform it, Moreau, "irritating charmer"[4] that he was, had had recourse to trimmings, to "winding ribbons everywhere, scattering flowers everywhere,"[5] thus stifling good painting under erudite knowledge.

A letter from Rouault which Mme. Coquiot kindly showed me, proves that, although he was warmly appreciative of Gustave Coquiot, who had been his early defender, he was upset by this critic's attack on Moreau. "You perhaps have no feeling for a particular nuance and hierarchy of values," Rouault wrote. "Don't forget that Gustave Moreau followed the Indépendants in the difficult days when it amounted to heroism to do so, and that already, several years ago, he urged me to try 'to find myself,' to leave the Beaux-Arts before the age of thirty, after which one no longer has the right to compete for the Prix de Rome."

And yet even Odilon Redon had noted that in Moreau's art "the figures he evokes have cast aside instinctive sincerity and remain fixed in a sort of visual rhetoric that has its own beauty, no doubt, but which is not the eternal thing in which humanity is constantly reflected and recognizes itself."[6]

And so Rouault wandered about Paris, face to face with a reality that he forgot when he had stood before his easel at the Beaux-Arts. One day, in Vollard's shop on the rue Lafitte, he saw Gauguin's *Yellow Christ*,[7] and he, too, felt the need to find himself in a profound truth. He was not yet thirty years old. But he would have liked to have the means of expression that would be adequate to his vision, "those that the apprentices in medieval trade guilds used to possess at such an early age."

In May, 1899, he drew a portrait of his mother whom, apparently, he resembled more than he did his father, of whom he also made a pencil sketch in June of this same year.[8] He made yet another self-portrait, in the Ingres manner, which shows him grown thinner, wearing a felt hat, and with a quizzical expression. Finally, he made a line drawing of the biblical head of Gustave Moreau's close friend, Rupp, who had been designated to obtain official recognition of, and to organize, the Moreau Museum on the rue La Rochefoucauld.

Then came a series of Rembrandt-like works, with something of the luminosity, even in the shadows, that Seurat obtains in his charcoals; some pastels ranging from a profile of Mme. Paul Flat reading, to a *Christ and the Disciples at Emmaus* which was shown at the Société des Artistes Français, along with an *Orpheus*, in April, 1899;[9] and the strange, detailed *Repast* at the Tate Gallery. This is painted

74

on a square sheet of paper and evokes a somewhat Maeterlinckian Middle Ages: two figures eating at a table, a young girl playing the lute, and a servant carrying a platter of fruit.

I should like, so to speak, to "read between the lines" of these early works. Is it because I know what followed that, beneath this charcoal line, or that touch of light, I seem to recognize a revealing indication of the future character of Rouault's work—a character that is so striking because it shows a vision, not dispersed like that of Moreau's, but centered and inward, interiorized, in the drawing, colors, and general harmony?[10]

But what is it that so moves me? Is it not that in these early works there is a radiance that derives, not from what they represent, but from something quite different—something that Gustave Moreau did not succeed in giving to his mythological works? Through the medium of the figures, everything speaks in a language of form and color. Then, too, we begin to perceive in the pupil a powerful feeling for people which was altogether lacking in his aristocratic teacher. Once he has found his expression, it is seldom that another's style colors his works, unless it be on occasion, the single guide, Rembrandt, for example. Being long familiar with the great themes of the Bible, Rouault was now, like Moreau before him, haunted by Herod's cruel, sacrilegious supper in the course of which the princess was given the head of John the Baptist.[11] But what became of this *Salome* of his no one knows.

Rouault tried square landscapes, and occasional night scenes, as in *Nocturne*. In these little pastels, which recall the English Romantics and Delacroix, the painter has very pungently localized his vision in landscapes and skies that evoke the presence of biblical personages.

Among the works that have remained unknown until now, *Daniel Defending Susanna*, a small vertical picture, still shows Moreau's influence, but its color is freer, its arabesques are less cramped, its drawing simplified. This is one of the rare works by Rouault that shows a woman in all her charm, "dainty and very beautiful to look upon." She had been persuaded to remove her veil in order that the Elders might feast upon her beauty.[12] At the top of the painting may be seen the dove of the Holy Spirit.

But what can the painter do in order to receive the breath of inspiration, so that the expression of his works may come to him not from outside the subject treated, but from the impetus of a faith that transcends reality? Would not the best plan be to follow the masters in the dialogue which they had begun with the visible world as life unfolds it before our eyes? It is interesting to compare this painting on a biblical subject with *Promenade*, from the Poignard collection. Here we see that the drawing is the same, with the same elegantly arabesque line as *Daniel Defending Susanna*. And yet, the latter picture has more accent, more resolution, more unity. One feels here the difficulty this lonely young man must have experienced in working from direct observation, in giving his figure groupings the animation of life. In this respect, the *Fisherman*, in the same collection, with its sepia tones heightened by blues and rose-grays, is even more emphatic. One feels

76

that it was painted from one of the rough sketches Rouault made along the banks of the Seine. And it is undoubtedly a study for *Paris (The Seine)* which, although the palette evokes Turner or Bonington, is unmistakably Parisian in spirit.

But even here, Rouault could not be satisfied with catching only a moment of visual truth. He sought the real significance of everything. Reality, his kind of reality, led to the very depths of being. And that is as it had to be. That was the justification of his existence, his essential purpose. He was not content just to look and set down what he saw. It was all very well to paint, but if it simply meant repeating what the Impressionists had done with talent, felicity, and a zest for life—and he was well aware of the charm of their work—what was the use? Rouault saw things differently. He was the kind who, in order to express himself through line and color, is obliged to close his eyes, to replace sight by vision.

Late in April, 1901,[13] Rouault made a pilgrimage to the little monastery that has been called an "object of fervor and passion" for Huysmans.[14] Located not far from Poitiers, in the Vienne *département*, it was at that time, as it is again today, a Benedictine abbey under the patronage of St. Martin.

Rouault[15] had come to Ligugé to join his friend Antonin Bourbon, a former classmate under Moreau, who was stopping at Smarves, not far from the monastery. The two friends lived there somewhat precariously, in peasant households, and attended religious services at the abbey. Bourbon was an oblate and was on intimate terms with Dom Besse and J.-K. Huysmans, who was known at the abbey as Joris-Karl. Three years earlier, in 1898, Huysmans (who had retired from his position of assistant director in the Ministry of the Interior) had gone to live in Ligugé where he joined two monks whom he had known at the Abbey of St. Wandrille, in Normandy: prior Dom Chamard, and Dom Besse, novice master.[16] Not far from the monastery, Joris-Karl had built the Maison Notre-Dame where he planned to house a working colony of artists.

"We were a few friends," Rouault told me, "who formed a little group around Huysmans, and we tried to lay the foundations for artistic and intellectual work that would be dedicated and selfless. Huysmans wanted to bring together men who, having abandoned the farce of Paris, would count neither on money nor on influence; no Bachelor's or Doctor's degrees, and no specialists; just men who had put behind them all that was nonessential in life: degrees, medals, prerogatives. He wanted to organize this with me, Antonin Bourbon, and a few others, among whom were Leclaire and Morisse, whom we called 'little Morisse.' "[17] The latter, who was an amateur, had a genius for exasperating Rouault with incessant questioning and, recalling him, Rouault spoke of the ravages of intellectualism to be found everywhere, even in Ligugé. "You know what I mean! You wind it up and whirr . . . you've got perpetual motion!"

It was a rule of the group to shun publicity, as well as everything that would ordinarily flatter one's vanity. In this, Huysmans himself furnished an example by refusing to contribute to an important newspaper, insisting that, by doing so, he would make the newspaper lose a number of its best-known subscribers. But

Joris-Karl found it hard to swim against the naturalistic current that had borne him along earlier. In Ligugé he lived among the same household effects that he had had in his apartment in the rue de Babylone, or in the rue St.-Placide, which was his last Paris address. In his *Souvenirs intimes*, Rouault has given the following description of Huysmans: "Cold, distant, exacting, crotchety at times, he walked along noiselessly, with mincing steps, his big head lolling on his sloping shoulders. At times, he would groan and sigh, or occasionally laugh in a strained or wary manner. In his slender, bony, parchment-like hands, he usually held a burnt-out cigarette."[18]

Comparing Huysmans to an "alley cat," Rouault describes him as "tense and fiercely devoted to his art," yet "good-natured," and with a considerable understanding of painting. Joris-Karl had "an early Forain and a small Cézanne, the size of your hand" hanging on his wall.[19]

Occasionally, Forain came to visit them (this delighted Dom Besse, who loved to go driving with him). A good ten years earlier, Huysmans had praised what he called Forain's "Japanese compositions" and the "behind-the-scenes" character of his work.[20] However, for the experienced eye of a Rouault, who had once admired this man nineteen years his senior, Forain was becoming too "restricted in scope in his painting and even in his drawing,"[21] while Rouault, himself, was evolving in the opposite direction. The older and more mature he grew, the more persuaded he became that the life at Ligugé, so opposed to the modern trend, was the only true life. It gave him renewed strength, and confirmed him in his resolution to make no concessions either to art or to the public. For him, more than for any other, truth could exist only in an inseparable association of soul and body. It was not enough for him to see with his eyes, touch with his hands, or verify things through the processes of reasoning. He believed, as St. Augustine did, that the more God is hidden to our senses, the more He is manifest. "We think we can know everything although we forget, ignore, or neglect the essential, which is love for every living creature under the heavens, whether in light or darkness."

It was in the name "reason" that Emile Combes pressed for a law banishing from France the occupants of all those holy places where one could meditate, pray, and conceive works that went beyond the Positivist outlook. Passage of the law against religious communities (July 1, 1901) put an end to the project for an artists' community which Huysmans (who had become an oblate on June 18) had conceived. But although the monastery was disbanded, three additional novices took the habit on September 12 by way of protest. The last Mass was said on June 27, and the following morning most of the monks entrained for Belgium. The artists remained behind with Father Guyot for a few weeks longer.

"We are going through days of nasty persecution," Huysmans wrote in his diary, on October 2, 1901. "We wander about the cloister and in the gardens, after services. We do nothing. . . . These services are wretched, sinister even, but we feel close. Evenings we can hardly see, and it's all we can do to read the antiphon. . . . Rouault, using siccative in a chamber pot, painted the following sign: 'Ligugé loafers' union.'"

And this note, dated the following day: "This evening, after a farewell lunch, Father Guyot came up to my study at five o'clock to read vespers, with Mme. Godefroy and Mme. Leclaire, Leclaire, Rouault, Morisse, Bourbon, and myself. A lugubrious service during which we were seated in chairs opposite one another. One would think we were back under the Terror."[22]

"Rouault will soon return to Paris," Huysmans noted on the 12th; at the end of the month, they both boarded the train for "the cesspool."

Meanwhile, the Gustave Moreau Museum was being organized. In February, 1900, a correspondent of *Le Journal*, after visiting the large room on the second floor, wrote: "It contains a profusion of Orpheuses, Helens in gold mail wandering about the ramparts of Troy, Salomes dancing before Herod, sirens flowering on a single stem, like three diademed flowers."[23]

When Léon Lehmann (who had left the Beaux-Arts in 1897 for reasons of poor health) visited his former teacher's atelier, he met Rouault there, and the latter invited him to come to live in his home. "For several years," Lehmann recalls, "I had the quiet life that I needed. Rouault's father and mother were kindness itself and I had a great veneration for them both. Rouault, himself, was extraordinarily friendly and tactful."[24] At that time Rouault was working on both a *Judas* and an *Orpheus and Eurydice* which, in 1901, were submitted to the Salon des Artistes Français,[25] and accepted. But he never forgot that his former teacher's last wishes remained to be fulfilled.

There were last-minute difficulties in obtaining official approval of Moreau's legacy. Finally, however, the decree was signed[26] and the whole matter settled, thanks to Henri Rupp. Rouault was named curator with an annual salary of 2400 francs, and it was understood that he would be present in person on Mondays. The Gustave Moreau Museum, in the rue La Rochefoucauld, was inaugurated on January 14, 1903.[27]

A short while ago, I went to visit this Museum. I wanted to see it again with my own eyes, accustomed as they are to the art of our own day. The influence exerted on Rouault by Moreau is recognizable in many landscapes with slashed skies and blood-red suns, as in certain compositions across which gallops the shade of the erlking. It is also impossible not to see the source of some of Rouault's themes in these Crucifixions enveloped in a sort of halo; in the little sketch entitled *Hercules and the Hydra*,[28] with its airy, violet-colored backgound; in the curious *Salome*[29] in which the effect is produced by streams of color. And one watercolor,[30] drawn with a thick brush, *The Council of the Rats* (a sketch for La Fontaine's *Fables*) could well have been signed by Rouault.

Moreau tried everything: line drawing, painting, chiaroscuro, what today we call "Tachisme," Blakian symbolism, Turner-like evocations, portraits à la Ricard —not to mention his Romantic, Delacroix side, frequently evident in his rough first drafts.[31] He was unable to resist the temptations of eclecticism, which included borrowings that ranged from Pompeiian art and Limoges enamels to the chill of the Pre-Raphaelites: too much confusion, too much "palette scraping."

Shortly after the opening of the Gustave Moreau Museum, Rouault made the acquaintance of Degas, whom he occasionally saw "climbing the twisting streets of old Montmartre, half-blind, tapping the ground with his stick like a latter-day Homer."[32] He writes: "Not wanting to disturb him, I had gone to see him at the hour when people told me he usually sorted out his pastels. But he was having lunch .... After having given him the message I had come to deliver, I started to leave. He came out to the landing with me, and we started to talk about painting. At five o'clock in the afternoon I was still there in his studio."[33] Degas, who was a solitary, timid man, "little interested in the trends of the time," said to Rouault, in referring to Jan van Eyck's technique: "We all paint like swine!" In this respect, Degas agreed with Moreau, and even with Renoir. "But although we must unceasingly learn from the great masters," Rouault said, "we must nevertheless never allow ourselves to be obsessed by technical perfection to the extent that all individual sensibility is obliterated."[34]

Later, Degas visited the Gustave Moreau Museum, where he saw *The Child Jesus Among the Doctors*, "which was hung in a large hall closed to the public. Because of his notoriously bad eyesight, his nose almost touched the canvas several times." Then, all of a sudden, he said: "Gustave Moreau certainly did not paint this picture!" "I was trapped," said Rouault, "and there was no getting out of it; so, admitting that I had done it, I criticized it rather severely, the Doctors: Albrecht Dürer; the Child Jesus: a bit like Leonardo; the picture as a whole: too reminiscent of Rembrandt ... though perhaps, in the background, the Virgin arriving like a wounded bird is a bit more of my own invention!" Degas turned and looked at me sternly, saying, "You had a father and mother, too, didn't you?"[35]

In the part of the museum where Moreau had had his private apartment, one day while browsing in the library Rouault came upon two novels by Léon Bloy —*Le Désespéré* and *La Femme pauvre*. In one of the books he read an inscription by the author, which contained an allusion to Folantin, a creation of Huysmans'. Folantin was a fussy old bachelor always on the lookout for a well-prepared dish, and Huysmans' attempt at a self-portrait. In that period of highly mannered Symbolism, Rouault liked the simple, direct, catapulting style of Bloy, this "ungrateful beggar" who, for all his emphasis on Divine love, was realistic enough to love his fellow men, and who exalted the Middle Ages.

All this helped the young painter-curator to perceive other forms, other kinds of expression, an art that would be on a totally different scale from the paintings under his custodianship.

The fact that Rouault haunted the banks of the Seine, that he went to the Cirque Medrano to see the clowns and the bareback riders, the fact that he observed life around the Moulin Rouge—all this was not due to the influence of Lautrec and the men who at the time were called *les modernes*. It was rather his reaction against an art which "a certain sly convention" had insidiously penetrated. Rouault was wary of all organized art, even a religious art, when it became an industry. And, in this respect, he was much closer to the profound outlook of Van Gogh

82

than to the trashy sacred art of the St.-Sulpice shops. For him "faith was a high wind; it was the faith that moves mountains, bearing with it a distaste for the social eyesores that besieged him on every side. . . . He felt that continuing to paint what people asked him to paint was wrongful. . . . The presence of evil, which infuriated him, held nevertheless every attraction for his art. Because he saw things darkly, he painted darkly. Tortuous contours and ungainly forms were charged with revealing the raw physical nature of sin. . . . It was a journey into Hell, but with faith in redemption."[36]

What Rouault himself called the "turn of the helm"[37] was the result of fairly continuous evolution rather than of a genuine revolution. The break with traditional religious art, with the religious "stage-setting," was caused by the spiritual power that the painter carried within him, and he was now preparing to communicate something beyond mere imagery. But what was there in Paris in the way of religious art at that time? Very little, really, since Manet's *Christ Among the Angels* and the *Flagellation* painted more than thirty-five years earlier; certain efforts by Moreau, Carrière, and Redon; the decoration that Maurice Denis made in Le Vésinet; and a few works that copied Emil Bernard's and Gauguin's stylized manner. But Rouault refused to be seduced by decorative mannerism. For him, continuous observation of life gave rise to effusions that could never be contained within the cold precision of form. What he wanted to do was suggest an entire physiognomy in a few lines. From this standpoint, the little *Duet* in the Poignard collection, a colored wash on canvas, points to the uninterrupted chain of artists (Da Vinci, Daumier, Rouault) who have been unusually interested in reproducing facial expression.

Now Rouault began to chronicle the story of human misery. But he went much farther and deeper than the Impressionists with their glittering substance, or than the Nabis with their druidic esotericism. At a time when the style was either for bright-colored painting, or stylized sensitivity, Rouault painted darkly and obscurely. He brought us back to the drama of existence, to the everyday lives of the clowns we all are, to the reality of the women of the streets, prowling the sidewalks.

Daumier had already discovered in these clowns and charlatans, in these bareback riders and hucksters, one of his families of characters whose grotesque play had been extolled by the Parnassian poet, Théodore de Banville. But Baudelaire, in his *Vieux Saltimbanque* (1861), seems to have been the first to use the theme from within, by drawing a parallel between the "poor buffoon, stooped, declining, decrepit, a wreck of a man, leaning against one of the posts of his shack," and the "old man of letters who has outlived his generation, after having been its most brilliant wit, . . . and whose booth a forgetful world passes by, without entering."[38]

Among the first experiments in this sequence is a series of pasteled watercolors, or watercolored pastels (it is often difficult to tell which dominates). This includes

probably because of this courage that posterity has recognized in his paintings how great an artist he really was underneath his less disturbing role of lithographer. Rouault always knew that the real creators are revolutionaries—to whom we grow accustomed. "You don't enter into tradition," he said, "the way you get on a bus, waiting for your number to be called. There must exist more secret affinities."[43] "All arrogance aside, it is legitimate to say that the language of form and color is a domain that is always waiting to be explored, and this despite the triumphs of the old masters."[44] Rouault was able to detect the force of innovation underneath the patina of the "damned" works that, with time, have become classics. It was not for nothing that the kindly administrator of the Gustave Moreau Museum, Henri Rupp—whose attitude toward Rouault was more or less paternal—replied to those who complained of his curator's bad disposition, his *mauvais caractère:* "*Mauvais caractère?* You mean that he has character! Today that's a rare quality!"

Indeed Rouault had character. He had character to spare! In his loneliness, he felt that he was brother to all the living and suffering, to every derelict. But he had no use for the extremes of humanitarian Socialism. Nor did he contribute to *L'Assiette au Beurre,* the anarchist paper which reproduced Steinlen's drawings of groups of women workers. He had soon understood that true brotherhood of man is not attained through polemics and proclamations.

However, as an individual without obeying any party line or going to any extremes, he could be counted on to break with the past and abjure all conformity. Now he pursued the line he had first taken in his big landscape, the one of the outlying quarters of the city bristling with scaffoldings. In reply to the hue and cry this raised, he merely confirmed his intentions. He realized that he was embarked on a perilous road "with precipices on each side," and "that to build one's art on the expression of a battered, old circus performer" [man or horse], was either "mad pride" or "perfect humility." But the die was cast. In this same year of 1903—when the last issue of *La Revue Blanche* appeared; when Vuillard and Vallotton exhibited at the Bernheim-Jeune gallery; when Gauguin died on the island of Dominique in the Marquesas; when Sérusier and Maurice Denis went to see Verkade in the Beuron monastery—a new annual avant garde exhibition called the Salon d'Automne (November-December) was inaugurated. Rouault modestly showed two paintings: a *Paris,* in a gray light, and a portrait which appeared in the catalogue under the title, *Etude.* His showings were rounded out by three pastels: *Christ and Disciples, Twilight,* and *Landscape.*[45] It is quite evident that he still hesitated to confront the public in his new role of a disturbing, disquieting painter. He wanted first to be quite clear about things in his own mind. But the works he created with such feeling and faith are still overwhelming.

The Dead Christ Mourned by the Holy Women · 1895

Nocturne (Landscape in Moonlight) · *1900*

Night Landscape (The Good Samaritan) · *about 1897*

1891 G. Rouault

The Promenade · 1901

94

The Kiss of Judas · 1895

The Nativity · about 1900

Face to Face · about 1900

Judges · 1901

4. Sins of Society

On March 16, 1904, Léon Bloy wrote in his diary: "I am told that Gustave Moreau's pupil, the painter Georges Rouault, is enthusiastic about me. When he found in Moreau's library a copy of *La Femme pauvre* which I had sent with the following inscription: 'To Gustave Moreau, to avenge him for M. Folantin,' this book left a wound in his heart from which he will never recover. I tremble at the thought of the punishment reserved for the poor wretch."[1]

In another note dated March 24 of the same year, Bloy mentions that Rouault had "shipped" another Moreau pupil, Georges Desvallières, to his "dark desert-island." (Rouault used this means to send small sums of money to Bloy.) And the "ungrateful beggar" added that he was indebted for these two compassionate people—*ces deux cœurs*—to Auguste Marguillier, secretary of the *Gazette des Beaux-Arts*,[2] who introduced Rouault to Bloy, in the rue Las Cases in Paris, as witness the following note from Bloy's unpublished diary: "April 21, 1904. Lunch at Marguillier's. He went to fetch Rouault who was still impatient to meet me. A nice face. Apparently he has a lot of talent, too much, in fact, not to remain poor. He is the devoted type who naïvely expresses his enthusiasm for me."[3]

Rouault, who was twenty-five years younger than Bloy, talked to all his friends of the pages this writer had devoted to the Middle Ages, to Byzantium, and to "holy poverty." After a long friendship with Huysmans, Bloy had now broken with him. (Huysmans was suffering from an acute ophthalmic inflammation that later confined him to a dark room with his eyes completely covered.) Bloy was writing *Belluaires et Porchers*. He "dressed like a carpenter, in a corduroy suit which, at that time, cost about two louis," and wore "heavy worker's shoes."[4] "I can still see him," Rouault wrote, "with his white forelock on his forehead, and large eyes that so easily became threatening and, as easily, compassionate."[5] This "wrecking contractor" now was on the warpath for all that was most famous, most highly placed; what we today should call our "sacred cows." Indeed, he went about as though he were deaf or blind, sometimes even like a madman, constantly inviting people's blows and involving himself with extraordinary courage.

Bloy had started to write at the age of thirty, after having earned his living making color illustrations. (He had begun to study at the Beaux-Arts, but had found the traditional hazing by older pupils so offensive that he had left.) He lived very simply. "One of God's witnesses, he hoped that the martyrdom to which he aspired would be a bloody one. He felt that he was the voice of all those who are abandoned or oppressed by the modern world," that it was his mission to interpret their lasting lament.[6]

This meeting was an important one for Rouault. For he too was attuning his ear to the "infinite clamor of all the mournful voices of all the downtrodden of every age, in a miraculously abbreviated formula that explained—through the necessity of a sort of divine sacrifice—the interminable postponements of Justice and the apparent inefficiency of the Redemption."[7] In him too there smoldered a permanent, profound revolt against the established order which constantly outraged his sense of equality. Finally, Bloy's style was loaded with the same explosive expressiveness that marked Rouault's new manner of painting. Writer and painter shared the same vision of reality, apparently terrible and relentlessly sordid. Both were drawn to the Middle Ages "with its gallows and basilicas, its shadows and gory blades, its prayers and sobbing, which for a thousand years had taken upon its shoulders as much as it could possibly bear of the weight of the immense Cross."[8]

Rouault, whose teacher had encouraged him to cultivate his mind, knew, nevertheless, how to forget what he had learned. Like Friar Marchenoir, he saw before him, stretching out, "the astonishing path of history with its countless crossroads," along which "erudition filled the libraries of Alexandria to feed countless bespectacled rodents whose function was to pick out the straws in the enormous mass of documentary manure dropped by larger animals."[9] Undoubtedly, this meeting with Bloy strengthened his courage to go against the current, and the prostitutes who proliferate in his painting of that period are, to a certain extent, sisters and daughters to Bloy. But it would also be a mistake to attribute more importance to this influence than it had. What Rouault may have admired in Bloy was the latter's need to transform "every event, every gesture, every individual into the pure symbol of some consuming spiritual reality."[10]

This writer, whose books Rémy de Gourmont said stood "somewhere between Saint Thomas Aquinas and Gargantua," could undoubtedly liberate both the mind and eye of the painter; he could also show him what is real underneath appearances. "In order to say something worth saying," Bloy declared, "as well as to give an impression of Beauty, one must appear to exaggerate, that is to say, direct one's glance beyond the object in itself."[11] Thus, in paintings as precious as silk, Goya "mocks the high Spanish officials of his time to such a degree that we are delighted to see their real humanness underneath their decorations."[12] Up until this point the revolutionary element in Rouault's art had been subterranean. But it had been already incubating beneath the harmless figures that he had painted under Moreau. Evident, for the first time, in *Night Landscape*, in his clowns it grew more individual. But it was not until he began to paint his *filles de joie* that it assumed its most socially terrifying aspect.

As we pointed out earlier, in his circus scenes Rouault is closely related to the author of *Les Fleurs du Mal*. When we look at his prostitutes, however, a very different name comes to mind, that of Dostoevsky, and particularly the Dostoevsky revealed in *Crime and Punishment*. Take this somber Rouault that says: "tragic is the light." It has "thrown convention to the winds, drawn all veils aside, torn off all masks; it has dared to do in painting what no one has yet dared to do."[13] And yet, at this point, turning to advantage "an inner wretchedness that should have finished him off," the artist could treat the most sordid, the most difficult, and the most poignantly moving of all themes.

Georges Charensol tells that already during Rouault's Montmartre years, after Moreau's death, "a few students together rented a studio on the rue Rochechouart. None of them being able to afford a model, they decided to invite the prostitutes on the nearby streets to come to their place to rest and get warm whenever they wanted. Rouault composed some of his most striking works from these human derelicts. They are paintings in ink, on paper, for the simple reason that he hadn't the means to buy canvas and paints."[14]

This evidence is important. For it explains why Rouault had no need to resort to the means used by Degas and Lautrec to acquire extensive knowledge of his subject. The dates of his early Prostitutes are the following: the first one was painted in 1903, as attested by the date that Rouault himself wrote on *Prostitute with Feathered Hat*. They were not shown in the Salons, however, until 1904 (Salon d'Automne), and 1905 (Salon des Indépendants).

In Joseph Müller's collection in Solothurn I saw a prostitute in profile which, in my opinion, may date from 1902. The canvas has been barely brushed by a thin transparent layer of color. The woman's face, which is turned toward the left and in shadow, is a striking one, and seems like the very incarnation of sin.[15] But in exposing the evil in a creature of flesh and blood who is marked by vice, Rouault adopts neither the attitude of the "customer" nor that of the scolding moralist. His position is more complex.

One might ask: why this theme rather than another? For what reason was Rouault haunted by it? Why, in the tradition of Baudelaire, Dostoevsky, and Bloy, was he fascinated by the riddle of prostitution? Answering these questions, Charles Journet believes that "the prostitute is the mirror in which all our coward-liness, all our self-indulgence is reflected, but at what a price!" (And it will be seen that this is how Rouault was to paint her.) "She reaches the point when she sells love, the love for which every creature thirsts as parched earth thirsts for water: human love, love of God, love of the dignity that was deposited in her the day her immortal soul was created, the day she was redeemed through the Cross of Christ. Truly, her poverty is a mirror-image in despair of the poverty of the saints."[16]

A delight in the lowest degree of evil may arise in a soul made for grandeur when it has apparently been frustrated by the world and its halfway measures. Jacques Maritain also wrote to Monseigneur Journet: "With regard to the question put to you by Pierre Courthion, I should reply as you have done. However, I wonder if, in the case of Bloy and Rouault, and perhaps in the case of Baudelaire and Claudel, there was not also the idea that these unfortunate women were the ransom of a bourgeois society and, in a certain measure, sacrificial victims . . . ."[17]

These last words reached us through a friend who was also Rouault's companion during the Versailles years, when his thoughts were much taken up with the theme of the prostitute as a victim of respectable society. In his work, Rouault recalls the searing words spoken by Jesus Christ two thousand years ago, against the hypocritical, the self-satisfied, and the lukewarm who neither despair nor hope: "Verily I say unto you, that the publicans and the harlots go into the kingdom of God before you."[18]

Rouault was to make a frontal attack on this theme for the first time. For the first time, he was to make of the prostitute a figure that was quite different from those that had been painted thus far. Indeed, his evocation of the harlot resembles that to be found in certain great passages of the Bible. Under his touch, the *fille de joie* becomes a symbol, the symbol of corruption, through money, of a great part of humanity, the expiatory victim of our society. He establishes a parallel between her and those travelers condemned to perpetual wandering: the itinerant players of the traveling shows. For Rouault identified himself with both clown and prostitute, as a reaction against people with "principles," as well as against the heros of Roman history, so dear to the Beaux-Arts and to the bourgeoisie. He identified himself with them.

Baudelaire once said: "Only strong men are intoxicated by the charms of horror." In protest against the ivory tower in which, consciously or unconsciously, his former teacher had lived, this young painter showed the reality of prostitution and the enslaved who wallow in it, motionless, monsters of indolence, "thick gelatinous masses of flesh, vacillating flesh, upon which no genuine kiss will ever be pressed again, flesh that seems rotten, abscessed. . . . For the man of sensibility, it is as though the artist were confronting him with dead women, or with dug-up corpses, for they have now entered into the realm of the abstract."[19] Gustave Coquiot spoke in defense of these "gutter Venuses" crouching "in poses assumed by epileptic toads," presenting "their fat bellies adorned with brushwood instead of soft hair." "As soon as Rouault gets hold of a woman," added this critic, who was friendly to the "damned" painters, "he leaves her to marinate in vinegar, in acid, in order to make her dry up like a stick, or swell like a bladder."[20] And the fact is that Rouault was haunted by these women. We see them reflected in his paintings as though in a game of mirrors, in full face, in profile, or in three-quarters, always

against the same dark, anonymous background. The flesh is always the same, as is the face, drawn in heavy, dark outline and presented in the most complex, subtlest of techniques: watercolor, oils, pastels, oil washes and, occasionally, all of them together.[21]

It is impossible to remain unaffected by so striking a reality, which has the force of an accusation, with its aura of dirty blue laundry water. Rouault's prostitute eventually takes on the shape of all that is perishable, transient in human nature. Léon Bloy's remark in reply to a visitor who, having noticed Rouault's presence at the interview, exclaimed: "That man represents the future!" "The future," Bloy retorted, "is death."

Although Cézanne and Daumier are the dominating influences, Rouault's painting clearly suggests an impending resurrection. He stigmatizes the dullness of the academic, anecdotic, representational art of his time, and calls upon the victims of run-of-the-mill justice to sit in judgment: "These prostitutes are the Fates and the court of last appeal," writes Michel Puy; "or, rather, they are so remote from life that one might think they were the dead awakened in their graves, to be held up to the covetous desires of all the males who have been hoping to see the image of real love appear before their eyes."[22]

Like Baudelaire, Rouault shocked the public. In 1904, visitors to the Salon d'Automne[23] found the opaque darkness of his painting repulsive, for he took an exactly opposite course to that of the Impressionists, for whom light was everything. This explains, too, the term *tableaux noirs* (blackboards, as well as black pictures) that was applied to his circus impressions and his landscapes, the latter described as "tiny, dim and, at the same time, delicately shaded, in the manner of the English school;[24] "syntheses à la Hogarth . . . impenetrable blackness."[25] For the anonymous critic of *La Revue illustrée*, Rouault was "the greatest and only tenebrist of his time." His warmest supporter, however, was Vauxcelles, in *Gil Blas*, and although he did speak of the "sneering crowds in front of three or four of Rouault's 'black pictures,'" (before which Luc-Olivier Merson, an "official" painter of the time, even went so far as to light a match) he nevertheless added immediately: "When Rouault paints a *fille de joie*, he doesn't rejoice cruelly, the way Lautrec does, at the vice the poor creature exudes; he seems rather to suffer, to weep over it."[26] In other words, beneath the blackness of this "paste made of caviar, blacking, and pitch," this critic was able to sense the immense pity the artist felt for the sinful creature. And although Péladan spoke of Rouault's nightmares, rejecting them along with the works of Odilon Redon and Lautrec, those "exaggerated scorners of reality," Elie Faure, after praising some small landscapes "hardly any bigger than your hand," which "are a sequel to the great Romantic school," wondered, as he looked at the clowns,[27] those "figures drenched in shadow, half marionette, half caricature, with something that is both comic and painful about them," why Rouault didn't go in for the demoniacal. "He has a feeling for monsters and gargoyles; and the temptations of St. Anthony, which look ridiculous when painted by Téniers, would overwhelm us if done by him."[28]

But many who had defended him earlier, appeared now to have deserted him, and even Gustave Geffroy took exception to Rouault's "opaque darkness." As for M. Delaunay, he poked fun at him: "Peals of laughter," he wrote, "may be heard in front of the seven frames—and if I say frames, it is because they are the only things one can see—that contain M. Rouault's entries. Black, beautiful inky black . . . and that's all!"[29]

But the severest criticism of Rouault's entries came from Léon Bloy. On November 5, 1904, after a visit to the Salon d'Automne, the "ungrateful beggar" made the following note in his diary: "A sermon on the subject of death would be a fitting inauguration speech for the Salon d'Automne, which I find very painful. To my sorrow, I understand literally nothing of the unfinished first studies by my friend Rouault, who was probably destined to be the greatest modern painter, but is now being dragged downward by some unbelievable mental aberration. After starting with Rembrandt, the poor devil has now taken a leap into utter darkness."[30]

Quite obviously, as regards the plastic arts, Bloy did not have as good an eye as Huysmans. "I never get any farther than *Olympia*," he said, "which for me was doing very well indeed." He thought Brou was a great sculptor because of his monument to Villiers de l'Isle-Adam; had compared Desvallières to a pelican bleeding for its young; and had admired Léon Bonhomme, who had painted his portrait.[31] "In artistic matters, Bloy followed his own sentimental impulses," Rouault explained. And he added: "You understand, I am sure, that there are things that remain a closed book to people who see very clearly in another domain. A deaf-mute could create something very beautiful and still be unable to speak except in grunts."

It was in 1905, however, that, following upon the exposition of Rouault's works in the Salon d'Automne, the conflict between the two friends reached really distressing proportions. That same year, Bloy had dedicated to Rouault the first chapter of *Belluaires et Porchers*, devoted to Lautréamont's *Chants de Maldoror*[32] with which Rouault's work offered a certain analogy. First of all, on May 1, on a visit to the Gustave Moreau Museum, Bloy had seen *The Child Jesus Among the Doctors*, which was stored there. Of this he wrote: "I didn't know that Rouault had such an immense talent. Now I know it, and I have told him so with enthusiasm."[33] Meanwhile, Rouault saw the famous recluse quite often. Then in the 1905 Salon d'Automne he showed a triptych entitled *Prostitutes*. One panel of the triptych was inspired by the Poulots, characters from Bloy's novel, *La Femme pauvre (The Poor Woman)*.[34]

When Bloy returned to his Montmartre apartment on October 31, after a second visit to the Salon d'Automne, he made the following entry in his diary, on the subject of Rouault: "This artist, whom one thought capable of painting seraphim, no longer seems to be able to conceive anything but atrocious, vengeful caricatures. The meanness of the bourgeois arouses such a violent reaction of horror in him that his art has apparently been fatally wounded by it. He thought he was doing my Poulots.[35] For nothing on earth would I accept such 'illustration' as this.

Something very tragic was called for: two completely bourgeois characters, male and female, guileless, peaceable, merciful, and good enough to make the chargers of the constellations foam at the mouth. Instead, he has made them into two cut-throats from the poor suburban districts."[36]

"I should have liked to please Léon Bloy," Rouault wrote in a letter to Joseph Bollery, which the biographer of the "ungrateful beggar" was kind enough to show me. "However, I failed miserably, at least with the characters in question.

"And if I gave an impression of 'assassins from the poor suburban districts with that awful man in the derby hat and that old harridan, it is because, although not a professional illustrator, I was first of all (at least I hope I was) a painter. Unless my memory fails me, in Bloy's book, the Poulot woman is depicted sitting astride the shafts of a street hawker's cart which, for the type of hypocritical bourgeois Léon Bloy imagined his Poulots to be, seems going a bit far. It seems to me, too, to be more in keeping with my two figures. However, my vanity on an author is not very great."[37]

Not only was Rouault completely lacking in false pride but, from then on, he was careful to avoid all subjects of dispute with this man who was his senior, and in whose presence he remained "standing, leaning against the wall, a slight smile on his closed lips, staring ahead of him, with an apparently impassive expression, but with a pallor that increased when the subject of modern painting was broached. Rouault grew pale but he remained heroically silent until the end."[38]

Indeed—and this was another proof of Rouault's strong character—he was to maintain this difficult silence until the death of Léon Bloy who, year after year, had made increasingly violent attacks on him. Bloy seemed quite unaware that in reality the attacks harmed only himself. "I have of course seen your unique and sempiternal canvas," he wrote Rouault, on May 1, 1907, after visiting the Salon des Indépendants. "It still shows the same sluts and buffoons, with one lamentable difference, that each time the amount of detritus is greater. . . . Today I have two things to say to you, and only two, the last I shall ever say, after which, for me, you'll be merely a chunk of likable meat. First: you are attracted solely by what is ugly; you appear to have a sort of vertigo of hideousness. Second: if you were a man who prayed, a religious man, a communicant, you could not paint those horrible pictures. A Rouault who was capable of profound sentiment would feel a bit terrified in this atmosphere. It is time for you to stop."[39] There was no doubt that Bloy was growing more and more aggressive, more and more a prey to the "burning, feverish, hallucinated passion" Charles Journet speaks of, "and which, every morning, made him call down upon the iniquities of this world the punishments of the Last Judgment."[40]

In spite of everything, however, Rouault kept on. He was well aware of Bloy's lack of flair for painting, and he was also determined to carry out what he had started. With his family he nevertheless continued to go to see Bloy on Sundays[41] until as late as June 11, 1917, which was the date of his last visit, for Bloy died that same year. But, in his painting, he never ceased to proclaim his sympathies for the disinherited of this world. For some, his wrestlers and prostitutes were "formless,

Next come the prostitutes. It should be recalled that about 1903, in a painting entitled *Prostitutes* in the Hahnloser collection, Rouault had made a sort of open-air attraction of these women, almost inseparable from the circus dancers and the ticket sellers. In 1906, in the *Prostitutes*, the watercolor in the Witziger collection, he presents, in fullface, two terrifying creatures who, themselves, are frightened under their grease paint and scarred in their nakedness by all the sins of this world. There are the women about whom Bloy said that "all that remains of their bodies is the silhouette line; a caress is practically inconceivable in these grimy pigments, redolent of the grave."[55] In the watercolor in the collection of Dr. and Mrs. Harry Bakwin, which dates from the same year, Rouault underlines the indolence that makes woman into a monster, a "pus-filled goatskin with slimy thighs," as one poet put it. Looking at these two flabby women, one has the impression that, being unable to use their legs, they can only get about by sliding along on their buttocks.

This woman of Babylon—it was her like that was called upon to entertain at the ancient feast—this woman is powerfully evoked in Rouault's *Nude with Pink Garters*. She was preceded by a *Nude*, of 1905, with the eyes of a rebellious slave, fastening her stockings with the gestures learned in her trade, beside a rumpled bed. In 1906 Rouault finished *Prostitute at Her Mirror* in which this woman's face, reflected in the glass, expresses the shame and pathos of her kind. "Beyond what is visible, a painter perceives the shadow of infinity projected on every creature."[56] This work recalls something Claudel told a friend,[57] and which he himself had been told by the priest who received him into the Catholic faith. A prostitute to whom this priest had just given the last sacraments said to him: "Open the wardrobe and you will see what kept me from suicide." What he saw was the statue of the Virgin Mary.

The watercolor and pastel *Prostitute Doing Her Hair* in the Petit Palais, as sort of Ceres bearing within herself the fruitfulness of Earth, precedes by one year the recumbent *Odalisque*, with it virulent greenish tonality. A little earlier, Rouault had prepared the way for this painting with the blue and russet *Olympia*, now in the Leclercq collection.

Finally, we come to the *Two Prostitutes*. (There are several variations of this painting; one of the most elaborate is in a Russian collection, and in a private collection in Switzerland, one of the most sketchy.) Here, in a spirit that recalls Cervantes, may be seen the fat and the thin, the bloated and the gaunt, filing along, like condemned ones being led to the rack. Among the critics of his time, Coquiot was the only one, perhaps, to realize what was so terrifying in these works. "You have dared," he wrote, "to torture the female who was so certain that she would always be adored! You have scourged her, flogged her, rent her in two; you have debased her in all her pride; you have emptied her breasts, creviced her belly, blown up her buttocks, twisted her legs, battered her face! And over it all you have spread a noxious color, composed of all the reds of blood and all the greens of putrefaction. You have executed, for a pope with genius, the rarest, the most eloquent, the most magnificent of windows for the cathedral to come."[58]

wrote Roger Marx, "bodies in soft flesh tints with ultramarine shadings may be vaguely seen, pressed one to another."[80] Gustave Kahn wrote that Rouault "paints vermilion rumps which bulge as though he had pummeled them into these shapes with his fists, and he conveys the synthesis of desire in the lines of a leg."[81]

The period of Rouault's obsession with the prostitute as a theme was now coming to a close. And, indeed, since he first treated it in 1902, he explored it so thoroughly that everything approaching it before him, from Pompeii to Constantin Guys and Lautrec pales beside his hallucinating figures. Just as Rembrandt's Saskia is rooted in our vision for all time, so are Rouault's prostitutes, in their own way. It was thus, too, that his friend André Suarès depicted them, in the book that he and Rouault brought out together:

> *Prends ma chair; sers-toi de mon corps; tue-moi, crêve la bête de louage; paye-la, mais tais-toi. Tu n'as pas à savoir d'ou je viens, ni pourquoi, ni comment.*
>
> *Plus de chair, plus de viande, plus de cette peau à soi, plus de ces viandes d'homme, avec leurs membres durs et ces poils de bête brute. L'eau légère, l'eau fraiche, salive de la nuit, l'eau profonde et l'oubli.*

> [Take my flesh; use my body; kill me; work the old hired horse to death; pay her, but keep quiet. It's none of your business where I come from, or why, or how.
>
> This flesh, this meat, this skin are no longer mine; no more male bodies, with their stiff limbs and animal hair.
>
> Sparkling water, cool water, the secretions of the night, deep water, oblivion.][82]

From now on, the big whore will be standing, fastening her stockings, or lazily moving her pleasure vendor's body about the room. She will be the vampire—but always ready to answer the call of mercy and of "God's incomprehensible benevolence toward to our sins, that led Bloy to say that the spirit 'prostitutes itself' to come and save us."[83]

Lust is a deadly sin, while false witness is a sin against God's eighth commandment. Better still, call it injustice; Giotto represented it as a livid sentinel with an angular, clawlike profile, hiding behind tiny shrubs too small to conceal him, under the ramparts of a dilapidated old château.

After the prostitutes came the judges, the defendants, and the tribunals. In 1907, Rouault began to portray the legal figures and other participants in the trials that he followed out of curiosity, being interested in the great variety of human types to be seen in the courtrooms. The judges, however, are no more respectfully

Dancer Lacing Her Slipper · *1906*

Circus Girl · 1902

Rugged Rosa · 1913

Ticket Sellers, Street Circus · 1904

Pitch-Ball Puppets (The Wedding of Nini-patte-en-l'air) · 1905

The Model · 1906

Prostitutes (study) · *1910*

Prostitutes · 1906

Prostitutes · 1906

122   *Prostitutes · (Composition) 1903*

Dancer · 1906

The Couple (also called The Loge) · 1905

Monsieur et Madame Poulot · 1905

Equestrienne · 1906

The Salon (also called At the Theater) · *1906*

Bathers · 1903

Prostitute · 1906

Clown with Inkwell · 1905

Head of a Tragic Clown · 1904

Clown and Child · 1905

Clown with Accordion (also called The Loge) · *1906*

134

Street-Fair Wrestlers · 1906

Parade · 1906

The Bridge · 1905

Fete at the Edge of the Pool · *1906*

Odalisque · 1906

138

Wrestler · about 1913

Monsieur X · 1911

142

Pitch-Ball Puppets (Puppets or The Bride) · *1907*

143

Head of a Clown · about 1907

handled than the gendarmes. "In these unforgettably terrifying pictures, both these representatives of authority have faces that are as sinister as those of the gangsters over whom their authority is exercised; all are grim and low-browed, battered by base passions and frenzied excesses. They look at us like so many live puppets in a burlesque marionette show, at once terrifying and splendid."[84]

A magistrate in the Seine courts, Deputy Prosecutor Granier ("They're all true to life," he said of Rouault's judges, "and I know them like a book."), arranged for Rouault to be present in the courtrooms. In fact, it was through Granier that Rouault witnessed the condemnation of a poor devil named Vacher. From this came the *Condemned Man* of 1907.[85] In this canvas, with a dark, purplish-red-russet background made warmer through the addition of reds and blues, the man who paid the price is put before us with terrifying effectiveness. The portrayal of the judges conveys just as lively a sense of pathos. Indeed, the dark, dramatic quality of this picture suggests that human justice is highly relative. What are we in its eyes? What are we worth? In other words, aren't we all equally tainted by sin? The head of the judge on the left appears to be the twin of the condemned man's head (the only distinguishing features being the shirt of the one, and the robe and jabot of the other). Above all, however, we must not think that Rouault was anarchically inclined to blame those who have a difficult and terrible role —those who must weigh, on the scales of justice, the assets and the debits of people who have struck a criminal blow at the community. On the contrary, in portraying his judges, he gave them the same uneasiness of expression that he himself had experienced: "The reason I gave my judges such woeful faces," he said, "was doubtless because I expressed the anguish I myself feel when I see one human obliged to judge another. And when I mistook the judge's face for that of the defendant, I was merely betraying my own distress. For nothing in the world would I accept the position of judge!"[86]

Courageously, insistently, caring nothing about censure, Rouault continued to protest against all forms of brutality and servitude, all vindictive retaliation, all humiliating degradation. Abbé Morel was right when he stressed the fact that Rouault's violent anger was "not that of an administrator of justice, but of a prophet."[87] He could be so incensed that he might almost have been guilty of committing a deadly sin had his outbursts not been as justified as that of Our Lord's when he drove the moneychangers from the temple.

"My father," Isabelle Rouault told me, "protested against the lack of insight of certain judges, against their inadequacy for the position they were called upon to fill. He had seen and heard some scandalous things in the courtrooms. With his profound knowledge of simple people (he had also had occasion to observe abandoned children and the ravages of alcoholism) he must often have been shocked by some particular decisions.[88] It sometimes happened, too, that Rouault saw lawyers as Daumier did, as men who occasionally, through clever eloquence, are able to obtain acquittal for criminals.

On this same theme of administrators of justice,[89] the watercolor on paper in the Petit Palais, entitled *Men of Justice* (about 1913), is expressive and moving in its delicate scale of browns and blues. The judge in the black cap, under the crucifix, recalls the poem Rouault published in *Paysages légendaires*, in 1929:

Le condamné s'en est allé
indifférent et fatigué
son avocat en phrases creuses
et imposantes
a clamé son innocence
un homme rouge tonitruant
et se dressant
a disculpé la Société
et chargé l'accusé
sous un Jésus en croix
oublié là.

[The condemned man went away
indifferent, weary
his lawyer in hollow
pompous phrases
had proclaimed his innocence
a red-robed prosecutor bellowing
rose up
held society blameless
and indicted the accused man
under a crucified Christ
now forgotten there.][90]

In connection with these courtroom scenes, we have already mentioned the name of Daumier and, undoubtedly, if there exists a master with whom Rouault has affinities, it is this son of a glass and picture-frame dealer from Marseilles. He too was a painter of lawyers and judges, he too portrayed the eternal dispossession of the poor and outlawed. And when Rouault mentions Daumier in his *Souvenirs intimes*, he seems also to be defending himself against philistine attacks: "People said of Daumier that his work was 'exaggerated and caricatural' but—except for Baudelaire and a few others—they forgot to look and see what an excellent craftsman he was, and how great and strong he could be with modest means, when so many others, who employed every pictorial means, remained poor and second-rate artists."[91] "My art is not based on any sort of compromise," Rouault said of himself, "and my greatest concern is not to exaggerate unduly. I agree that the grotesque and the tragic are juxtaposed in my works, but aren't they also inseparable in life?"[92] It is true that Daumier was "discovered" as a painter posthumously. With regard to his prints, one is obliged to recognize, as Rouault did, that "after a while, this series of powerful crocodiles lithographed by Daumier may become boring, except for a carefully selected few."[93] It is as a painter that

Daumier was to attain to the rank of a great artist, a designation which will never again be disputed.

Although, at first sight, a comparison between these two painters would appear to be obvious, it cannot bear close scrutiny. First of all, women are generally absent in Daumier's work, whereas in Rouault's, woman is everywhere present even though she is seldom seen in the role of Aphrodite or as hostess of elegant little dinner parties. With Rouault we pass from the streetwalker to what could be the wives and consorts of biblical kings, whose profiles look as if struck in metal by the artist.[94] But whereas Daumier's fraternal kindliness and humanistic religion are conditioned by love of the Republic and of humanity according to the gospel of the men of "Forty-eight," the charity of Rouault, who was an avowed Christian, penetrates beneath the surface and strikes at the very heart of what is most incomplete, most imperfect, and vulnerable in all of us. I do not, of course, mean to disparage Daumier's kindliness, which is so manifest in a work like the *Washerwoman*, depicting both the wretchedness and the dignity of the worker. Nor do I wish to belittle the faith that was his. But this faith was perhaps somewhat limited. It was perhaps less capable than Rouault's of including the employer as well as the employee, the judge as well as the man condemned to die. The only thing about the two painters that may at times seem comparable is the treatment; but here again, by virtue of certain refinements in his work, Daumier may appear to be a vigorous epigone of the Fragonard wash technique, whereas Rouault set out to destroy the aristocratic, pleasure-seeking charm of the eighteenth century that, for the French, had become taboo. With him, we enter into the domain of all that is "antipretty, antigraceful, antipolished. . . . We are confronted with the expression of power."[95] But like Daumier, Rouault uses a line that surrounds form, a thick line in which background and foreground are integrated, so to speak, with the contour.

Attempts have also been made to associate Rouault with the German Expressionism of Jawlensky, and especially of Nolde, whose proletarian, hallucinatory Christ, painted in a vulgar, waxlike color, has no real relationship to Rouault's except that it is contemporary. But apart from the fact that his work reflects the spirit of the age, the *Zeitgeist*, Rouault differs from these Germanic painters who proudly called themselves "barbarians," in his "Latin sense of strict, definite form."[96]

The date of Rouault's great encounter with the public was approaching, and it was doubtless because he wanted to show a large group of his works that he sent nothing to the 1909 Salon d'Automne. His first one-man show, consisting of 121 paintings, eight drawings, forty-three ceramics, and ten glazed terra cotta pieces, took place at the Galerie Druet,[97] from February 24 to March 5, 1910.

The catalogue had a preface by Jacques Favelle.[98] After commenting upon the gravity of these works, "this strange assemblage of evil or pitiable heads" which are just the opposite of "low caricature or derision," Favelle declared that they "bore the mark of a patient workman who loves his tools as well as the raw materials he works with." Then, after having noted in Rouault's painting the absence of "Nativities to adore" and "glorious Assumptions," he stated very aptly that Rouault had "created sequels to the 'Dance of Death' sequences of the late Middle Ages and to Callot's 'Beggars.'" He made the point, however, that Rouault was aware that since the Renaissance the crafts had been replaced by the fine arts and that "the continuity of an almost religious discipline" had been replaced by the somewhat disorderly, convulsive movements of individual genius." He interprets Rouault's constant state of anxiety, his habit of working "nervously, by fits and starts, continually correcting himself, filled with a quivering, almost frenzied passion," as due to "the feeling of isolation that forces all modern artists to look for their means of expression in themselves alone."

The exhibition was presented in the following manner: *The Child Jesus Among the Doctors* and the *Dead Christ Mourned by the Holy Women* formed a backdrop against which Rouault stands as a young man who has reached maturity. A.S. (André Salmon) gives a summary of the paintings, among which he cites: *Street Group; Peasant; Old Man; Wrestlers; Pierrot; Circus Ticket Seller; Courtroom; Judges; Punch; Dancer; Lecture;*[99] *Clowns as Motley as Their Talk Is Crazy.*[100] He forgets to mention, among the works shown, a certain number of likenesses of dour professors, and six paintings entitled *Automobilist.* J.-F. Schnerb compared Rouault to Poe, in that all his details already contain the final effect.[101] The critic of *Le Siècle* considered that, after the period spent in Moreau's atelier, Rouault had taken refuge "in amorphous, unformulated, confused daubing." Vauxcelles, who was disappointed, spoke of hallucinating sketches, drawn with painful frenzy," of "obscene negresses," and "grimacing judges." "Listening to M. Rouault's cries, outbursts and raucous stammerings, one is reminded of a Huysmans or a Bloy, spewing out their disgust for their times, or else of some mystic who both abhors life and is terrified by it."[102] "It can't be helped," wrote S. Bender, in the *Courrier Français*, "to be true to one's self and to be a success—these are incompatible. At the Druet gallery the public is struggling to understand Rouault, who enjoys seeing the gloomy side of things and insists upon stewing in his own dark juices, even in his ceramics. And Methey does not seem at all reluctant to go along with these concoctions."[103]

In general, people preferred academic paintings to what they called Rouault's "collection of horrors."[104] The *Echos parisiens*, however, criticized the reliance of the old-fashioned academic school on Henner's mannerisms, and almost fulsomely went on to say that "Toulouse-Lautrec, despite his keen perception, was little more than a maker of posters, whereas Rouault is proving to be quite as discerning, with greater power—a real painter."[105] Others spoke of Rouault's *Cackling Country Women*, *Newsboy*, the unforgettable *Old Man*, the *Pierrots*—as a relief from the insipid prettiness of Chéret's work.[106] On the other hand, *L'Indiscret* declared that interest in Rouault was "a real crime when a country has such masters [believe it or not!] as Roll, Albert Besnard, La Gandara, and Paul Chabas."[107]

Jacques Rivière, writing of this exhibition in the *Nouvelle Revue Française*, spoke of Rouault's "lines that, although they do not follow the form precisely and

148

continuously, nevertheless, by repeating, retreating, and crossing one another, succeed in capturing the form in their countless interlacings. This is why Rouault's images always seem to have been summoned with feverish fingers from the very depths of the canvas; not laid down quietly on the paper, but wrested from it by a slashing technique of incisions, spurts, and violent deformations. These images are immutable; they derive basic strength, as though through roots, from nature in which they are founded, and whose massive organization they borrow."[108]

The above article was undoubtedly the fairest and the most penetrating of all those that were written about Rouault in 1910 on the occasion of this exhibition. Jacques Rivière, whose intuition penetrated the hidden side of human beings, also spoke of the bluntness of Rouault's statement. "Form as he sees it is not the contour of things as ascertained by the palm of the hand. On the contrary, it is hidden under an outer covering, withdrawn shyly into the very heart of being. In the first stages Rouault adheres closely to his model, encompasses it with docility, woos it with the utmost devotion. But this is only to provoke it to self-revelation. Then suddenly, the vivid secret gesture he had been watching for, an inner tension is released, and the form is there before him, trembling, fleeting, like startled game that scampers away."[109]

Lastly, the ceramics. Rouault had exhibited a first collection at the Salon des Indépéndants in 1907. In the same year, in the autumn Salon, he had shown a series of paintings on semiglazed pottery, under the name of Metthey, with the following remark: "The earthenware pieces belong to M. Vollard."[110] Then, in the exhibition at Druet's, in 1910, it will be recalled that he showed other ceramics. The following year, at the Salon d'Automne, Rouault showed a rather large number of ceramics made to decorate M. André Mare's polished walnut dining room, in addition to the paintings, among which were *Winter* and the *Baptism of Christ*.[111] A critic who signed himself "La Palette" saw in these plaques, platters, plates, and vases "Monsieur Ubu descended into hell, with his cousins from the legal, military, financial, governmental, and cat-house worlds." And he added: "Baudelaire would have liked to meditate like this upon human infamy while relishing his pear and his cheese."[112]

In general, Rouault's friends, as well as the more informed critics, were most enthusiastic about these ceramic pieces, to the point, even, of neglecting what was essential. "Bonnard is the only one (and yet I hardly know him)," Rouault wrote later, "who didn't go into ecstasies over the ceramics at my first show in Druet's gallery, but insisted on my painting."[113]

At Rouault's second one-man show, held at Druet's in 1911, a collection of ceramic wares was exhibited, together with paintings. In *Paris-Journal* there was the following note: "Rouault exhibition tomorrow, December 11. It will be an important one, containing 45 canvases, 11 monotypes, 16 glazed pottery pieces and a few humerous comical plates on one of which is written: 'Quite overdone, the Gioconda's smile!'"[114] And André Salmon, the author of the article, added: "M. Rouault takes pleasure in reproducing his compositions on china, in order that the wicked, recognizing their monstrous faces in their plates, as in a mirror, should lose their appetites in consequence."[115] A round platter, with the title *Wrecks*, bears the motto, under an old lady with a lorgnette: "I posed for La Belle Zelie."[116] "Haunted as he is by the grotesque," wrote the critic of *Action*, "Rouault only conceives of beauty as being distorted, bloated, worm-eaten. He likes what is ugly and portrays it in extraordinarily rich, subdued colors which he employs with the mastery of a great painter."[117]

As usual, Vauxcelles spoke well of both the painter and his exhibition: "This is the art of a visionary and a satirist who destroys his victims while moaning and suffering himself. Magnificent colors flash like lightning against the black depths of his backgrounds. . . . For Rouault, modern humanity is composed of swarming larvae, of the epileptic contortions of the damned. And this bitter pessimist flagellates and disfigures his fellow men only in order to throw himself at the feet of a fierce Christ, whom he has represented in the really unforgettable Baptism."[118]

In 1912, Rouault had his third exhibition at the Druet Gallery. Régis Michaud was made uneasy by his "misshapen, grimacing faces that were often too long, with their out-of-joint bone structures, slashed as though by a scythe, full of bumps and hollows, reddish at the top and greenish at the bottom."[119] Gustave Kahn, who was the first to write free verse, noted that "M. Rouault is one of the most searching, the most disturbed, the most hungry for true art, the most experimental, the most picturesque, the most debated and, in the better sense of the word, the most debatable among present-day painters."

We have seen in Rouault's painted ceramics the gradual development of the caustic, but yet teasing, side of his nature. Soon, however, this tendency toward wit and humor became quite apparent in pieces other than ceramics, as, for instance, in his *Ubu* suite; and it was to have even freer rein in series of "caprices" which he called "albums." Rouault had begun these sequences in 1910, if we are to believe Guillaume Apollinaire, who tells us that they were called: *Versailles*, *Gentleman-Painters*, *Miserere*, *Provincial and International Types*, *Familiar Types*. These "terrible, distressing drawings," wrote Apollinaire, "which are so filled with pity and irony, alternate with tart, bitter little comments, with strange poems that recall those recited in Umbrian villages by followers of St. Francis of Assisi, the 'minstrels of God,'[120] whose songs rose to a new, heart-rending lyricism."[121]

But painting is not everything in this world. There is also life—family life, in particular. On January 27, 1908, Rouault married Marthe Le Sidaner, whom he had met at the home of friends. She was a delicate, highbred, witty woman, the sister of a Pointillist painter belonging to Henri Martin's circle. Two days before the wedding the groom-to-be had received the following letter from Léon Bloy:

Paris, Montmartre
January 25, 1908

My dear Rouault,
   I believe I know you well enough to be sure that you are not counting on my presence at your nuptial Mass on Monday. I hate these purely

social ceremonies during which no one really prays, not even those immediately concerned, and least of all the immediately concerned; to which people go out of idle curiosity, with their minds full of stupid or dirty thoughts; or else they shake hands with any- and everybody while mouthing stereotyped good wishes that are enough to make a tapir vomit.

You know I am fond of you, Rouault. All I can do is to pray for you, and that I intend to do.[122]

Rouault always deprecated the attempts of art critics who sought to find analogies between his painting and certain magnificent, if somewhat extravagant and occasionally uncharitable, pages from Bloy's works. "Don't compare me too much with Bloy," he wrote Gustave Coquiot. "He never liked what I did, and he had a horror of modern art, or at least what people call modern art."[123] But it should not be forgotten that Bloy had become a great spiritual support for Rouault, just as Huysmans had been a few years earlier. So the young couple did not fail to pay a call on this friend who had already become the "pilgrim of the Absolute." According to Mme. Rouault, their reception was an icy one, but fortunately Bloy's two daughters were also present. One of them, Véronique, seventeen at the time, played a hymn of her own composition. Mme. Rouault,[124] who was a pianist by profession, paid Véronique the type of compliment that only a real musician could. This made Bloy glow with satisfaction.

Then, in 1912, the Rouaults moved to Versailles, where their address was 36, rue de l'Orangerie. Along with Rouault were his aging parents, his wife, and two daughters: Geneviève, born in 1908, and Isabelle, born two years later.[125] Mme. Rouault undoubtedly did more than her share to support the household at this time. When she left home in the morning to give piano lessons in Paris, or at the Lycée de Versailles, her still active mother-in-law took charge of the household.

Rouault reproached himself at that time for not being able to provide sufficiently for his family, a circumstance that made him oversensitive. As a result, when a tactless priest suggested to him that he should "make paintings that would sell,"[126] his conscience was upset. Fortunately, his friends Jacques and Raïssa Maritain, at whose home he dined once a week, succeeded in convincing him of the error of this point of view. He used to arrive alone at their apartment, after his day's work, and would usually begin with a long monologue on whatever was uppermost in his mind. He "would start by pouring out his grievances about everything that had exhausted or irritated him. Then, little by little, he would calm down and his tone would grow more cheerful, he would even recapture his irony and gaiety, begin to tell funny—but never vulgar—stories. . . . At these moments, he would often take from his pocket illegible scraps of paper on which he alone could decipher his latest poems."

He also showed the Maritains his "satirical drawings" which, in their way, constitute a sort of "exegesis of the commonplace" imbued with the same tremendous irony that is to be found in the works of Bloy. Rouault was grateful to these

line of administrators, architects, gardeners, and artists of all kinds who fulfilled the royal desire for buildings and formal walks. But, to tell the truth, he made some rather curious pictures of the place. Because of their heavy outlines one's first impression is that they represent no particular place. Then, as one looks more closely, something seems to grow clearer, more precise, something that suggests an atmosphere of leisure, wealth, and tradition. We begin to distinguish small bodies of water, figures leaning idly against railings. Previously, in 1910, he had painted the *Parc de Versailles, the Staircase* (or *The Terrace*) with a lady carrying a parasol coming down the steps. Here we have a Versailles seen as if for the first time, unmasked, and here too we have a Rouault who has meditated on Versailles' harmonious balance, bewitching charms, and architectural poetry. At the same time he is aware of all the toil, tears, and tenacity that this must have cost. Am I mistaken? Like a watermark, through the fountain, beneath the green, gleaming in the spray of the basins, I seem to see in contrast[133] the face of the young worker, painted at about this same time, the *Head of a Laborer* (1911) in the Ralph F. Colin collection. This head, with its tense youthful expression, is bandaged; as though wounded by a shot fired at some barricade, it is marked by the stigmata of poverty and hard work.

"I know my technical resources," Rouault wrote to Suarès. "I know that I can do unusual things, both strong and noble. . . . More and more alone, and in Versailles—that is, the North Pole of art—never any responsiveness at the opportune moment; I have, of course, one devoted friend (Maritain) but he is more overwhelmed than I by the burden of his interminable, daily labors."[134]

A few days later Suarès answered Rouault, reproaching him for finding fault with others. "You have always been inclined to see the world in terms of your own rebellious thoughts and indignation," he wrote. "But these things were inside you and you had to be delivered of them. . . . You came from a background of pinched circumstances, cellars, and all the other accursed, monster-haunted places. Don't go back to all that."[135]

Rouault knew that his "gloomy depths" irritated Suarès, but he also knew that Suarès accepted the fact that he must work with the somber and the sinister. His "Women" and his "Prostitutes" were now epitomized in Salome. What he was thinking, though he did not put it down, was that this Salome was very different from Gustave Moreau's: this one was less pleasing, had broken with tradition and, at the same time, there was nothing historical about it. This Salome was in fact very alive, to be found on any street corner. He therefore defended himself against Suarès' criticisms. "If, for a long while, I have seemed to be drifting," he wrote, "it was partly for the following reason: I had accumulated so many forms, figures, feelings, and emotions that they constituted an insuperable obstacle, and it all had to come out one way or another. The day of my deliverance, my friends —or rather, those I believed to be such—threw up their hands in horror. When people have stuck a label on a poor devil's back, he is expected to act the part; I was 'a mystic,' and now I had brought into the world a self-assertive, untamable offspring who, from birth, shook his fist at society; for some of them I was a man

156

list was by now a brilliant one, including such names as M. and Mme. Marcel Sembat, MM. Olivier Saincère, Stéphane Piot, Gustave Coquiot, Baignières, Dutilleul, Leclanché, John Quinn, Dr. Girardin, M. and Mme. Henri Simon, Mme. Hédy Hahnloser, and Mme. Louise Hervieu.

Vollard became interested in Rouault and was planning to purchase his entire atelier. For the painter this would mean some security and the possibility of plunging "without guilt feelings" into his daily work; he could also feel stimulated by the fact of having been singled out by this man who had championed Cézanne, Renoir, Pissarro, and Degas, and who was now making advances to him.

In April, 1914, Rouault had come to Versailles, the city of kings, where he moved into "modest diggings," with a little garden, "seven minutes from the lycée"[140] where his wife taught piano. The address was the Impasse des Gendarmes, a one-story house which was "tumble-down, very damp,"[141] unhealthy, and flimsily built. André Lhote recalls spending an evening there with Rouault, the painter of prostitutes and judges. "Having followed him into the children's room," he writes, "I saw three or four delightful creatures, with thick shocks of blond hair, pale and blue-eyed, either kneeling on their beds or about to drop off to sleep."[142] Claude Roulet tells us that it was there, when he could not sleep, that Rouault really began to write.

It was while living here that Rouault sent three poems to Apollinaire's magazine, *Soirées de Paris*, and they appeared in the July-August number. One of them, entitled *L'Artiste*, ends on the following lines:

> *Tomorrow will be fair*
> *He sang through his tears*
>   *holding his heart*
>   *with fervent hands*
>   *like a Host.*[143]

But alas, the future boded **no** good, for a fresh crime was soon to be committed that plunged the world into darkness. On August 4, following the invasion of Belgium by the Kaiser's troops, war was declared.

Conjurer · 1907

Woman's Profile · 1908

Mother and Child (Mme. Baignères and Her Son) · *1906*

164

Olympia · 1905

Bathers · about 1910

Seated Nude · about 1910

Mythological Composition · *about 1910*

Head of a Laborer (or The Injured Man) · *1911*

The Baptism of Christ · 1911

Landscape · about 1912

De Profundis · 1912

171

Homes of the Wretched · about 1912

African Landscape · about 1912

Village in the Snow · about 1912

Winter Landscape · about 1912

174

Landscape · 1902

Judges · 1908

Men of Justice · about 1913

Christ Mocked · 1912

The Widow · about 1912

The Faubourg of Toil and Suffering · *1912*

Woman with Hat · about 1912

"Stuck-Up" Lady · about 1910

181

Christ Mocked · about 1913?

Tragic Clown · *about 1913?*

184

5. Miserere

From now on, Rouault was championed by the dealer whom all the most important painters and sculptors of the time desired as dealer—even at the risk of being exploited. Who was this Vollard, where had he come from, how had he made his reputation? He was a curious man who generally started his sentences with a questioning and slightly stuttering "Tell me, now. . . ." I knew him in his last years. With twenty francs to his name, he had started his career as a picture dealer at the age of twenty-two, living on sea biscuits and camping out in two garrets in the rue des Apennins, one of which served as his shop and the other as living quarters. In 1893, he moved to 39, rue Lafitte, where he showed a few sketches by Manet, given him by Mme. Manet herself. Nobody wanted them. In 1895, on the advice of Odilon Redon and Maurice Denis, he organized an exhibition of works by Cézanne who, like Van Gogh, was then a drug on the market. Then, in 1898, Vollard moved to No. 6 in the same street, to the incredible place which in no way resembled a picture gallery. Gertrude Stein described it: "Inside there were a couple of canvases turned to the wall, in one corner was a small pile of big and little canvases thrown pell-mell on top of one another, in the centre of the room stood a huge dark man glooming. This was Vollard cheerful. When he was really cheerless he put his huge frame against the glass door that led to the street, his arms above his head, his hands on each upper corner of the portal and gloomed darkly into the street. Nobody thought then of trying to come in."[1]

There was something curious about the behavior of this picture dealer of whom Picasso made a Cubist portrait; a certain difficulty of adaptation to Paris, a piratical side to his character. And I remember hearing that Suarès, arriving one day in the rue Lafitte and seeing Vollard getting out of his carriage in front of his shop, had muttered between his teeth: "Salammbô, the slave merchant!"

Vollard, who was born on Reunion Island, had preferred the picture market to the career of law. He "did anything and everything" in order to sell and, at that time, invited everybody who was anybody in Paris to come to his famous "cellar" where Cézanne, Renoir, Degas, Redon, Forain, Pissarro, and many others came to dine. He sold some excellent paintings indeed and he always had some amusing things to tell about each canvas—about how he had acquired it, and the different deals it had been mixed up in.

At that time, when the painters who are recognized today as being the most important were not yet appreciated, Vollard bought paintings, if they had real quality, which the other dealers did not want and which were scorned then, for instance, as being "unfinished." In other words, this man, whom Forain called "the rue Lafitte tripe-seller" because of his rather disorderly window displays, was at the time the most clear-sighted of dealers and certainly the most open-minded that a young artist could find.[2]

Vollard had one overriding ambition: to produce books. He had a sort of presentiment of the oblivion into which a picture dealer inevitably falls after the generation he helped with his flair and astuteness has passed on. By becoming a publisher of books, Vollard hoped to make his name. He had the good taste and the foresight to choose the right artists to illustrate his books. He "did not hesitate," Rouault said, "to burden the poor pilgrim with literary and art projects it would have taken three centuries to carry out."

After the appearance of his first portfolio,[3] Vollard proceeded to more ambitious ventures.[4] His limited editions, which were no doubt the handsomest of all produced in the first half of this century, required taste, intuition, and daring. For Vollard did not look for illustrators "to whom he assigned a particular manuscript, but painters who consented to illustrate a work of their own choice."[5]

He nevertheless made so bold as to ask Rouault to do a series of etchings for a text by himself—Vollard—the hero of which was to be the resurrection of Jarry's hero under the title *Les Réincarnations du Père Ubu*, to be printed in special type chosen to match the drawings.[6] Vollard had made fruitless overtures to Forain and to Derain for this book, before concluding with Rouault. The first plate (an etching showing a Negro with upraised arms) fired him with enthusiasm, and Rouault himself became so absorbed in his work that he disappeared from view. "M. Vollard has done with him what he did with Cézanne," wrote Louis Vauxcelles, "he has stored him away in the cellar."[7]

As it happened, Rouault had been well prepared to undertake such a task as this by the numerous drawings, the quick sketches he had made according to his mood of the moment, which had so interested Guillaume Apollinaire. An idea of these early "grotesques" may be had from the sheets in the Quinn collection, which were sold at auction at the Hôtel Drouot.[8] Here, among the drawings made in 1915, we have the pensive, frightened face of the *Judge*, and a gesticulating *Prophet;* the *Eunuch* seems to be meditating on the end of all things, and the *Old Turk* is, as we say, a veritable spit and image. The 1918 output includes, together with the sketches

186

for a bestiary, the *Man with Glasses, Ubu,* and the extraordinary *Mère Ubu,* the latter a combination of concierge and lady's companion.[9]

Preparation of these illustrations for the *Réincarnations du Père Ubu* took no less than fourteen years, although Rouault started engraving the plates the very day after Vollard had decided to take him under his wing.[10]

In this series, there are many Negro characters. "They are more like Negroes than real ones" was Odilon Redon's comment. Much later, when the work was well ahead Rouault went at least ten times to the Théâtre du Châtelet to see an operetta entitled *Malikoko, roi des Negres* (Malikoko, King of the Negroes). On these occasions, the picture dealer thought it great fun to go and keep an eye on his painter. "Vollard invited all of us, one after the other, to go with him," Marie Dormoy said, "in order to let us get a good look at Rouault and, at the same time, not disturb him in his work."

Rouault, who could be caustic and often mockingly ironical, had an opportunity to disport himself at the expense of Vollard's prosaic text, the mediocrity of which had not escaped comment. Replying to a critic on *Comoedia,* who had suggested that he might do an *Ubu marchand de tableaux* (Ubu as a picture dealer), Rouault wrote in a tone of urbane banter: "Monsieur de *Comoedia,* in asking me to write the story of *Ubu marchand de tableaux,* I imagine you had a secret hope that I would disembowel him. What a mistake on your part! I am no administrator of justice, nor do I want to be one, and if I were, monsieur, to how many literary-prize Ubus, parliamentary Ubus, university Ubus, traditional or pretended liberal Ubus, even critical Ubus, I should have to pay my respects. But I shall stop there, being fearful lest I might recognize an Ubu side in myself, whether full-face, three-quarter, or one-quarter view."[11]

In the *Réincarnations du Père Ubu* Rouault exposes the stupidity and dishonesty of the very rich. For him, evil "is not so much sordid, loathsome vice," as pharisaical satisfaction. "It is putting up readily with the physical and moral wretchedness of others, and even taking advantage of it, in order to excuse oneself."[12] Ubu, in fact, has an ancestor in Henri Monnier's character, Monsieur Prud'homme, whose fame has all but eclipsed the personality of his creator. Monnier, who was a subtle chronicler of the manners and customs under Louis-Philippe and the Second Empire, was extremely witty. However, his causticity, in contrast with Daumier's or Rouault's, was not so much transformed into design and expression, as it resolved itself into a flogging of the *bourgeoisie,* "the gentlemen who will not accept an idea until it is covered with dust."[13]

The war confirmed Rouault in his skepticism about "progress," which was still on the lips of every sort of rationalist. And indeed, it was not at all by chance that, apart from the diversion he derived from his "album pieces" and his variations on the character of Ubu, he concentrated momentarily on drawing, for color was at that time too much of a distraction for him. He sought now a consuming visual balance to the horrors of war, not as a refuge, but to bring out his own active thought.

Thus Rouault plunged headlong into meditation on the Psalm of Penitence. Moved by this cry of distress, he imagined his own *Miserere* in a series of engravings

Dancers with White Dog · about 1925

that summarized the sufferings and hopes of contemporary man. Indeed, for many long years, he was to be deeply absorbed in a work based on David's sacred text (Ps. 50 [51] : 10), with which he mingled the horror of war:

> Let me hear the sounds of joy and gladness;
> the bones you have crushed shall rejoice.

In *Miserere and War*, Rouault undertook a work which, in vigorous black-and-white tones, was intended as a dialogue between the quick and the dead. It was to be a sort of vast *danse macabre* recalling those that the Dominicans and Franciscans of the fifteenth century used to stage in churches.

Little by little in Rouault's mind, between the experiences of sin and redemption there came into being a universe peopled with unforgettable evocations, scenes, and visions. In this universe the poet, the priest, and the soldier (the man who sings, the man who offers up in sacrifice, and the man who sacrifices himself—Baudelaire's triad of human heroes) play the leading parts. However, this is no mere drama they are enacting—it is the essential action of human existence.

Miserere and *War* were originally intended to consist of two volumes of fifty plates each: those were the titles intended—the first, *Miserere*, and the second, *War*.[14]

Rouault composed the majority of the plates between 1914 and 1918. Then, after many vicissitudes, they finally appeared in 1948 in one volume.

He first made a series of drawings in India ink. Copperplates were made of all these. However, as work on the etchings proceeded, the original drawings were radically changed. In fact, Rouault tells us he used a great variety of tools and went over and over each of the plates, sometimes making "as many as fifteen successive states."[15] (At Vollard's request he later made paintings of many of the subjects.)

In this series, the plates alluding directly to the war—for the first time called a world war—are rare. Rouault rose above the events of the day,[16] discovering the universal in the particular and the permanent in the temporal. Everywhere are references to the life, the Passion, and death of Christ. Sin is constantly present, inherent in the human condition. In an unforgettable etching titled *Are We Not All Convicts?*, a man with a raised head and tensed neck, strikingly reminiscent of the *Ordeal of Samson*, appears. Like some animal destined to a more noble fate, he seems to be waiting for the intervention of supernatural grace. Always—and this is what distinguishes him from Matisse—Rouault subordinates technique to expressive intent.

His friend, the poet André Suarès, was Rouault's confidant and occasionally an inspiration through this long and arduous labor. What Rouault liked in him was his detachment from mundane current affairs. He was himself, in a certain sense, a man of the Middle Ages, and he was attracted by the "Renaissance" spirit that characterized Suarès' thinking. He did not, of course, share the latter's fondness for the decorative, nor his dandy's interest in dress. But he appreciated the delicacy of taste and the isolation of this long-haired, independent soul, whose unaffected

190

diction "recalled the ripple of running water."[17] These two artists also had in common a strong antagonism to regionalism. "The language of the greatest number of people is the soil in which thought grows, in which art becomes purified and represents nature, in which science furnishes food for both heart and mind. There is no gainsaying this, and the champions of regionalism are mistaken."[18]

When Rouault asked Suarès what he thought of *Miserere and War* as a title, Suarès insisted that *Miserere*, by itself ,would be better, and it avoided the mixture of Latin and non-Latin. "The shorter the title, the better," he wrote, "particularly for a collection of plates . . . true artists in every connection observe the law of sacrifice."[19]

But times were hard, and the war had aroused the basest, shrillest passions. "I have learned what hatred is," wrote Rouault to his friend. "The deeper it lies hidden the more diabolical hatred is; and I often have the impression that so-called justice, the golden mean, tolerance, and agreeable eclecticism—in a word, whatever scales have ever been invented are, in reality, instruments of torture."[20]

Suarès, like Rouault, suffered from the relativism of justice and, although he did not share his friend's Christianity, he was a man whose spirit tended toward a high moral plane in consequence of an intense inner life.

"Of all the men I know today," he wrote Rouault, "you are the least pagan." And he went on to speak of the "ascension" of Rouault's own nature "to the higher plane where prayer and ardent search for ideal truth fuse. What is least known about you is doubtless your desire to attain to a religious sentiment clothed in lasting beauty, however horrifying or scandalous to the Pharisees. In art the temple of the Pharisees is the Academy. But they will not have you, for you are not so much seeking form, as expression. Yet from the very first I grasped this search as the meaning of your life and work; you only cultivate material beauty in order to make it the handmaiden of sentiment, *ancilla Domini*. I like the beauty of your paint and I like your concern with redemption, pursuit of which you sometimes carry as far as Hell itself. This is what rescues your tramps and prostitutes, your poor wretches, and indeed all your monsters, from the horror and mire of their lives: the beauty of paint with which you make them visible vouches for their souls, and gives assurance that their wretchedness is also worthy of salvation. My dear Rouault, it seems that that kind, noble man, Gustave Moreau, made no mistake about you. . . ."[21]

Beauty of substance! It is certain that Rouault was most sensitive to it. And now that he was struggling with his copperplates, the etcher's craft took on great importance for him. He took care of his tools as meticulously as a head cook takes care of his pots and pans. "One morning," Vollard writes, "I met Rouault hauling an enormous load of files, scrapers, engraving needles, and sandpaper. 'What are you going to do with all that? Etchings, aquatints?' 'Call it what you please. . . . Somebody hands me a copperplate . . . and I go at it.'"[22]

About this same time—independently of this vast work that was to require so many trial proofs and successive states, and so much patience to the very end,[23] Rouault began two series of lithographs based on visits to the industrial suburbs.

In them, he treated landscape as a means of spiritual expression. Suarès had recognized his gift for evoking the atmosphere of the outlying districts where the workers lived. "In my opinion," he wrote, "you can achieve something that has not been done for a long time. That is, the religious landscape . . . the mystic landscape. For centuries—since Rembrandt, in fact—not a single painter has succeeded in conveying this."[24]

Thus, *Legendary Landscapes* (six lithographs and fifty reproductions of drawings)[25] form a series of "symbolical images, treated with large, flat patches of lithographic ink, on the surface of which float whites that are more or less pure, according to whether they were specially protected or came out mottled as a result of the effects of scraper or sandpaper."[26] Ornamental borders, vaguely Byzantine in style, alternate with very realistic landscapes depicting a roving, leisurely, drifting life:

> *The bargeman's daughter combing her hair,*
> *Leans gently over the stagnant water*
> *Gazing upon her image.*

Here the delicate, tapering trees have been sketched in vigorously with the brush. However, the six lithographs that compose *Depressed Suburbs*[27] are in a grayer tonality, for they represent Rouault's recollections of the Belleville of his childhood, "where man's work is never done," to which he made so many allusions. Many themes which were to be expanded in the painted versions later on are foreshadowed here:

> *Always Christ in the suburbs,*
> *Wretchedness transpierced by grace,*
> *Human toil, and pain . . . .*

Lastly, there should be added to these lithographic works a certain number of plates made for Frapier. Among these are: *Christ on the Cross, Parade, Clown, Equestrienne, Prostitute, Charles Baudelaire, Léon Bloy, J.-K. Huysmans, Gustave Moreau in His Little Hat, Gustave Moreau with His White Beard, André Suarès*, and a *Self-Portrait*.[28]

During the time that he was working like this for his dealer-publisher, Rouault was in excellent spirits and comparatively prosperous. Of course, Mme. Rouault helped. She was an admirer of Debussy and Ravel, and herself an excellent pianist who had given concerts in Versailles. She also appreciated Cézanne, grasping the talent of this great leader who had singlehandedly upset so many ideas about painting. "She was an admirable woman, patient in the face of adversity."[29] In the seated, three-quarter portrait that Léon Lehmann made of her in the rue Blanche (around 1911) we see her looking not exactly sad, but filled with care. "You know," she said to me, not without a certain coquetry, as we looked at this portrait together, "I was more sprightly than that."

When they moved back to Paris, they found a flat in the rue Blomet.

Mme. Rouault had to leave early every morning for the Dominican convent in Asnières, where her daughters were in boarding school and where she herself gave piano lessons all day.[30] Meanwhile her husband was working in the rue Martignac, at Vollard's. He didn't go home for lunch. "When times were hardest," Rouault told me, "I never mentioned my family to Vollard, and he did not fail to notice it. 'You are lucky,' he said to me one day, 'to have children who raise themselves.'"

And yet the family had increased. Michel was born, as I said before, in 1912, and Marthe Rouault gave birth to Agnès, the last of the four children, on December 10, 1915. Rouault composed the following poem to his family:

> *Faithful Marthe,*
> *Geneviève, my chiming bell,*
> *Make themselves heard*
> *At break of day.*
> *In these bloodthirsty times*
> *I tremble for us all.*
> *Isabelle, my little dove,*
> *Michel, frail pillar of the house,*
> *Agnès, my little pigeon.*
> *Should the Byzantine celebrities*
> *Tell you that your father is beyond hope,*
> *Pray, do not be too disturbed.*[31]

Mme. Rouault well recalls Vollard's first visit to the rue Blomet in 1917, when he purchased Rouault's entire output. "The drawings and paintings were all he could see," she told me. And the fact is that the dealer recognized at once what treasures he was acquiring. He knew the paintings were not finished, but he had said, "All or nothing!" and Rouault agreed on the condition that he could take as long as he liked to complete them. For the moment Vollard expected Rouault to devote himself body and soul to him. This makes me think of Faust and the pact with the Devil. That a work of art should be sold for money has, in itself, something diabolical about it.

"A voluntary prisoner, shut up from dawn to dusk for years without a vacation, working all day long in the premises of a dealer who spied on him and kept prodding him, Rouault saw nothing of the city except the crazy pattern of rooftops with their chimneys and weather vanes."[32] For quite a while the relationship between the painter and the dealer was peaceable enough. "Rouault nevertheless found his bondage irksome. There was a great deal to be done and he wished he had more time to retouch earlier works.[33] However, he put up with Vollard's greed without complaint, as later he was to put up with the dealer's impatience. But Vollard did keep his patience for many years, even though he did not always understand the psychology of the artist. Rouault, after all, realized that in the end he would be the gainer, so long as he was permitted to bring to a successful issue that disinterested form of work we call art. Replying to a critic who came to

Old Clown with White Dog · about 1925

interview him for a newspaper, and asked about his relationship with the dealer, he made the following shrewd statement: "People say that M. Vollard is burying me alive. . . . 'Lazarus come forth! and Lazarus came forth.' The symbolism here is generally misunderstood. What it really means is that sometimes the dead come to life and sometimes the living are dead."[34]

But tongues went on wagging. Vollard was accused of keeping Rouault "behind bars." And even Suarès reproached his friend for wasting his time with more and more "Ubu" subjects. "Six months at that sort of thing," he wrote, "well and good. But six years is five too many. What are you working so hard at? You're getting bogged down in the lowest circles of Hell, where the demons mock and the soul can register nothing but degrees of infamy. . . . When we try to give birth to monsters, we end poisoned ourselves. We break out in abscesses and ulcers. . . . I have the impression that Vollard is trying to come between us. He wants to keep you under his thumb. If you let him do it, you will be morally damned. Make use of him, don't become his slave. He is not dangerous to your life, and you know how to look after yourself, but he might be dangerous to your mind. . . . Vollard's taste and understanding of painting are unique. He has real talent in a trade where it is enough to be clever. But Vollard is a reprobate. Vollard is a vampire."[35]

How did Rouault cope with the situation and preserve his independence? Sooner or later the gossip columns would be carrying items like this: "M. Vollard, having the patience of an Indian on the warpath, will exhume for 25,000 francs the Rouaults he bought for thirty louis."

Since 1916, when *A Lady of High Degree* was shown at the Bernheim-Jeune gallery, no one had seen any of Rouault's paintings. The result was that when, in November, 1920, a Rouault exhibition was held in a new gallery, La Licorne (organized by one of his earliest collectors, Dr. Girardin), it created quite a stir. It included fifty canvases, representing every stage in the painter's development since the *Dead Christ*. Among them were portraits of prostitutes, scenes of street circuses, and courtroom scenes.

Gaston Varenne, writing in *Bonsoir*, tried to define Rouault's art in terms of his damned or forsaken creatures. "We have only to look at this circus dancer lifting a provocative leg to the public . . . this greenish nude whose legs show the marks of blood-red garters; this idiotic old clown smiling toothlessly; these pasty-faced murderers being questioned by malevolent judges. . . . All these damned, corrupt human beings, abandoned to their dismal fates with no star to guide them, are victims of the exacerbating power of the senses.

"But Rouault expresses more than that. Weary of debauchery and the gutter, he has lifted up his eyes to heaven, to Christian heaven, and revived its touching legends. He has gone back to the subjects of his adolescent years, only now he treats them with a piety that is more personal and, at the same time, no less orthodox. His tormented heart has found peace, the dark clouds are rent apart and have vanished, dispersed by the light of a new sun." This critic also observed: "Here we are as far from trashy popular religious art as we are from the crucifixions of M. Maurice Denis, whose imitations of the Primitives are too often slavish.[36] What is generally called religious art resembles Rouault's as little as a prayer learned from a book resembles a cry that goes directly from the heart to God."[37]

"Georges Rouault," wrote Jean Pellerin, "has no use for the petty, the dull, or the base, such as Degas paradoxically exploited without impairing his essential lyricism. Rouault's more wholesome conception occasionally recalls Daumier's fine wash drawings which, while they convey summarily to the eye an impression of harshness and savagery, are never without grandeur. M. Georges Rouault has the gift that critical jargon has dubbed 'breeding'." And, in reference to Rouault's sprawling line: "At times Rouault broadens a spot to obtain an effect of shadow, to define an eye socket, or to deepen the crease of a groin." Jean Pellerin concludes authoritatively: "M. Rouault's excesses are but a means. And the end is genuinely tragic beauty."[38]

We have come some way from the time when this same Jean Pellerin had heard the public at the Hôtel Drouot shouting its reprobation of three nudes by Rouault up for auction. "I never understood so well as I did then," this poet wrote, "just how powerful a misunderstanding separates the public at large from the original artist. To these curiosity seekers, landscapes were colored photographs and their conception of the nude was satisfied by the blond, pink ladies in the perfume advertisements."[39]

From then on, all the writers and critics of importance, all those who saw clearly, undertook the defense of this painter whose "unpopularity" was "a source of unique delight" to Coquiot.[40]

In 1921, Michel Puy published the first book on Rouault in the N.R.F.'s little collection entitled *Les Peintres français nouveaux*. In it the author touched on how far Rouault had gone since he left the Beaux-Arts. "Like Dante," he wrote, "Rouault invented an Inferno." Referring to the frequently leveled charge of Rouault's exaggeration, he stated: "His zest for caricature often takes the form of buffoonery, and yet his laughter is short-lived and lacks gaiety. He is full of suffering and pity."[41]

Only a few persons at this time felt the "passion and profound pity expressed in these masks, these stupid, sickly faces of slaves and executioners." Nor could many grasp "what a powerful colorist has matched these deep blues, wine purples, and inky blacks."[42] We now find the names of the musician, Parent, and M. Grignard added to the list of Rouault collectors.

During this period when he was preparing his *Miserere* as well as other important illustrated books, Rouault did little painting. But although his painted works are less numerous, they are perhaps for this reason doubly important. This was the epoch during which he composed the *Old Clown*, in the Niarchos collection. This picture, which is one of Rouault's most important works, concentrates in its black-grays, shot with purple, a vision of the whole of human wretchedness. In order to find an equivalent expression of suffering, we should have to look to the summits at times reached by Dante, Rembrandt, or Shakespeare. And Suarès had Shakespeare in mind when he wrote Rouault, distinguishing the buffoon from the clown with admirable acumen: "You conceive of buffoons and simpletons the way a lyrical poet imagines the horror and wretchedness of a landscape.... But one day you will see the gulf that separates the clown from the buffoon. Banquo, Polonius, Shylock, and Caliban are, for me, all clowns.

"The buffoon is a victim of society. As such, he is a serf. He is wretched. He is an object of compassion, and you have made him that. You have looked at him with charitable eyes.

"The clown, on the other hand, is a leader, the very opposite of a victim. The clown is wisdom or its parody, folly; full of a sometimes terrible irony, full of eternal laughter. And the clown of clowns, of course, is the death's-head."[43]

This timeless figure is indeed the "clown of clowns." Incidentally, the clown is one of the most insidiously difficult of all subjects. How many experiments, how many ineffectual or vulgar attempts we have seen and continue to see! The Salon has produced as many bad clowns and second-rate buffoons as the latter-day popular song writers. A well-nigh impossible theme, even some of the best painters have failed with it. The chief pitfalls are melodrama and ridiculousness. Rouault appears to have been successful, however, once and for all, for he always went deeper than the mere surface trappings.

Rouault's visionary, evocative powers are combined with a gift for generalization far greater than Toulouse-Lautrec's, with whom he is often compared. "Lautrec," wrote Suarès, with some severity, "does not go beyond what nature gives him; he limits his choice to the vulgar traits and impure contours that correspond to his own temperament; perhaps this is the only way he could see life. He was a minor early Huysmans (i.e., before Huysmans' conversion and his mysticism).... Whereas you, my dear Rouault, the risk you run is that of never being realistic, not that of being too much so.... You always interpret and give play to your imagination; and you are right in thinking that yours is a poet's vision. You are a poet by the sting of your satire. At bottom—and to the extent that a painter can be one—you are a prophet."[44]

Rouault painted a certain number of portraits, the list of which has been drawn up by Bernard Dorival.[45] Among them, the most poignant is probably that of Lebasque, a painter whom Rouault saw frequently and who, although very gifted to start with, became a sort of academic Bonnard. Rouault made two portraits of him, one fullface in watercolor (1917), and the other in oil, also known as the *Sick Man* or *Comedian* (1914–30), which shows a face with curious, painfully contracted features.

What a contrast with Rouault's own face, which had such frank, open features! Rouault painted himself several times, not, however, from the narcissistic motives that inspired Courbet. Like Rembrandt, Rouault tended to see in his own face the personification of man in general, and the last such likeness we have of him is the color lithograph (1928) reproduced as frontispiece in his book *Soliloques*. After that, being no longer able to identify himself with a sufficiently generalized type of humanity, as he had when he executed *The Worker's Apprentice*, Rouault lost

interest in the self-portrait, limiting his quest to expression of universal religious feelings. Rouault never shared the curious personalism of Léon Bloy for whom "the disturbing tombstone words 'Here Lies . . .' required a supernatural interpretation." Bloy also wondered "if the Holy Ghost does not dwell on the remains of the dead, like the column of invisible light that was manifested to the seeress of Dülmen."[46]

Rouault continued to be friends with Suarès, who was more capable of understanding Henri de Groux's anecdotal painting than his own. However, the friendship between the two men had risen above their differences of taste. In May, 1917, Bloy sent Rouault a copy of the last book of his that was to appear during his lifetime: *Au Seuil de l'Apocalypse (At the Threshold of the Apocalypse)* and in a letter dated June 28, Rouault thanked him.[47] Bloy, for whom the war was a veritable martyrdom, was to die of an attack of uremia on November 3 of the same year. For Rouault (who was now forty-two years old), a part of his youth died along with the recluse of Bourg-la-Reine.

A few years later, Rouault finished (in his own way, which consisted in intensifying his earlier versions) one of the pictures that immediately comes to mind when we think of him: *Christ in the Suburbs* of 1920, in the Fukushima collection, Tokyo. This is a night scene set in Belleville, as Rouault remembered it. The moon is rising behind the ramshackle dwellings of the poor, between the factory chimney and the silvery street. Christ is present in the feeling for common people that permeates the picture, though there is no halo to be seen.[48] From this same time we also have the *Faubourg* in the Leclercq collection, in which we see tired workers walking along a street lined with tall buildings.

Following the *Four Bathers*, which is in a broader rhythm and slightly Egyptian in character (about 1920), Rouault went back to a series of paintings on circus themes, and made three drawings for Henry Church's book, *Clowns*.[49] He gave the final touches to *Circus Trio* (1924), and to the *Profile of a Clown* (about 1925), which is both roughhewn and meditative. He also finished *Two Acrobats with White Dog* (about 1925), vigorously and densely painted in greens, grays, and reds, and *Acrobat in Yellow Tights* (about 1925), shown fullface with raised arms, the sweater painted over the flesh tones. Then comes the moving *Old Clown with Dog* (1926), which is one of Rouault's major works. Here we find a deep, intimate understanding between man and beast, at the heart of which is posed a question as subtle and yet basic as that raised in *Hamlet*. The clown is painted in claret reds with chalky highlights. The thinly applied color stands out against the heavy outlines that link it with the English greens of the background. It is a picture of extraordinary strength.

Rouault seems now to have attained his full power. Was this because the artist suffered at not being able to devote more time to his canvases? Coquiot, who stressed the importance of this stage in Rouault's career, went so far as to write that, whereas "the work of both Guys and Lautrec has become dated and is now a thing of the past, Rouault's, on the contrary, will belong to every epoch."[50]

Rouault must have recognized himself in the following word-portrait that his friend and neighbor in Versailles, Jacques Maritain, drew of him: "A pale complexion, clear, alert eyes that seemed to be looking inward rather than at anything around him, a forceful mouth, prominent brow, and large skull covered at that time with abundant blond hair[51] (which he does not at all regret having lost), there is something that recalls a moonfaced clown—an astonishing mixture of pity and bitterness, of mischief and ingenuousness—in the physiognomy of this painter who is opposed to coteries and conventions and, in general, to all contemporary usages. Meanwhile, fame is dragging him out of his cellar—he actually was born in a cellar, in 1871, during the bombardment of Paris."[52]

Rouault's "antimodern" painting, which had sprung spontaneously from the very depths of his being, in the course of efforts to break away from gloom and to attain the light of grace, had greatly appealed to this subtle young philosopher who had now become the leader of Neo-Thomism. Indeed, Maritain found in Rouault something altogether lacking in our time: profundity of thought, a gift for seizing things in their deeper reality and defining them, as also for suggesting humanity's eternal aspirations for redemption. He had recognized immediately in Rouault a man of the "explosively timid" type who is extremely reserved in matters of love and religion and "insists upon hiding" from others. It was, in fact, with Rouault in mind that he wrote *Art et Scholastique (Art and Scholasticism)*, the first edition of which appeared in 1919.[53]

These two men were made to understand each other. Rouault's art reminded the philosopher that before it becomes anything else, art is first and foremost the creation of tangible things, and not aesthetic speculation. Maritain's thinking confirmed in Rouault the conviction, if not that art has frontiers, at least that there arrives a moment when it is confronted with a force stronger and greater than itself. Art, though it does not serve the State or some other political body (as Proudhon mistakenly believed), sustains humanity's better self and constitutes, for the religious man, a means of approach to that which is beyond him, a quest for the supernatural. Rouault expressed it with great humility in his letter-preface to a book by Georges Charensol: "Don't mention me unless it be to glorify art; don't present me as a firebrand of revolt and negation. What I have done is nothing, don't make much of it. A cry in the night. A sob that miscarried. A strangled laugh. Throughout the world, every day, thousands of obscure, needy people who are worth more than I am, die at their tasks.

"I am the silent friend of all those who labor in the fields, I am the ivy of eternal wretchedness clinging to the leprous wall behind which rebellious humanity hides its vices and its virtues alike. Being a Christian in these hazardous times, I can believe only in Christ on the Cross."[54]

As a frontispiece to this book, Rouault used the self-portrait titled *The Worker's Apprentice* (about 1925–26).[55] The face is mostly forehead rounded under a little hat pushed back on the head. But the most striking thing about it is the willful line of the mouth, which is emphatically horizontal. The eyes show depth and suffering but are open to human contact. Here Rouault identifies himself with human toil in every age, as well as with all who have ever toiled. This work makes me think of Baudelaire's poem *Tableaux parisiens*. Rouault made a portrait lithograph of Baudelaire as frontispiece to another book, *Souvenirs intimes*,[56] which appeared the same year. In the chapter devoted to the poet, the painter showed awareness of the reservations regarding Baudelaire and his poetry then held in some orthodox circles. What he wrote was: "Although men like Baudelaire or Verlaine may appear to some to have fallen very low, they nevertheless retain so much natural distinction (in comparison with those who censure them, flatter them, or consider themselves their peers) and give off so spiritual a fragrance, that they need but a word or a glance to put everything in its proper perspective."[57]

Close "association" with Baudelaire, Poe, Rembrandt, and Goya had kept Rouault at a distance from the canvas-deep sensibility of the Impressionists, and from their subtlest "eye," Claude Monet. Rouault, far from being one-sided, was always open to every approach, however foreign or even opposed to his own art, and he was never niggardly in his admiration of a genuine artist. Hence the following note written on the occasion of Monet's death in Giverny in 1926: "For those who are under the exclusive spell of 'the aggravated desires of the eye,' nothing is too violent." And he recalled:

> "*Light winter frost over the French countryside,*
> *Fog-drenched Londons,*
> *A green Thames against a pale ashen sky,*
> *Water lilies on the transparent waters of the lonely island where Monet dreamt his dreams.*"

Himself a painter who tried to find a single image with which to express the different aspects of morning and evening, Rouault added: "He liked to record the time of day, but it seems to me that Monet was aware of a 'pictorial time.' I mean a vision of form, subjective or objective according to the gifts granted each of us. It is a vision independent of the time of day."[58]

Although it has never occurred to anyone to classify Rouault among the Impressionists, there have been many who consider him a typical Expressionist. But this painter cannot really be labeled. At the time of the Berlin exhibition in the Alfred Flechtheim gallery,[59] the German critics were prompt to point out his affinities with the *Brücke* group. Dr. Kurt Glaser observed that Rouault "rises well above his subject matter."[60] The critic on the *Berliner Tageblatt* (was it Meier-Graefe?) asked rather shrewdly—the Expressionist movement was then at its height in Germany—if there had not been "a certain malice on the part of the organizers of the exhibition." Now, he went on to say, "Everyone can see where all these emotional German artists found how to express themselves!" And the author of the article concluded—doubtless with Nolde, Kirchner, and even Jawlensky in mind (all three of whom were well-known in Germany at this time): "It all comes from Rouault! The biting line, the ravaged faces, the compositions in which we always find two or three figures. Even the technique of dark brush strokes in black, and touches of watercolor added here and there to lighten the whole."[61]

As may be seen, for several years now Rouault had achieved critical recognition. Only Maurice Raynal, perhaps, still took exception. Ready enough to defend the Cubists, he reproached Rouault for grinding out one work after another, and even accused him of "artiness" *(artisterie).*[62]

Although art criticism is occasionally blind, there are also a few clear-sighted critics. "Rouault," wrote Georges Chabot, "places his characters on the edge of bottomless pits, from which they carry on a dialogue with the viewer. . . . Certain of his works seem to have been catapulted onto the canvas."[63]

In 1929, going back to one of his earliest themes, Rouault painted the sets and designed the costumes for Serge Diaghilev's production of *The Prodigal Son* for the Ballet Russe. In Monte Carlo, he composed a backdrop that showed a long road with a small bell tower in the center, and at the side, two other structures. At a given moment, a tent was supposed to come down like a big bird and inside it the prodigal son was to be robbed by the companions who had urged him to leave his father's house. Rouault wrote: "I, who, according to some, am supposed to be the painter of horrors, hesitate to say how enchanted I was with the rhythms and movement patterns of the girl dancers in Monte Carlo . . . rehearsing on the stage while I sat planning my settings. . . . I saw the entire ballet company perform: friezes, bas-reliefs, pediments, compositions of every sort were formulated in space. Indeed, the mind was carried far away from mere sensual spectacle."[64]

The ballet was given at the Sarah Bernhardt Theater in Paris on May 21, 29, 31, and on June 4, 6, and 12. The libretto in three scenes was by Boris Kochne, and Balanchine was the choreographer. The music was by Sergei Prokofiev, whose sharp, percussive rhythms Rouault admired. "At the time I was painting my sets," he told me, "a certain very famous art patron decided that because I was French and Parisian for generations back my taste must run exclusively to things like *La Fille de Madame Angot,* since I used to hum tunes from it under my breath. To this 'noble' foreigner the French were a race of cabaret entertainers."

For the last performance, the one that took place on June 12, at eight o'clock, Rouault wrote to Suarès that he had asked Diaghilev to reserve seats for him. *The Prodigal Son* came third on the program, between *Le Renard* and the suite from *Prince Igor.* Evening dress being obligatory, Rouault wanted to reassure his friend on this score. "About the dress suit," he wrote, "I want you to know that I myself went once in street clothes although, true enough, I had on a white collar and a black bow tie. In any case, should you have any difficulty, ask for M. Diaghilev, in my name, and don't walk out with your ticket the way you did the other time."[65]

With regard to the manner in which his settings were carried out, Rouault expressed "certain reservations about the central part," adding that he had sent a long letter to Diaghilev on the subject.

"Certain conditions beyond my control were imposed:

"1) By those awful stagehands. As I planned it, the tent was to be like a bird descending from heaven. As it is, it hides my setting for the greater part of the performance. They have made it look like a sentry box, only a bit squarer, fortunately! (I had to spend three nights repainting it so it would not be too frightful looking.) There is also the matter of the dancers' bar which was added.

"2) Chirico (for *Le Bal*) painted all his own settings in Monaco, where he had everything he needed within easy reach. Whereas when I came back to Paris, the set dresser and the choreographers went to Monte Carlo and worked on their own. And once they were back in Paris, nothing could be changed! All that within two or three days of the opening. In my opinion, the man who writes the libretto should be the choreographer and the set decorator as well."

Toward the end of the year Rouault went for a rest in Switzerland. He had already spent some time at Gryon, in a chalet belonging to the painter Werner Feuz. On this, his second visit, Rouault went to Montana-sur-Sierre, in the Valais. On Christmas Eve, to amuse the children in the place, Rouault dressed himself up as Santa Claus, repeating his performance the next day for the daughter of the Japanese collector Fukushima. The cotton wool on the coat caught fire from the lighted candles on the Christmas tree, and Rouault's hands were badly burned.

"What an adventure!" Vollard wrote him when he learned that the accident had had no grave consequences. "In the old days, the wizards used to plunge into the flames in order to acquire a new science; you, however, had no need of this experience, having a talent that constantly renews itself.

"But it was doubtless to keep up the tradition that the gods decided to envelop you in flames.

"As for your idea about the Académie, I think it first rate, by which I mean necessary, in order to force those fellows to live up to their responsibilities. You can count on me to let each one of them know—tomorrow I will have a list of them—that I shall be happy to show them specimens of your graphic works and a few paintings which I shall fetch from the atelier, and choose carefully. . . .

"You do not have to tell me that you will present your candidature as a painter. Furthermore, if you had done nothing but graphic works, there is more painterliness in a square centimeter of one of your prints than in the largest canvases by three-fourths of the honorable members."[66]

This letter would seem to prove that the two men, the painter and the dealer, got along very well together.[67] As for this affair of the Académie, there was a farcical as well as a serious aspect to it.[68] In any case, the news began to be whispered about Paris. "Rouault is settling down," his opponents went so far as to say. Or was he sounding them out? Had he been encouraged to present his candidature by his old friend, Pierre Termier, the geologist, who was a member of the Académie des Sciences? The differences between the various branches of the Institut, however, are considerable and, whereas in certain sections membership is a considerable honor (Académie des Sciences, Inscriptions et Belles-Lettres), the Académie des Beaux-Arts (with the exception, perhaps, of music) is as worthless as

the Prix de Rome that it confers. Fortunately for Rouault, the whole thing came to nothing. He never became a member of that "slave ship" that had carried off his teacher, Moreau. For Rouault to have become a member of the Académie, extensive reforms would have been needed. And not only Rouault, but Matisse, Bonnard, Braque, and Dufy as well would then have been admitted.

Rouault spoke of his candidature, half in earnest, half in jest, in *L'Intransigeant*. "I have presented my candidature to the Institut," he said. "To clear up all misunderstanding, I am doing this because my teacher, Gustave Moreau, said to me on his deathbed, with tongue in cheek, but also with genuine good nature, 'I would leave you my Institut uniform, only you would burst it at the seams.' "[69]

Bursting through inherited conceptions—wasn't that exactly what this painter of prostitutes, clowns, judges, and workers' Christs had always done? He never belonged to the official society that has dishonored French art from Delacroix onward. Rouault the recluse, Rouault the independent, Rouault the seer, Rouault the believer never consented to have anything to do with art officialdom. His art was one long protest against the formulas and the slackness it represented.

But let us get back to the Valais, where Rouault had started a few canvases just before the affair of the Academy[70] began to be talked of. When he undertook the difficult theme of mountains, he did not let himself be crushed by it. He showed me the sketches he had finished before his accident. A scene showing a mule against an Alpine background became, for him, an excuse to recall the Flight into Egypt. From a stay of several weeks in Sion he brought back the rough sketch for a Valère and Tourbillon landscape, painted in a range of silver-grays. Then there is the Valère church, seen from the other side of the Rhone, drawn with a hard line and shot through with reds. His daughter Isabelle told me: "He was very fond of the Valais landscape with its vineyards."

Self-Portrait · 1925

Russian Ballet · 1929

Circus Women · 1925

212

The Old Clown · *1917*

213

Spanish Woman · 1930

Christ in the Suburbs · 1920

Pierrot · 1920

Woman with Red Flower · *1925*

Judges (Danse Macabre, or Fleus du Mal) · *about 1926*

Circus Equestrienne · 1927

Georges Rouault 1915

The Reformer · 1915

Figure (study for "Miserere et Guerre")

Landscape (With Large Trees) · 1929

Trio (Mother and Children) · *1929*

Two Heads in Profile · 1929

Composition: Two Women · 1929

Ile-de-France Landscape · 1926

Cemetery · 1930

227

The Road Is Long (Leftist Neighborhood) · *1929*

Faubourg · 1930

Clowns · 1930

Leftist Neighborhood (Depressed Suburban Area) · 1930

Portrait of the Painter Lebasque · 1917

6. Greatness and Accomplishment

After a long period devoted principally to etching, Rouault returned to painting exclusively. However, he continued to supervise the printers who had been entrusted with his engravings. Alone in his rue Martignac studio, he settled down to producing a series of important paintings.

As for his technique, I shall draw upon what he himself told me, as well as such information as he gave in the course of newspaper and magazine interviews; but I shall mainly rely on my own study of his work. Rouault did not like to talk about his art. "It is painful for me to analyze and explain myself," he wrote to Vollard, "and especially in front of other people. According to some, I am good at it, but it makes me uncomfortable and I don't like to do it."[1] His natural reserve was accentuated when he was directly questioned about his way of working. "An artist," he said, "pays no attention to theories, whether his own or other people's. In front of the canvas he forgets everything."[2]

Very often when chatting with him I could feel his resistance to going on, his reluctance to spoil things by analyzing or even putting a name to them. In his heart of hearts, Rouault wanted to keep his conceptions of art intact.

And yet, with regard to more or less "impersonal" aspects of his art, he often gave his opinions. He contributed of the physical survival of paintings. At this time he was living in the rue de l'Orangerie at Versailles. "Many artists," he wrote, "labor under the mild and harmless delusion that their works will of course survive." There are so many artists that if all were to use good paints and good canvas, "how our descendants would suffer, both spiritually and physically!" Rouault went on to pay tribute to Cézanne. "This great, lonely worker was never exposed to the indignity of official recognition, never wore that bit of red ribbon in his lapel . . . at a time when many a today-obscure or failed dauber was flaunting his decorations in compensation for his artistic mediocrity."[3]

Nothing is predictable in this profession. "You know how it is with painting," he told me. "Sometimes you advance like the tortoise, sometimes like the hare. But it is perhaps a good thing," he added, "to practice both methods. Faced with the white canvas, a man ponders and tries to collect his thoughts; he hesitates to take the plunge. When he finally gets to work, there is no more hesitating. The work may come rapidly, or he may have a long hard struggle with his medium."[4]

"The head of a clown, the figure of a Pierrot, should it take on a certain gravity (by virtue of the drawing and the color), would thereby be something unusual. (A good example of the importance of color is my *Christ à la Passion*.)"[5]

Rouault was always consumed by desire to go beyond what he had already achieved. "The terrible thing about me," he wrote, "is that I am never content with myself, I never derive complete satisfaction from bringing something off. I can always see or think of further improvements."[6] He was ever dissatisfied, ever afraid of not proving adequate to the work at hand.

In words that recall Van Gogh, he wrote Suarès: "I create—in my own way, of course, and I don't say that it is the best way—I create the way wind blows or fire burns.

"I am aware of the objections that may be raised.

"Also, that every critic, even artists and art teachers, will bristle . . . at any rate, I know I'm rubbing them the wrong way.

"I can hear them: virtuosity, finish, and so on . . . honesty, sincerity . . . they talk until it comes out of your ears. . . .

"But none of it is of the slightest importance.

"And, since I create in this way, you are probably going to say: 'Why, then, do you keep me waiting—Suarès, so genuinely drawn to your work—for years,[7] you must have thousands of works to show. Even though they may be poor things, they are nevertheless products of your heart and your mind.'

"Right here we touch upon my secret.

"When children play at hide-and-seek, they say, 'You're getting warm, you're getting hot, you're cold.'

"My dear Suarès, you are getting warm.

"Shall I tell you something? You believe that I am often distracted from my work, but it isn't so. When I am, it just makes me stay up a little later. 'Well, then, what have you got to show for it? You work until you drop, but where are the results? . . .' Well, I'm going to tell you now.

"I have for years been working on the same canvases, the same works. But this is very fortunate! I have also been working 'on the side' and, occasionally, I have made more than one version of the same subject."[8]

Rouault was an artist who found his inspiration in himself. Indeed, his subjects come down to a few themes, and the emotion his works always convey surges from within. When we examine a Rouault, what strikes us first? Above all, the way the paint has been applied: very thickly and with passion, with great sureness, and with spontaneity; these move us. However, it is clear that Rouault does not have the rapid brilliance, the *fa presto* that we see, for instance, in the work of

234

Tiepolo. Technically, Rouault was a painter who pondered long and then set down his vision very quickly. In this he greatly resembles Rembrandt, whose work has the same character. Rouault spreads the paint on the canvas like modeling clay, working it with palette knife, brush, and fingers, the marks of which remain on the finished pictures. Sometimes the paint is as sleek and brilliant as freshly applied enamel. More often, however, it gives the impression of a battlefield: piled up, kneaded and rekneaded, touched and retouched, pounded mercilessly. The result is an agglomeration of tone upon tone, a thick, warm integument of the richest texture. Here we recognize the marks of hard labor, the sweat of the artist's brow tinged with his lifeblood, in an almost sculptured relief. The entire picture surface vibrates with the painter's touch. Indeed, the thickly applied pigment achieves a hitherto unknown degree of energy; every form—man, flower, vase—seems to flow directly from the artist's hand into our own sensibility. Rouault's world, with its figures of passion, powerful heads, and cadmium suns expiring behind hills, becomes an integral part of our vision. Over and above the wretchedness and inexorableness of man's fate, Rouault's art glows like a chalice of serenity.

The earliest works had been composed of subtle mixtures of gouache, pastel, India ink and colored inks. Then Rouault began to "paint in oil, applying it thinly, frequently on paper or tracing paper later mounted on cloth or on board." Lastly come the works Chabot likened to "congealed lava," in which "luminous tones . . . crackle among dark, rugged impastos. . . . The light does not come from without, does not fall upon the forms, but emerges from the canvas itself."[9]

Rouault invented a strange and original alchemy to achieve an almost tactile type of painting. When the canvas is looked at up close, it brings to mind an uneven, broken terrain. Starting with a powerfully sustained, rhythmic drawing, the painter builds up deposit after deposit, sometimes mixing his mediums to such an extent that it is no longer possible to identify them. "His line flicks like a whip, on occasion; on other occasions it is broken up and suggests form without defining it too clearly. Swirls, spatterings, spots, a sort of pictorial underground rumbling, suddenly produce the decisive line."[10] No wonder, when we look closely at these works, we find our imaginations oddly stirred. Mirages loom up in the vitalized pigment, asserting themselves more strongly each time we look at the picture. "In front of certain canvases, with their accumulated thicknesses of paint, so many layers of it like silt, buckling like the surface of some volcanic landscape, we are suddenly gripped by the visions they evoke, visions like those of a dying man. We are reminded of Degas' epigram that nothing so resembles a daub as a masterpiece."[11]

It has often been said that Rouault's manner of accentuating his contours in such a way that a broad line encloses each light-colored area like the leading of stained glass,[12] derived from his experience as a *peintre-verrier*—a worker in stained glass. Rouault himself pointed out this analogy to me, but I felt that he was none too convinced of it. In fact, I am rather inclined to see in this heavy line that keeps forms inside their contours, an affirmation of generous, obvious, powerful ex-

pression which is anything but in conflict with nature. Cézanne once said, "The contour eludes me." Contours existed for Rouault, but they were entirely of his own making—almost a background which establishes the form. The latter is pushed back within the black lines variously spread, smeared, or splashed on the paper.

Rouault took a very broad, objective view of style and technique. "Not everyone can paint Michelangelo's *Last Judgment*," he said. No one was quicker than he to recognize an artist's originality.[13] He liked Claude Lorrain's drawings in *Liber Veritatis*, their use of "sepia wash, touched up with gouache." He also admired Rembrandt, who "in three triumphant lines on a ten-centimeter surface, brings out the essential atmosphere charged with inner feeling."[14]

Sharing Baudelaire's opinion, Rouault recognized that nowadays each artist must invent his own technique, rather than rely upon tradition. "It used to be," he said, "that you were a craftsman before you became an artist, acquiring at an early age the manual means for expressing yourself without difficulty—before you had ideas, good or bad." But right after this backward glance, lest he be confused with the Neo-Classicists, Rouault added: "However, one should not let oneself be bewitched by the old masters." For Rouault painting was not an exercise of virtuosity or mastery, nor yet a demonstration of knowledge, but a "harmony between the visible world and inner light."[15]

Rouault neither hated nor defended the academic preparation he had had. He knew he was lucky to have found a good teacher and, being poor, he had been "glad to be able to draw from a live model."[16] He never joined any group or clique of painters. He declared he was "happy to belong" to the "very unpedantic" French school. He distrusted those who looked upon him as a kind of primitive, sensing phoniness. "I feel that I belong to the Île-de-France, by birth and inclination."[17] Rightly proud of being the least conformist of the artists of his time, he had confidence in the young revolutionaries of art—however violent their techniques. "Whether they will or no," he thought of them as "sons, brothers, great-nephews, distant cousins bound by some secret tie not always visible."[18] And never, even when he was in his eighties, did Rouault suppose that painting would cease to go on evolving. He knew that, although art may become "atrophied, may deviate into deformed vulgarization" or be swamped by overproduction, "the pathway has been kept open, nevertheless. No rare or original seed fails to come to flower, no matter where or when."[19]

To the very end, Rouault's attitude toward the things that endure remained that of a young man. He never abandoned the idea of universal brotherhood. No Pharisee, he remained as he had been when he wrote: "The mere dream of a superior humanity, so imperfectly realized, makes us no better than any poor, ignorant man who feels sincere compassion for his fellow men. In terms of eternity, the perfect work of art is no better than the most moving."[20]

With regard to the exaggerated importance attached to signatures in our time, a situation grossly abused in some quarters, Rouault once said this to me: "I had hoped to remain an anonymous artist,[21] but, alas, everybody keeps asking me to

Head of Christ · 1937 or 1938

sign things! You'll see me yet wearing a Homburg, with an umbrella like that of M. Joseph Prud'homme, the very picture of a Parisian bourgeois. . . . I would have you know that at twenty I was handsomer than Alfred de Musset, and so beamingly foolish that traces survive today."[22]

Rouault was as reluctant to talk of poetics (I use this word purposely, since "aesthetics" seems too intellectual a term to apply to an art that is as direct and naturally transcendent as this one) as he was reluctant to talk of painting. "The art I create is dumb," Nicolas Poussin had said, and Rouault, who liked tangible realities, often quoted it. "What we are here for is to create beautiful or expressive form. Controversy, criticism, negations of every sort—secular or sacred—are beside the point. Art cannot be explained."[23] Observe that Rouault said "beautiful or expressive." Here he supplies us, to some extent, with a key to his own poetics. For he had not hesitated to break with the traditional definition of the word "beauty," the extreme relativity of which had been pointed out by Voltaire. "If you ask a Chinaman to give an example of a beautiful thing, he will name a toad," we read in the *Dictionnaire philosophique*. And the fact is that there are as many possible interpretations of the term "beauty" as there are varieties of humor, passion, sentiment, and other expressions of man's nature, major or minor, comic or tragic, reflecting joy or sorrow, satisfaction or surprise, certainty or doubt. Rouault was familiar with all this. Indeed, he felt the same admiration for "the enthusiasm and communal spirit of the workmen who built the cathedrals as for Watteau's charm, Corot's Vergilian breadth, and for Cézanne's modulated harmonies . . . the realistic force of Courbet, the austere form of Papa Ingres."[24]

Rouault's reaction to nature was a very personal one, in that he did not look at it with the intention of copying it, but rather of becoming imbued with it—as he himself said—of being enriched by its forms and colors. "Nature inebriates some and puts others to sleep, but even in a mythological art, patient, continual observation of nature is as necessary as breathing."[25] And Rouault summarized his goal in a few words: "I am not pursuing beauty, but expressiveness."

He acknowledged that beauty—"changing, multiple, undefined"—is not always easy to distinguish; the harder to distinguish because" blind men love talking about colors,"[26] and because every artist has his own conception of beauty. "We should not demand of one artist the same thing another artist gives us. We should not force artists of either the present or the past into a strait jacket of our own leanings, ideas, and ways of feeling. Above all, we must have eyes to see with, before promulgating our own intellectual and spiritual directives."[27]

Questioned as to his favorite landscape, Rouault was reminded of country fields—at once romantic and classical—which he had painted when he was just out of the Beaux-Arts. In them he had discovered a cosmic affinity between man and his natural surroundings:

*"The broad valleys over there
Lead I know not where."*[28]

240

Rouault was a cultivated man, in the best sense of the word, a circumstance that saved him from many mistakes. He had the rare gift of being able to grasp the painting of the old masters, of being able to recognize the living elements in the past. The public, on the other hand, too often is impressed by superficial brilliance, by display of "taste" and ostentation, by the familiar and reassuring. It hates being upset.

But the root of the evil is the fact that, in art, people have always sought to define and limit what is by nature infinite. If possible, they would reduce art to a single manner of seeing and expressing. This situation, of course, is largely the fault of the aestheticians, every one of whom presents his own individual formula which he then makes into a general rule. "Whether lettered or unlettered [the critic] may say what he will of charm, beauty, order, restraint, nobility, and the ideal," Rouault said. "We do not know the first thing about it—whether the earliest artist who tried to draw his shadow on the wall was deliberately or inadvertently anything more than a highly gifted humorist. All the same, there is in art a certain order, a hidden hierarchy, of which people seem to be increasingly unaware."[29]

Rouault's paintings are of average dimensions for the most part, rarely over six feet in length. He used to say: "Genius does not lie in the format. Many large surfaces which have received official praise have nothing great about them except their mathematical dimensions!"[30]

Rouault disliked vague terms like "decorative." A "decorative" work as far as he was concerned, might be commonplace, or then again might be unforgettable. In the same way—and here he was in agreement with Henri Matisse—he had a horror of "vagueness, a tendency to mawkish sentimentality." He made the following rejoinder to an article by Marcel Arland, objecting to the labels that were constantly being attached to him: "I have always liked wide open spaces, and my solitude is so densely populated that I have never for a second been bored. Now a certain critic claims that I am melancholy, morbid, and Lord knows what else. I am as gay a dog as ever trod this earth. Painting, my dear Mediterranean friends, does not necessarily resemble a pretty plate hanging on the wall (whether well crafted or not). There are other delights besides that of an arabesque traced against an untroubled sky."[31]

However, this cheerful profession of faith did not prevent him from describing himself at the same time (October, 1931), as an "Early Christian painter" in *Portrait spiritualiste de terre d'ombre*, a poem sent to an American magazine:

> *He loved light*
> *Serene features*
> *The charm of color*
> *And more delicate tones. . . .*
> *Remote from rhetoric*
> *Deep, muted tones*
> *Also the sounds that sometimes*

242

Echo
In shadow or in light.
But he was born in a certain gloom
And marked by a certain seal.

When he shall be cleansed
Of the apocalyptic world
Which has haunted him since birth
And when at last he shall have set down
With more or less felicity
The expressive form
He loved
For forty years
Should he not yet be dead

Dearly beloved son of light
Without ever pleasing you
Then he will sing another song.

Tragic is the light.[32]

Rouault, like Rembrandt, always wanted to live his art, and to live it day and night (night scenes are rather frequent). He never tried to turn out a handsomely finished product, but—this is also like Rembrandt—sought to express, through painting, his innermost feelings. And just as Rembrandt always evoked analogies to his own life (his features may always be found among the figures that people his religious scenes), in the same way Rouault, with greater modesty, however, always included himself among his clowns and prostitutes, judges and convicts, biblical characters, even among his figures of the *Ubu* cycle. Religious faith, which was his *raison d'être* as a man, was always the justification of his work as an artist. But, as he has said himself: "Honestly, I have painted with my eyes open night and day to the visible world, closing them from time to time merely to bring order to it. . . . It was always beautiful to me, even late at night when saints and sinners alike are asleep—if, after all, there really are persons wholly good or wholly bad."[33]

As we have seen, Rouault never believed in art for art's sake. For him, painting was a means by which a gifted man could elevate his own spirit and that of others. "I feel a need to affirm, not to deny or criticize," he wrote to Vollard. "A whole world of thoughts and feelings awakens in me when I am in the presence of life and nature. By such means as I possess (not the means I might wish to possess) I try to express this world as best I can."[34] Rouault's art is a concentrated art, an art that confines itself to essentials, an art that rejects eclecticism, confusion, snobbishness, and display in order to bring out what is undying. Rouault's hand

244

enhances and transubstantiates the physical medium, impregnating it with human heart and mind.

Needless to say, this pure, generous, and spiritual talent was not at ease in the climate of the Paris art market. It was utterly opposed to that market. In an age of frenetic activity, this painter followed the rhythm of his own nature. He avoided facility, faithful to his urges, indifferent to those "apostles of 'Eternal Beauty'" whose works "for fifty years were hung in the privileged places at every official exhibition, over and over again, year after year—almost literally the same paintings."

Rouault had forebodings of a dark time for mankind. "A new world is dawning," he wrote. "Tragic is the light I see on the horizon. Egged on by hypocritical politicians and their shrewd hangers-on, material appetites have gone beyond all bounds. The entire universe is out of joint, spiritual values are being destroyed ever more rapidly. There is scarcely any time left for leisure or higher things. New speed records. Talking movies. Charlie Chaplin is Shakespeare. Hollywood is the navel of the world. Man is wolf to man— *Homo homini lupus*—under the guise of civilization."

Rouault did not feel at home in this period of transformation. He was the very opposite of the robot-like machine-age figure, the "modern automaton without heart,"[35] the caricature of Cartesian rationalism. That is why he kept aloof, withdrew into himself and worked in peace, trying to keep from producing too much and be diverted from his goal."[36] Referring to the enormous quantities of knowledge today and the difficulty of understanding all of it, he wrote: "In these gaudy times, we think we will shortly reach the point where everything is known, but the fact is we are ignoring the essential, which is love of all living things, of all beauty both visible and hidden. People before us, though they may have simplified things, were well aware of this."[37]

Amid this confusion, Rouault sometimes liked to recall "the gentle Corot taking his morning stroll under the trees in Ville d'Avray." He also turned his thoughts to Cézanne in the following lines:

> *At sight of the green laurels*
> *Adorning the heads of future "stars"*
> *In a beauty contest*
> *"Brr! It's cold!"*
> *Said the recluse*
> *Blowing on his numbed fingers*
> *High up on Mont Sainte-Victoire*
> *Way up where awards*
> *Don't reach.*[38]

This reminds me of a conversation I once had with Rouault. I said to him that as a student he had probably not been overwhelmed as we were by an avalanche

246

of reproductions from everywhere in the world, in black-and-white and color. "You didn't have to look at a real Tower of Babel, documents from every time and place," Rouault replied. "Oh, all we had was the *Magasin pittoresque*. But we had some good books in the Beaux-Arts library. There was one on Ravenna and another on Agrigento. The vice today is that people can talk about just anything, and say whatever comes into their heads. In art, for instance, everything is frightfully jumbled together. When Manet and Courbet were hung in the Salon des Refusés, the point was clear. Nobody was misled then; but today, the confusion is greater. Large or small, the cliques simultaneously congratulate and despise each other. I can tell you, I do my best to stay independent. What is lacking at times today, even among the critics, is a really free critical sense. Even when a work is the opposite of what I like, I am capable of speaking in its defense. Actually, I can be very eclectic, though not, of course, the way Moreau was.... But I do try to be fair.

"Naturally, a lot of things have changed. What people no longer respect today we probably respected too much. The cultivated *bourgeoisie*, for instance, is finished. There aren't any more of them. Ingres, Degas, Moreau were all such superior bourgeois types, and they were just the contrary of the petty bourgeois who believes that art is dangerous. When you get to my age, you understand better, perhaps, the shades of difference between the generations. You mistrust short-lived celebrity. Don't forget that I knew Etex and Aimé Millet. I have also seen certain Bonnats that were not bad at all, as well as some rather good Ziems (not the 'Venice' series, needless to say!). I knew Maurice Denis when he was considered an *avant gardiste*, and Frantz Jourdain, who headed the jury at the Salon d'Automne, when he had to reconcile the conventionally brilliant painting of a Guirand de Scevola (Bonhomme called him 'Garland of Cervelas') with the vital work of Matisse and Vlaminck.... You understand, there are things that simply do not go together."

Rouault's respect for traditional values did not diminish his love for the common people.[39] In other words, he loved his country in all its nobler manifestations. He did not, however, put quantity ahead of quality and, contributing to a discussion in *La Vie*, he wrote: "Why should universal suffrage obtain in matters of art? How many artists have gone unappreciated to their dying day with the full approval of public opinion?"[40]

Rouault was in constant opposition to the "successful mediocrity" that satisfied so many of his contemporaries. He always defended "the most precious of all freedoms, that is, the one that seems natural, yet is never mentioned for the reason that no one knows its exact formula. For there exists a domain in art that escapes our best critics, in which ordinary intelligence plays no role. Indeed, I should go so far as to say that a certain sort of intelligence and learning can actually be harmful and disturb the magnificent balance of the artist who can express himself through his art."[41]

But neither did he like those who are content with a minimum of effort, cultivation, and knowledge. "Mediocrities," he used to say, "are afraid of not being

themselves but, alas, that is just what they are."[42] "Beautifully plumed parrots, or peacocks spreading their tail feathers—many artists are little else."[43] He wondered why people always seem to mention the same conceited men over and over again, rather than pay tribute to real talent. "Why should we not be more grateful to the man who brings an entire world to life on a small canvas and who succeeds in moving and interesting us, than to one who spends his life at tedious tasks that bring him all the honors and please everybody more or less, but never move anyone?"[44]

To a disorderly civilization which encourages shoddiness, to the increasingly frenzied intoxication with speed, Rouault opposed the wholesome attitude symbolized by moving under one's own power at one's natural pace. "What I like about peasants," he wrote, "is the slowness with which they move and the hardness of their lives, though I myself was born and bred in the city. I like the age-old sight of two fine oxen moving slowly under their wooden yoke plowing a deep furrow steadily, taking their time about it."[45]

Because of the distracted, restless, noisy life we lead today, craftsmanship and genuine disinterestedness are more important than ever. Spiritual things are devalued; mechanical, stupidly exhausting work is richly rewarded. Rouault was unwilling to accept this state of affairs. In a society which smugly indulges in vain pursuits, where people kill time in order to get away from themselves, where all that might remind us of death has been disguised—Rouault stood out solitary and strong, a Christian monolith, towering above a mongrel culture.

Between the years 1930 and 1939, Rouault finished a number of very important paintings based on religious and circus themes, some of which are still not known to the public. They range from Old Testament characters to images of Christ and families of clowns and other circus figures.

The *Christ and the Fishermen*, in the Beyeler collection, Basel, is the first of a series of paintings which give the impression that the artist is at home. We are reminded sometimes of T. S. Eliot's poetry. Rouault, however, painter of the Paris industrial suburbs, sworn enemy of intellectualism, is very different from the subtle, St. Louis-born poet. Certain analogies, however, are discernible. Both make lasting impressions. The scenes they evoke do not refer to specific localities; they exist in the artist's own world. This is as true of landscapes in Eliot's "East Coker" as of Rouault's working-class quarters where Christ appears. The remarkable *Christ in Profile* (Bourdon collection) has the force of the New Testament account of the Passion. Here is the Word incarnate, bent under the weight of all human suffering, clothed in human form, molded of earthly clay. Dripping with sweat and tears, he is walking to his crucifixion for the salvation of mankind. *Christ Mocked*, painted at the same time, sums up everything we have ever heard of the humiliating episode with the soldiers. The *Head of Christ* (*Passion*) in the Cleveland Museum, and the *Crucifixion* (formerly collection Farra) show to what extent Rouault is able to convey his own religious feelings in painting through color and pigment alone, apart from all representation. Anticipating the redemp-

250

tion of all men through supernatural love, he unites what went before with what is to come after. Certain of his works are stamped with an Old Testament grandeur that is either fiercely patriarchal or cruelly feminine, and the question arises whether we do not have here the remote influence of Gustave Moreau's tiaraed idols. In any case, Rouault's *Roussalka* makes me think of the Queen of Sheba, with her unctuous grace and flowing curves.

The most notable of these biblical figures is *The Old King* in the Carnegie Institute, Pittsburgh. Matisse attached great importance to this painting, a color reproduction of which hung in the hall of his apartment at Cimiez, near Nice, beside another reproduction, Van Gogh's *Self-Portrait with Bandaged Ear*. As we stood looking at the two of them, Matisse pointed out to me that compared with Rouault's dense, powerful painting, Van Gogh's self-portrait looked like something from the eighteenth century. *The Old King*, which recalls King David, is striking in its directness. And nothing is more moving than the contrast between the very masculine features and the bouquet of white flowers the king is holding.

Jean Grenier found an excellent phrase for this aspect of Rouault. He compared him to "rain falling upon freshly mown fields"—the rain, thanks to which "the just man shall flourish like the palm tree, like a cedar of Lebanon shall he grow. . . . They shall bear fruit even in old age. . . ."[46]

These works were finished at the same time as certain circus scenes such as *The Injured Clown* (about 1933, private collection, Paris) and *The Little Family*, both of which are serenely moving, for the circus figures symbolize the painter's own life. I have kept a clear, haunting memory of both these pictures, having seen them often in the Rouault home. To my knowledge, they are the largest canvases Rouault ever painted.[47]

During this same period Rouault's graphic activity began to bear fruit. One after another, the plates he had been working on for so long were published. After the lithograph that served as frontispiece to Marcel Arland's *Carnets de Gilbert*,[48] the *Réincarnations du Père Ubu*,[49] which he had started in 1916, was finally published. With their heavily inked blacks, Rouault strikes a note of universality that is opposed to the provincial particularism of the writer. For Vollard, whom Berthe Weil had nicknamed "Dolikhos," had "let his *Ubus* simmer in a dozen different sauces in a French worthy of a Bombala kangaroo."[50] Whereas the text ends with the banal episodes *Ubu chez Lénine*, Rouault brings in figures that suggest the life of the spirit. In Rouault's introduction it is made clear that he was never taken in by the dealer-writer. "Now tell me, Monsieur Vollard, just what are you letting me in for?" he wrote. "Is there still time for fun in this damned life?"

In 1938 appeared *Le Cirque de l'étoile filante*.[51] It comprised a sequence of 17 etchings in color, and 82 woodcuts, composed partly from childhood memories of circuses. Here the clowns Frizzy-Chicken and Boom-Boom appear with dancers and acrobats: "Carmencita, Raissa, little Conchita, Pale-Dawn, Bitter-Sweet the nurse of luckless women, Calm-Morning, the female blossoms from all lands, in

Christian Spirit (Christ in the House of Martha and Mary) · *about 1945*

the bud or gone to seed." The colors are shrill: the etchings might almost be folk art. The woodcuts are massive, powerful, serve as ornamental borders and tail-pieces and are occasionally extremely wide. The chapter headings are: *Shows, Hawkers, Pigeon Wings,* and *Arabesques.* "In the blue-gold night, her black and saffron-yellow tights making her look like a wasp," seen in profile on horseback the bareback rider appears under a red curtain. Then come jolly Hortense and Benito "holding wide both arms . . . declaring that he is a decent fellow." Rouault's poetic prose runs throughout:

> *Tomorrow, Lord of the Sad Bones,*
> *The gypsy wagon will rattle along*
> *Till it reaches the next turning*
> *Where it will get caught in the ruts.*

The seventeen color etchings were printed by Lacourière. Rouault painted in addition 82 gouaches to go with the 82 woodcuts that were made by Aubert (from Rouault's drawings on wood). Among these one shows a skeleton lying in a crypt, with crosses in the distance.

Passion,[52] by André Suarès, is a companion volume to the *Cirque.* The two volumes form a kind of diptych, the one sacred and the other profane.[53] *Passion* is probably the most carefully executed of all the books Rouault did for Vollard. Suarès' tight, orientally poetic prose is quite on a par with the etchings. Indeed, at times, Suarès treats scenes of Christian communion somewhat in Rouault's own manner. It is a book in which the life of the worker and the religious life are prized as highly in the poetry as in the illustrations. Even Rouault's earlier theme of the prostitute is recalled in the poet's impassioned style: "You are sacred for them who are willing to understand. You are not sinner but victim, the receptacle of all our sins. Nor are you the guiltiest. Rather, you are the cesspool of our sins and lies. All other women, your sisters—the rich, the fashionable, the married, the highly esteemed, the very moral—you are the ransom for them all. Not one of them would possess the jewels and the gold she is so proud of—nor modesty, nor purity, nor vain plumage, nor the aigrette of her fair name, nor the hand-kissing and other marks of respect—if you, the victim, were not on the auction block for all women."[54]

Although with fame Rouault was much sought after, he nevertheless led the same retired life as before. In 1932, at a banquet organized in honor of Maillol, the following note from Rouault was read aloud: "My dear Maillol, all things come to him who waits—that is, who waits fifty or a hundred years, under the cold slab of the grave."

During the summer of 1937 a small retrospective exhibition of Rouault's work since 1905 was held at the Petit Palais for three months. It was a separate room within a larger exhibition called "Maîtres de l'Art Indépendant," organized in connection with the Paris World's Fair. It was generally believed at the time that

Vollard had loaned all the canvases for this show, but actually only fifteen of the forty-two items that appear in the catalogue came from Vollard.[55]

For many people this exhibition was a revelation. When Lionello Venturi saw the fifteen canvases Vollard had loaned—canvases never shown before—he decided to devote an important critical study to Rouault. This was a source of great satisfaction to the painter. In fact, even the attitude of the authorities was becoming less hostile and, in May, 1939, a portrait of Rouault by Jules Joëts, (true, it was a harmless one) in which he is shown three-quarters, was bought by the Musée du Luxembourg. I much prefer, however, the word-portrait by Claude Roulet, who saw in this painter an "eccentric whose very head changes shape. When he hunches up his shoulders, lowers his head a bit and raises one eyebrow, it is round! When he draws himself up, it is long and pale; his features become more sensitive and delicate and his face takes on a very warm expression. With crow's-feet at the corners of his eyes, and that ironic mouth, he radiates subtle good nature, a mixture of kindliness and evasive self-absorption."[56]

The critics were becoming more and more sympathetic. Paul Fierens wrote that Rouault was "closer to the Middle Ages than to modern skepticism, closer to Baudelaire and Dante than to Racine. Rouault paints man," he added, "as a mixture of spirit and clay, of heart and guts."[57] "No painter's work is at once less exact and more true," wrote another.[58] In his preface to the catalogue of the Rouault exhibition in Munich (August, 1930), Will Grohmann no doubt went somewhat too far when he compared Rouault, the "French Catholic," to Beckmann, the "German Protestant." Raymond Escholier came nearer to the truth when he wrote that Rouault's art is "consumed in flames, covered with live ash and blue tinged shadows, crystalline and transluscent and, at other times, saturated, thick, entirely in depth."[59] A Belgian critic (was it Charles Barnard?) wrote: "Rouault practices a terrible, explosive art, and the 'Messieurs Homais' of this world would have been quick to protest: 'Here is the terrorist of painting! This is Jack the Ripper!'"[60] Finally, Waldemar George, in a thorough study of Rouault's painting, accused the Dominican fathers, admirers of Picasso and the Surrealists, of having "turned their backs on Rouault."[61] This accusation was later denied by one of the Dominicans.[62]

On July 22, 1939, the car in which Vollard was riding skidded on the Pontchartrain road and crashed into a ditch. Vollard, who had suffered a fractured skull, died shortly afterward in the Franciscan nursing home at Versailles.

It was not until the next day that Rouault heard the news. He was leaving for his studio, and he was "so shocked that he had to sit down." In fact, he was so deeply affected that when he got back home in the rue de Courty, near the Chambre des Députés, he asked the concierge to go up ahead of him and let his daughter Isabelle know (she was alone with him in Paris at the time).[63]

Vollard's death—as Rouault realized—was not going to simplify matters. Since 1922 Rouault had not dated any of his works; he had been taking them up and working on them from time to time, and never bothered to sign them. Over a period of twenty-two years he had delivered to Vollard, in addition to the graphic works, 563 finished, signed paintings. In the course of time, relations between the artist and his "manager"[64] had become somewhat strained. However, after several rather painful discussions, they had finally come to a clear understanding.

The question now was how was he going to get along with Vollard's heirs? He was an extremely conscientious painter and never allowed a work that dissatisfied him to go out of the studio. Something of all this may have crossed his mind while he was attending Vollard's funeral at the Eglise Sainte-Clotilde. Vollard had been at once his exploiter and his salvation, had both urged him on and bullied him.[65]

In order to give him a change of scene his friend Claude Roulet suggested that he come to Geneva for a visit. Rouault accepted, having kept a certain liking for this city which reminded him of the atmosphere of the Protestant school he had attended as a child. After a few days, he was himself again. "That was Vollard's ghost," he commented, as he swatted a mosquito at the so-called Rousseau Island in the Lake of Geneva. Then, in that amusing way he had whenever he said something a bit ironical, he added: "In reality, Vollard was very fond of the old masters and he particularly liked me to talk to him about them, since his own knowledge was very superficial."[66]

Benito · 1937

The Injured Clown · 1932

The Holy Countenance · 1933

Passion · 1937

Judge · *1937*

Dancer · 1932

The Wandering Jew · *1934*

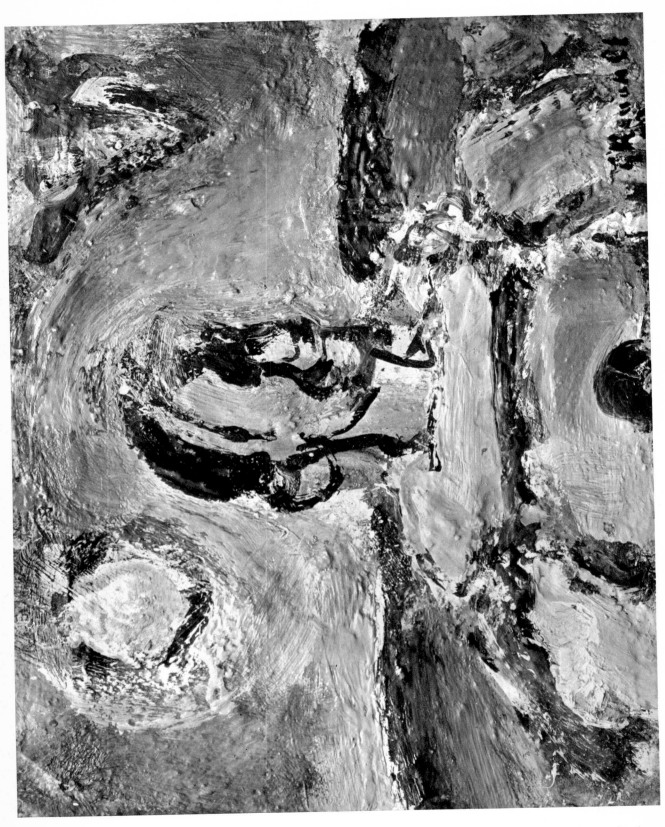

Pierrot · 1938

In the Press the Grape Was Trampled · *1934*

266

Twilight · 1937

Old Faubourg · 1937

Pierrot · 1937

Pierrot · 1937

Nocturne (Danse Macabre) · *1937*

Interior · 1937

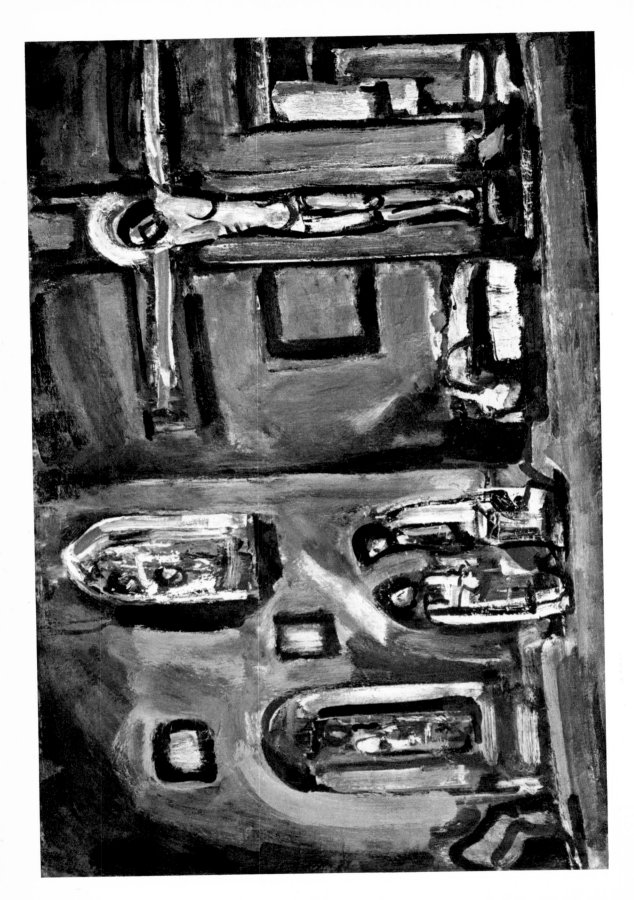

Interior of a Church in Brittany · 1938

In the Old Faubourg · 1937

Crucifixion · 1939

Peasant Woman · 1938

Gouache for "Le Cirque de l'étoile filante" · *1932*

Gouache for "Le Cirque de l'étoile filante" · *1932*

Frontispiece · 1938

Frontispiece for "Fleurs du Mal" · 1938

278

Nocturne · 1937

279

Christ and a Doctor · 1937

Head of Christ (Passion) · *1938*

Tramp · 1937

Pierrette · *1937*

284

Gouache for *"Les Réincarnations du Père Ubu"* · *1931*

Pierrot · *1938*

Street Circus · about 1937

Composition for "Le Cirque de l'étoile filante" · 1933

Old Faubourg · 1938

7. Rouault: Painter of the Human Condition

I have the impression that Rouault felt the Nazi invasion of France more deeply than his friend Matisse. He suffered, in fact, both in mind and body as a result of the German occupation. He realized, however, that although weakened, France still possessed a strong inner vitality.

"Modest, silent, hard-working France, it is up to us, your spiritual sons, to see that you do not appear to the rest of the world in a false light.

In this new Byzantium, sedentary for seventy years, having lived through three wars, O my gentle France, I still feel for you as the Prodigal Son felt in his old father's arms."[1]

Rouault wrote this after a visit to Chartres Cathedral, which he had not seen before. Before the spectacle of this "beautiful, chaste stone, the work of anonymous craftsmen," he reflected upon the multiple aspects of suffering. Invoking the poet of the cathedral's "irreproachable spire," he cried: "Péguy, devoted son of Chartres, I walk in your footsteps and can hear your voice."[2]

But he had a moment of apprehension. Enumerating the works such as the Rembrandts, Grünewalds, and the Greek pieces that deeply moved him, he wondered whether he would ever again see them. "Far from earthly conquests, will it be my privilege to contemplate once more the *Descent from the Cross* (school of Avignon); the 'Smile' in Reims—which I prefer, even mutilated, to the *Mona Lisa;* Chardin's little *Saying Grace;* the *Embarkation for Cythera* by Watteau; Corot's *Old Bridge* over a light ocher road; Le Nôtre's gardens at Versailles; and how many other works of the infinitely various French school, not forgetting Cézanne."

Rouault spent the relatively calm year of the "phony war" with his family at Beaumont-sur-Sarthe, where he had a country place. At his request, Vollard's heirs brought him a number of canvases to finish, and he kept on working. Then, before the lightning advance of the German tanks, he fled across France as far as

Golfe-Juan in a car driven by his daughter Geneviève. The long procession of refugees who took to the roads at that time was an episode Rouault had often foreseen. Most of us, as long as things seemed to be going well, had forgotten that to the believer this world is no more than a transitional stage. And now the roads were streaming with the homeless. "Endless herds of refugees are still trudging the dreary roads, up hill and down dale. Night and day the tide rumbles ceaselessly on, without respite, heading for arid, wretched, or fantastic regions such as we had never dreamed of in our wildest imaginings."[3]

Once he had reached Golfe-Juan he again asked for unfinished canvases to be sent him.[4]

During the collapse and invasion, Rouault never ceased to think of Paris:

"*Notre-Dame de Paris*
My patron saint
Doesn't this warring world
Shrivel away
Like the wild ass's skin?"[5]

At a time when people were first awakening to a sense of the community of all mankind, as individuals fallible but subject to redemption through grace, Rouault saw his prophecy of "Man is Wolf to Man" come true. Man had indeed become a wolf to other men. Always present to Rouault's mind was the Fall of Man. The spirit of François Villon, the spirit of the Middle Ages, which many had thought never to see again, reappeared.

"*Sinner am I, I know it well;*
And yet God does not will my death. . . ."

"Kind mother, old crone, we shall all one day be turned to dust,"[6] wrote Rouault about the time he painted *The Hanged Man*, now in the Musée d'Art Moderne, Paris,[7] showing a village in flames under a blood red sun. On the black gallows death performs a grisly dance ("May God keep his soul! Let his body rot!").

And one feels that night has really covered everything with its chill blanket. The drama lies in the opposition of the blue-greens to the livid white of the hanged man's shirt. The thick pigment itself seems to contain the dregs of all crimes and vices that have ever existed.

Rouault's painting, with its harlots, judges, and clowns all bound to one another in a sort of universal interdependence, animated by the eternal debate between body and soul, brings to mind the poems of François Villon. The same is true of Rouault's writings, which are concise, clipped, and occasionally use earthy colloquialisms.

Ten of the works painted by Rouault during his stay at Golfe-Juan—circus scenes and religious scenes—were shown in the Galerie Louis Carré, Avenue de

Messine, between April 15 and May 9, 1942. On a handwritten page reproduced in the catalogue,[8] the painter alluded to the German occupation and to the "still-distant time when the spirit and heart of the pilgrim will find really sincere peace, without prostituting the word, when power will not be flaunted but employed with insight and discretion. There are more things in this complex, mechanized world than we can see with our eyes or touch with our poor hands."

Many were cheered by this exhibition, coming as it did in those gloomy days. It gave a foretaste of defeat of the enemy and the end of the occupation. Also, it had been a long while since any of Rouault's paintings had been exhibited. On this occasion he showed, among others, *Pierrot as Aristocrat*, painted in enamel blues, combining suppleness and grace with a certain firmness. This "Gilles," shown fullface against a setting sun with his hands on his knees and a player's cape over his shoulders, ranks, along with Watteau's *Gilles*, among the great works of French painting.

Other canvases shown at the same time were *Pablo the Spaniard*, the delightful *Little Equestrienne*, *Stella Vespertina*, which has the radiant serenity of his last works, and *Thousand and One Nights*, portraying the Shulamite as the very essence of feminine charm.

The exhibition was well received, even though Pierre du Colombier,[9] who never understood Rouault's work, spoke of him as an "imitation genius,"[10] and a certain R. Fechy noted in that disgraceful sheet *Le Pilori* (a collaborationist paper): "They're still making their messes: hideous forms, splashes of dung."[11]

Paris was liberated on August 25, 1944. For Rouault, as for many others, the German defeat meant the end of a long succession of privations. Little by little things began to resume their normal course. In 1946, in a group exhibition called "For a Religious Art," at the René Drouin[12] gallery in the Place Vendôme, in the company of Bonnard's *Saint Francis de Sales* (painted for the church at Assy) and a *Vanity* by Georges Braque, Rouault showed a number of works, among them *Joan of Arc*, *Veronica*, *Christ on the Cross*, *Flight into Egypt*, *Christian Spirit* (or *Christ in the House of Martha and Mary*), as well as twenty or so plates from the *Miserere*. In *Christian Spirit*, the figures have a flower-like delicacy expressing human brotherhood in the presence of the supernatural.

Sometime before 1948 Rouault did a flower painting, composed of sonorous, soft colors, and the remarkable *Holy Countenance*, which was used as the basis for a tapestry now in the chapel at Hem.

I first saw this last-named work in the Rouault apartment opposite the Gare de Lyon. It was hung in a darkish room which it fairly lighted up with its presence, and from it I understood better what his daughter meant when she said, "My father's inner life was so intense . . . that the reality of his surroundings escaped him. And although he regretted at times the ugliness and banality of this neighborhood, he was quite able to dismiss it from his thoughts."

The *Holy Countenance* with its elongated features, owes its light to drawing and pigment alone. I sense in it a profound emotion—the same emotion that had made of the *Christ Mourned by the Holy Women* something more than a mere academic exercise. Indeed, this olive-complexioned head[13] resembles no other Christ in painting. Although it brings to mind Giotto, El Greco, and Rembrandt, and although it attains to the elevation of these masters, it has been achieved through other means in a totally different spirit. (It is perhaps most closely related to El Greco.) This is a new way of seeing the subject. Two elements dominate: the extremely plastic form of the face, and the richness of the pigment which, one feels, has been subjected to continuous change, slowly built up out of alluvial deposits. Here the painter would seem to have abandoned all pride of accomplishment, and even of authorship. Rouault was never taken in by his own fame. In the course of his long life, he had seen fashion sweep up and then desert many a famous man, Gustave Moreau and Puvis de Chavannes, for example. "As time goes by," he wrote, "the work alone remains and has to fend for itself. Its loudest defenders will be quite forgotten. So much for the press, the dealers, the critics, the artist's friends, and the coteries!"[14]

In addition to the above, Rouault brought out two series of reproductions grouped under the titles *Divertissements* (1943) and *Stella Vespertina* (1947). The first of these collections, in which the figure of Harlequin keeps recurring, strikes a note of elegance which the artist's work does not often possess. Indeed, there are paintings in *Divertissements* as charming as Watteau's. There are blue, half-length figures against backgrounds of green and gold. There are delightful Pierrots shown side by side with bareback riders whose red costumes accentuate the pallor of their complexions. The flesh tones radiate a subtle light. Rouault's text, printed in holograph, is highly personal:

> *Harlequin*
> *I love to see you golden yellow*
> *and ivory black*
> *Sharp as the sting*
> *of a lustful wasp.*

Stella Vespertina,[15] the other portfolio, appeared in June, 1947. Here are some excerpts from the text:

"We keep going faster and faster, without time for a sigh even on our deathbeds. Art in this mechanical century would seem at times well-nigh a miracle. . . . True beauty remains hidden, and this has always been so.

"If there is nothing new under the sun, nonetheless we can sing a different tune in a different key. . . .

"Between the Institut and the Louvre flows the Seine."

Maurice Morel, in his short but striking preface to this volume, speaks of the pictures as being "overwhelming evidence" of Original Sin. "Viewed in this light," he writes, "Rouault takes on his full significance. There are few maladies he has not explored, few types of wretchedness he has not come to grips with, nothing that concerns mankind he has not probed with his brush. . . . And if this old man," he adds in conclusion, "today pauses to gaze with the intensity of a child at the

292

evening star, it is because he sees in it neither an outworn allegory nor a diversion, but an entirely fresh, entirely ineffable symbol of Hope such as he himself found in the Cross which once loomed against a Near East horizon."

Stella Vespertina is a carefully produced sequence of reproductions. The themes are religious, and the dense, vehement colors have the brilliancy of brass instruments. Wholly invented by the painter, his colors never imitate nature. The powerful structural lines—verticals and horizontals crossed by diagonals, roads leading to bell towers under moonlit, light copper skies—create a curiously impressive, timeless atmosphere. Not even the costumes detract from this total effect.[16] The most striking of these works is probably the little *Nocturne*,[17] the original of which is in the collection of M. Philippe Leclercq, near Lille. Its dark blue-greens create a highly poetic, suggestive atmosphere.

Rouault was never a real Fauve. Nevertheless, the *Stella Vespertina* prints exhibit an intensity and a resonance with respect to color pushed to their extremes, without ever seeming strained. Rouault has occasionally been compared to Nicolas Poussin, to whose work he was introduced by Gustave Moreau. In fact, there are certain early landscapes by Rouault that invite comparison with those of the master who composed the *Arcadian Shepherds*. However, in Rouault's late landscapes the spiritual tension communicated to the paint itself is no longer derived from the story, or from the action of the characters, but from the interrelationships of proportions, planes, and colors. These of themselves create the dramatic intensity. "When I escape into pictorial poetry," Rouault wrote, "the silence is filled with images and sounds, with unexplored vastness, and with delightful groves like those of Fra Angelico."[18]

The exhibitions now began to follow one another almost without interruption. Since Vollard's death, Rouault had been entirely caught up in his work. His daughter Isabelle, whom he called his "Antigone," aided the museum curators in connection with his exhibitions.

In April, 1946, Rouault had a joint exhibition with Georges Braque at the Tate Gallery in London, in which he showed 18 oils and watercolors, one gouache, and 25 etchings from the *Miserere*. Then in 1947 Odette des Garets showed some 40 paintings by Rouault in her gallery. These included flower pictures, a few Pierrots, and some biblical landscapes, all in very vivid colors that sparkled with an entirely new brilliance.

My first meeting with Rouault took place at Mme. de Garets' gallery in the rue de Courcelles. I jotted down the following impressions right afterward:

"Despite all the people coming and going (Paulhan, who thought the light was too harsh, Villon, Gromaire, my fellow critics) I had a long, pleasant talk with Rouault, during which he showed no trace of impatience. We were sitting in a sort of little recess and, as I listened to him, I could watch his face. People have said of him that he looked like a *notaire* or an official from the *état civil*. This seems to me to be a somewhat hasty judgment. Rouault is a rather pensive-looking man and being neither very tall nor very short, one does not notice his height. Certain characteristics, however, attract attention, such as his sensitive, wrinkled hands, which he looks at and moves while speaking. Particularly striking, too, is his very high forehead which stands out like a dolmen in the fields of Brittany. In short, he has a meditative expression which is further accentuated by a rather short, slightly hooked nose, a thin, straight mouth with lips that go down at the corners, and a strong chin. The expression as a whole is one of stubbornness and inner concentration. His conversation included reflections about his work, memories of the past and, at the same time, extreme curiosity about everything that was going on.

"The way he looks at you and his tone of voice are, perhaps, what I am least likely to forget. His frank, understanding way of looking you in the eye has about it a certain mischievousness. As for his voice, it can be muted at times, or suddenly become loud and resonant, when he wishes to give stress to what he is saying. Rouault speaks with his entire body in a sort of monologue. He asks himself questions and supplies the answers. He has none of the slightly distant, executive manner of Matisse, nor has he Bonnard's look of chilly, wide-eyed bewilderment. You feel he treats you as an equal.

"As for the paintings exhibited, my general impression is one of rich color. Rouault knows when to stop; he doesn't overdo the sumptuousness. The colors are at once delicate and vehement, with great density. He knows where to inject a note of brilliant yellow, a dead white, or a deep, mat blue. Sweat and blood, and big feminine faces. This is not Byzantium, but the compact style of the Bible, the clotted blood of the 'very old new,' as Delacroix put it."[19]

At this time the lawsuit Rouault had brought against Vollard's heirs was coming up again. The legal situation was as follows. As we said before, for thirty years Vollard had been stockpiling Rouault's works, taking them out of the studio whenever the painter considered that they were finished. Vollard accepted Rouault's decision in these matters.

It was feared that the court would refuse to accept the arrangement according to which, when an unfinished canvas was sold, the artist has a right to take it back, even when the contract stipulates the distinction between rough drafts and finished pictures. Rouault's lawyer in court used Vollard's term for himself: "slave-driver." Counsel for the defense meanwhile spoke of Rouault as "a lazy genius." What was at stake in this trial was the moral right of the artist with respect to his work. On May 19, 1947, the Paris Court of Appeals decided in favor of the artist. He was the owner of his work so long as he had not of his own accord disposed of it otherwise. The Court considered that the unfinished, unsigned canvases in Vollard's keeping were in the nature of "future" works, and that this being the case, they could not change hands once and for all but, at the most, be promised. With this decision a new legal precedent was set. Vollard's heirs were therefore ordered to return all Rouault's unfinished canvases to the artist. However, about one hundred of them were not returned to him, and certain of these latter paintings were occasionally shown or sold against the will of the artist and his family, despite the court order forbidding it.

Rouault had really acted disinterestedly. On November 5, 1948, at a factory in Montreuil-sous-Bois he threw some 315 canvases into a furnace. This was out of the seven hundred or so paintings that Vollard's heirs had returned to him.[20] It was done in the presence of a court official and a photographer. Thus, after having been called first "damned," then "a new Machiavelli," Rouault now was called "a disciple of Bernard Palissy" in the public press.[21] Léon Treich compared Rouault's gesture to Rimbaud's destruction of the first edition of *A Season in Hell*.[22] The editor of the magazine *Esprit* wondered if it was not "a dangerous precedent for a great creative artist to take upon himself the judgment of the ages, saving this work and destroying that one, leaving behind him no traces of the doubts and hesitations through which the human side of the artist could be grasped."[23]

The editor of *Esprit* supposed Rouault's motives to have been dictated by taste or policy. Actually, his motives were at once more simple and more complicated. Abbé Morel has mentioned somewhere Rouault's "rejects, his false starts." He even spoke of "overworked" canvases.[24] Isabelle Rouault has told me what criterion Rouault applied when he pitched out the works to be burned. It was simply a question of how much time would be needed to finish them. Conscientious as he was, what worried him was not doubt that he would not be able to finish a particular canvas to his satisfaction, but fear lest he would never have the time to do so. His principal concern in making the painful choice (the canvases had been returned to him some months earlier) was the stage of progress of each painting. Thus it was only after long hesitation, and not without great anxiety, that Rouault decided to burn those works which he felt so little advanced that completion would demand too long a time.

But to come back to the lawsuit. One striking fact deserves to be pointed out. In awarding the verdict to Rouault, the judges showed "Christian" justice to an artist who must have seemed to many of them as their cruelest portraitist. At the same time, when they passed legal judgment on the painter's rights as opposed to the dealer's, they rendered a real service to all future artists.

We come now to one of the high points of Rouault's art, the work that combines all his themes, both those based on human passions, violence, and vice, and those based on divine grace, hope, and mercy. As Georges Chabot has written: "Here faith, love, and charity, vanity and cruelty, hypocrisy and pharisaism, life and death, are synthesized. . . . This work is striking, even frightening. Every element in it has greatness. In the *Miserere*, in this ensemble of aggressive, sparse, grandiose compositions, Rouault has perhaps expressed himself most completely."

Rouault had begun work on the *Miserere* during the war of 1914–18 but dissatisfied, he kept going back over his subjects, "sometimes making as many as fifteen trial drafts."[25] Now this work of the painter's maturity finally was published. We have already discussed the early stages. Actually, the engravings were executed between 1917 and 1927.

A first presentation of the book took place at the Galerie des Garets from November 27 to December 21, 1948.[26] Then, four years later, on February 26, 1952, a second exhibition of this series of etchings was held at the Galerie Louis Carré.[27]

296

Jean Cassou spoke of Rouault's "secret, strange, stubborn rage." And Jean Wahl, after noting that in Rouault's painting there were "colors from behind the sky, colors that we are unable to name," recalled that the painter himself had said: "The desire to exhibit is an incurable disease, and an artist will always be at a certain distance from the Promised Land."

This reminds me of a question I once put to both Matisse and Rouault: would you continue to paint on a desert island, where you had lost all hope of ever again communicating with your fellow men? Matisse's reply was emphatically in the negative: "There are no artists without a public. . . . An artist wants to be understood, a painter to be looked at." Rouault, however, was more reserved: "I am sure I would continue to paint, even without a single viewer, even with no hope of one." I understood that for him, after the inevitable period of withdrawal into himself, which is the source of all works of art (although this may, at first, appear to be egotistical), creation leads to an act of generosity, a gift to the community, visible or invisible. This must be so for any man whose genius derives from God alone.

We have already observed how modest a man Rouault was. When driven to show his work, he was always torn between his natural reserve and his need for understanding. His daughter Isabelle recalled, for instance, that he was reluctant to show his work even to Suarès, who mistook this reluctance for lack of confidence.

Rouault's last works, that is, those done after 1948, are inspired by the New Testament. A deep sense of poetry permeates their simple, powerful subject matter in which "everything remains only half-said, almost reticent. The sacred landscapes are pastoral scenes from the Bible, occasionally Oriental in character. Blazing stars plunge through night-blue skies. Little figures wander here and there, along the banks of a river or down some dim road. Around them are buildings of no particular period or style. Although the figures wear no haloes, their saintliness is unmistakable. They are whispering meaningful words to each other."[41]

Now a number of important Rouault exhibitions were held.[42] First was the show in New York[43] in 1945, with a catalogue listing 161 items (a number of American collections were represented). Next came the one in Prague in 1947. The city had not as yet been taken over by the Communists, the exhibition was a warm tribute to French art and culture. In 1948 at the Venice Biennale, Rouault showed 25 paintings. But the most important of these exhibitions was the one held in Zurich, in April-June, 1948 (266 items).[44] This included, for the most part, works from Swiss private collections, among them those of Joseph Müller (Solothurn), Max Bangerter (Montreux), Werner Feuz (Clarens), Witziger (Basel) and Mme. Heddy Hahnloser (Winterthur), Rouault's earliest Swiss collector. Then came the exhibition at the Boymans Museum in Rotterdam, where the press made frequent mention of Rouault's visionary gifts, comparing him to Bernanos. C. Doelman found his art more Nordic than Southern, "closer to Faust than to Apollo, in spite of some Byzantine features." Commenting on the *Miserere*

Where all is harmony
To the eyes, the heart, and the mind.[70]

We find the theme of death and resurrection in Rouault's earliest efforts, where it is a sort of emanation in certain of his biblical landscapes. But these early landscapes are still imbued with romantic symbolism, whereas in the thick layers of impasto of the last paintings, which seem already to open to another world, Rouault expresses himself, despite his age, with full genius.

I have a series of photographs of Rouault taken shortly before his death,[71] when he had become the last surviving painter of his generation.[72] A patriarchal figure with a thin nose, a play of expression at the corners of the mouth, creases under the chin. His eyes hold the indulgent look of an old eagle poised for its last flight. The pictures show him as I had known him. When he spoke, his eyes—which were at once turned inward and outgoing, as is often the case with those whose thoughts are more and more preoccupied with the past—seemed to encompass his whole lifetime, the various stages of which we have been trying to reconstruct.

According to Mme. Rouault, the painter suffered more when he was unable to work than from any physical pain during the last years of his life. Indeed, one felt in him a certain impatience, similar to that of the traveler all packed and eager to leave.

Rouault died on February 13, 1958, at the age of eighty-seven. The funeral took place on February 17, in the church of St.-Germain-des-Prés, which was crowded on that occasion. Abbé Morel delivered the eulogy, bidding farewell to a fellow Christian whose art he had admired passionately for a long time. He emphasized Rouault's "artisan" side, drew the analogy between him and Péguy, and recalled the works he had left behind, a trail blazed for subsequent explorers. He also spoke of Rouault's capacity for anger, "which was always resolved in God's gentle pity."

I myself, in the French weekly, *Arts*, tried to say how much humanity had lost, for all that his work remains among us. In concluding, I remarked that in Rouault's generation—which was that of Matisse and Bonnard, Valéry and Claudel— "Rouault was the only Christian painter who, in his work, had contemporized the real drama of our time—which, whether we like it or not, is essentially a religious one. For after the long sleep of lukewarm faith—the illness—we are conscious again of the 'stumbling block' of Christianity. With Rouault, art becomes weary of providing no more than an exhibitionist entertainment, however 'angelic.' It has returned to its real function. What this means, in the last analysis, is that it must give up its own life in order to be born again."[73]

Harlequin · 1947

Judges · 1948

Christ Mocked · *1942*

The Flight into Egypt · 1942

Biblical Landscape · *1948*

Decorative Flowers · 1946

Stella Vespertina · *1946*

Legendary Trio · 1945

313

Christ on the Cross · 1942

"Man is Wolf to Man" · *1948*

Pablo, the Spaniard . 1942

Teresina (or Agnes) · *1945*

Carmencita · 1947

Head of a Clown · 1948

Harlequin (Divertissement) · *1943*

Autumn in Versailles · 1948

322

Teresina · 1947

The King of the Golden Isles · 1947

Bouquet with Fruit · 1945

Thousand and One Nights · *1942*

Dancers · 1948

Duet · 1947

Bluebeard · 1948

Profile of Christ · about 1949

Harlequin · 1956

Pierrette · 1953

Christian Nocturne · 1952

End of Autumn (III) · 1952

Seraphine (Old Traveling Circus) · *1952*

Profile · 1953

Old Street Circus · 1951

Duet · 1951

337

Pierrotins · 1953

Maternity (Faubourg of Toil and Suffering) · *1950*

The Sea of Galilee · 1950

8. Salvation and Redemption

"I am sorry for my own generation, which is empty of all human substance; having known nothing but liquor, mathematics, and sports cars in the way of spiritual life, it has become completely gregarious and devoid of all character.

"A century of advertising, mass production, totalitarian regimes, armies which go into battle with no flags flying and hold no masses for the dead. I hate my period with all my being, for in it mankind is dying of thirst. . . .

"Give us back spiritual purpose, spiritual disquiet. Give us something as refreshing as Gregorian chant. Were I a believer, I should certainly find Solesmes a vast improvement over this workaday world. It is no longer possible to live by electric refrigerators, politics, financial statements, and crossword puzzles! It just isn't. Nor is it possible to live without poetry, color, or love. . . .

"I have the impression that we are moving into the world's blackest time."
(Antoine de Saint-Exupéry, "Que faut-il dire aux hommes?" *Le Figaro Littéraire*, April 10, 1948).

Rouault, for whom "Beethoven's death mask or the look in Rembrandt's aged eyes was more disturbing than a whole century of epic, heroic action,"[1] did not allow himself to be diverted from his art, even by what might appear to us as "necessity." He lived completely in and for his work. "I never rush things," he told me. "It was not until 1940, the beginning of the last war, that I saw Chartres for the first time, I found the door locked; they were taking out the stained-glass windows to store them in safety." Having first admired the Christian primitives, Rouault repudiated "the classical hierarchy that puts man at the center of the universe."[2] There is nothing surprising, therefore, in the reply Paul Valéry made

341

to Marcel Arland who, at a publisher's luncheon, had spoken to him of Rouault: "But you surely do not take him seriously!"[3] Rouault's and Valéry's poetic systems were utterly incompatible. Valéry still clung to a secular view of man as the king of creation, radiant with beauty, intelligent by virtue of his logical powers, capable of cataloguing (like Leonardo da Vinci) all the physical wonders of the world as they appear to the senses, distrusting whatever cannot be demonstrated and thereby reconstructed. Rouault, on the other hand, was entirely rooted in religious mystery. He was haunted by such questions as, "Where do we come from?" "What are we?" "Where are we going?" He did not, however, succumb to Gauguin's primitive symbolism. He recognized in Baudelaire "the affectionate smile of a brother in the spirit"[4] who, like himself, was moved by lost women, old clowns, and romantic sunsets.[5] Rouault knew quite well that his own poetics was in no way founded on physical proportions, however sublime the harmonies to which these may attain (as the temples at Paestum). No, what moved him especially were spiritual relationships, the naked love that plumbs the heart and soul and is manifest even among the most unfavored, the basest, and (physically) the most unsightly of our fellow men. Unlike the physical vision of the Renaissance, to which we owe so many masterpieces that, in their own domain, will never again be equaled, Rouault's vision was a spiritual one. Thus he upset all the conclusions to be derived from study of Greco-Roman antiquity at its height, and from frequenting museums oriented almost without exception to appreciation of a single aesthetic canon. Incidentally, today's academicism is nothing but a degenerate form of this aesthetic.

On the other hand, Rouault, more generous and clear-sighted than Paul Valéry, did not hesitate to praise him for the strong features of his personality, that is, for his deductive, almost mathematical intelligence (although he realized the dangers of Valéry's position). Rouault was well aware of the limitations of organization, and of art conceived as a game. Unlike the author of *Eupalinos*, Rouault did not deify human understanding. "For men who work hard," he wrote Suarès, "at times both eyes and mind grow weary. Who is to judge him? Whatever the schoolmasters, the critics, and the rationalists may say, the unconscious plays a role in all creation. . . ."[6]

In point of fact, Rouault was not interested in the type of art dependent upon calculated allusion. His own painting makes us forget its own surface. It is not surprising, therefore, that Rouault's art should have failed to appeal to Valéry, for whom even the idea of God could be no more than a "logical deduction."

But Paul Valéry was not the only critic. No intellectual descendant of the Encyclopédistes, no follower of Descartes could have approved of Rouault's pessimism, his emphasis on ugliness, his exposure of a world in which there is no room for the pretty, the agreeable, or the witty—not even for that "delectation" which, according to Poussin, is the supreme aim of the plastic arts.[7]

The special feature of Rouault's painting is that it is made from our flesh, from the same clay that our flesh is molded. It is as strident as the cry of an animal suddenly startled. But there exists in it, in the blood that colors it and the leaven that

342

makes it rise, a transcendent conviction that all is charity and, at the same time, impatience for the resurrection. Here at last is an art that is the material embodiment of the spirit. Why, then, should anyone be surprised that Rouault's entire career, once his apprentice years were over, was a reaction against his age? This lonely painter was always against: against false ideas, against technique understood as accomplishment, against explanations, against academic teaching, against all cocksureness of judgment. Today, as is only just, he finally appears as the most faithful mirror of his time; year after year, he collected his evidence, grasping the real character of the present. He was never sidetracked by the fashionable or the ephemeral. While Rouault makes us conscious of the dark side of the human condition—in all its variety—of life as a handful of dust, he has also opened our being to aspiration and the supreme harmony.

Rouault was sensitive to criticism. At first he suffered from the incomprehension of the public that attended his exhibitions, as well as from the injustice of newspaper critics. At the end of his career, he was much moved by expressions of respect and admiration. Lonely and shy though he was, Rouault was not indifferent. He accepted all the risks of being an artist, including the the capriciousness of inspiration. He recognized that no artist can be all things to all men. "O fortunate artist," he wrote in *Soliloques*, "even though your art be an art of unhappiness, keep on! . . . the artist is not trying to make over the world. The only soul he saves is his own."

Rouault knew too that "what distinguishes a great work from a merely good one sometimes seems a trifle. Actually, however, it makes all the difference—the sensitive touch of a pianist, a violinist's bowing—in other words, his approach to his subject." Indeed, the path that leads from the original intention to the final result is a mysterious one. "How many poor devils of artists, present or future, will look back with identical sighs to the blessed vision they once glimpsed or thought they had glimpsed!" Rouault knew how to stop, look, and reflect. He defended "sustained, loving effort . . . never as vain as it appears to men of action, who consider it a waste of time to fold one's arms and close one's eyes for a moment so that some imaginary composition may take shape."

Today we are better able to judge of the position of a painter of this caliber. His art and his life touched upon everything that has been of any importance in the evolution of thought and expression since the end of the nineteenth century. Indeed his audacious art was now to take its place in the real tradition, as is the case with all art deeply rooted in living reality. We are inclined to forget that it takes a great contempt for fashion, and even extreme boldness, to come to grips with the future. Truly original forms and ideas possess such power of novelty that they inevitably frighten the contemporary public. At first they give the impression of hopelessly ill-behaved children: they are the damned, the antisocial members of the community. Then, time blunts their edges and smooths out their roughness. What had seemed to be a crime against the art of painting is eventually integrated with it, and the *enfant terrible* who "disgraced his teachers and dishonored the profession" takes his place among the masters of all time.

344

Like Dante, Rembrandt, Daumier, Dostoevsky, and Cézanne, Rouault went back to the wellsprings of creation, never seeking to produce a merely pleasing art. He explored mankind's essential nature, and I know of no artist whose conduct of life, like his work, exhibits greater consistency. He was all of a piece.

"Every man," he wrote Vollard in 1922, "has his cross to bear. Mine is my art. If there is pride or simple-mindedness in confessing this, I don't care. But the fact is that it constitutes my only outlet, however inadequate, and expresses my better self.

"My one good quality, unless I am mistaken, is that I am not afraid to make a fool of myself.

"...But try to explain that to all these fellows who are turning themselves inside out to fall into line with the taste of today or the day after.... The basic human condition does not interest them. Whereas for me, it is my very life. And if I'm not wrong, I am becoming something of a classic! Not that I mean to, or even know whether I deserve to be one. Certainly I am not trying to do so through the use of tricks, preconceived ideas, and the gift of gab."[8]

The believer always heads directly for the essential, leaving aside the lesser features of life, for he knows that the goal is not to be reached in this world. What difficulties he encounters, even to come close to it! And Rouault wrote quite rightly that "a long, persevering, and sometimes tragic effort is required not to succumb before the Promised Land is in sight."[9]

Rouault was a religious artist in the same sense that Van Gogh was. But whereas the Dutch Protestant sought to converse directly with God, at the risk of being consumed by the sun, the Catholic Rouault, realizing that he would never attain to God through his own efforts, relied on grace to help him. The result was that the Dutchman's vision became confused and frightened, whereas the Breton Rouault's faith grew constantly firmer. Yes, Rouault showed sympathy for everything that lives even in utter darkness, "where one encounters so many ravaged faces, so many backs bent under their burdens." But "despite so much visible wretchedness, he would never despair, but keep on believing, tomorrow as today, in the hero, the martyr, and the saint." One must turn his back on comfortable, consoling appearances in favor of a reality that is deep and permanent. "The quest of the real is unending," wrote Rouault, "and there is no need to travel in order to satisfy it. Those whose eyes and hearts are closed can go to the ends of the earth without meeting anyone."[10] Joseph Pichard noted somewhere the following: "I see neither Annunciation nor Resurrection in Rouault's work, which is surprising. Even Rembrandt, who was also peculiarly limited in his subject matter, had nevertheless more curiosity or, shall we say, was more hospitable."[11] This is true as regards the Annunciation. But one of the last woodcuts in *Passion* is a scene of the Resurrection, and another version of this same picture is a painting belonging to Mr. and Mrs. S. S. White, in Ardmore, Pennsylvania.[12] In this latter work, which is wrongly titled *Christ with Raised Arms*, the Lord's face is turned heavenward, whereas in *Passion*, it is shown frontally. In both versions, however, the tomb guarded by the soldiers appears. The subject and the

346

characters are really not important. Everything about Rouault is so Christian that his choice of one subject or another adds nothing in depth to the uniqueness and truth of his art. "Everything you do is religious," Suarès wrote him, "even your clowns. You present one miserable prostitute exactly as she is: she gets only crumbs of sensuality from the banquet table of life. . . . Your faith becomes the less obvious the more ardent it is. You never capitalize on it, never trade on it." [13]

This, I believe, sums up Rouault's achievement. He was the painter of inwardness, of the supernatural light that glows in the profoundest depths. He never took God's name in vain. Indeed, Rouault made the most circumspect use of this name which writers and painters who call themselves Catholic employ only too readily. His work is filled with consciousness of God, but also with great pity for His creatures and their unworthiness. To believe is to suffer, according to Rouault, who revealed God in all things—but from within, as a vision, not as an image. Rouault often said that the finest among the Primitives had not consciously sought to create a religious art. "It was their nature, or perhaps their way of looking at things, their way of feeling—of loving. Religion and life were one for them, faith their reason for living." [14] And Rouault was sure that true faith, the deepest sense of religion—an unassuming, secret love of the Savior—is often to be found "in the hearts of the damned." [15]

When people tried to discuss sacred art with Rouault, he invariably replied that there is no such thing. It is merely some by artists who have faith. In fact, he insisted that he would never "classify all art on religious subjects as 'sacred art'." Sacred art, according to him—and I believe that he was right—is the work of creators who never for a moment imagine they are turning out something really sacred. He made a partial list of works which he felt would last. These were: Grünewald's *Resurrection* and *Crucifixion* in Colmar; and *Christ's Agony* "by old workers whose names are no longer known." "When I was but a child, some stained-glass windows in need of repair passed through my hands. From them I learned to prefer the anonymous old masters of stained glass to the contemporary ones much admired and honored around 1889—'do-nothing kings,' most of whose names are now forgotten." [16]

Regarding the purely theoretical efforts made in his lifetime to urge a revival of a communal art like that of the cathedrals, Rouault knew that nothing is ever accomplished in art by simply desiring it. "We can do something else, but we cannot re-create what the collective, spontaneous effort of generations built with the faith that was theirs." [17] In other words, we cannot do over what has already been done. "There is far too much imitation of the past, a superficial approach to the beautiful and the sublime. Just as we do not wear the same clothes as our ancestors, it would be artificial to imitate at all costs the faith of the Middle Ages." [18]

There was also talk of reviving the art of the fresco, for mural painting. "That's not for me," Rouault said. "I'm not interested in murals. . . . Formerly, things were a little different. A painter began as an artisan. He did his work and when the

348

Rouault was an artist who challenged such attitudes, still too widespread today. There is not a trace of frivolity, of anything "entertaining" in his work, nor is there any of the age's simple-minded faith in the inevitable victory of quantity over quality. Indeed, he always reacted with the same spiritual force that his painting radiates, against the powers of destruction, pride, profit, or science-worship. Rouault reminded us that life is tragic, that the human condition is a matter of serious concern, and that the world has gone mad. The spectacle of peoples playing at frightening one another, the constant efforts on the part of the press to play upon the fear of death, brought the following comment from Rouault: "Is it impossible that the atom bomb will become our next idol . . . for people have ceased to believe in the efficacy of the spiritual and, only too often, material force is visibly, hypocritically victorious."[32]

When we try today to see Georges Rouault's accomplishment as a whole, we realize that the painter is wholly present in everything he did, from his first theme of *Samson* in chains to that of *The Old King*. (Rouault was "one of the people, but he was also an aristocrat."[33]) We see him in the dolorous faces of his prostitutes; in the clowns whose seriousness under the grease paint shows a terrifying sincerity; in his eternally wandering tramps; in the faces of workers engaged in unsatisfying labors, moving along streets dotted with factory chimneys; in his bareback riders at the circus; and finally, in carnival settings, in his old acrobats with their dogs, meditating on life's ironies.

In every one of these characters, Rouault saw an image of humanity. They are our counterparts, the "expressive vehicles of our suffering."[34] It is well known that Rembrandt, at different periods of his life, had a tendency to compare the events in which he himself was involved with episodes from the life of Christ. His own face is skillfully introduced somewhere in all his scenes from the New Testament. It was his manner of experiencing what is essential in Christianity, of extracting "light from the dark depths of night." But in the case of Rouault, whose "beings and things seem to be lighted from behind,"[35] the identification is less direct, more complex. Rouault would doubtless have felt that it was a lack of modesty on his part to show the symbol of his belief too clearly. Nor should we forget that he was less interested in portraying his religious feelings than in asserting his faith. He identified with the humble, the poor, the betrayed, the damned, but also with those who are willing to assume the impossible role of settling disputes. Jean Grenier wrote of his judges that "however monstrous they may be, and by their very monstrosity, they make us think about real justice. His prostitutes, in their disgrace, recall both their degradation and real love, while his sad, bewildered clowns evoke by contrast innocent children at play."[36] Always, however, and even in his most grotesque and terrible works, Rouault maintains a certain tenderness. It may be said that if today his work "has become all love, it has always been quite free of malice."[37]

Rouault's frankness in protesting social and moral injustices was due to the fact that he had always opposed the lies, deceit, and hypocrisy of society. "How

352

often," he wrote, "I have found not only modesty and delicacy, but the capacity for tenderness and love among people of whose very existence the pundits and hairsplitters of this world are unaware!"[38]

Rouault was closer to Dostoevsky than to Balzac. He was not so much interested in creating multiple social types—to the point where we are wholly caught up in them—as to grasp the meaning of life in a few typical figures. In Dostoevsky, as in Rouault, we find a transcendence of fate, a certain unity of aim which entirely overshadows the descriptive, picturesque elements. The parallel between Dostoevsky and Rouault, therefore, seems to me quite different from the customary one drawn between Balzac and Daumier. For however different they may be, Rouault and Dostoevsky both follow a system of Christian aesthetics which shows us our own imperfections,[39] the Hell of a man-made world. They also share the conviction that deep down in the hearts of the most repugnant drunkards, prostitutes, or criminals, by virtue of their suffering and capacity for charity, they may participate in the communion of saints.

In other words, Rouault's vision of life was on a grand scale. He never lost sight of the impressive spectacle constituted by the endless chain of our iniquities. Once he had recovered from the religious aestheticism and pious but affected intellectualism of Huysmans, he did not seek out human suffering in cathedrals or among the crowds at Lourdes, but rather among street peddlers, among those who sell their bodies on street corners, among the ill-housed, the ill-fed, the homeless— in other words, among the very poor, among those who adopt children besides their own, not reckoning the cost.

Rouault's understanding of things was always very sound. His immense shyness and his "unconquerable fear of sullying with words what is purest and most beautiful,"[40] may occasionally have kept him from telling us all we should like to know about him. Like most men of faith, he was surprised to see cultivated people make a god of intelligence, a pretext for special privilege. He felt that, given the great unknown that lies before us and the ignorance of even the wisest, the most extraordinary among us has little more understanding than the most backward. We need only consider for a moment the force of penetration of the divine spirit.

Some ten years before Rouault died, I had several conversations with him. I would usually turn up at nine o'clock in the evening and find him and his daughter Isabelle waiting for me in the large back room of their apartment. More often than not he was wearing a dressing gown with a blue scarf around his neck. His prominent forehead contrasted with his small, delicate hands which he kept on the table in front of him, moving them as he talked. His conversation was extremely entertaining, particularly when he got on the subject of the terms critics applied to him. "Some say 'individualist.' Others, not at all, he derives from classical art. You must be joking! He's an Expressionist!" And so it went. "He would start a story," wrote Marcel Arland, "leave it for another, go on to a third, then come back to the first. 'What do you think of Degas?' 'Who? Degas? Yes. By the way, that reminds me . . . .' Then would come a new clutch of stories and remarks, in

354

which not so much as the shadow of a *danseuse* could be glimpsed. You only had to wait awhile. I would gently come back to the question. 'What about Degas?' 'Degas; of course! Well, Degas! You see, it's like Derain. One day when . . . that is to say, no, it was another day, the day when Roussel, Cadet-Roussel, unless it was Maxence, you know, the fellow with the drooping moustaches. . . .' And he would keep on talking. I decided to let him wear himself out. Finally, I tried once more: 'And what about Degas, Rouault?' 'Why, I was just about to tell you, but you keep interrupting me!' The moment comes at last. Rouault gathers his strength and, with a look both thoughtful and keen, replies to the question."[41]

These conversations would have completely baffled anyone who was not familiar with the gossip of the art schools, the studios, and the Ecole des Beaux-Arts, not to mention Vollard, the other dealers, and all the rest of the shop-talk. Fortunately, I was able to obtain a more complete view of his personality. Rouault spoke in fits and starts in a lively, animated manner, punctuating his remarks with murmurs and bursts of anger, as well as with the kindliest of smiles. As I said before, it was all extremely entertaining, but he never tried to dazzle or impress you. When Rouault did talk about himself, it was to get the facts straight with regard to erroneous stories making the rounds about him. His rambling interior monologues, spoken aloud, were full of substance. Rouault's language was direct and compact. It was also larded with many striking phrases (there are a number in his writings) and original turns of speech. At times he would say emphatically, "Understand me, I don't want to be set among the 'great.' I don't want to give lessons. I am made of Breton granite, which is resistant. I also have sharp edges. Sometimes I try to smooth them down, but it doesn't work."

I can summon up today the various stages of his physical appearance, some of them with the aid of his self-portraits. Here we see him, a slender young man, wearing a Ligugé student's cape, at the same time when he was still a pupil of Gustave Moreau. Then, as the "working apprentice," as he called himself at a moment in his life when many with a tenth of his talent would have put themselves forward as distinguished painters. Lastly, comes the old man with the white eyebrows, the great artist of the *Miserere*, who "can take it, who never runs away."[42] His capacities for sympathy, as well as his sense of universal comprehension, led Rouault to identify himself with every suffering creature. He himself wrote: "They never heard as intensely as I—neither in peace nor war—the death rattle of a slaughtered animal, its mouth hanging open without emitting a sound, as in a nightmare."[43]

Rouault lived his art, for he realized that immense knowledge is of no use without that gift for second sight which is characteristic of every true artist. "As soon as you paint," he said, "you have to forget everything: father, mother, sisters, brothers, friends, enemies, old works and modern ones . . ." because "nothing is old and nothing is new except the ray of grace beneath which a man's heart is beating." There was rare harmoniousness between Rouault's creative capacities and what is called common sense. "The more imagination you have," he wrote, "the more necessary it is to be a realist."

356

A Selection of Prints

Equestrienne · 1925–1927

362

Buffoon · 1926

Depressed Suburbs · 1929

364

Parade

Roualt

Parade · 1925–1927

366

Les Réincarnations du Père Ubu: page 186 · 1928

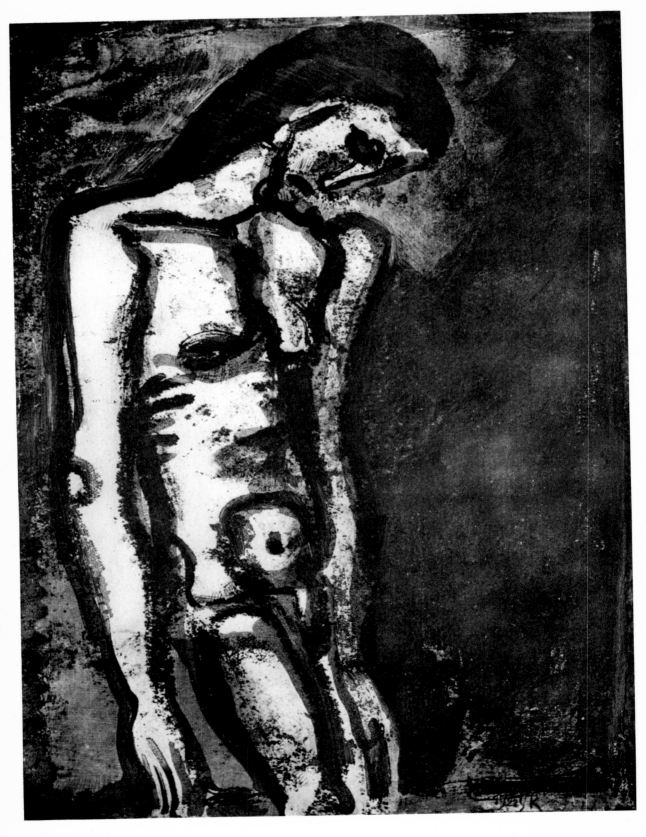

Miserere (No. 3) · 1922

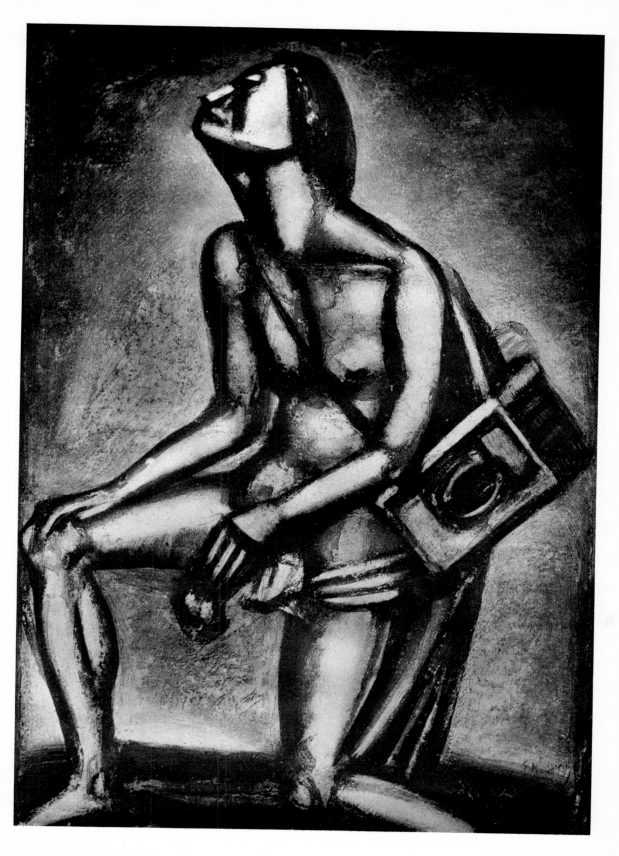

Miserere (No. 27) · *1926*

370

Miserere (No. 16) · 1922

Miserere (No. 47) · 1927

Reclining Skeleton · 1932

Notes

1. Birth and Apprenticeship

1 Georges Rouault's birth certificate, taken from the files of the nineteenth *arrondissement* of Paris, and dated 1871, reads as follows: "The second of June, 1871. Birth certificate of Georges Henri, of the male sex, born on the twenty-seventh of May in the house of his father and mother, in Paris, 51, rue de la Villette, son of Alexandre François Joseph Rouault, aged thirty-one, cabinetmaker, and of Marie-Louise Alexandrine Champdavoine, his wife, aged twenty-seven, day worker. On presentation of the child, and based on the declaration made to me, an official of the Registry Office of the nineteenth *arrondissement* of Paris, by the father, in the presence of Bernard Sabourin, aged forty-six, painter, 51, rue de la Villette, Paris, who has signed this declaration, after reading it, together with the father and myself."
Signed: Rouault, Sabourin, Febvet, and Richard.

2 Léon Lehmann says that when he was born they called him Georges l'Obus (Georges the Cannon Ball).

3 Personal conversations with the author. This reference will not be repeated. The reader will kindly note that, hereafter, the numerous other statements by Rouault, presented between quotation marks without indication of reference, are from the same source.

4 Letter from Rouault to Suarès, dated August 21, 1911.

5 Georges Rouault, "Souvenirs du jeune âge gravés dans mon cœur," *Le Point*, August–October, 1943, p.20.

6 Georges Rouault, "Visage de la France," *Verve*, 1940.

7 Unpublished letter, dated August 24, 1925, from Georges Rouault to André Suarès.

8 "Georges Rouault," *Revue Universelle*, May 15, 1924.

9 Georges Rouault, "Souvenirs du jeune âge sont gravés dans mon cœur," *op. cit.*, pp.20–24.

10 *Ibid.*, p.24.

11 Mme. Georges Rouault showed me a collection of drawings made during these evening classes. They are stamped with the official stamp of the National School of Decorative Arts and are dated and marked on the margin with the pupil's grading. For the most part, they are drawings made from engravings or from the antique. The first one is signed G. Rouault, and is dedicated: "To my dear Uncle [M. Charles Rouault], January 1, 1885." He already knew what he wanted. It shows the nude bust of a man, in a three-quarter view, turning as though to designate a point in space. A *Bacchus* profile that constitutes the face of a medallion is dedicated: "To my dear Aunt [Mme. Charles Rouault], January 1, 1886." The drawing has already become firmer in a sketch of a nude man, drawn from a live model and dated February 9, 1886 (grade 10), morning. On the evening of November 9, Rouault finished a sketch of a man standing, with the columns of light and shade well separated, and marked grade 14 (the drawing has written on it, in the pupil's own handwriting, the date and the following inscription: "To my dear Uncle and Aunt for New Year's. December, 1886."). These indications show that Rouault also attended morning classes.

373

12 "Sur Forain," *La Vie*, 1913, note on the Forain exhibition held at the Museum of Decorative Arts, Pavillon de Marsan, Paris.

13 This information was obtained from the Ecole des Beaux-Arts in the file marked "Georges Rouault, No. 7139." Rouault's arrival is noted as follows: "Pupil of E. Delaunay. Enrolled December 3, 1890, for the Library, oral classes and the Gallery .... Admitted to the atelier, December 3, the same day."

14 Georges Rouault, "Gustave Moreau," *L'Art et les Artistes*, April, 1926, special issue devoted to Gustave Moreau.

15 "Souvenirs du jeune âge sont gravés dans mon cœur," *op. cit.*

16 It was probably under Gustave Moreau's direction that Rouault painted the *Road to Calvary*, in 1891 (Collection Walter P. Chrysler, Jr., New York), in which he tried to give variety to the substance and reduce it to its very essence. But the painting is still a resemblance.

2. Gustave Moreau: Inspiration and Guide

1 Gustave Moreau presided over Georges Rouault's entrance examinations and saw to it that he was officially admitted "to the school properly speaking," in the Painting Section, on March 13, 1892 (Beaux-Arts, file no. 7139). It should be recalled that there are three stages of admission to the Beaux-Arts: 1) A candidate is admitted to the Gallery, that is, into the halls and glassed-in courtyard in which are the casts of antique statues, from which he makes charcoal sketches that are corrected by the drawing instructor. 2) He visits one of the professors acting as *chef d'atelier*, in order to show him his work (drawings made at the school or paintings done on the outside), and this professor takes him into his class. 3) The student admitted to an atelier is admissible for the preparatory competitive examination (a test that will decide his admission into the section he has chosen). If he passes this examination, he is admitted to the school proper.

2 Louis Vauxcelles, "L'Enseignement de Gustave Moreau," *ABC*, November, 1936.

3 Charles Chassé, *Le Mouvement symboliste dans l'art du XIXe siècle*, Paris, 1947.

4 Roseline Bacon, *Odilon Redon*, Vol. I, 1956.

5 Antoine Orliac, *Mercure de France*, April 15, 1956.

6 Here Degas would appear to have been a bit harsh. According to Rouault's recollections, Moreau became a member of the Institut as the result of pressure on the part of his colleagues.

7 *Sensations et Souvenirs*, Paris, 1895.

8 "Gustave Moreau," *Certains*, Paris, 1889, pp. 18–19.

9 Edouard Schuré, *Précurseurs et révoltés*, Paris, 1930.

10 Léon Thévenin, *L'Esthétique de Gustave Moreau*, Paris, 1930.

11 *Ibid.*

12 *Précurseurs et révoltés.*

13 Gustave Larroumet, "G. Moreau et le symbolisme dans la peinture," *Etudes de litterature et d'art*, Paris, 1895.

14 The movement known as Symbolism developed in the following manner: 1) Through music and operas of Richard Wagner. 2) Through the painting of Gustave Moreau (*Oedipus and the Sphinx*, 1864, *The Young Man and Death*); through Odilon Redon's collection of lithographs entitled *Dans le Rêve*, published in 1879, and, in the same year, through the decorations by Puvis de Chavannes in the Panthéon. 3) Through literature. In 1884, Huysmans published *A Rebours* and in the same year, Fénéon published the first issue of the *Revue Indépendante*. In 1885 appeared the first volumes of poems by Jules Laforgue and Henri de Régnier, and also the *Revue Wagnérienne*, edited by Edouard Dujardin. Finally, in 1886, Jean Moréas published the "Manifeste Symboliste" in *Le Figaro* of September 18.

15 Georges Rouault, "Gustave Moreau," *L'Art et les Artistes*, April, 1926, special issue devoted to Gustave Moreau.

16 "Souvenirs sur Degas," *L'Intransigeant*, March 9, 1937.

17 Georges Rouault, "La Toison d'Or" (Carrière), *Mercure de France*, November 16, 1910. Carrière's moral influence was short-lived and people forgot him. Degas contributed momentarily to his "execution" by a remark he made before one of Carrière's anaemic mother-and-child pictures, painted in an exaggeratedly ethereal manner: "One really should not smoke in a sickroom," commented Degas. More generously, Rouault said that one Sunday, in a museum, he had caught a child rubbing a badly stretched Carrière canvas with his fist, and shouting to his mother, who protested, "There's fog on it, there's fog on it." (*Soliloques*, p. 63.)

18 Charles Floquet, who was an enemy of "Boulangism," was Président du Conseil in 1888.

19 "Souvenirs du jeune âge sont gravés dans mon cœur," *Le Point*, August–October, 1943, pp. 37–40.

20 Henri Matisse, personal conversations with the author.

21 André Michel, *Le Journal des Débats*, April 22, 1898.

22 Louis Vauxcelles, "L'Enseignement de Gustave Moreau," *op. cit.*

23 Georges Rouault, "Gustave Moreau," *Le Correspondant*, April 10, 1926.

24 Statements made by Rouault on the subject of Moreau, *Beaux-Arts*, October 16, 1936.

25 Personal conversations with Henri Matisse. This was the only time I ever saw Matisse's intent eyes slightly moisten. Recollection of Moreau had sufficed for this to happen.

26 *Ibid.*

27 *Ibid.*

28 Henri Evenepoel, "Gustave Moreau et ses élèves" (letters from 1894 to 1898), *Mercure de France*, I. XV. I., 1923, pp. 22–23.

29 *Ibid.*

30 *Ibid.*

31 Bonhomme, who was born in the Faubourg du Temple quarter in 1870, one year before Rouault, was a nephew of Gaston Boissier, the author of *Cicéron et ses amis*. He entered the Beaux-Arts in 1890, under the instruction of Henner, whom he later left for Gustave Moreau.

32 Paul Seguin-Bertauld, as said to André Warnod; "Léon Bonhomme," *Arts-Documents*, No. 41, 1954.

33 Bernard Dorival, *Cinq Études sur Georges Rouault*, Paris, 1956, pp. 32–33.

34 *Ibid.*

35 In a letter to Rouault, Matisse speaks of "our friend Bonhomme, whom I saw copying Leonardo da Vinci with linseed oil in different stages of dessication" (each one to be used for a special work by Leonardo). Quoted by Dorival, *ibid.*

36 Vouched for, according to Dorival, by a letter from Bischoff to Rouault, dated April 5, 1944.

37 Léon Bonhomme died poor, in September, 1924, in St.-Denis (Seine).

38 Debay, *Demain*, June 11, 1896.

39 Evenepoel, *op. cit.*

40 Georges Rouault, *L'Art et les Artistes.*

41 Georges Rouault, "Gustave Moreau," *Souvenirs intimes,* Paris, 1927.

42 Evenepoel, *op. cit.*

43 Georges Rouault, *L'Art et les Artistes.*

44 Henri Matisse, personal conversations with the author.

45 Georges Rouault, *Souvenirs intimes,* p. 32.

46 Recalled by Rouault in *L'Art et les Artistes.*

47 Statement made by Rouault to *Beaux-Arts*, October 16, 1936. When he was in Italy in 1948, Rouault especially admired the portraits of Raphael, to be seen in Florence. He found in them a very different quality from the so-called "divine" Raphael of the Beaux-Arts.

48 Statement made by M. Rupp to Léon Deshairs (Léon Deshairs, "Gustave Moreau," *L'Art de notre temps*, Paris, n. d.).

49 Henri Matisse, personal conversations with the author.

50 Georges Rouault, in an open letter to Matisse, "Matisse," *Les Chroniques du Jour*, April, 1931.

51 Henri Matisse, personal conversations with the author.

52 Evenepoel, *op. cit.*

53 Georges Rouault, *L'Art et les Artistes.*

54 Louis Vauxcelles, *L'Ere Nouvelle*, April 24, 1924.

55 Henri Matisse, personal conversations with the author.

56 Georges Rouault, *L'Art et les Artistes.*

57 Evenepoel, *op. cit.*

58 Rouault said elsewhere: "Gustave Moreau knew about my *realistic* experiments, he saw them and never did take as much exception to them as those who, for the last thirty years (this was written in 1926), have continued to say that I have not fulfilled the early promise my works gave." *L'Art et les Artistes.*

59 *Ibid.*

60 Léon Lehmann, "Hommage à Rouault," Palais de Chaillot, June 6, 1951.

61 Georges Rouault, *L'Art et les Artistes.*

62 Henri Matisse, personal conversations with the author.

63 Georges Rouault, *L'Art et les Artistes.*

64 Ecole des Beaux-Arts, file no. 7139.

65 *Ibid.*

66 Rouault depicted, in his own manner, the episode when Samson had lost his vigor as a result of Delilah's trimming his hair and the Philistines "put out his eyes and sent him down to Gaza. They chained him up with a double bronze chain and he turned the millstone in prison." (Judg., 16, 21)

67 This painting is hanging in the office of Monsieur Untersteller, director of the Beaux-Arts, where he kindly allowed me to examine it at my leisure.

68 *L'Invendable*, 1904.

69 Salon de la Société des Artistes français, 1895, No. 1661, *The Child Jesus Among the Doctors*, No. 2715, *Study of a Head.* Drawing.

70 In connection with the name of Rouault in the list of painters, it should be noted, for the record, that in addition to the great artist who is the subject of this volume, there are two other painters named Rouault. One, Gustave Rouault, the son of a Rennes railway employee, was an official painter who made portraits of the Czar, Félix Faure, Pope Leo XIII. The other, Arsène Dominique Rouault, is a landscape painter and lives in Montmartre.

71 "Les Arts Plastiques," *La Troisième République 1870 à Nos Jours*, Paris, 1931, p. 135.

72 Jacques-Emile Blanche adds the following pertinent remark: "But that's just it! Why on earth did Gustave Moreau take such pains to paint the way the old masters did? He hadn't sufficient confidence in himself. And he succumbed under the weight of his vast knowledge." (*Ibid.*, p.134.)

73 *Sensations et Souvenirs.*

74 "Gustave Moreau," *Études de littérature et d'art*, Paris, 1895.

75 *Le Matin*, July 18, 1895.

76 The date of this charcoal sketch, which belongs to the Rouault family in Paris, poses a problem. Could Rouault have sketched it after having sold his Prix de Rome picture, painted in 1895, to Sembat? The dates would appear to agree. But Mlle. Rouault, to whom I spoke about it, considers this unthinkable. She suggests another possible explanation. Like many painters, Rouault hardly ever dated his works until they left his atelier to be shown in an exhibition. He might thus have made an error of two years in dating this sketch, which appears to have been made in preparation for the painting. I myself am inclined in favor of this explanation by the fact that in the preparatory sketch the face of the Virgin is larger than that of the Christ, whereas, in the painting, Rouault has reduced this feminine face to its proper proportions. The Beaux-Arts has always taught that a woman's face should appear to be smaller than a man's.

77 I should like to take this opportunity to finish once and for all with this loathsome farce of the Prix de Rome for painting, which, true enough, few people take seriously any longer, unless it be, from time to time, some naïvely honest young man. The best thing to do is to print the list of the winners. Since David, whose Prix de Rome was won after great difficulties, in 1774, and Ingres who, having missed it once, was given it in 1801, neither Géricault, nor Delacroix, nor Daumier, nor Courbet, nor Manet received so-called distinction which, thenceforth, was only conferred upon second-rate painters. From 1884 to 1914, that is to say, over a period of thirty years, the Académie des Beaux-Arts awarded the Grand Prix de Rome to Pinta, Axilette, Lebayle, Danger, Thys, Laurent, Devambez, Lavalley, Lavergne, Mitrecey, J.-A. Leroux, Billetey, Emile Aubry, Lefeuvre, Déchenaud, Larée, Moulin, Gibert, Laparra, Roger, Sabatté, Jacquot-Defrance, Sieffert, Guétin, Monchablon, Roganeau, Bodard, J.-T. Dupas, De Gastine, G.-C. Girodon. During that time, the Société des Artistes indépendants, founded in 1884, counted among their exhibitors: Bonnard, Cézanne, Cross, Van Dongen, Van Gogh, Henri Matisse, Laprade, Marie Laurencin, Maximilian Luce,

Marquet, Odilon Redon, Seurat, Signac, Toulouse-Lautrec, Vallotton, Vuillard, and Vlaminck (not to speak of other "independents" such as Degas, Monet, Renoir, etc.).

78 These paintings are in the museum at Avallon. The Conservator, M. Pierre Poulain, has kindly furnished the following information concerning them. They each measure $8' 10^1/_4'' \times 5' 11''$. Both are signed: "Henri Georges Rouault," but only the *Stella Mattutina* is dated: "1895."

79 Henri Matisse, personal conversations with the author.

80 Georges Rouault, *L'Art et les Artistes.*

81 Salon de la Société des Artistes français, 1896, Rouault, Georges-Henri, 155, rue de Sèvres: *The Dead Christ Mourned by the Holy Women.*

82 *La Revue Bleue,* June 6, 1896.

83 *Demain,* June 11, 1896.

84 *Le Public,* May 1, 1896. We learn from the *Revue Encyclopédique* of May 2, 1896, in an article also by Roger-Marx, that the landscape in question is "the setting for a *Return of the Prodigal Son.*"

85 This is certified by Rouault himself. See "Souvenirs du jeune âge sont gravés dans mon cœur," *Le Point,* p. 15.

86 Ambroise Vollard, *Souvenirs d'un marchand de tableaux,* Paris, 1937.

87 Mlle. Rouault informs me that this sketch was crumpled and torn in 1940, under the German occupation, when it got mixed with some pastels. The brown color on the right is an oil spot, and the tear on the left (now repaired) was made then. There are a few scratches on the face. But having now been mounted on cloth, this great, moving sketch is once more ready to confront the years.

88 This photograph of Moreau's atelier appeared in *Vogue,* April, 1958, with identification and information concerning the students in the atelier.

89 The catalogue has a preface by Sâr Péladan entitled "Mandement graalesque," roughly, "Mandate from the Holy Grail."

90 E.L., *La Revue Blanche,* March 15, 1897.

91 This we learn from *Le Thyrse,* April, 1897.

92 Statement made by Rouault to *Comœdia,* 1911.

93 *Rapide,* April 20, 1897.

94 Arsène Alexandre, *Le Figaro,* April 19, 1897.

95 *Le Journal,* April 19, 1897.

96 Compare the *Paysage d'Auvergne* in the Beurdeley collection, which shows that Rousseau was influenced by the English painter, John Constable.

97 In 1897, as though he sensed his time was short, Moreau wrote notes for the catalogue of his pictures.

98 André Michel, *Journal des Débats.*

99 Gustave Geffroy, *Le Journal,* undated clipping in the Rouault family archives.

100 Jacques-Emile Blanche, *op. cit.*

101 Louis Vauxcelles, *L'Ere Nouvelle.*

102 Georges Rouault, *Souvenirs intimes,* p. 19.

103 *Ibid.,* p. 20.

104 Like Proust's Swann, who resembles him. In fact, Proust was very much attracted by Moreau, who was one of his first models for the character of Elstir.

105 Léon Thévenin, *L'Esthétique de Gustave Moreau,* Paris, 1897.

106 *Ibid.*

107 Georges Rouault, *L'Art et les Artistes.*

108 Marcel Proust, *Contre Sainte-Beuve,* Paris, Gallimard, 1954.

3. The Search for Self

1 Statement made by Rouault to *Spectateur,* June 18, 1946.

2 Rouault, as quoted by Georges Chabot, *Revue d'Art,* Antwerp, September, 1928.

3 One of Rouault's sisters had married in Algiers, and had just lost her husband.

4 André Salmon, *L'Europe nouvelle,* November 28, 1920.

5 Gustave Coquiot, *Des Gloires déboulonnées,* 1924.

6 Odilon Redon, letter to Mme. de Holstein, January 29, 1900.

7 Rouault told this to me, and he repeated it in a letter to Suarès. Vollard was personally acquainted with Gauguin to whom, in 1893, he had introduced the model for his painting entitled *Javanaise.* As regards the Crucifixions in various shades of yellow, they were one of the themes of the new painting of the time. Gauguin's *Yellow Christ* was painted in 1889. It was started in Pont-Aven and finished at Pouldu, and a watercolor of it exists in the F. Durrio collection. This Christ was inspired by a polychrome statue in the chapel at Trémalo, near Pont-Aven (reproduced by John Rewald, in *Post-Impressionism,* New York, 1956, p. 305). The picture itself, which was part of the former Schuffenecker collection, is now in the Buffalo Museum. The *Yellow Christ* appears again in the background of Gauguin's *Self-Portrait,* painted about 1890 (in the former Maurice Denis collection). But there is also a *Yellow Christ* by Emile Bernard, which dates from 1886 (reproduced in *Lettres de Paul Gauguin à Emile Bernard,* Geneva, Cailler, 1954, in which it is erroneously dated 1888). This is the *Yellow Christ* that Bernard gave Gauguin, when they first met in 1886.

8 These family portraits were made before his parents left for Algiers. Mlle. Rouault informs me that they had difficulty bringing their grandmother back from Algiers, as she had been sent there as a civil servant employed in the Caisse d'Epargne.

9 Société des Artistes français, 1899: Rouault, address, 131, rue des Fourneaux. No. 1703: *Le Christ et les disciples d'Emmaüs.* No. 1704, *Orphée.*

10 Form, color, harmony; these are the three major qualities that Rouault emphasized in speaking of his métier.

11 Salon des Artistes français, 1900. Rouault, address 24, rue de Buci: *Salomé.* During his entire life, Rouault was haunted by the theme of Salomé. In 1933, he made a lithograph of *John the Baptist,* the theme of which he took up again in a painting.

12 Dan., 13, 32.

13 Dom Jean Coquet, who welcomed Rouault back to Ligugé, September 1, 1949, thought that Rouault had made his first pilgrimage to the abbey some fifty years before (preface to the catalogue of an exhibition of Rouault's enamels, executed in their atelier by the monks of Ligugé, that was held at Creuzevault's, in Paris, June 1 to 30, 1956). Jean Jacquinot, in "Trois amis: Huysmans, Rouault, Bloy," *Bulletin de la Société J.-K. Huysmans,* No. 34, 1937, pp. 168–81, published a very precise article on this subject. M. Jacquinot obtained his information about Ligugé from the monastery's archivist, Father Gazeau. The record shows that Rouault spent six months in Ligugé, and that he left there in late October, 1901. He must, therefore, have arrived there at the end of

April, or at the beginning of May. As for Huysmans, according to Dom Pierre de Monsabert, he settled there in 1898 (see *Le Monastère de Ligugé*, Abbaye Saint-Martin de Ligugé, 1929).

14 Dom Robert.

15 It should be recalled that Rouault, although he had been baptized on June 25, 1871, in the parish of Saint-Leu, had not made his First Communion at the usual age. While he was working under Gustave Moreau, he met the Dominican, Father Vallée, at the home of a friend and co-disciple, René Piot, and asked him to give him the necessary instruction and preparation.

16 Elie Chamard, "Les Étapes de la foi chez deux écrivains; Musset et Huysmans," *Ecclesia*, Paris, May, 1957.

17 I imagine that "big Morice," for them, was Charles Morice, the art critic who defended Gauguin in the *Mercure de France*.

18 Georges Rouault, "Huysmans," *Souvenirs intimes*, Paris, 1927.

19 Georges Rouault, "Sur Huysmans," *Bulletin de la Société Huysmans*, No. 27, 1928.

20 "Forain," *Certains*, Paris, 1889.

21 Statement made by Rouault to *L'Intransigeant*, undated clipping in the Rouault family archives.

22 "Ligugé," *Journal intime*, August 16 to October 19, 1901, unpublished manuscript, Collection P. Lambert, published by Jean Jacquinot, "Trois amis: Huysmans, Rouault, Bloy," *Bulletin de la Société J.-K. Huysmans*, No. 34, p. 177.

23 Raitif de la Bretagne, *Le Journal*, February 12, 1900.

24 Léon Lehmann.

25 Extract from the Salon catalogue: Rouault, address, 215 bis, Boulevard Saint-Germain: No. 1746, *Judas*; No. 1747, *Orphée et Eurydice*.

26 The legacy was accepted by decree on February 28, 1902.

27 Marcel Fouquier, *Le Journal*, January 15, 1903.

28 No. 795 in the Musée Gustave Moreau catalogue, 1926.

29 No. 759 in the catalogue.

30 No. 396 in the catalogue.

31 Moreau even left at least ten wax sculptures, among which are: *Hercules, Salome, Prometheus, The Apparition*, which he probably used for a series of paintings on these different themes. One of them, *Venice*, is curiously like the sculpture of Henri Matisse, with its well-defined planes. On this subject see, "Gustave Moreau sculpteur," by Ragnar V. Holten, in *Revue des Arts*, Nos. 4–5, Paris, 1959.

32 Georges Rouault, "Degas," *Souvenirs intimes*, p. 94.

33 Rouault's recollections of Degas, as reported in *L'Intransigeant*, March 9, 1937.

34 Statement made by Rouault on the subject of the Musée Gustave Moreau, in *Beaux-Arts*, October 16, 1936.

35 *Ibid.*

36 Lionello Venturi, "Georges Rouault," *L'Europeo*, Milan, April 25, 1954.

37 Georges Charensol, "Rouault," *Chroniques du Jour*, p. 23.

38 Charles Baudelaire, "Le vieux saltimbanque," *Le Spleen de Paris*, Paris, La Pléiade, 1938, p. 420.

39 Georges Rouault, letter to Edouard Schuré, with no date, published in *Goëland*, Paramé, June, 1952.

40 Georges Rouault, *Demain*, December 9, 1931.

41 Georges Rouault, preface to *Stella Vespertina*.

42 Jacques Maritain, *Art et Scolastique*, Paris, 1947, p. 177.

43 Georges Rouault, preface to *Stella Vespertina*.

44 *Ibid.*

45 They are indicated, in the order given, by the following numbers in the catalogue: 482 and 483; and, for the pastels, 746, 747, and 748.

4. Sins of Society

1 *Quatre ans de captivité à Cochon-sur-Marne*, Vol. I (1900–1904), Paris, 1905.

2 Auguste Marguillier, who was born in the Aube *département*, in 1862, was translating Wilhelm Bode's book on Rembrandt, the French version of which appeared in 1906. Marguillier was a real friend to Rouault, and it was in his company that the latter first visited Belgium.

3 This unpublished fragment of Bloy's diary was kindly furnished by his daughter, Madeleine Edouard Souberbielle.

4 Georges Rouault, *Souvenirs intimes*, Paris, 1926.

5 Georges Rouault, letter to the *Cahiers du Rhône*, Neuchâtel, 1944, special number on Léon Bloy.

6 Interviews with Jacques Maritain by Max Frantel, in *Comœdia*, undated clipping in the Rouault family archives.

7 Léon Bloy, *Le Désespéré*.

8 Léon Bloy, *Le Salut par les juifs*.

9 Léon Bloy, *Le Désespéré*.

10 Jacques Maritain, *Quelques pages sur Léon Bloy*, Paris, 1937.

11 *Journal*, Paris, 1919. We shall see later that Bloy did not at all apply to painting the ideas that he tended to proclaim with regard to his own métier.

12 Georges Rouault, *Les Chroniques du Jour*, April, 1931.

13 Georges Chabot, unpublished criticism.

14 "Georges Rouault," *Revue des Deux Mondes*, March 1, 1958.

15 1902 would also appear to be the date of a very dramatic *Clown in Profile*, in the same medium, in which the edge of the ruff is tinted. Perhaps, too, of a *Bust of a Woman*, in blue and flesh tints, which is at once close to nature and deeply expressive.

16 In a letter to the author.

17 Jacques Maritain, in a letter to Mgr. Charles Journet, which was kindly communicated to the author.

18 Matt., 21, 31; cf. 21, 32.

19 Georges Chabot, *Revue d'Art*, Antwerp, September, 1928.

20 *Des Peintres maudits*, Paris, 1924.

21 Léon Lehmann, in an article on Rouault published in *Beaux-Arts*, August 9, 1935.

22 *Georges Rouault*, in the series entitled "Les Peintres français nouveaux," Nouvelle Revue Française, 1920.

23 Rouault contributed brilliantly to the 1904 Salon d'Automne, in which there was an Odilon Redon room, a Renoir room, and a Toulouse-Lautrec room. The catalogue gives his address as the rue Pierre Leroux, in the Invalides neighborhood, and lists 44 entries by him which are divided as follows: 8 oil paintings (prostitutes and circus clowns), 36 pastels and watercolors (clowns, acrobats, prostitutes, dancers, old nurses and some landscapes, for the most part in twilight tones). It might be of interest to the reader to consult the complete list of works by Rouault that were shown that year. Unfortunately, at the time, the dimensions were not mentioned, and this makes identification difficult.

Accordingly, we give the titles in French. PAINTINGS: Nos. 1090, *Une Fille, robe rouge;* 1091, *Une Fille, plume rouge;* 1902, *Clown et clownesse;* 1093, *Croquis de cirque;* 1094, *Croquis de cirque;* 1095, *Croquis de cirque;* 1096, *Croquis de cirque;* 1097, *Croquis de cirque.* DRAWINGS and WATER-COLORS: Nos. 1619, *Monsieur Auguste* (pastel); 1620, *Fille attablée* (pastel); 1621, *Clown* (pastel); 1622, *Mlle. Irma* (pastel); 1623, *Monsieur Clown* (pastel); 1624, *Deux Femmes* (pastel); 1625, *Fille de cirque fumant* (pastel); 1626, *Fille de cirque fumant* (pastel); 1627, *Pierrot à table* (pastel); 1628, *Pierrot et sa famille* (pastel); 1629, *Danseuse* (pastel); 1630, *Monsieur Gugusse* (pastel); 1631, *Femme au trapèze* (pastel); 1632, *Acrobate en jaune* (pastel); 1633, *Tête d'homme* (pastel); 1634, *Tête de danseuse* (pastel); 1635, *Effet du soir* (aquarelle); 1636, *Ciel rouge* (aquarelle); 1637, *Effet de lune* (aquarelle); 1638, *Rivière* (aquarelle); 1639, *Nounous* (aquarelle); 1640, *Grosse femme* (aquarelle); 1641, *Pêcheur* (aquarelle); 1642, *Rivière* (aquarelle); 1643, *Homme* (aquarelle); 1644, *Paysage* (aquarelle); 1645, *Coucher de soleil, montagne* (aquarelle); 1646, *Prairie* (aquarelle); 1647, *Meules* (aquarelle); 1648, *Plaine* (aquarelle); 1649, *Paysage roux* (aquarelle); 1650, *Petit Village* (aquarelle); 1651, *Arbre et prairie* (aquarelle); 1652, *Le Soir* (aquarelle); 1653, *Crépuscule* (aquarelle); 1654, *Paysage* (aquarelle).

24 M. Fouquier, *Le Journal*, October 14, 1904.

25 Léon Riotor.

26 *Gil Blas*, October 14, 1904.

27 Called *Croquis de cirque* in the catalogue.

28 Elie Faure, *Les Arts et la Vie*, November, 1904.

29 *Le Journal de Caen*, December 20, 1904.

30 "L'Invendable" *Mercure de France*, Paris, 1919, p.43.

31 "I introduced Léon Bonhomme to Bloy," Rouault told me, "and Bonhomme painted a portrait of Bloy which, at my insistence, was accepted by the Salon d'Automne."

32 M. Joseph Bollery contributes the following details: The article in question entitled "Le Cabanon de Prométhée," had appeared originally in *La Plume*, undedicated, in September, 1890. In the same book, the article on Paul Bourget entitled "L'Eunuque" is dedicated to Léon Bonhomme, while "Un Brelan d'excommuniés" was dedicated to Georges Desvallières.

33 *Mercure de France*, pp. 70–71.

34 The titles, as listed in the catalogue, were as follows: *Filles;* 1) *Monsieur et Madame Poulot, Léon Bloy, La Femme pauvre,* peinture; 2) *Prostitute,* peinture; 3) *Terpsichore,* peinture.

35 *Monsieur et Madame Poulot* figure in the catalogue as a painting, which usually means oils. But this is undoubtedly the watercolor in the Philippe Leclercq collection, which Rouault, according to his daughter, always recognized his entry in the 1905 Salon d'Automne. There exists a sketch in watercolors of *Monsieur et Madame Poulot*.

36 *Mercure de France*, p. 132.

37 Letter from Georges Rouault to Joseph Bollery, dated August 29, 1937.

38 Raïssa Maritain, *Les Grandes Amitiés*, New York, 1941.

39 Léon Bloy, "L'Invendable," 1904–1907, *Journal*, p.289.

40 "Léon Bloy et *Le Salut par les Juifs*," *Nova et Vetera*, Fribourg, October-December, 1958, p.285.

41 Mlle. Rouault remembers perfectly the visits she made as a child to Bloy's home in Bourg-la-Reine, and she recalls especially how he looked seated under a tree.

42 Anner, *L'Intransigeant*, March 28, 1905.

43 *Mercure de France*, April 15, 1905.

44 *Gil Blas*, March 23, 1905.

45 In December, 1905, Rouault was named with four other members to sit on a subcommittee of the Salon d'Automne. The President for 1906 was Frantz Jourdain and the Vice-President, Georges Desvallières.

46 Beneath this title, Rouault wrote on a press clipping: *La Noce à Nini-Patte-en-l'air*, to show that it was one and the same picture. (Today it belongs to Monsieur Coutot.) "At each exhibition," Isabelle Rouault told me, "my father would ask me to verify the titles. He insisted, for instance, on adding the expression *Jeu de massacre* (Pitch-Ball Puppets) to this same *Noce à Nini*, and *Têtes à massacre* to *La Mariée*, in the Tate Gallery, in order to show that he himself assimilated these painted figures to puppets." But Rouault gave these names to his figures simply by analogy for they may be distinguished from puppets, properly speaking, by all that separates art from reality. It should be recalled, however, that Rouault liked to classify his paintings according to category. There is the series of circus players, street players, prostitutes, and buffoons; then there is also the series of puppets or heads to be thrown at. These are the unbreakable dolls to be seen in the back of certain booths in street fairs. The game is to bombard them with hard beanbags and, if possible, knock them all over at once. The beanbags may be seen, in fact, in the foreground of the painting entitled *La Noce à Nini-Patte-en-l'air*. This game is also called "Noce à Thomas."

47 Thiébaut-Sisson, *Le Temps*, October 17, 1905.

48 *Gil Blas*, October 17, 1905.

49 Maurice Raynal, *Peinture moderne*, Skira, 1953.

50 Louis Vauxcelles, "L'Atelier Gustave Moreau," preface to the exhibition catalogue, *Les Fauves*, November-December, 1934.

51 *Ibid.*

52 Léon Lehmann, "Souvenirs du temps des Fauves," *Beaux-Arts*, August 2, 1935.

53 On the reverse side is another heavy, dark figure of a clown leaning on his elbows, with one cheek resting in his hand. (The figure 5 is written at the top, to the right.)

54 At that time, blue amounted to an obsession with Rouault and with Picasso. To what is this due? Perhaps to the profound, irresistible influence of Cézanne. *The Fountain* is the earliest of the great Versailles subjects by Rouault, so far as I know today. The others are: *Fete at the Edge of the Pool* (1906, watercolor, $22^1/_4 \times 25''$, Collection Netter), and *The Staircase*, also called *The Terrace* (1910, watercolor, $27^1/_4 \times 21''$, Paris, Musée d'Art Moderne).

55 Quoted by Hubert Colleye in *La Métropole* (Antwerp), Nos. 22–23, February, 1958.

56 There exist several preparatory versions of *At the Mirror*, which date from 1905: among others, the gouache and watercolor, painted in the width of the canvas, in the collection Leclercq ($19^9/_8 \times 25''$), in which the woman is seated, not ungracefully, on a red cushion. On the back of this same picture, painted in height, is a woman standing, of which a more perfected study, the *Prostitute with Red Stockings*—a Spanish nude, seen from the back, with hat and fur-piece—used to belong to the Albert Sarraut collection. (A reproduction of this latter painting may be consulted in the Museum

of Modern Art volume entitled *Rouault*, New York, 1945, p. 42.) Another variation that preceded *At the Mirror* is *The Fallen Eve*, in the width of the canvas, pastel and China ink, in the Petit Palais. This is a work that is full of gentleness.

57 Charles Journet.

58 *Vagabondages*, Paris, 1921, pp. 118–19. Another time, despite the fact that he had little sympathy for matters pertaining to religion, Coquiot made the following lucid observation, in Rouault's presence: "It would take a saint to understand!"

59 Ernest Hello; Hello would appear to have had a presentiment of Rouault's painting when he wrote: "In modern art, idea disturbs form. Being unable to be contained by the form, the idea bursts and breaks it. But beyond the ruins of the broken forms may be glimpsed immense horizons."

60 Ernest Hello, *L'Homme*, 1872.

61 Claude Roulet, "Le peintre français Georges Rouault, II," *Revue de Belles-Lettres*, Neuchâtel, December, 1936.

62 Rouault, foreword to a special number of the review *Kunsten-Idag*, No. 2, 1954.

63 Mr. Alley, assistant curator of the Tate Gallery, has made an excellent catalogue of Rouault's London works.

64 *Gil Blas*, February 2, 1906.

65 The Salon ran from March 20 to April 30, 1906. As listed, Rouault exhibited the following: 4357, *Trois Études pour les Trois Graces*; 4358, *Études de nu*; 4359, *Fille*; 4360, *Baigneuse*; 4361, *Filles*; 4362, *Fille dansant*.

66 *Mercure de France*, April 15, 1906.

67 *La Revue Théâtrale*, April, 1906.

68 At the Salon d'Automne in 1906, Rouault's entries were as follows: 1489, *Paysage*; 1490, *Clown*; 1491, *Filles*; 1492, *Filles de cirque*; 1493, *Études*; 1494, *Filles*; 1495, *Études*; 1496, *Baigneurs lutteurs*; 1497, *Clowns et filles de cirque*; 1498, *Filles et paysages*. All these numbers were indicated as paintings.

69 Rouault's entries in the 1907 Salon des Indépendants were the following: 4262, *Paysage*; 4263, *Filles*; 4264, *Fille*; 4265, *Fille*; 4266, *Clowns*. A glass cabinet containing: a) 3 stannous china plates; b) 12 stannous enamel plaques; c) 6 stannous enamel plaques; d) stannous enamel candy box (ceramic by Metthey).

70 *L'Amitié de France*, May–June, 1907.

71 Rouault's entries in the 1907 Salon d'Automne were the following: 1482, *Accusé et avocat*; 1483, *Accusé et juges* (fantoches); 1484, *La Mariée* (fantoches); 1485, *Accusé et avocat*; 1486, *La Cour*; 1487, *La Foule*; 1488, *Fille de cirque*, pastel; 1489, *La Péniche*, pastel; 1490, *Clown*, pastel. There exists another *Péniche*, a watercolor dated 1906 (22 × 24³/₄″). It was bought by the subscribers of the *Peau de l'Ours*, along with two other watercolors of the same date: *Fille de cirque* (29 × 20¹/₂″) and *Rollin le lutteur* blowing on a cornet (27³/₄ × 22″).

72 *Le Tintamarre*, October 13, 1907.

73 *Le Beffroy*, December, 1907. In his book on Tristan Corbière (*Le Divan*, Paris, 1925), Martineau quotes verses by the author of *Amours jaunes*;

> Encloué je suis sans cercueil
> On m'a planté le clou dans l'œil
> L'œil cloué n'est pas mort
> Et le coin entre encor.

74 Under this same title, they are numbers 5221 to 5226. Rouault's address is given here as: 11 bis, rue Mansart.

75 *New York Herald*, May 20, 1908.

76 Rouault's entries in the 1908 Salon d'Automne were as follows: 1787, 1788, *Figures décoratives*; 1789, *Condamné à mort*; 1790, *Juges*; 1791, 1792, *Figures décoratives*; 1793, a glass case containing ceramics decorated by Rouault on Metthey stannous pottery: 13 small plaques, 2 flasks, 1 frieze landscape, 1 frieze decorative figures, 7 cupels, 9 small candy boxes, 1 small cream pitcher.

77 *Le Petit Parisien*, October 10, 1908.

78 M. Habert, *Revue des Arts*, October 18, 1908.

79 *Les Hommes du Jour*, October 30, 1908.

80 *Chronique des Arts*, October 10, 1908.

81 *Le Radical*, September 30, 1908.

82 André Suarès, *Passion*, illustrated by Georges Rouault with 82 woodcuts in black-and-white and 17 colored etchings.

83 Charles Journet, correspondence with the author.

84 Louis Vauxcelles, *Gil Blas*, September 30, 1907.

85 M. Joseph Müller told me that Rouault, in reminding him that *Le Condamné* had been shown at the 1908 Salon d'Automne, confirmed the fact that he had painted it after having been present at the sentencing of a man named Vacher. (We found the following in the Salon d'Automne catalogue, under No. 1789: *Condamné à mort*, painting.)

86 Statement made by Rouault to Jacques Guenne, *Nouvelles Littéraires*, November 15, 1924.

87 From the funeral oration delivered by Abbé Morel in the church of Saint-Germain-des-Prés, Paris. *In memoriam* was published for Rouault's family and friends, by L'Etoile Filante, February 10, 1959.

88 Today, individual cases are given more conscientious study, particularly when it is a question of juvenile deliquents.

89 Rouault also painted some lawyers (there was an *Accusé et avocat* in the 1907 Salon d'Automne; and there is another one, painted in watercolor, dated 1908, in the Collection Rouault).

90 "Oublié là." After the separation of Church and State, the crucifixes in courtrooms had been removed.

91 "Daumier," *Souvenirs intimes*.

92 Statement made to Jacques Guenne, *Les Nouvelles Littéraires*, November 15, 1924.

93 "Daumier," *op. cit.*

94 I refer especially to the *Tête de femme* (1930, oil, 12⁷/₈ × 9″, former Collection Werner Fenz, Clarens), which constitutes such a worthy pendant to the *Old King*.

95 Guichard-Meili, *Temoignage chrétien*, July 25, 1952.

96 Gotthard Johansson, *Svenska Dagbladet*, January 31, 1951.

97 In a personal conversation with the author, Henri Matisse recalled that "Druet had started with a big bar-café and tobacco shop on the Place de l'Alma, where Rodin, who was working nearby at the marble depot on the rue de l'Université, usually went for lunch. As it happened, Druet was also a photographer and he asked permission of Rodin, who had a special pavilion at the 1900 World's Fair, also on the Place de l'Alma, to photograph all of his sculpture. This beginning and his subsequent association with artists gave Druet the idea of selling paintings. He gave up his tobacco shop and rented a gallery on the corner of the rue Matignon and the Faubourg St.-Honoré. His first exhibition was devoted to the Neo-Impressionists. He later moved to the rue Royale."

98 Who was Jacques Favelle? Was he a critic who is now forgotten, or was he an invented character?

99 Is this the admirable *Conférence* (1908, 12$\frac{1}{2}$ × 8$\frac{1}{4}$", on paper) in the Petit Palais?

100 *Paris-Journal*, March, 1910.

101 *Chronique des Arts*, February 26, 1910.

102 Louis Vauxcelles, without further indication, in the Rouault family archives.

103 *Courrier Français*, March 5, 1910.

104 *Le Progrès*, March 15, 1910.

105 *Les Echos parisiens*, March 10, 1910.

106 *Ibid*.

107 *L'Indiscret*, March 30, 1910.

108 *Nouvelle Revue Française*, April 1, 1910, pp. 49–51, reprinted in *Etudes*, Paris, Nouvelle Revue Française, 1924.

109 *Ibid*. Concerning the ceramics, Rivière spoke of the "plenitude of these nudes seated amid dark sparkling landscapes."

110 Vollard met Rouault at Metthey's as Dorival and Raynal have already recounted, and it occurred to him to ask him to decorate some pieces of pottery. Vollard added the following note: "Thus it was that I acquired these vases, plates and platters that looked as though they had come from some Renaissance potter's hand." The Vollard estate was, in fact, the source of the two large vases decorated by Rouault with women bathers, that I saw being delivered to the Musée d'Art Moderne, some ten years ago, and I think that I have rarely experienced such pleasure at the sight of simple vases. An extraordinary unity relates the paintings on them—women crouching comfortably in what might be undersea poses—to the pottery itself, the blues of which have been given unusual savor by the firing. I understood then the satisfaction, the simple artisan's pleasure, that Rouault must have felt while working with the potter.

111 That year (1911), Rouault, who lived at 51, rue Blanche, sent the following, listed among the entries to the Salon d'Automne: 1381, *Groupes campagnards*, p.; 1382, *Petite famille*, p.; 1383, *L'Hiver*, p.; 1384, *L'Hiver*, p.; 1385, *Nuit d'hiver;* 1386, *Baptême du Christ;* 1387, *Tête de clown* (plate); 1388, *Tête de femme* (plate); 1389, *Nu* (plate); 1390, *Nu* (platter); 1391, *Nu* (platter); 1392, *Nu* (platter); 1393, *Nu* (platter); 1394, *Pierrot* (platter); 1395, *Nu* (large vase); 1396, *Clown* (small plaque); 1397, *Cheminée* (large plaque); 1398, *Cheminée* (four small plaques). The ceramics were shown in M. André Mare's dining room (with decorative works by La Fresnaye, Marie Laurencin, etc.).

112 *Paris-Journal*, October 22, 1911.

113 "Correspondance de Rouault et de Suarès," letter from Rouault dated November 10, 1913, *Nouvelle Revue Française*, April 1, 1959.

114 *Paris-Journal*, December 10, 1911.

115 *Ibid*.

116 This platter was in the Girardin collection.

117 *L'Action*, December 17, 1911.

118 *Gil Blas*, December 15, 1911. The *Baptism of Christ* mentioned is probably the one in the Petit Palais, painted in 1911.

119 *Revue du Mois*, January 10, 1912.

120 Elsa Bonan has furnished me with the following account: In the thirteenth century the Franciscans created a poetic form that was at once religious, mystic, and popular. The *giullari di Dio*, the most famous of whom was Fra Jacopone da Todi, recited their *laudi* in order to exhort people to charity and repentance. These *laudi* are of a pathetic nature

and, at times, they are in dialogue. *Giullari di Dio* might be translated as "God's jugglers."

121 According to Apollinaire, these albums "were shown at the Druet Gallery in 1911, when this painter had his one-man show." And in the same article he adds that Rouault sent abroad, "where doubtless he will have sensational success, 40 projects for colored etchings"; he recalls that these albums are still in France. (Guillaume Apollinaire, *Paris-Journal*, July 5, 1912.) Mlle. Rouault tells us that the first of these colored etchings were made by Joseph Florian, a friend of Léon Bloy. Florian had a hand press on which he himself printed the etchings. The Florian family, who live in Stara-Rise, in Czechoslovakia, still own certain of the originals.

122 Letter published by Maurice Chapelan in *Figaro Littéraire*, March 22, 1952, on the occasion of the "Exposition Léon Bloy," at Loyse, rue Bonaparte.

123 Letter from Rouault to Gustave Coquiot, which was kindly communicated to the author by Mme. Mauricia Coquiot.

124 Marthe Rouault came from a half-bourgeois, half-artistic family named Le Sidaner, of Saint-Malo. Her father was a seafaring captain and, in his leisure hours, also a painter and a sculptor. Her mother, who was a cultivated musician was left a widow with seven children, whom she brought up conscientiously and well. Mme. Rouault was the youngest of the daughters, and certainly the only one of them who could have adapted herself to the life of an artist. She got along marvelously with Rouault's parents, in whose home she was obliged to live. "I still miss them," she told me only recently. "My husband's mother was a model of self-abnegation."

125 They were to be followed by Michel, born in 1912, and Agnès, in 1915.

126 Raïssa Maritain, *op. cit.*

127 Bloy went to live on the Place Condorcet, in Bourg-la-Reine, on May 15, 1911. In January, 1916, he moved to lodgings on the rue André-Theuriet, also in Bourg-la-Reine, in the same house in which Péguy had lived.

128 Raïssa Maritain, *op. cit.*

129 "Correspondance de Rouault et de Suarès," letter from Rouault, dated June 22, 1912, *op. cit.*

130 *Ibid*.

131 *Ibid*.

132 At this same moment Rouault saw his mother as *The Widow* (Petit Palais). This shows that he shared deeply the life of his family, and that art, for him, was a means of self-revelation. A composition that is apparently similar to the above-mentioned *De Profundis*, exists in the Collection Philippe Leclercq (at the left we see a priest saying Mass and, against the wall, a Holy Face). In reality, however, this latter work has quite another significance, which is: the *Dead Soldier*, one of the subjects used for the *Miserere* engravings. Lastly, there is Rouault's Tokyo *De Profundis*, but which is quite different, with a black cross that is a variant of the *Stella Vespertina* cross.

133 *I see* this converse image, but no doubt it did not exist in the mind of the painter. Rouault, as we have seen, was always absorbed in what he was doing; he devoted himself wholeheartedly to the work of the moment.

134 "Correspondance de Rouault et de Suarès," letter from Rouault, dated June 25, 1913, *op. cit.*

135 "Correspondance de Rouault et de Suarès," letter from Suarès, dated June 29, 1913, *op. cit.*

136 "Correspondance de Rouault et de Suarès," letter from Rouault, dated July 4, 1913, *op. cit.*

137 Rouault had sent Suarès a rough copy of this text. It should also be recalled that there exists an article on Ingres by Suarès, which appeared in the *Grande Revue*, July, 1911. It was in connection with this latter article that Rouault first came in contact with Suarès, whom he met later at the home of Letellier, a mutual friend. Letellier directed, in Paris, a school for boys, which he later moved to the country. In the first letter to Suarès, dated July 16, 1911, in speaking of the rough copy of his future article, which he mentions as his "petit Monsieur Ingres," Rouault wrote that he had composed it "in a moment of enthusiasm for the fellow's strength, skill, and determination, as well as irritation against his compatriot, the southerner Lapauze, who keeps repeating, in vain, that 'our young men will understand what a lesson, this was' etcetera."

138 Georges Rouault "Ingres Ressucité," *Mercure de France*, December 10, 1912.

139 According to Georges Chabot, it was the art critic Gustave Coquiot who first spoke of Rouault to Vollard.

140 "Correspondance de Rouault et de Suarès," letter from Rouault, dated January 17, 1914, *op. cit.*

141 Claude Roulet, "Georges Rouault," *Soliloques*, Neuchâtel, 1944.

142 "Georges Rouault," *L'Amour de l'art*, December 12, 1923.

143 Georges Rouault: "L'Artiste – Miserere – Mère," *Les Soirées de Paris*, July-August, 1914, double issue, Nos. 26 and 27.

5. Miserere

1 Gertrude Stein, *Autobiography of Alice B. Toklas*, New York, Harcourt Brace and Company, 1933.

2 I am indebted to Henri Matisse for these details concerning Vollard's gallery, as well as the dealer himself. There is also, unless I am mistaken, a caricature by Forain of Vollard's shop: *Rue Lafitte*, in which we see an old broken comb, together with other junk from the Flea Market.

3 Vollard's first album was composed of two engravings of *Bathers* (Cézanne), a *Béatrice* by Redon, a *Laundress* and a *Canoeing* by Bonnard, *The Tuileries Gardens* and *Children's Games* by Vuillard, *Apparition* and *Young Girl at a Fountain* by Maurice Denis, *Iris* by Sisley, and *The English Cart* by Lautrec.

4 There followed *Vues de Paris* by Bonnard, *Intérieurs* by Vuillard, *L'Apocalypse* by Redon. His first very important book was *Parallèlement* by Verlaine, illustrated by Bonnard (1900).

5 "I first choose the painter who, himself, chooses his author, and I leave the artist complete liberty to carry out his book as he would a succession of pictures." (Declaration made by Vollard and quoted by Marcel Zahar.)

6 Plantin type was chosen for *Les Réincarnations du Père Ubu*, and the printing was done by Jourdes et Fils.

7 *L'Ere Nouvelle*, April 24, 1924.

8 On Thursday, October 28, 1926, "Pinturicchio" informs us that at this sale (most of the Rouaults were reproduced in the catalogue) the collectors among the general public "booed the supermen, *Mère Ubu*s, and other terrifying rough sketches made by this genuinely great artist. But what really made them indignant was that people should be paying eight and ten thousand francs for rapid wash drawings that were but a form of relaxation for the artist who, after a hard day's work, amused himself in the evening while chatting with his family. And I thought," the critic went on, "as I looked at those wild-eyed booers: 'Why, they themselves are models for Rouault, genuine Ubus, with their bloated faces, their thick lips, and their spleen.'" (Pinturicchio, *Carnet de la Semaine*, November 7, 1926.)

9 These sheets (gouache and watercolor) run from $12^3/_{16} \times 7^7/_8''$ to $15^7/_8 \times 10^1/_4''$. There are some in the Petit Palais and Mme. Henri Simon also owns several.

10 For these details, as well as most of those that concern Vollard, we are indebted to a lecture given by Marie Dormoy at the Feuille Blanche, on January 17, 1946. A typed copy of this lecture may be consulted at the Bibliothèque Nationale.

11 To André Warnod, *Comœdia*, 1926. Clipping without further indications in the Rouault family archives.

12 Joseph Pichard, *L'Art de l'Eglise*, No. 1, Bruges, 1953.

13 Léon-Paul Fargue.

14 Rouault recalled on his plates the titles of his original project, which is to say: *Miserere* (Plate I) and *War* (Plate 34). This second part contains all the subjects that are especially related to war. *Face to Face* is a draft board; *Civilian Soothsayers Chatting* speaks for itself; *Bella Matribus* shows us the mother rather than the Virgin; *The Just* is a wounded soldier being borne away by angels. In the *De Profundis*, we see the soldier dead and, to the left, members of Parliament discoursing. This plate is dated 1927. Twelve years later, in 1939, in the oil belonging to M. Philippe Leclercq, Rouault replaced the speeches by a priest saying Mass. *At the Wine Press* brings together the wounded man and the nurse. *With Nails and Beak* is an allusion to Big Bertha, the famed German cannon. *The Angel of Reims* presents a contrast to the German. *Dura Lex* is a homage to the soldier who does his duty without asking for an explanation. The *Virgin with Seven Swords* is the Virgin of Suffering. Lastly, in *Our Lady of Land's End* may be seen a reference to Finistère and Brittany, which was the native province of Rouault's father.

15 Georges Rouault, preface to *Miserere*, 1948.

16 There were, nevertheless, a few exceptions: *The Nobler the Hearth, the Softer the Collar* is an allusion to "Junker" Germany; and *My Gentle Land, Where Are You?* pictures a village in flames, recalling the invasion.

17 Henri Petit, "Suarès," *Le Parisien Libéré*, December 13, 1955.

18 "Correspondance de Rouault et de Suarès," letter from Suarès, dated January 30, 1916, *Nouvelle Revue Française*, April 1, 1959.

19 Letter from Suarès, dated from La Simiane, May 21, 1922, *ibid.*

20 Letter from Rouault, dated July 30, 1916, *ibid.*

21 Letter from Suarès, dated from Carqueiram (Var), December 19, 1923, *ibid.*

22 Ambroise Vollard, *Souvenirs d'un marchand de tableaux*, Paris, 1927.

23 When the printing was finished, a United States ambassador asked Rouault to gold-dip a certain number of these copperplates in order to have them inlaid into the walls of his embassy.

24   Letter from Suarès, dated from La Simiane, May 21, 1922, *op. cit.*

25   Editions Porteret, Paris, 1929. Printing was completed on May 8. The full-page engravings were printed by Duchâtel, and the edition was composed of: 6 copies numbered 1 to 6 including in each one, 6 original lithographs and 2 retouched by hand; 12 copies numbered 7 to 18, including 6 original lithographs and 1 retouched; 132 copies numbered 19 to 150, with 6 original lithographs, 15 copies *hors commerce* CLI to CLXV.

26   Pierre Mornand and J.-R. Thomé, "Vingt Artistes du Livre: Georges Rouault," *Le Courrier Graphique*, Paris, November, 1950.

27   Edition des Quatre Chemins, Paris, 1929.

28   Details of the printings made by Frapier may be found on the advertising pages of Frapier publications added to *Souvenirs intimes*, second edition (1927). Mention should also be made of the 6 original lithographs that accompany the first edition of *Souvenirs intimes* (1926), the lithograph that forms the frontispiece of the second edition of this book (*Baudelaire*), and, lastly, *Buffooneries*, an album of 12 original lithographs (first series), all printed by Frapier.

29   Raïssa Maritain, *Les Grandes Amitiés*, New York, 1941, p. 169.

30   Mme. Rouault told the author that she gave piano lessons until 1929.

31   Georges Chabot, unpublished text, quoted by Maritain in a more shortened form and revised by Rouault in a more detailed form, in *Soliloques*, Neuchâtel, Ides et Calendes, 1944.

32   Abbé Maurice Morel, foreword to *Stella Vespertina*.

33   Georges Chabot, in an unpublished text.

34   To André Warnod, *Comœdia*, 1926. Undated clipping in the Rouault family archives.

35   "Correspondance de Rouault et de Suarès," letter from Suarès, dated September 20, 1919, *op. cit.* Suarès was always objective. On May 11, 1923, he wrote to Rouault: "Thank God, you have Vollard. There are no Vollards for poets."

36   This seems to the author to be an exaggeration. Even if we do not like Maurice Denis' painting, he never made servile imitations of the Primitives. He interpreted them, calling our attention to them and to the real values among them, somewhat the way Bourdelle did for the Archaic Greeks.

37   *Bonsoir*, November 16, 1920.

38   *La Lanterne*, December 27, 1920.

39   *Ibid.*

40   *Vagabondages*, Paris, 1921.

41   *Georges Rouault*, 1921. "At the N.R.F., in the little book about me, they rubbed out the clown's hat that I have on my forehead. You never know who is responsible in those big houses." (Georges Rouault, interviews with the author.)

42   Louis Vauxcelles, *Excelsior*, September 28, 1924.

43   "Correspondance de Rouault et de Suarès," letter from Suarès, dated October 11, 1917, *op. cit.*

44   *Ibid.*

45   "Autoportraits et portraits de Rouault," *Revue des Arts*, No. 4, December, 1953.

46   *Dans les Ténèbres.*

47   Joseph Bollery, to whom we are indebted for this information, was kind enough to let the author see this letter.

48   *Christ in the Suburbs* is very close to this line of Maritain's: "The reason why Christ wanted to be a worker in a little village was that he wanted to take upon himself the ordinary estate of humanity." (Jacques Maritain, *Art et Scolastique*, Paris, 1927, p. 33.)

49   *Clowns*, Paris, Deux Mondes, 1923.

50   *Des Peintres maudits*, Paris, 1924.

51   Matisse was mistaken when he spoke of Rouault's "red" hair.

52   Jacques Maritain, *Revue Universelle*, May, 15, 1924.

53   Raïssa Maritain tells this in her book *Les Grandes Amitiés*. The text on Rouault, which appeared in *Revue Universelle*, was incorporated in a new edition of *Art et Scolastique*, brought out in 1927.

54   Letter-preface to the book entitled *Georges Rouault, l'homme et l'œuvre*, by Georges Charensol, Paris, Quatre Chemins, 1926.

55   Mlle. Rouault pointed out the fact that her father had later made certain changes in the work that was reproduced in the 1926 volume, having given it greater depth and seriousness.

56   Rouault, *Souvenirs intimes*. The first edition comprised 385 copies: 35 *hors commerce* numbered from I to XXXV, and 350 numbered from 1 to 350, illustrated with 6 original lithographs, Paris, Frapier, 1926. The second edition appeared in 1927 and contains only one lithograph, Baudelaire's portrait, which is used as frontispiece. Both editions contain a preface by André Suarès.

57   "Baudelaire," *ibid.*, p. 65.

58   "Claude Monet," *L'Amour de l'Art*, No. 8, 1927.

59   The exhibit opened on May 30, 1925.

60   *Börsenzeitung*, March 18, 1925.

61   *Berliner Tageblatt*, March 27, 1925, copy with no indication of the author's name, in the Rouault family archives.

62   Maurice Raynal, *L'Intransigeant* (with regard to the exhibition of gouaches and watercolors by Rouault, at the Quatre-Chemins, 18, rue Godot-de-Mauroy, in 1929). Raynal did not change his opinion, and there is not a separate chapter devoted to Rouault in *Peinture moderne*, Skira, 1953.

63   "Georges Rouault," *Cahiers d'Art*, No. 3, 1928.

64   Preface to *Stella Vespertina*.

65   Letter from Rouault to Suarès, June, 1929, kindly communicated by Mlle. Rouault.

66   Unpublished letter from Vollard to Rouault, dated January 18, 1930, kindly communicated by Mlle. Rouault.

67   Later, Vollard termed Rouault an "executioner of work" and the expression was repeated at the time of the lawsuit that Rouault brought against Vollard's heirs. It was, in fact, an argument in favor of the painter. (See Ambroise Vollard, *Souvenirs d'un marchand de tableaux*, p. 260.)

68   Being ill and away from France, Rouault could not undertake the visits. He would thus appear to have deliberately placed himself in a position that made it impossible for him to succeed.

69   "Pourquoi je me présente à l'Institut," *L'Intransigeant*, May 27, 1930.

70   During his convalescence, Rouault made a series of pastels: *Faubourg of Toil and Suffering*, composed of landscapes and heads. He was tempted by the astute and probably quite factitious idea of a proposed film on the subject of his painting.

6. Greatness and Accomplishment

1 Letter from Rouault to Vollard, dated from Saint-Palais-sur-Mer, October 3, 1922.

2 Georges Rouault, preface to *Stella Vespertina*.

3 *Gil Blas*, undated clipping in the Rouault family archives.

4 *Ibid.*

5 "Correspondance de Rouault et de Suarès," letter from Rouault, dated April 27, 1913, *Nouvelle Revue Française*, April 1, 1959.

6 Letter from Rouault to Suarès, dated November 1, 1913, *ibid.*

7 Rouault did not like to show his work until he himself felt the need to do so. Even Suarès was made to wait.

8 Letter from Rouault, dated September, 1915, *ibid.*

9 Georges Chabot, unpublished article.

10 *Ibid.*

11 Georges Chabot, "Georges Rouault," *Revue d'Art*, Antwerp, September, 1928.

12 Claude Roulet, "Le peintre français Georges Rouault, II," *Revue des Belles-Lettres*, Neuchâtel, December, 1936.

13 "It is better to be mistaken in our own way," he said, "than in that of the great masters." (Reply to an inquiry on the métier, *Beaux-Arts*, October 16, 1936.)

14 *Ibid.*

15 I remember a conversation on the same subject that I had with Pierre Bonnard. "Nowadays," this great Nabi remarked, "a painter must learn everything anew by himself, beginning with the ABCs of the métier. There is no longer any real instruction and there was none for me and my friends, who, *unlike Rouault and Matisse, did not have the privilege of working with such a teacher as Gustave Moreau. We* had to experiment on our own, at the risk, frequently, of wandering astray, and this was true from the very beginning of the métier."

16 Reply to an inquiry on "1830–1930," conducted by *L'Intransigeant*, November 23, 1929.

17 *Ibid.*

18 *Ibid.*

19 Unidentified clipping in the Rouault family archives.

20 Text by Rouault quoted in 1924 by Louis Vauxcelles. In *Verve*, November 15, 1938, under the title "Anciens et Modernes," Rouault wrote: "Many an artist has sighed at the discrepancy between his inner vision and the world of emotions facing the poor little work he has given birth to; on the edge of an abyss, without realizing it, at other times in complete joy, or secretly sobbing, according to the gifts that have been granted him."

21 This was a figurative reference to the humility an artist must possess to return to the simple, generous conception of the sculptors on cathedrals, as well as of the poor taste constituted by the signing of famous names at the bottom of works that are often without distinction. But it does not apply to signatures, as such, which may be indispensable in some particular cases. In 1939, for instance, Rouault used this means to distinguish between the works delivered to Vollard and those that were not. The signed ones were those that the artist himself considered as finished, whereas the others were kept for further work. In other words, the signature indicated that the work had been delivered to the dealer, and thus distinguished finished from unfinished work.

22 Preface by Georges Rouault to Georges Charensol's book, *Georges Rouault, l'homme et l'œuvre*, Paris, Quatre Chemins, 1926.

23 *Art Présent*, Paris, 1945.

24 Inquiry on the "Ecole Française," *L'Eclair*, August 29, 1924.

25 Preface to *Stella Vespertina*.

26 *L'Intransigeant*, February 8, 1932.

27 On the Musée Gustave Moreau, in *Beaux-Arts*, October 16, 1926. Rouault added to these declarations: "Vermeer of Delft painted only a very small number of works, but they were of a quality that is rare; whereas Tintoretto, whose verve was incredible, covered miles of painting."

28 "Quel est votre paysage préféré?" *L'Intransigeant*, April 2, 1929.

29 Georges Rouault, "En Marge des doctrines," *L'Intransigeant*, November 15, 1932. Rouault added the following paragraph, which is still timely: "But let us not speak of order, nor poke fun at the ignoramuses, the hacks, and the hawkers when the would-be elite finally learned yesterday, at the Institut, that there had existed a remarkable painter named Manet, whom they honored with an appropriate 'gabfest.'"

30 Statement made by Rouault in the review *Art Présent*, No. 1, 1945.

31 Georges Rouault, "En Marge des doctrines," *Nouvelle Revue Française*, October, 1931.

32 To this Rouault added: "With the kind regards of the solitary G. R.," and dated his poem "Saint Malo, October, 1931." This was published in *Tomorrow, Homage to Rouault*, December 9, 1931, volume 2, Upper House, Lawrenceville, New Jersey; review founded by Mrs. Wayne Andrews and James Douglas Peck.

33 *Revue d'Art*, Antwerp, 1928.

34 Letter from Rouault to Vollard, from Saint-Palais-sur-Mer, dated October 3, 1922. A copy was kindly furnished by the Rouault family.

35 Georges Chabot, *Revue d'Art*.

36 Georges Rouault, "En Marge des doctrines," *Nouvelle Revue Française*, November, 1931.

37 Preface to *Stella Vespertina*.

38 *L'Intransigeant*, February 8, 1932.

39 He once wrote, "I am a man of the faubourg, very much so, on the one hand, and so little, on the other."

40 *La Vie*, on the subject of the Forain exhibit, held at the Musée des Arts Décoratifs in 1913.

41 "En Marge des doctrines," *op. cit.*, October, 1931.

42 Preface to *Stella Vespertina*.

43 *Ibid.*

44 "On Forain," Rouault's reply to an inquiry organized by *La Vie*, 1913.

45 Georges Rouault, "Anciens et Modernes," *Verve*.

46 Jean Grenier, "Georges Rouault et la Bible," *Preuves*, April, 1958; and Ps., 91 (92); 13–15.

47 Mme. Cuttoli plans to have tapestries of these two canvases made in the Aubusson ateliers.

48 Marcel Arland, *Les Carnets de Gilbert*, Paris, Nouvelle Revue Française, 1931. This printing included, as frontispiece, an original lithograph by Rouault, in addition to four copper-plate engravings and five in color. The 216 copies consisted of: 3 on super-lustrous Japanese vellum, numbered I to III; 14 on Imperial Japanese vellum, numbers IV to XIII and marked A to D *hors commerce*; 19 on Van Gelder

Dutch vellum, 15 of which were numbered XIV to XXVIII and 4, *hors commerce* E to H; 180 on Arches vellum, 150 of which were numbered 151 to 180. The text was printed by Darantière, the engravings by Haasen, and the lithos by Desjobert.

49 *Les Réincarnations du Père Ubu*, text by Ambroise Vollard, Paris, Ambroise Vollard, 1932; with 22 etchings and 144 drawings by Georges Rouault, engraved on wood by Georges Aubert, preface by Georges Rouault, dated 1930, set in Plantin type, and finished February 15, 1932. 305 copies numbered in Arabic numerals, that is: 55 on Monval by hand, from 1 to 55; 250 on Vidalon, from 56 to 305; *hors commerce*, 30 from I to XXX, 15 from A to O; 225 sequences of etchings, 50 of which on lustrous Japanese vellum and 175 on Van Gelder. Printed on Aimé Jourde's hand-press, woodcuts by Aubert.

50 Berthe Weil, *Pan! dans l'œil*, Paris, Lipschütz, 1933, p. 42. This is a book of memoirs in which, by way of introduction, the author, who was herself a picture dealer, published her pamphlet on Vollard that the *Mercure de France* had refused when it was submitted in reply to "Figures d'Amateurs" (December 16, 1916), in which Vollard had written most ungratefully of Camondo, who had been one of the early sources of his fortune. Under the title: *Les Débuts de Dolikhos*, Berthe Weil first brought out her reply in a small pamphlet that cannot be found today. She then decided to print it at the beginning of *Pan! dans l'œil*.

51 *Le Cirque de l'étoile filante*, text and illustrations by Georges Rouault, edition of 250 copies, 1 to 35 on Japanese vellum, 36 to 250 on Montval, I to V on Japanese vellum, VI to XXX on Montval. Printing was finished on March 5, 1936.

52 André Suarès, *Passion*, set in Elzevir-Plantin, with 17 colored etchings, 17 in black-and-white, 17 figures for the List of Plates, and 82 drawings engraved on wood by Georges Rouault. 245 copies were printed, 25 of which were *hors commerce*, from I to XXV. Printing was finished February 19, 1939. For *Passion* Rouault made 82 drawings for the woodcuts, and executed the same subjects in oil on cardboard. Two of the latter were removed from the series by Creuzevault to be set in bindings, among them, the *Magnificat des trois Marie*, in the possession of Philippe Leclercq.

53 Pierre Mornand and J. R. Thomé, *Vingt artistes du livre*, Paris, 1950.

54 "No, it is rather He, robed in pale linen, who approaches these weeping women, no longer as the gardener who comes at morn, but the visitor who comes at night." (André Suarès, *Passion*.)

55 The other works loaned on this occasion belong to the Collections Piot, Marcel Fleischmann, Girardin, Bangerter, Sacher Stehlin, Joseph Müller, MacSweeny, Bellanger, Druet, and Rosenberg.

56 "Georges Rouault à Genève," *Revue de Suisse*, December 20, 1951, pp. 84-85.

57 Paul Fierens, without further indication of source, in the Rouault family archives.

58 Louis-Léon Martin, *Art et Décoration*, April, 1930.

59 *La Peinture française au XXe siècle*, Paris, 1937.

60 November 2, 1931, without further indication of source, in the Rouault family archives.

61 "Georges Rouault," in a special number of *La Renaissance*, October-December, 1937.

62 Father Couturier who, later, in about 1942, gave Rouault his entire support and invited him to design stained-glass windows for the church at Assy, in the Haute Savoie. These designs were carried out by Paul Rony. On the other hand, Father Régamy, who wrote on Géricault and Delacroix, had the courage to express his regret at not having appreciated Rouault at his full value at the time when his painting was still being opposed.

63 "Georges Rouault à Genève," *op. cit.*, p. 76.

64 Rouault, who was now under exclusive contract, used to say of his relationship to Vollard: "It is a heavy cross, I am behind barbed wire. . . . In chains! How am I to work normally?"

65 Maurice Coutot.

66 This remark was quoted by Claude Roulet in "Georges Rouault à Genève," *op. cit.*, p. 81.

7. Rouault: Painter of the Human Condition

1 Georges Rouault, "Visage de la France," *Verve*, Paris, 1940.

2 *Ibid.*

3 Georges Rouault, *Soliloques*, Neuchâtel, Ides et Calendes 1944, p. 192.

4 When he came back to Paris in 1942, Rouault finished, among other paintings: *Christ Mocked* and *Passion* (reproduced in *Le Point*, August–October, 1943, p. 79). He was extremely anxious about his unfinished works, so much so, in fact, that after trying to reach an agreement through conciliation, he was finally obliged to resort to legal procedure. In this he was assisted by the jurist Maurice Coutot, his two lawyers, Lucien Baudelot and Jacques Baraduc, and his daughter Isabelle, all of whom, together, assumed responsibilities which otherwise would have made it impossible for Rouault to continue painting.

5 *Les plus belles prières*, Paris, Amiot-Dumont, 1953.

6 *Les Peintres du cirque d'hiver*, poem by Georges Rouault, in the exhibition catalogue, May, 1937.

7 The title of the picture is: *Homo homini lupus*, oil on canvas, $25^8/_{16} \times 18^1/_8''$.

8 The catalogue contains, in addition to the autograph page by Rouault, dated Easter, 1942, an important note by Bernard Dorival.

9 "One either has grace or one hasn't. One is moved or one remains cold. It is either something great or it is nothing. But by this perilous attitude Rouault remains a very isolated phenomenon in French painting." *Beaux-Arts*, April 20, 1942.

10 *Comœdia*, May 9, 1942.

11 *Le Pilori*, May 7, 1942.

12 From April 12–30. The exhibition was organized by Abbé Morel who also wrote the preface to the catalogue. Rouault's contribution, which was listed along with that of the other artists shown on an inserted page, consisted of 17 paintings, 21 prints from *Miserere*, 6 etchings in black-and-white and 3 in color.

13 This *Holy Countenance* was especially mentioned, after Rouault's death, at the memorial meeting organized at the "Centre Catholique des Intellectuels Français," in the rue Madame in Paris, by the center, the family, and a few friends of the painter. On this occasion, J. Plasse-le-Caisne recalled that he had made several attempts in his workrooms to translate it into tapestry. He said that he had begun with rather rich materials, wools that went "from black to white, with at least ten gradations in between." Finally, after several failures, he succeeded in making a satisfactory version which, strangely enough, was finished on the very day of Rouault's death, in three tones of ordinary hemp, black, gray, and natural-colored. It may be seen today, monumental in size, in the church in Hem. This was the first work of Rouault's to be used as an altarpiece. This memorial evening, which took place May 19, 1958, was addressed, among others, by R. P. Régamey, Bernard Dorival, Georges Charensol, J. Plasse-le-Caisne, Alfred Manessier; and fragments of the roneotyped texts were published in *Sociologie et Religion*, No. 25, published by Fayard, Paris, December, 1958. Jacques Maritain's preface to the Museum of Modern Art, New York, catalogue for the 1953 exhibition, was read on this occasion and is included in the Fayard publication.

14 Letter to Christian Zervos, *Cahiers d'Art*, No. 3, 1928.

15 *Stella Vespertina*, album of 12 reproductions in color by Georges Rouault, printed by Draeger. Text by Georges Rouault, preface by Abbé Morel, Paris, René Drouin, 1947. Printing was finished in June, 1947.

16 A certain number of the canvases reproduced in the album *Stella Vespertina* were finished by Rouault before the end of the lawsuit and delivered to Ambroise Vollard's heirs.

17 *Nocturne* was shown at the René Drouin gallery, in the Place Vendôme (May, 1947), together with the other paintings reproduced in *Stella Vespertina*. It was stolen during the exhibition, then returned to a painting expert without it ever having been possible to identify the strange temporary lover of this little masterpiece. *Nocturne* was also reproduced in enamels in the Ligugé ateliers.

18 *Stella Vespertina*.

19 Exhibition Georges Rouault, from February 7 to March 1, 1947, Galerie des Garets, 31, rue de Courcelles, Paris VIII. The catalogue contained a preface by Marcel Arland and, as frontispiece, a profile of the artist drawn by his daughter Isabelle. This exhibition was followed immediately by one in Prague, which opened March 23, 1947, in the gallery of the Circle of Intellectuals where, among others, were shown four paintings done in 1914 (Collection Josef Florian, Moravia), one of them his *Paul Verlaine*. The catalogue contained a preface by Miroslav Mičko which mentioned 10 paintings and 24 etchings from *Miserere*.

20 Many more canvases were destroyed a few years later.

21 Georges Chabot, unpublished text.

22 Rimbaud had in his possession 47 copies of this 53-page booklet printed by the Alliance Typographique, Brussels, all of which he destroyed in November, 1873.

23 *Esprit*, February, 1949.

24 "Quand Rouault détruit ses brouillons," *Carrefour*, October 16, 1948.

25 Georges Rouault, presentation of the *Miserere*.

26 The catalogue gives the following description of this edition: 58 plates, 500 copies of which were printed between 1922 and 1927 on tinted Arches vellum, for Ambroise Vollard. War conditions having resulted in the loss or deterioration of a certain number of proofs, the edition was limited to 425 copies, numbered 1 to 425, plus 25 copies *hors commerce* I to XXV. The dimensions of the plates are $25^7/_{16} \times 19^{11}/_{16}$". The paper is watermarked for Vollard. The book was published by L'Etoile Filante. This information is followed by a detailed account of the *Miserere* and a few press quotations. A certain number of the prints in this book were shown before 1948 in Europe and in America.

27 The catalogue has a preface by Thierry Maulnier.

28 Gotthard Johansson, *Svenska Dagbladet*, January 31, 1951.

29 Claude Roger-Marx, *La Gravure originale en France, de Manet à nos jours*, Paris, Hypérion.

30 *Georges Rouault*, Museum of Modern Art, New York, 1947.

31 Carl O. Schniewind, *ibid*.

32 "Le Miserere de Rouault," *La France Catholique*, January 11, 1952.

33 *Ibid*.

34 *L'Art Sacré*, March–April, 1952.

35 Georges Rouault, reply to an inquiry conducted by Maurice Brillant, published in *La Croix*, May 11 and 12, 1952.

36 After the *Miserere* was published, Abbé Morel directed the artistic part of the film that reproduced the work *in extenso*. This is the most striking documentary film made to date on the subject of a work of art.

37 *Hommes et Mondes*, No. 2, March, 1949.

38 Dom Jean Coquet, preface to the catalogue of the exhibition of enamels and prints held at the Creuzevault gallery, Paris, from June 1 to 30, 1956.

39 The speakers were: Léon Lehmann, Georges Salles, René Huyghe, Jean Cassou, Jean Wahl, and Alfred Manessier. A poem by Jean Cayrol was read aloud and Abbé Morel introduced the film based on the *Miserere*, which was shown for the first time. (This film was produced by the Comptoir des Techniciens du Film and the Société des Films du Temps; technical director Frédérique Duran; and artitistic director, Abbé Morel.)

40 Preface to the catalogue of the exhibition held in Brussels in 1952 at the Palais des Beaux-Arts; La Connaissance, publishers.

41 Georges Chabot, from an unpublished note.

42 A list of all the exhibitions of the works of Georges Rouault may be consulted in the back of this book.

43 The book catalogue (161 numbers, 81 of which were oil paintings) contains an important foreword by James Thrall Soby; an account of Rouault's prints by Carl O. Schniewind, and a bibliography by Hanna B. Muller, Museum of Modern Art, New York, 1947. (This latter date, although it is that of the book we have in hand, refers to the exhibition of 1945.)

44 Kunsthaus, Zurich, April–June, 1948. The catalogue contained 266 items, a foreword by W. Wartmann, and a bibliography.

45 *Groene Amsterdammer*, November 19, 1949.

46 This exhibition, organized by Robert Giron, was the result of co-operation between the directors of museums in Brussels, Amsterdam, and Paris, assisted by Mlle. Rouault.

47 *Le Soir*, Brussels, undated clipping in the Rouault family archives.

48 H. R. R., *Trouw, Amsterdam*, May 9, 1952.

49 *Alkmaarse Courant*, May 10, 1952.

50 H.V.G., *Algemeen Handelsblad*, May 24, 1952.

51 H.V.C., *Het Gooi en Ommelander*, May 31, 1952.

52 The catalogue listed 135 items, with the same prefaces as for the Brussels exhibition, published by the Musées Nationaux, Paris, 1952. Before the close of this retrospective exhibition, Marcel Arland gave a remarkable talk on Rouault at the Musée d'Art Moderne.

53 *Témoignage Chrétien*, July 25, 1952.

54 *Le Monde*, July 9, 1952.

55 Christian Zervos, "Approche de l'œuvre de Rouault," *Cahiers d'Art*, No. 27, December, 1952.

56 In Los Angeles, of particular interest was the *Road to Calvary* (1871), loaned to the Wadsworth Athenaeum, Hartford. This is one of the paintings that is most closely related to the symbolism of Gustave Moreau.

57 This exhibition was composed of 149 items: 85 paintings (oils, gouaches, watercolors, etc.). A luxurious catalogue, containing 10 colorplates, was brought out by the newspaper *Yomiuri*, dated October 1, 1953. In his foreword, Shigetaro Fukushima tells how he became acquainted with Rouault after having admired one of his pictures, a gouache, in the window of the Georges Bernheim gallery, rue de la Boétie. This meeting took place in 1929.

58 Catalogue with a preface by Abbé Maurice Morel.

59 *Corriere della Sera*, April 22, 1954.

60 Tilo Soini, *L'Eco di Bergamo*, April 22, 1954.

61 *La Libertà*, Piacenza, April 22, 1954.

62 Guiseppe V.Grazzini, *Il Nuovo Cittadino*, Genoa, May 7, 1954.

63 Constantino Baroni, *Il Popolo*, Milan, April 22, 1954.

64 Enzo Fabiani, *ibid*.

65 *Epoca*, Milan, May 2, 1953.

66 *L'Avenir d'Italia*, Bologna, April 29, 1953.

67 Account in *Sud-Ouest*, signed Jean Rocques, who also spoke of the last paintings by Rouault, "these vespertine landscapes bathed in calm and gentle happiness." ("La joie de Rouault après avoir entendu Madame Nouaille," *Sud-Ouest*, July 24, 1956.)

68 This description of the last Rouaults recalls somewhat the poems that André Suarès published in *Passion*, poems that were inspired by his own emotion in the presence of his friend's paintings:

> About him, so white, light spreads its feathers . . .
> Your foldless robe is the lantern on the prow,
> And your mute step the ship of guilelessness.

69 Dom Xavier Botte, *L'Art de l'Eglise*, No. 1, Bruges, 1953.

70 Georges Rouault, *Stella Vespertina*, Drouin, Paris, 1947.

71 These photographs were made by Roger Hauert. They were collected in a small brochure that appeared in Geneva in 1956, published by René Kister.

72 Bonnard and Matisse died before him.

73 This address was published the following year under the title *In memoriam (In memory of Georges Rouault)*, printed by M.Fequet and P.Baudier. On February 23, 1958, a memorial Mass, organized by the Italian Catholic Artists' Union, was celebrated in Rome, in the Basilica of Santa-Maria of Montesanto. On this occasion, Fortunato Bellonzi recalled in a few words "Rouault's anticlassicism and his protest against the bourgeois spirit." An account of this service appeared in the *Osservatore Romano* of March 2, over the signature of Mgr.Ennio Franca.

8. Salvation and Redemption

1 Georges Rouault, *Stella Vespertina*, Drouin, 1947.

2 Waldemar George, "Georges Rouault," *La Renaissance*, October-December, 1937, special issue devoted to Rouault.

3 "Georges Rouault," *Fémina-Illustration*, October, 1956.

4 Georges Rouault, "Baudelaire," *Souvenirs intimes*, Paris, Frapier, 1926.

5 Rouault considered composing a suite on the *Fleurs du mal*, but he abandoned the project.

6 "Correspondance de Rouault et de Suarès," letter from Rouault, dated June 11, 1913, *Nouvelle Revue Française*, April 1, 1959, pp.674-75.

7 Unless it be for the "delectation in knowing" (*délectation dans le connaître*) that Maritain speaks of in *Art et Scolastique*, Paris, 1927.

8 Letter written from Saint-Palais-sur-Mer, dated October 3, 1922, a copy of which was kindly communicated by the Rouault family.

9 *Divertissements*, Paris, Tériade, 1943.

10 *Ibid*.

11 "Georges Rouault," *L'Art de l'Eglise*, No. 1, Bruges, 1953.

12 This painting is reproduced in E.A.Jewell's book *Georges Rouault*, Paris, Hyperion, 1945, p.27.

13 Letter from Suarès to Rouault in *L'Art et les Artistes*, special number devoted to Gustave Moreau, April, 1926.

14 "Pour ou contre Matisse," in *Les Chroniques du Jour*, April, 1931.

15 Georges Chabot, *Revue d'Art*, Antwerp, 1928.

16 "Anciens et Modernes," *Verve*, November 15, 1938.

17 Preface to *Stella Vespertina*.

18 Quoted by Dorival in "Hommage à Rouault," *Sociologie et Religion*, Paris, December, 1958.

19 *Panorama de la peinture française contemporaine*, Paris, Kra, 1927.

20 Rouault authorized Hébert Stevens and, later, Paul Bony, to execute the five stained-glass windows destined for the church in Assy (Haute Savoie). It should be noted, nevertheless, that in 1937, because of his obligations toward Vollard, Rouault had to refuse the proposal made by the architect, Henri Vidal, to design a stained glass window for the church in the *cité ouvrière* (workers'-town) of Tavaux, in the Jura *département*.

21 Reply to "L'Art sacré," an inquiry conducted by Maurice Brillant, *La Croix*, May 11 and 12, 1952.

22 Georges Rouault, Preface to *Stella Vespertina*.

23 Georges Chabot, unpublished text.

24 "Rouault nous parle," interview with Waldemar George, *Figaro Littéraire*, January 3, 1948.

25 Quoted by Lionello Venturi, "Art religieux et art sacré," n.p., n.d.

26 *Ibid*.

27 Quoted by Lionello Venturi, *ibid*.

28 R.P.Régamey, *Art sacré au XXe siècle*, Paris, 1952, p.245.

29 Quoted by Jacques Maritain in *Art et Scolastique*.

30 Dom Xavier Botte, *L'Art de l'Eglise*.

31 In this church, Le Corbusier has undoubtedly succeeded in creating genuine religious emotion, by means of distribution of light in a solid material.

32 Reply to an inquiry on sacred art, Maurice Brillant, *La Croix*.

33 Preface to *Stella Vespertina*.

34 Georges Chabot.

35 Jean Grenier, "Georges Rouault and the Bible," *Preuves*, April, 1958.

36 *Ibid.*

37 Marcel Arland, "Soleil," *Arts et Métiers graphiques*, April, 1958.

38 Georges Chabot, *Revue d'Art*, Antwerp, September, 1928.

39 In *Crime and Punishment*, Sonia introduces the murderer, Raskolnikoff, to the New Testament account of the death and raising of Lazarus.

40 Georges Chabot, unpublished text.

41 "Georges Rouault," *Fémina-Illustration*, October, 1956.

42 Georges Chabot, unpublished text.

43 *Ibid.*

44 Roger Fry, *L'Amour de l'Art*, 1924, p. 154.

45 Quoted by Lars Erik Aström, *Expressen*, January 28, 1951.

46 Preface to *Stella Vespertina*.

47 The comment is that of Vincent van Gogh, and he sums up the whole problem of religious art: "To give an impression of anguish," Vincent wrote to Emile Bernard, "one can try to do it without aiming direct at the historic garden of Gethsemane."

48 Léon Bloy, *Le Sang du Pauvre*, Paris, 1909.

49 Fathers Lucien Marie of Saint Joseph and Albert of the Sacred Heart, *L'Art Sacré*, March-April, 1952.

Chronology

1871   May 27. Georges Henri Rouault was born in Paris in a cellar (51, rue de la Villette, Belleville) during a bombardment of the northern section of the capital by the troops of the "Versailles government." Paris itself was in the hands of the Commune. His father, Alexandre Rouault, from Montfort in Brittany, was thirty-one, and a cabinetmaker by trade. His mother, Marie-Louise Alexandrine Champdavoine, born in Paris, was twenty-seven.

1881   Georges often visited his aunts who lived in the rue de Sévigné with their father, Alexandre Champdavoine. The latter was an ardent admirer of Daumier, Courbet, and Manet.

1885/90   Period of his apprenticeship as a stained-glass painter, first with Tamoni, then with Hirsch. He worked on the restoration of medieval windows and attended evening classes at the Ecole des Arts Décoratifs in the rue de l'Ecole de Médecine. Albert Besnard, a painter who was famous at the time, wanted him to execute the stained-glass windows for the Ecole de Pharmacie from his cartoons. Rouault refused the offer due to loyalty to Hirsch. He decided to paint, and on December 5, 1890, entered the Ecole des Beaux-Arts, in the studio of Elie Delaunay.

1891/92   Delaunay died on September 5, 1891 and was succeeded by Gustave Moreau, who thus became the teacher of Rouault, Matisse, Marquet, Lehmann, Evenepoel, Manguin, and others. Series of religious subjects, treated in a Rembrandtesque style.

1893   March 31. Gustave Moreau, whose favorite pupil he was, made him compete for the Prix de Rome. The subject: The Ordeal of Samson. Rouault failed.

1894   On February 6 Rouault was awarded second prize in the Fortin d'Ivry competition for his painting *Coriolanus in the House of Tullius*. In July he won the Chenavard prize for *The Child Jesus Among the Doctors*.

1895   Rouault competed for the Prix de Rome a second time. The subject was the Dead Christ Mourned by the Holy Women. Failed to win a second time. The Prix was awarded to an inferior painting by a pupil of Bonnat.

1896   Rouault exhibited his painting for the Prix de Rome at the Salon des Artistes Français.

1897   He was represented at the Salon de la Rose Croix by *The Dead Christ*, a drawing. To the Salon for this year he sent some landscapes and the *Bathers*.

1898   On April 18 Gustave Moreau died of cancer at the age of seventy-two. He bequeathed his studio and his collections to the government on condition they be transformed into a museum bearing his name.

1901   Rouault painted romantic landscapes, religious compositions, and Paris scenes. Late in the year he retired to a Benedictine abbey at Liguge, near Poitiers, where J.-K. Huysmans was trying to organize a brotherhood of artists.

1903   January 14. Inauguration of the Musée Gustave Moreau, rue La Rochefoucauld, Paris. Rouault was appointed curator. He participated in the foundation of the Salon d'Automne with Desvaillières, Matisse, Marquet, Piot, and the critic Rambosson. He was represented by two paintings in the first exhibition.

1904   In March he met Léon Bloy, of whom he eventually became a close friend. At the Salon d'Automne he exhibited a large number of watercolors and drawings, paintings of prostitutes, clowns, and acrobats in dark tones in his new manner, and landscapes. The public sneered at these "gloomy" paintings.

1905   Exhibited, at the Salon d'Automne, a triptych entitled *Prostitutes*. One of the panels represents Monsieur and Madame Poulot, characters from Léon Bloy's *La Femme pauvre*. The other two panels show a prostitute and Terpsichore. At the same Salon, in the "Cage aux Fauves," Rouault exhibited street and circus performers, and clowns.

1906   Exhibited works at the Berthe Weil gallery and at the Salon d'Automne.

1907   Rouault met Vollard through the ceramist Metthey.

1908   On January 27 he married Marthe Le Sidaner, by whom he was to have four children: Geneviève, Isabelle, Michel, and Agnès. Series of Judges and Tribunals, begun in 1907 *(Condemned Man)*, inspired by the Tribunal de la Seine where he followed courtroom procedure for nearly a year, thanks to his friend Granier, a deputy public prosecutor. He also painted poor people, peasants, workers.

1910   February 24-March 5. First one-man show at the Galerie Druet, 10, rue Royale, Paris. Article by Jacques Rivière in the *Nouvelle Revue Française*.

1911   He moved to Versailles, 36, rue de l'Orangerie. Jacques and Raïssa Maritain, whom he had met at Léon Bloy's, were his neighbors. The same year he began his friendship with André Suarès. On December 11, second one-man show at the Galerie Druet; enthusiastic article by Louis Vauxcelles in *Gil Blas*.

1913 Ambroise Vollard, who had first become interested in Rouault as a ceramist, bought his entire production to date.

1917 Vollard became Rouault's dealer. Later he set up a studio for him on the top floor of his house, 28, rue Martignac, Paris, to enable the painter to complete several hundred canvases. Between 1917 and 1927 the dealer commissioned him to illustrate a number of books, including *Les Réincarnations du Père Ubu* and *Miserere*. These works took up a large part of the artist's time for several years.

1918 Rouault abandoned watercolor and gouache and painted in oil. Religious subjects, the Passion. His palette became more colorful. He rarely exhibited.

1919 October 17. *The Child Jesus Among the Doctors*, acquired by the government in 1917, was placed in the museum of Colmar. This was Rouault's first museum representation.

1920 Exhibition at the Galerie La Licorne, organized by D. Girardin, one of his principal collectors. Among his other collectors were M. and Mme. Marcel Sembat, Mme. Olivier Saincère, Stéphane Piot, Gustave Coquiot, Baignères, Dutilleul, Leclanché. John Quinn, M. and Mme. Henri Simon, Mme. Heddy Hahnloser, and Mme. Louise Hervieu.

1921 First monograph on Rouault by Michel Puy in the collection *Les Peintres française nouveaux*.

1922 Exhibition at the Galerie Barbazanges.

1924 April 22-May 2. Big retrospective exhibition at the Galerie Druet. Jacques Maritain published important essay on Rouault in *La Revue Universelle*.

1926 Rouault published *Souvenirs intimes*, illustrated with lithographs. Publication of Georges Charensol's book with thirty-nine reproductions of works by Rouault.

1929 Settings and costumes for Diaghilev's ballet *The Prodigal Son*, with score by Prokofiev and choreography by Balanchine. Performed at the Sarah Bernhardt Theater on May 21, 29, and 31, and June 4, 6, and 12. Toward the end of the year Rouault went to Montana-sur-Sierre in the Valais (Switzerland). Burned his hands severely while playing Santa Claus.

1930 The Undersecretary of State for the Fine Arts refused to acquire a painting by Rouault recommended by the committee on selections for the Musée du Luxembourg. Rouault began a series of color etchings for *Cirque de l'étoile filante* for which he wrote the text, and for André Suarès' *Passion*. First exhibitions outside France: London (St. George gallery), Munich (Neumann gallery), New York (Brummer gallery), Chicago (Art Club).

1932 Painted *The Injured Clown* and *The Little Family*, which Mme. Cuttoli had reproduced as a tapestry by the Aubusson craftsmen. Mrs. Chester Dale gave the Musée du Luxembourg a canvas by Rouault, his first in that museum.

1937 From June to October a Rouault retrospective was held in a special room at the Petit Palais. It included forty-two canvases of which fifteen were on loan from Vollard. On seeing this, Lionello Venturi decided to devote an important study to Rouault (it was published in New York in 1940).

1938   Exhibition of Rouault's graphic works at the Museum of Modern Art, New York.

1939   Ambroise Vollard died on July 22, shortly before the outbreak of the Second World War.

1940/41   Exhibitions in Boston, Washington, and San Francisco.

1943   Publication of *Divertissement*.

1945   Retrospective at the Museum of Modern Art, New York (161 items).

1946   In April, Braque-Rouault exhibition at the Tate Gallery, London.

1947   March 19. Rouault won his case against Vollard's heirs when the court decreed that the painter is owner of his work until such time as he handed it over unconditionally to another person. His many unfinished canvases were to be given back to him, but 119 were never returned.
Stella Vespertina published by René Drouin. Exhibition of forty paintings at the gallery of Odette des Garets, rue de Courcelles.

1948   April-June. Retrospective at the Kunsthaus, Zurich (166 items). Twenty-five paintings and twelve etchings by Rouault sent by France to the Venice Biennale. On November 5, in the presence of a court official, the painter burned 315 canvases from among those returned to him by court order. First presentation of *Miserere* at the gallery of Odette des Garets (November 27-December 21). Trips to Switzerland and Italy.

1949   First maquettes for the enamels executed in the workshop of the abbey at Ligugé. Trips to Belgium and Holland.

1951   June 6. On the occasion of the artist's eightieth birthday, the Centre Catholique des Intellectuels Français organized a "Tribute to Rouault" at the Palais Chaillot. First public showing of the film on *Miserere*.

1952   Retrospectives at the Palais des Beaux-Arts, Brussels, the Stedelijk Museum, Amsterdam, and the Musée National d'Art Moderne, Paris.

1953   Retrospective exhibitions at the Cleveland Museum of Art, the Museum of Modern Art, New York, the County Museum, Los Angeles, in Osaka, and in the National Museum, Tokyo.

1954   Retrospective show at the Galleria d'Arte Moderna in Milan.

1956   Exhibition at Albi, Musée Toulouse-Lautrec (Palais de la Berbie).

1958   February 13. Georges Rouault died in Paris at the age of eighty-seven. The government decided to give him a state funeral. In the course of the ceremony at the church of Saint-Germain-des-Prés (February 17) there were speeches by the Abbé Maurice Morel, and M. Billières, minister of public education. A message from André Lhote in the name of French artists was read.

comme s'il voyait soudain
le soleil se lever

la Tradition
dont ils parlent tant
et le classicisme
dont nos petits Poussin
sont si friands
qu'ils en perdent
l'entendement
pictural
la Tradition est aussi bien
et peut-être encore plus
dans l'air que tu respires
Sourire de Reims
hier encore
ne l'as tu pas retrouvé
dans les yeux clairs
et le sourire perlé
de cette bergerette

. . .
comme s'il voyait soudain
le soleil se lever

La Tradition
dont ils parlent tant
et le classicisme
dont nos petits Poussin
sont si friands
qu'ils en perdent
l'entendement
pictural
la Tradition est aussi bien
et peut-être encore plus
dans l'air que tu respires
Sourire de Reims
hier encore
ne l'as tu pas retrouvé
dans les yeux clairs
et le sourire perlé
de cette bergerette

[. . . as though he saw suddenly
the rising sun

Tradition
that they talk about so much
and the classicism
that our small-fry Poussins
are so fond of
that they lose
all
pictorial sense
Tradition is as much
and perhaps even more
in the air you breathe
"Smile" of Reims
even yesterday
did you not see it again
in the bright eyes
and the pearly smile
of this little shepherdess]

Rouault's Writings: A Selection

"Noli Me Tangere"

> Under this title, Rouault refers to Cézanne's dread of physical contact. Some critics had thought that Rouault was publishing a conversation between the two artists. However, Rouault had never met Cézanne and this fragment is to be considered as a kind of homage to Cézanne.

"Do not come near me, do not touch me: within myself I carry all the beauty that the world is unaware of or misunderstands . . . .

"Do not come near me: I am the leper who avoids men and whom men avoid; far from them I have experienced the happiness of devoting all my efforts to attaining my spiritual absolute. This isn't much. My art was a means, not an end; I fell upon it like a lion on his prey and I have never been fully happy; had I lived several centuries, the result would have been the same. A few rare artists found my work beautiful and profound; I have not known them, I have lived with the dead, with the great dead, those whose works disclose glimmers of eternity. I was truly happy when I was at one with them and with nature. The ideal that filled my heart was so high, however, that even when I did my utmost to copy what I saw, all I could achieve was an imperfect, fleeting reflection. Thus a beautiful face perceived in a limpid stream can be dispelled by the slightest breath of air.

"Do not come near me: I am dying. What more can a dying man do for those who survive . . . than what I have tried to do—to leave behind the best of myself?

"Do not come near me: I can teach you nothing. My life was hidden, but luminous and pure, modest and grave and meditative; my art was its most absolute, most discreet expression. Look in my imperfect work for what you vainly ask of the old, the infirm, the suffering, man.

"Do not come near me: do your task as well as you can, in your turn, whether far from men or among them, but without giving too much credence to their teachings and admirations, for if you lived two or three consecutive lives, you would see your fellow men repeatedly destroying what they have adored and adoring what they have destroyed. And yet be full of compassion for them, for you too are weak, and it may very well happen that after having sincerely admired me, you will deny me tomorrow! Who can answer absolutely and forever for himself without incurring the sin of pride?

"Do not suppose that our most high and noble art can be taught or learned in schools and academies: the knowledge you acquire there will pale as soon as you are able to observe forms and colors lovingly. The pundits who practice the errors they teach are to be less trusted than those errors themselves: the latter are sometimes merely old truths distorted and would seem magnificent could they be resurrected from the ashes.

"Believe even less those who after my death will speak in my name or wrangle over my unfortunate corpse: the poorest and least accomplished of my works is more trustworthy. After the battle, prowling jackals and hyenas always take advantage of the night . . . .

From "Trois Artistes" in *Mercure de France*, Nov. 16, 1910

★

. . . All these people are at their wits' end. In their frenzied hurry they don't even take time to think before they act.

"I just want to enjoy life," says the wretched larva, "were it only for one day, one hour, one minute, one second before I must go to my grave."

Like the ostrich, head under wing
When the roaring storm breaks,
So many people take refuge
  Under the soft pillow
  Of specious arguments.

★

Every delicately shaded movement
Harmonizes with color.
The experienced painter in whose mind
Every image is so well imprinted,
  Will he realize at last
That at the end of the long road
Our Lady of the End of the Earth
Stretches out her arms to the poor devil?

Our Lady of the End of the Earth, I honored you before your modest chapel was swallowed up by the sands. The tears on your sweet face have furrowed seams like steep ravines.

★

The label matters little. Gauguin is right when, referring to the décor, he says that "an apple is a ball." But Cézanne says more than that by his superior pictorial rendering of harmonious relationships. The subject takes on more or less importance according to the gifts, the sensibility, the power of the artist who treats it. The apple is no more than a pretext. The white cloth serves only to strike a minor or major chord or perhaps to evoke a distant echo of the tree on which the apple grows.

From Le Cirque de l'étoile filante,
Editions Ambroise Vollard, Paris, 1938

★

The ancient canons, the noble proportions, the serene balance of Greek statues are hardly sufficient. Moreover, although we have fine examples of this antique statuary, we also have a whole false Greece, conventional and worthless . . . .

★

In 1897, when Moreau died, I was less than thirty years old. It would have been easy for me to found an academy. I was urged to do so, but I thought I was too young, not practiced enough in the games of life and art. But I would have been unwilling in any case. I was determined (and I was particularly criticized for this, though it is perhaps my only merit) not to fall under the spell of certain old masters, despite my admiration for them, precisely because of my admiration . . . .

Certain cycles are so complete than there is nothing left to say after them, unless in other nuances.

The old masters are perfect and admirable examples, on condition that we remember that the spirit gives life and the letter kills, and that even the best pastiche is inferior to the harmonious stammering or incoherence of a child trying to speak.

★

The medieval craftsman loved his stone, his wood, and wrought lovingly. The anonymous builders of our great cathedrals were vastly superior to many pseudo-personalities of our day, when the ideal collaboration between architect, painter, and sculptor has been abolished. The art of the cathedrals is at once collective and personal, but the way of life, the modes of feeling, understanding, and loving that were at the root of this art cannot be artificially revived. We can do other things, but we cannot re-create what the spontaneous collective effort of generations built with the faith that was theirs.

It is no exaggeration to say that in spite of the achievements of the ancients, the language of forms and colors is a realm that still remains to be explored.

★

The conscience of an artist worthy of the name is like an incurable disease which causes him endless torment but occasionally fills him with silent joy . . . .

★

This is how Degas described the methods of an ancient Chinese or Japanese school: A model is presented, a flower in a vase. The pupil must copy it within a certain time, though a quite long time, then recopy it again and again in a shorter and shorter time. Finally the table, the flower, and the vase are removed, and he must begin again from memory . . . . That is what explains Ingres' words on the culture of the eye. There is in nature such a variety of atmospheres, a range of values so rich and subtly shaded, that direct observation necessarily involves choice and the assertion of a hierarchy . . . .

★

I know that there is such a thing as a "carnal" love for pigment. But are there no muscles and bones beneath the flesh? If you pursue "the pulp of the fruit" too exclusively, with immoderate anxiety and passion, you run the risk of producing an invertebrate art in which you take such delight that you forget many other essential points . . . .

★

Colors are sold in tubes, but it is we who compose our tones, and they correspond to a need for full harmony. As we progress or believe that we are progressing, we become more silent and clloected . . . . Just as in other domains, the more we know, the more we see what we don't know yet.

★

The richness of the world, all artificial pleasures, have the taste of sickness and give off a smell of death in the face of certain spiritual possessions.

★

The painter who loves his art is ruler in his own kingdom, even if he be in Lilliput and a Lilliputian himself. He transforms a kitchen maid into a fairy, and a great lady into a brothel matron, if he wants to and sees them so, for he is a seer. His vision includes everything that is still alive in the past.

★

The artist discards all theories, both his own and those of others. He forgets everything when he is in front of his canvas.

From *Stella Vespertina*, Editeur René Drouin, Paris, 1947

Balance, order, and proportion are not achieved by external means alone, from the outside, oh! exhibitionists of my heart. They begin inside. Not only must we give the most secret and loving tribute of ourselves throughout our lives, but we must not rest on our laurels, our transient successes or honors. Nor dare we become proud, too impressed with all the mother-of-pearl buttons that glitter on the ceremonial robes of the most celebrated mandarins.

★

I was like a peasant in the field, attached to my pictorial soil, like the man hanged by his own hempen rope, like an ox under the yoke. Though terribly restless, I never took my nose out of my work save to ascertain the light, the shadow, the half-tint, the curious features of certain pilgrims' faces. I noted forms, colors, fleeting harmonies until I was sure they were so indelibly impressed in my memory that they would stay with me beyond the grave . . . .

★

Images and colors, to a painter, are his way of being, living, thinking, feeling.

This is why—no matter what the doctrinaires say, endlessly discussing, weighing, testing, measuring, with their glasses (magnifying or not), their binoculars or even their telescopes, their weights and measures, their compasses and water-levels—let one poor devil of a painter appear on the scene, and all their specious theories and calculations are null and void. The most insignificant little picture —done in prison or palace, by anyone at all (perhaps by this poor devil of a painter who did not ask to be born or to be a painter)—this insignificant little picture, however technically inexpert, will rebuff all our sensible, reasonable doctors of the arts for maybe a hundred years.

★

Even if it is true that there is nothing new under the sun, do not make use of this thought, solitary artist, lest you close your eyes too soon to all living things. Always take time to enjoy the sight of the slightest, tiniest, little creature . . . .

★

A painter who loves his art must be careful not to see too much of critics and men of letters. These gentlemen, however unconsciously, distort everything, thinking that they are explaining it—the artist's thought, sensibility, and intentions. They take away his strength, just as Delilah took away Samson's. They have no gift for nuances, and they have an instinctive aversion for everything that is beyond their reach and baffles them.

★

I believe neither in theories nor in the vast, vague ideas that haunt an extra-terrestrial world and, in the last analysis, have neither life nor viable form. I particularly abhor the slovenliness of thought and action which leads to a facile, sticky idealism that softens angles and robs every drawing of consistency.

★

Nothing is old, nothing is new, save the light of grace underneath which beats a human heart. The way of feeling, of understanding, of loving; the way of seeing the country, the faces that your father saw, that your mother knew. The rest is chimerical . . . .

★

Another very modern error is to deprecate those who used to be called "minor masters," and to pay attention only to the very greatest ones. Artists who fall into this error, like those who become infatuated with a theory, end up affected, dessicated, too tightly strung—especially when their own natural talents are "minor" ones . . . .

★

The tradition is not academic. I can admit without the slightest hesitation that it could become academic, but only for a time. Life with its hidden forces makes this impossible . . . .

★

You shall celebrate all living things:
The smile of the newborn infant
When he begins to stammer
The first buds in spring
The smell of the hawthorn
The first work you created,
Apprentice, even if it was a failure,
In the hope of doing better.
Don't conceal your pleasure
Over a color harmony
Even if you hit on it by chance.
Celebrate the long road
In the golden summer sun
The friendly white house
By the little path
And its cheerful occupants
Who rejoice over
Your imaginary successes
First fruits of a lifework
Slow to be born
But steadily growing
Some new trouble every day.
Celebrate the living source
The bark that drifts by noiselessly
Over the sleeping waters
The wheat swaying under the wind

Which is to be harvested tomorrow
Everything is occasion
For serene joy or toil
According as your heart and mind decree

>   (In the desolate meadows of Unhappiness
>   The tiniest flower fades and dies.)

★

Be by turns
Romantic
Fauve
Cubist
Orphist
Futurist
Rhomboidist
Classical tomorrow—why not?
See how rich you are
My dear son!
I am but a will-o'-the-wisp
Which trembles in the wind and vanishes
Then is reborn once
To vanish forever.
There are also difficult victories
Very somber defeats
And famous retreats
More glorious than victories
Blessed meditations
Long infinite patiences
Dumb victims
Thanksgiving after childbirth
And obscure loves
In this beloved art.
Some are pampered
Others excommunicated
But no matter — provided your heart
Unhappy artist
Keeps holiday!

From *Soliloques*, Neuchâtel, Ides et Calendes, 1944

Rouault's Signatures

Paysage · 1905 (au pinceau)
Landscape · 1905 (brush)

Clown et clownesse · 1905 (au pinceau)
Male and Female Clown · 1905 (brush)

Nu (esquisse) · 1906 (au pinceau)
Nude (sketch) · 1906 (brush)

Tête d'ouvrier (ou Le Blessé) · 1911   (au pinceau)
Head of a Laborer (or The Injured Man) · 1911   (brush)

Crucifixion · 1936   (signature gravée dans le cuivre d'une eau-forte en couleurs)
Crucifixion · 1936   (signature engraved on the plate of a color etching)

Signée avec pinceau, sur les toiles, et avec la plume à l'encre sur les photographies · 1937 à 1939
Signed with a brush on the canvases, and with pen and ink on photographs of the canvases · 1937–1939

Pierrot

Faubourg

Pierrot

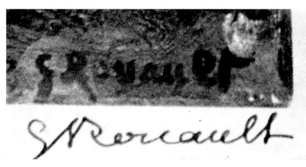

Crépuscule
Twilight

Signée avec pinceau sur les toiles, et avec la plume à l'encre sur les photographies · 1937 à 1939
Signed with a brush on the canvases, and with pen and ink on photographs of the canvases · 1937–1939

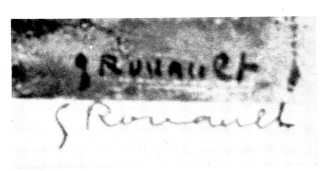 

Tête de femme · 1939 (au pinceau)
Head of a Woman · 1939 (brush)

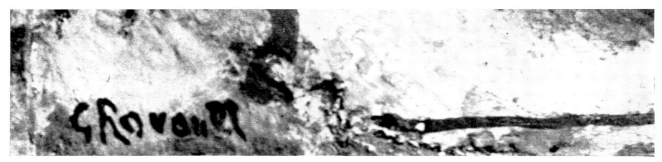

(au pinceau)
(brush)

(au pinceau)
(brush)

(au pinceau)
(brush)

Classified Catalogue

Until 1930, Rouault signed and dated most of his gouaches, pastels, and water-colors. The oil paintings, however, were rarely dated, and he was known to have continued working on them for as long as ten, or even twenty, years. Indeed, his intensity, his exigent nature, made it very hard for him to let his paintings leave his atelier. This explains the fact that when he signed a number of canvases at the same time (as, for instance, in 1937 or 1938) they were usually the product of many years of work.

On the other hand, certain paintings that served as models for woodcuts and etchings based on the same themes bear a later date than the engravings, because Rouault retouched them after he had given his final approval to the prints. In fact, he returned time and again to some of these themes, long after they had been printed, and at different times in his career.

Rouault usually signed his works as he delivered them. An exception is, for instance, a series of "album leaves" in the Girardin collection, which remained unsigned while others were signed a long time after they were finished.

With regard to the canvases in the Vollard collection, a special agreement was reached between painter and dealer according to which Rouault considered as finished only the works which he had signed; for these Vollard then gave him a receipt. When Vollard died, 819 unfinished, unsigned works were stocked in his house in the rue Martignac, in the atelier he had turned over to Rouault. The fate of these pictures was decided by lawsuit and, as the result of a decree handed down by the Paris courts on March 19, 1947, Vollard's heirs were ordered to return them all to Rouault, since, not having been finally released by Rouault, the paintings remained his property. When the order was ostensibly executed, 119 paintings were missing.

The result was that, in defiance of the court decision, several of the "undelivered" works appeared on the market, usually with forged signatures which were intended to hide their source.

Mention should be made of the fact that, according to the terms of Rouault's will, the co-signer of this Catalogue, Isabelle Rouault, was given the power to authenticate the unfinished, unsigned canvases that would appear to her to be sufficiently advanced not to be destroyed. She also has the power of affixing a stamp on the sketches that were in her father's atelier at the time of his death, and which, after careful selection, were retained. This stamp gives evidence of the work's origin and guarantees its authenticity.

Because of the great variety of media that Rouault used in the course of his career, it has at times been difficult to give an exact description of his techniques, which were often used in combination. In the chronological order of their appearance, these processes may be summarized as follows: charcoal, charcoal and crayon, watercolor and pastel, colored inks, oil paints and monotypes, tempera, wash, gouache and pastel, gouache and oils (occasionally), drawing and wash with India ink. In the end, however, except for a few odd series, Rouault confined himself to oils. In addition to his paintings, prints, and drawings, Rouault, during different periods of his life, also produced ceramics, tapestries (carried out under the supervision of Madame Cuttoli), stained glass, and enamels.

Rouault's graphic work occupies a predominant place in his general production. He left many lithographs in black-and-white and, very rarely, in color *(The Cavalcade, La Chevauchée)*, as well as a great many copperplates etched with aquatint, in a variety of processes that were both complicated and original. Lastly, it should be recalled that Rouault made many drawings for woodcuts which were carried out, under the artist's close supervision, by George Aubert.

In conclusion, there are three further remarks that should be made. Rouault often painted a border around his subjects, in a single color. Since it was his rule to measure the works he presented without the border, this is what we, too, have done. However, with regard to the more complicated, ornamented borders, which were painted with a view to tapestry reproductions, Rouault considered the borders to be part of the picture, and we have done the same. Lastly, Rouault sometimes amused himself—particularly toward the end of his career—by painting certain frames which we have not included in our measurements, for they were not intended as a part of the total picture.

The works which were painted on paper were frequently given a cloth, then a thin panel backing, changing the original dimensions. Thus, slight differences that may be found between the dimensions quoted in certain exhibition catalogues and those given here are easily explained. Occasionally, too, certain works that had been signed and exhibited were later taken back to Rouault's atelier and even, at times, enlarged, as in the case of the *Little Magician*, and the *Christ Mocked* which was painted for the church at Assy.

1891–1901

Sujets religieux (compositions)
Religious Subjects

1 Gethsémani · 1892
Gethsemane

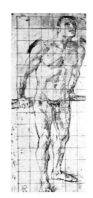

2 L'Enfant Jésus parmi les docteurs · 1893
The Child Jesus Among the Doctors

3 Ermite · 1893
Hermit

4 Etude pour l'Enfant Jésus parmi les docteurs
1894
Study for "The Child Jesus Among the Doctors"

5 Etude pour Samson tournant la meule · 1893
Study for "The Ordeal of Samson"

6 Etude pour Samson tournant la meule · 1893
Study for "The Ordeal of Samson"

Paysages
Landscapes

7 Paysage · 1900
Landscape

8 Paysage · vers 1900
Landscape · about 1900

9 Paris (La Seine) · 1901
Paris (The Seine)

407

10 Paysage · 1901
Landscape

11 Paysage · 1901
Landscape

12 Christ et disciples · vers 1900
Christ and Disciples · about 1900

Divers · **Miscellaneous Subjects**

13 Stella Vespertina · 1895

14 Portrait de Madame Paul Flat · vers 1900
Portrait of Madame Paul Flat · about 1900

15 Pêcheur · vers 1900
Fisherman · about 1900

1902–1914

Christ: La Sainte Face et compositions
Christ: The Holy Countenance and **Compositions**

16 Christ et disciples (esquisse) · 1905
Christ and Disciples (sketch)

17 Christ aux outrages · vers 1912
Christ Mocked · about 1912

18 La Sainte Face · 1912
The Holy Countenance

19 Christ en croix · vers 1913
Christ on the Cross · about 1913

20 La Sainte Face · 1913
The Holy Countenance

21 Tête de Christ · 1905
Head of Christ

Filles · Prostitutes

22 Nu sur fond bleu · 1905
Nude on a Blue Ground

23 Fille vue de dos · vers 1905
Prostitute, Back View · about 1905

24 Au café · 1906
At the Café

25 Filles · vers 1907
Prostitutes · about 1907

26 Fille au fourneau · 1906
Prostitute (With the Stove)

27 Fille (et deux personnages) · 1906
Prostitute (With Two Figures)

28 Fille se coiffant · 1906
Prostitute Doing Her Hair

29 Nu (esquisse) · 1906
Nude (sketch)

30 Trio · 1906

409

31 Nu au bras levé · 1906
Nude with Arm Raised

32 Intérieur (dit aussi Filles au salon) · vers 1910
Interior (also known as Prostitutes in the Salon)
about 1910

33 Fille · 1908
Prostitute

Clowns et Pierrots · Clowns and Pierrots

34 Le Clown rouge · 1903
The Red Clown

35 Clown au chien · 1903
Clown with Dog

36 Le Clown au tambour · 1903
Clown with Drum

37 Polichinelle · 1906
Punch

38 Tête de clown · vers 1907
Head of a Clown · about 1907

39 Tête de clown · vers 1908
Head of a Clown · about 1908

40 Le Petit Clown · 1908
The Little Clown

41 Le Clown au singe · 1910
Clown with Monkey

42 Le Clown tragique · 1911
Tragic Clown

43 Pierrotin · vers 1913
Little Pierrot · about 1913

44 Monsieur Loyal et Danseuse · 1905
Monsieur Loyal and Dancer

45 Le Pierrot blanc · 1911
The White Pierrot

Scènes et personnages de cirque
Circus Scenes and Characters

46 Numéro de cirque · 1903
Circus Act

47 La Parade · 1906
The Parade

48 Trois Personnages de cirque · 1906
Three Circus Performers

49 Personnage de cirque (homme debout) · 1906
Circus Performer

50 Acrobate · vers 1913
Acrobat · about 1913

51 Acrobate · vers 1913
Acrobat · about 1913

52 Lutteur · 1913
Wrestler

53 Caissières de cirque forain · 1905
Ticket Sellers, Traveling Circus

54 Polichinelle
Punch

411

Paysages · Landscapes

55 Paysage (Chute d'eau) · 1904
Landscape (Waterfall)

56 L'Inondation · 1910
The Flood

57 Paysage (Maison derrière les arbres) · 1913
Landscape (House Behind Trees)

58 Paysage · vers 1913
Landscape · about 1913

59 Le Palais d'Ubu roi
The Palace of Ubu

60 Paysage · 1911
Landscape

Paysages (avec figures)
Landscapes with Figures

61 La Traversée du pont · 1905
Crossing the Bridge

62 Parc de Versailles, escalier (dit aussi La Terrasse)
1910
Parc de Versailles, the Staircase (The Terrace)

63 Hiver · 1910
Winter

64 Paysage (La Péniche) · vers 1910–1912
Landscape (The Barge) · about 1910–1912

65 Paysage · 1911
Landscape

66 Petit Port (avec groupes de personnages) · 1913
The Little Port, with Figures

412

67 Versailles (esquisse) · 1913
Versailles (sketch)

68 Paysage (Hiver) · 1913
Landscape (Winter)

69 Banlieue parisienne (Bords de Seine) · vers 1914
Parisian Suburb (Beside the Seine) · about 1914

Nus (et compositions) · Nudes and Compositions

70 Nu (esquisse) · vers 1905
Nude (sketch) · about 1905

71 Nu aux bras levés · vers 1906
Nude with Arms Raised · about 1906

72 Nu aux bras levés (esquisse) · vers 1906
Nude with Arms Raised (sketch) · about 1906

73 Nu · vers 1906
Nude · about 1906

74 Baigneuses · 1908
Bathers

75 Nu assis · 1909
Seated Nude

76 Composition · 1909

77 Nu au collier
Nude with Necklace

78 Deux Baigneuses · 1912
Two Bathers

413

79 Nu (esquisse)
Nude (sketch)

80 Figures décoratives · vers 1907
Decorative Figures · about 1907

81 Le Modèle · 1908
The Model

Figures décoratives · Decorative Figures

82 Nus (Figures décoratives) · 1911
Nudes (Decorative Figures)

83 Arabesque (esquisse)
Arabesque (sketch)

84 Arabesque · 1911

Gens de Justice
Men of Law

85 L'Accusé · 1907
The Accused

86 La Cour · 1908
The Court

87 Avocat plaidant · 1908
Lawyer Pleading

88 Les Juges · 1908
The Judges

89 En Pleine Envolée · 1908
Carried Away

90 Juriste (dit aussi L'Avocat) · 1911
The Jurist (also known as The Lawyer)

91 Duo · 1904
Duet

92 Homme en habit · 1905
Man Dressed Up

93 Automobilistes · 1908
Motorists

Types (hommes) · Men

94 Automobiliste (au volant) · 1909
Motorist (At the Wheel)

95 L'Orateur · 1908
The Orator

96 Le Banquet · vers 1910
The Banquet · about 1910

97 Deux Profils · 1910
Two Profiles

98 Pédagogue · 1912
Pedagogue

99 Le Financier · 1911
The Financier

100 Laquais · 1913
Lackey

101 Travailleurs (intérieur) · 1914
Workers (Interior)

102 L'Avantageux · vers 1912–1913
The Fop · about 1912–1913

415

103 Invectives (esquisse)
Invective (sketch)

104 Le Régisseur (dit aussi Hector)
The Manager (also called Hector)

105 Le Père de famille · 1913
Father of the Family

Types (femmes) · Women

106 Femme au chapeau · 1905
Woman with a Hat

107 Mère et enfant (dit aussi La Femme du clown)
1905
Mother and Child (also called The Clown's Wife)

108 Femmes au théâtre · 1906
Women at the Theater

109 Faubourg (marchandes des quatre-saisons) · 1906
Faubourg (Street-Hawkers)

110 Femme aux gants blancs · 1906
Woman with White Gloves

111 Silhouette de femme au petit chien · 1908
Silhouette of a Woman with a Small Dog

112 Femme accoudée · 1908
Woman Leaning on Her Elbows

113 Figure de femme (buste) · 1909
Woman's Figure (bust)

114 Femme au chapeau à plume · 1909
Woman in a Feathered Hat

115 Femme au rideau bleu · 1909
Woman and Blue Curtain

116 Femme au chien · 1909
Woman with Dog

117 Maternité (vieux faubourg) · 1912
Motherhood (Run-Down Faubourg)

118 Madame X · vers 1912–1913
Madame X · about 1912–1913

119 La Belle Hélène (esquisse) · vers 1913
La Belle Hélène (sketch) · about 1913

120 Discussions · 1913

121 La Cuisinière · 1914
The Cook

122 Métisse (esquisse)
Half-Caste Woman (sketch)

123 Hortense (esquisse)
Hortense (sketch)

124 Madame Euphrasie (esquisse)
Madame Euphrasia (sketch)

125 Buste de Femme · vers 1914
Bust of a Woman · about 1914

126 Profil de femme
Woman in Profile

417

Faubourg des longues peines (petite banlieue)
Faubourg of Toil and Suffering (Depressed Suburban Areas)

127 Femme malade · 1910
Sick Woman

128 Exode · 1912
Exodus

129 La Pauvre Famille (Exode) · vers 1911
The Poor Family (Exodus) · about 1911

130 La Mère de famille · 1912
The Mother of the Family

131 Romanichelle (esquisse)
Gypsy Woman (sketch)

132 Petite Banlieue (Femme et enfants)
vers 1910–1912
Depressed Suburb (Woman and Children)
about 1910–1912

133 Le Taudis · vers 1913
The Hovel · about 1913

134 Faubourg des longues peines
(Rue de la Solidarité) · 1911
Faubourg of Toil and Suffering
(Rue de la Solidarité)

135 Faubourg des longues peines
Faubourg of Toil and Suffering

Grotesques

136 Léandre · 1912
Leander

137 La Famille Zéphirin (esquisse)
The Zéphirin Family (sketch)

138 Grotesque à la robe de chambre · 1913
Grotesque Figure in a Dressing-Gown

Divers · Miscellaneous Subjects

139 Les Nourrices · 1904
The Wet Nurses

140 Esquisse pour Les Poulot . 1905
Sketch for Monsieur et Madame Poulot

141 Dans La Rue · 1908
Street Scene

142 Petit Breton · 1912
Breton Boy

143 Trio · vers 1912–1913
Trio · about 1912–1913

144 Verso du Trio, Un Breton vu de dos (esquisse)
vers 1912–1913
Verso of "Trio": Breton, Back View (sketch)
about 1912–1913

145 La Promenade
Promenade

146 Duo · 1906
Duet

147 Jean-Pierre

419

1915–1930

Compositions religieuses · Religious Compositions

148 Crucifixion · 1918

149 Christ en croix · 1929 ou 1930
Christ on the Cross · 1929 or 1930

150 Les Disciples d'Emmaüs · 1929
The Disciples at Emmaus

Ténèbres (Satan) · Satan and Darkness

151 Satan · 1930

152 Christ aux outrages · 1930
Christ Mocked

153 A Pantin · vers 1930
To Pantin (The Funeral) · about 1930

Clowns et Pierrots · Clowns and Pierrots

154 Le Clown rouge · vers 1915
Red Clown · about 1915

155 Clownerie · 1917
Clowning

156 Trois Clowns · vers 1917
Three Clowns · about 1917

420

157 Clown (au nez rouge) · vers 1926
Red-Nosed Clown · about 1926

158 Clown (au nez vert) · vers 1926
Green-Nosed Clown · about 1926

159 Tête de Clown · 1929
Clown's Head

Scènes de cirque · Circus Scenes

160 Danseuse · 1923
Dancer

161 Petite Ecuyère · vers 1925
Little Equestrienne · about 1925

162 La Famille du Clown · 1930
The Clown's Family

«Ubu» · "Ubu"

163 Agent des moeurs (pour «Ubu») · 1918
Vice Squad (for "Ubu")

164 Pour «Ubu» · 1918
For "Ubu"

165 Mau-mau (esquisse)
Mau-Mau (sketch)

Types (hommes) · Men

166 L'Homme content · 1915
Satisfied Man

167 Von X · 1915

168 Moine (profil) · vers 1915
Monk, Profile · about 1915

421

169 Bureaucrate · 1917
Bureaucrat

170 Le Juif errant · 1918
The Wandering Jew

171 Monsieur Z · 1915

Types (femmes) · Women

172 La Belle Madame X · 1915
The Lovely Madame X

173 Femme au corsage vert (de face) · 1915
Woman in a Green Dress

174 Buste de femme · vers 1926
Portrait of a Woman · about 1926

175 Portrait de Maria Lani · vers 1929
Portrait of Maria Lani · about 1929

176 Eve déchue (profil) · 1930
The Fallen Eve (profile)

177 Tragédienne · 1930
Tragedienne

Petite Banlieue · Depressed Surburban Areas

178 La Pauvre Eglise · 1929
Church in a Depressed Area

179 Le Vieux Mur n'en finissait pas N⁰ 1, Faubourg
1929
The Old Wall Went on and on N⁰ 1, Faubourg

180 Le Déménagement · 1929
Moving House

422

181 Le Prophète de malheur (Zone rouge) · 1930
Prophet of Evil (Leftist Neighborhood)

182 Le Vieux Mur n'en finissait pas N⁰ 2, Faubourg
1929
The Old Wall Went on and on N⁰ 2, Faubourg

183 Cimetière · 1930
Graveyard

184 Rencontre · 1930
Meeting

185 Le Retour d'Ulysse · 1929
The Return of Ulysses

186 Revendication (Zone rouge) · 1930
Workers' Demands (Leftist Neighborhood)

Grotesques

187 Grotesque · 1916

188 Grotesque · 1916

189 Grotesque · 1917

190 Grotesque · 1917

191 Grotesque · 1917

192 Grotesque · 1929

423

Divers · Miscellaneous Subjects

193 Bestiaire · 1916
Bestiary

194 Les Réprouvés · 1915
Outcasts

195 Bestiaire · 1916
Bestiary

196 Nu · 1917
Nude

197 Avocat plaidant · 1920
Lawyer Pleading

198 Arabe · 1918
Arab

199 Quatre Baigneuses · vers 1920
Four Bathers · about 1920

200 Danseuse · vers 1926
Dancer · about 1926

201 Trio de cirque
Circus Trio

424

Le Visage du Christ
Christ: The Holy Countenance

202 La Sainte Face · vers 1931
The Holy Countenance · about 1931

203 La Sainte Face · 1933
The Holy Countenance

204 Le Saint Suaire · 1937
The Holy Shroud

205 Le Saint Suaire · 1937
The Holy Shroud

206 Christ · 1937

207 Le Saint Suaire · 1937 ou 1938
The Holy Shroud · 1937 or 1938

208 Christ · 1937 ou 1938
Christ · 1937 or 1938

209 Le Saint Suaire · 1937 ou 1938
The Holy Shroud · 1937 or 1938

210 Christ · 1937 ou 1938
Christ · 1937 or 1938

425

Passion · The Passion

211 Christ en Croix · vers 1935
Christ on the Cross · about 1935

212 Paysage (Passion) · 1937
Landscape (The Passion)

213 Christ aux Outrages · 1937
Christ Mocked

214 Passion · 1937
The Passion

215 Paysage (Passion) · 1937
Landscape (The Passion)

216 Passion · 1937
The Passion

217 Passion · 1937 ou 1938
The Passion · 1937 or 1938

218 Passion · 1937 ou 1938
The Passion · 1937 or 1938

219 Passion · 1937 ou 1938
The Passion · 1937 or 1938

220 Passion · 1937 ou 1938
The Passion · 1937 or 1938

221 Passion · 1937 ou 1938
The Passion · 1937 or 1938

222 Passion · 1937 ou 1938
The Passion · 1937 or 1938

223 Tête de Christ · 1939
Head of Christ

224 Passion · 1938
The Passion · 1938

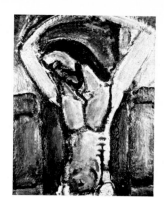

225 Christ aux Outrages · 1938
Christ Mocked

Christ et personnages · Christ and Figures

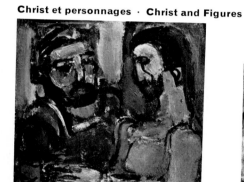

226 Christ et docteur · 1937
Christ and Doctor

227 Christ et pêcheurs · 1937
Christ and Fishermen

228 Christ et docteur · 1937
Christ and Doctor

229 Christ et docteur · 1937
Christ and Doctor

230 Christ et pêcheurs · 1937
Christ and Fishermen

231 Christ · 1937

232 Christ · 1937

233 Christ et disciple · 1937
Christ and Disciple

234 Christ et pêcheurs · 1937
Christ and Fishermen

427

235 Christ et pauvre · 1937
Christ and Poor Man

236 Christ solitaire · 1937
Solitary Christ

237 Christ et enfant · 1937
Christ and Child

238 Christ et docteurs · 1937 ou 1938
Christ and Doctors · 1937 or 1938

239 Christ et disciples · 1937 ou 1938
Christ and Disciples · 1937 or 1938

240 Christ (e t deux personnages) · 1937 ou 1938
Christ and Two Figures · 1937 or 1938

241 Christ et disciples · 1937 ou 1938
Christ and Disciples · 1937 or 1938

242 Christ (dans un intérieur avec trois figures)
1937 ou 1938
Christ in a Room with Three Figures · 1937 or 1938

243 Stella Matutina (Passion) · 1937 ou 1938
Stella Matutina (The Passion) · 1937 or 1938

428

244 Christ et lépreux · 1938
Christ and Lepers

245 La Fuite en Egypte · vers 1938
The Flight into Egypt · about 1938

246 Christ et malade · 1939
Christ and Sick Man

247 Faubourg des longues peines · 1937 ou 1938
Faubourg of Toil and Suffering · 1937 or 1938

248 Christ et docteur
Christ and Doctor

249 Vieux Faubourg · 1937 ou 1938
Old Faubourg · 1937 or 1938

Ténèbres (Satan) · Satan and Darkness

250 Le Prince des ténèbres · 1937
The Prince of Darkness

251 Ténèbres · 1938
Darkness

252 Satan · 1937

253 Satan · 1938

254 Satan · vers 1933
Satan · about 1933

255 Satan

Danse Macabre

256 La Baie des trépassés · 1938
The Bay of Departed Souls

257 De Profundis · 1938

258 Debout les morts · 1938
The Rising of the Dead

429

Clowns et Pierrots · Clowns and Pierrots

259 Danseuse et Clown · 1932
Dancer and Clown

260 Les Deux Frères · 1937
The Two Brothers

261 Duo · 1937
Duet

262 Clown et Clownesse · 1937
Male and Female Clowns

263 Cirque forain · 1937
Street Circus

264 Trio, Clowns · 1937

265 Clowns · 1937

266 Clowns · 1937

267 Clowneries · 1937
Clowning

268 Clown anglais · 1937
English Clown

269 Clown · 1937

270 Polichinelle · 1937
Punch

430

271 Grotesque · 1937

272 Clowns · 1937

273 Trio · 1937

274 Pierrot guerrier · 1937
Pierrot Warrior

275 Polycarpe · 1937 ou 1938
Polycarp · 1937 or 1938

276 Pierrot · 1937 ou 1938
Pierrot · 1937 or 1938

277 Pierrot · 1937 ou 1938
Pierrot · 1937 or 1938

278 Pierrot · 1937 ou 1938
Pierrot · 1937 or 1938

279 Pierrot · 1937 ou 1938
Pierrot · 1937 or 1938

280 Pierrot · 1937 ou 1938
Pierrot · 1937 or 1938

281 Pierrot · 1937 ou 1938
Pierrot · 1937 or 1938

282 Pierrot · 1937 ou 1938
Pierrot · 1937 or 1938

283 Pierrot · 1937 ou 1938
Pierrot · 1937 or 1938

284 Pierrot · 1937 ou 1938
Pierrot · 1937 or 1938

285 Pierrot bleu · 1937 ou 1938
Blue Pierrot · 1937 or 1938

286 Pierrot · 1937 ou 1938
Pierrot · 1937 or 1938

287 Pierrot · 1937 ou 1938
Pierrot · 1937 or 1938

288 Pierrot · 1937 ou 1938
Pierrot · 1937 or 1938

289 Pierrot · 1937 ou 1938
Pierrot · 1937 or 1938

290 Pierrot et Polichinelle · 1937 ou 1938
Pierrot and Punch · 1937 or 1938

291 Pierrot · 1937 ou 1938
Pierrot · 1937 or 1938

292 Pierrot · 1937 ou 1938
Pierrot · 1937 or 1938

293 Pierrot · 1937 ou 1938
Pierrot · 1937 or 1938

294 Arlequin · 1938
Harlequin

295 Jeune Pitre · 1938
Young Clown

296 Pierrot et dompteur · 1938
Pierrot and Animal Trainer

297 Pitre · 1938
Clown

298 Pierrot · vers 1938
Pierrot · about 1938

299 Grotesques (cirque) · vers 1938
Grotesques (Circus) · about 1938

300 Le Clown Jaune · vers 1938
Yellow Clown · about 1938

301 Pierrot

302 Gilles · 1939

303 Pierrot · 1937 ou 1938
Pierrot · 1937 or 1938

Scènes de cirque · Circus Scenes

304 Composition pour «Le Cirque de l'étoile filante»
1932
Composition for "Le Cirque de l'étoile filante"

305 Fille de cirque · 1937
Circus Girl

306 L'Ecuyère · 1937
Equestrienne

433

307 Fille de cirque · 1937
Circus Girl

308 Le Nain · 1937
The Dwarf

309 Cirque forain – Parade · 1937
Street Circus: Parade

310 Fille de cirque · 1937 ou 1938
Circus Girl · 1937 or 1938

311 Le Clown blessé · 1932
The Injured Clown

312 Cirque de l'étoile filante · 1938

«Fleurs du Mal» et «Ubu» · "Fleurs du Mal" and "Ubu"

313 Homme en habit vert · 1933
Man in a Green Coat

314 Fleurs du Mal · 1937

315 Fleurs du Mal · 1937

434

316 Promenade du Père Ubu · 1939
Père Ubu out for a Walk

317 Réveil d'Ubu · 1938
Ubu Awakening

318 Grotesque pour «Ubu»
Grotesque for "Ubu"

Compositions (avec figures) · Compositions with Figures

319 Automne · 1937
Autumn

320 Bacchanale · 1937
Bacchanal

321 Figures décoratives
Decorative Figures

Paysages (avec figures)
Landscapes with Figures

322 Paysage légendaire · 1937
Legendary Landscape

323 Crépuscule · 1937
Twilight

324 Crépuscule · 1937
Twilight

325 Paysage (Crépuscule) · 1937
Landscape (Twilight)

326 Couchant · 1937
Sunset

327 Christ et pêcheurs · 1937
Christ and Fishermen

328 Crépuscule · 1937 ou 1938
Twilight · 1937 or 1938

329 Automne · 1937 ou 1938
Autumn · 1937 or 1938

330 Crépuscule · 1937 ou 1938
Twilight · 1937 or 1938

331 Automne · 1938
Autumn

332 Paysage · 1937 ou 1938
Landscape · 1937 or 1938

333 Stella Matutina · 1938

334 Paysage légendaire (Christ et forains) · 1938
Legendary Landscape (Christ and Fairground
People)

335 Paysage (dit aussi Paysage légendaire)
1938
Landscape (also known as Legendary Landscape)

336 Stella Matutina · 1938

337 Matin · 1938
Morning

338 Automne · 1938
Autumn

339 Paysage légendaire · 1938
Legendary Landscape

436

340 Stella Matutina · 1938

341 Paysage biblique · 1938 ou 1939
Biblical Landscape · 1938 or 1939

342 Stella Vespertina · 1938

343 Matutina · 1939

344 Nocturne · 1939

345 Nocturne · 1937 ou 1938
Nocturne · 1937 or 1938

Juges · Judges

346 Les Trois juges · 1936
The Three Judges

347 Le Tribunal de province · 1937
The Provincial Tribunal

348 Juge · 1937
Judge

349 The Provincial Tribunal · 1938
Le Tribunal de province

Types (hommes) · Men

350 Tête d'homme · 1931
Head of a Man

351 Antonio · 1937

352 Le Dernier Romantique · 1937
The Last Romantic

437

353 Père Boeuf · 1937
Father Ox

354 Bouchers · 1937
Butchers

355 Soldat · 1937
Soldier

356 Chinois · 1937
Chinaman

357 Profils · 1937
Profiles

358 Petit Page · 1937
Little Pageboy

359 Paysans · 1937
Peasants

360 Paysans · 1937
Peasants

361 Paysans · 1937
Peasants

362 Soldat · 1937
Soldier

363 Soldats · 1937 ou 1938
Soldiers · 1937 or 1938

364 Soldats · 1937 ou 1938
Soldiers · 1937 or 1938

438

365 Fonctionnaire · 1938
Civil Servant

366 Diplomate · 1938
Diplomat

367 Monsieur Louis · 1938

368 Paysans · 1938
Peasants

369 Tzigane · 1938
Gypsy

370 Les Deux Amis · 1938
The Two Friends

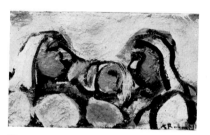

371 Guerre (Deux soldats) · 1939
War (Two Soldiers)

372 Moine · 1939
Monk

373 Tête · 1939
Head

Types (femmes) · Women

374 Reine du cirque · vers 1933
Queen of the Circus · about 1933

375 Madame X · 1937

376 Face à face · 1937
Face to Face

439

377 Carlotta · 1937

378 L'Espagnole · 1937
Spanish Woman

379 L'Italienne · 1937
Italian Woman

380 Petite Campagnarde · 1937
Little Country Girl

381 L'Espagnole · 1937
Spanish Woman

382 La Petite Servante · 1937
Little Serving-Girl

383 Marie · 1937

384 L'Espagnole · 1937 ou 1938
Spanish Woman · 1937 or 1938

385 Figurante · 1937
Walker-On

386 Véronique · 1938
Veronica

387 Figure de femme (pour le Miserere) · 1939
A Woman (for "Miserere")

388 Pierrette · 1939

440

389 L'Orientale · 1937
Levantine Woman

390 Vieil Arabe · 1937
Old Arab

391 La Marocaine · 1937
Moroccan Woman

392 Arabes · 1937 ou 1938
Arabs · 1937 or 1938

393 Arabes · 1937 ou 1938
Arabs · 1937 or 1938

394 Arabes · 1937 ou 1938
Arabs · 1937 or 1938

395 Arabes · 1938
Arabs

396 Orientale · 1938
Levantine Woman

397 Seigneurs arabes · 1938
Arab Noblemen

398 Oriental · 1938
Levantine Man

Petite Banlieue · Depressed Suburban Areas

399 Vieux Faubourg · 1937 ou 1938
Old Faubourg · 1937 or 1938

400 Vieux Faubourg · 1937 ou 1938
Old Faubourg · 1937 or 1938

401 Vieux Faubourg · 1937 ou 1938
Old Faubourg · 1937 or 1938

402 Au Vieux Faubourg des longues peines · 1939
Old Faubourg of Toil and Suffering

403 Faubourg des longues peines · 1938
Faubourg of Toil and Suffering

404 Petite Banlieue · 1939
Workers' Suburb

Divers · Miscellaneous Subjects

405 Fleurs · 1937
Flowers

406 Grotesque · 1931

407 Guerre · 1937
War

408 Projet pour une fontaine Cézanne · 1938
Project for a Fountain in Memory of Cézanne

409 Fauve · 1938
Wild Animal

410 Nature morte · vers 1938
Still Life · about 1938

442

411 Ballets russes · 1939
Russian Ballet

412 Au Pressoir le raisin fut foulé (Miserere) · 1939
In the Press, the Grape was Trodden (Miserere)

413 Acrobate · vers 1939
Acrobat · about 1939

1940-1948

Le Visage du Christ
Christ: The Holy Countenance

414 Passion · vers 1948
The Passion · about 1948

415 Pax · vers 1948
Pax · about 1948

416 Béthanie · 1946
Bethany

Compositions religieuses · Religious Compositions

417 Fragment pour «L'Enfant Jésus
parmi les docteurs» · vers 1945
Fragment for "The Child Jesus
Among the Doctors" · about 1945

418 Intérieur d'église · 1945
Church Interior

419 De Profundis · 1946

443

420 La Fuite en Egypte · vers 1946
The Flight into Egypt · about 1946

421 La Petite Eglise · vers 1947
The Little Church · about 1947

422 Ecce Homo · vers 1948
Ecce Homo · about 1948

Paysages bibliques
Biblical Landscapes

423 Christ et pêcheurs · 1942
Christ and Fishermen

424 Stella Vespertina (Paysage) · 1942
Stella Vespertina (also known as Landscape)

425 Christ et disciple · 1942
Christ and Disciple

426 Paysage biblique · 1944
Biblical Landscape

427 La Route · 1946
The Road

428 Le Pont · 1945
The Bridge

429 Nazareth · vers 1946
Nazareth · about 1946

430 Paysage aux grands arbres · 1946
Landscape with Big Trees

431 Aux Rives du Jourdain · vers 1947
On the Banks of the Jordan · about 1947

432 Paysage biblique (aux deux groupes) · vers 1947
Biblical Landscape · about 1947

433 Paysage biblique · vers 1947
Biblical Landscape · about 1947

434 Crépuscule d'hiver · vers 1947
Winter Twilight · about 1947

435 Paysage biblique · vers 1947
Biblical Landscape · about 1947

436 Tibériade (au portique) · vers 1948
The Sea of Galilee · about 1948

437 Laissez venir à moi les petits enfants · vers 1948
Suffer the Little Children to Come Unto Me
about 1948

438 Automne (dit aussi «Tibériade») · vers 1948
Autumn (also known as "The Sea of Galilee")
about 1948

439 La Route · 1947
The Road

440 Automne · vers 1947
Autumn · about 1947

Clowns et Pierrots · Clowns and Pierrots

441 Petit Pierrot au bouquet · 1942
Little Pierrot with Bouquet

442 Pierrot sage · 1943
Reflective Pierrot

443 Trio · 1943

445

444 Duo · vers 1943
Duet · about 1943

445 Pierrots · vers 1943
Pierrots · about 1943

446 Les Deux Frères · vers 1943
The Two Brothers · about 1943

447 Pamphile · 1945
Pamphilius

448 L'Aristocrate · vers 1945
The Aristocrat · about 1945

449 Clown · vers 1945
Clown · about 1945

450 Jim · 1946

451 Pierrotins · vers 1946
Little Pierrots · about 1946

452 Le Rouquin · 1947
The Redhead

446

453 Duo des frangins · vers 1947
Brother's Duet · about 1947

454 Duo · vers 1947
Duet · about 1947

455 Pierrot · vers 1948
Pierrot · about 1948

456 Pedro · vers 1948
Pedro · about 1948

457 Duo · vers 1948
Duet · about 1948

458 Au Clair de la lune · vers 1948
In the Moonlight · about 1948

Scènes de cirque · Circus Scenes

459 Petite Ecuyère · 1942
Little Equestrienne

460 Cirque · 1942
Circus

461 Pierrot au bouquet · vers 1945
Pierrot with Bouquet · about 1945

«Divertissement» · "Divertissement"

462 Gentil Bernard · 1941
Kindly Bernard

Ces quatorze gouaches forment, avec
«Arlequin» que nous donnons en hors
texte, la totalité des oeuvres reproduites
dans «Divertissement», édité par Tériade,
à Paris, en 1943

These fourteen gouaches, together with
"Harlequin" which is reproduced separa-
tely, form the complete corpus of works
reproduced in "Divertissement," published
in Paris by Tériade, 1943

463 Les Deux Têtus · 1941
Two Stubborn Men

464 Pierrot blanc · 1941
White Pierrot

465 Mange-tout · 1941
Wastrel

466 Petit Page rouge et or · 1941
Little Pageboy in Red and Gold

447

467 Le Moqueur · 1941
The Mocker

468 Madame YXE · 1941

469 Les Deux Anciens · 1941
The Two Elders

470 Danseuses · 1941
Dancers

471 Acrobate · 1941
Acrobat

472 Quiquengrogne · 1941
Wotthehell

473 La Roussalka · 1941
Russalka

474 Margot · 1941

475 Pierrot noir · 1941
Black Pierrot

«Fleurs du Mal» · ''Fleurs du Mal''

476 Fleurs du Mal (Figure de face) · 1945
Fleurs du Mal (Figure Seen from the Front)

477 Fleurs du Mal (Figure de profil) · 1945
Fleurs du Mal (Figure Seen in Profile)

478 Frontispice pour «Les Fleurs du Mal» · 1945
Frontispiece for ''Les Fleurs du Mal''

448

«Stella Vespertina» · "Stella Vespertina"

These nine paintings figure among the twelve reproduced in color in the book "Stella Vespertina," published by René Drouin, Paris, 1947

479 De Profundis (dit aussi «Hiver») · 1945
De Profundis (also known as "Winter")

480 Automne · 1945
Autumn

481 Orientale, ou Vieil Orient · 1945
Oriental Woman, or The Old Orient

482 Christ et disciples · 1945
Christ and Disciples

483 Nocturne · vers 1945
Nocturne · about 1945

484 Puits de Jacob · 1945
Jacob's Well

485 Crépuscule · 1945
Twilight

486 Le Fugitif · 1945
Fugitive

487 Clair de lune · 1945
Moonlight

Paysages (avec figures) · Landscapes with Figures

488 Cimetière · 1946
Graveyard

489 Vieux Versailles · vers 1946
Old Versailles · about 1946

490 De Profundis · 1948

449

491 Au fil de l'eau (Ile-de-France) · 1948
By the Waterside (Ile-de-France)

492 Hiver · 1946
Winter

493 Soleil d'hiver
Winter Sun

Juges · Judges

494 Juge · 1947
Judge

495 Juges · 1947
Judges

496 Juge · 1947
Judge

Types (hommes) · Men

497 Le Napolitain · 1945
Neapolitan

498 Joyeux Drille · vers 1945
Gay Dog · about 1945

499 Songe-creux · 1946
Dreamer

500 Maître Testu
The Advocate Testu

501 Vétéran (en souvenir d'H. Rupp) · vers 1946
Veteran (In Memory of H. Rupp) · about 1946

502 Patrice · vers 1948
Patrice · about 1948

450

Types (femmes) · Women

503 Profil · vers 1945
Profile · about 1945

504 Sainte Marthe · vers 1945
Saint Martha · about 1945

505 Louisette · 1946

506 Figure de femme de trois-quart · vers 1947
Three-Quarter Portrait of a Woman · about 1947

507 Monique · vers 1947
Monique · about 1947

508 Reine de cirque · vers 1948
Queen of the Circus · about 1948

509 Figure de femme au chapeau à plume · vers 1948
Head of Woman in Feathered Hat · about 1948

510 Theodora · vers 1948
Theodora · about 1948

511 Carmencita · vers 1948
Carmencita · about 1948

512 Reine de cirque · vers 1948
Queen of the Circus · about 1948

513 Tête de femme · vers 1948
Head of a Woman · about 1948

451

Fleurs décoratives · Decorative Flowers

514   Petite Fleur pour tapisserie · 1942
Little Flower for a Tapestry

515   Fleurs décoratives · 1946
Decorative Flowers

516   Fleurs décoratives · 1946
Decorative Flowers

517   Fleurs décoratives · vers 1946
Decorative Flowers · about 1946

518   Fleurs décoratives · 1947
Decorative Flowers

519   Fleurs décoratives · 1947
Decorative Flowers

520   Fleurs décoratives · 1947
Decorative Flowers

Faubourg des longues peines · Faubourg of Toil and Suffering

521   Jacques Bonhomme · vers 1946
John Everyman · about 1946

522   Hiver · vers 1946
Winter · about 1946

523   Automne · vers 1946
Autumn · about 1946

452

524 Exode · 1948
Exodus

525 Exode (La Route est longue) vers · 1948
Exodus (The Road Is Long) · about 1948

526 Vieux Faubourg · vers 1947
Old Faubourg · about 1947

Divers · Miscellaneous Subjects

527 Le Courtisan · 1945
Courtier

528 Bestiaire · 1945
Bestiary

529 Testu fils · 1947
Testu's Son · 1947

1949–1958

Le Visage du Christ
Christ: The Holy Countenance

530 Passion (Tête de Christ) · vers 1951
The Passion (Head of Christ) · about 1951

531 Ecce Homo · 1952

532 La Sainte Face · 1954
The Holy Countenance

453

Le Christ et compositions religieuses · Christ and Religious Compositions

533 Notre Jeanne · 1948–1949
Joan of Arc

534 Passion · 1949
The Passion

535 Le Sacré Coeur · vers 1949
The Sacred Heart · about 1949

536 Crucifixion · 1950

537 Intimité chrétienne (Christ et enfants) · 1952
Christian Spirit (Christ and Children)

538 La Fuite en Egypte · 1952
The Flight into Egypt

Paysages bibliques
Biblical Landscapes

539 Automne · vers 1949
Autumn · about 1949

540 Nocturne d'automne · 1952
Autumn Nocturne

541 Fin d'automne (I) · 1952
End of Autumn (I)

542 Fin d'automne (IV) · 1952
End of Autumn (IV)

543 Fin d'automne (V) · 1952
End of Autumn (V

544 Crépuscule · 1952
Twilight

454

545 Paysage biblique · 1953
Biblical Landscape

546 Paysage biblique aux deux arbres · 1952
Biblical Landscape with Two Trees

547 Paysage biblique au tronc d'arbre · vers 1953
Biblical Landscape with Tree Trunk · about 1953

Clowns, Pierrots et scènes de cirque · Clowns, Pierrots, and Circus Scenes

548 Magloire · 1952

549 Clown · 1952

550 Petit Louis (Vieux Cirque forain) · 1952
Little Louis (Old Street Circus)

551 Songe-creux · 1952
Dreamer

552 Mistigri · 1952

553 Gentil Bernard · 1952
Kindly Bernard

554 Pierrot · 1953

555 Clown · 1956

556 Profil de clown (vieux cirque forain) · 1953
Profile of a Clown (Old Street Circus)

455

Types (femmes) · Women

557 La Petite Magicienne · 1949
The Little Sorceress

558 Yoko · 1952

559 Douce-Amère (Vieux Cirque forain) · 1952
Bitter-Sweet (Old Street Circus)

560 Blanche-neige · 1952
Snow-White

561 Rosine · vers 1952
Rosine · about 1952

562 Reine de cirque · vers 1952
Queen of the Circus · about 1952

563 Profil · vers 1952
Profile · about 1952

564 Orientale · vers 1952
Levantine Woman · about 1952

565 Profil · 1956
Profile

List of the Works Illustrated

Before 1891

Drawing. École Nationale des Arts Décoratifs, Paris. Page 22
Drawing. École Nationale des Arts Décoratifs, Paris. Page 22
Drawing. École Nationale des Arts Décoratifs, Paris. Page 22

Period 1891–1901

1891

Paris. Small size. Page 92
The Road to Calvary. Oil. $15^3/_4 \times 26''$. Wadsworth Athenaeum, Hartford, Conn. Page 58

1892

The Return of the Prodigal Son. Charcoal. Page 71
Job. Oil. $21^1/_4 \times 26^1/_2''$. (inscribed: first sketch made in the Gustave Moreau atelier). Page 59
Gethsemane. Oil. $16^1/_4 \times 13''$. Signed lower center, and inscribed: "To my old friend Letra, in affectionate remembrance." (Letra was a custodian at the Ecole des Beaux-Arts.) Private collection, Paris. C.C. 1

1893

The Ordeal of Samson. Oil. $57^1/_2 \times 44^3/_4''$. Los Angeles County Museum. Page 60
The Child Jesus Among the Doctors. Watercolor and gouache. $26^1/_2 \times 21^1/_4''$. Collection Hahnloser, Winterthur, Switzerland. C.C. 2
Hermit. Oil. $16^1/_4 \times 13''$. Inscribed: "To my old friend Letra." Private collection, Paris. C.C. 3
Study for The Ordeal of Samson. Pen drawing. $7^7/_8 \times 3^1/_8''$. Signed with a monogram, bottom left. Private collection, Paris. C.C. 5
Study for The Ordeal of Samson. Pencil drawing. $7^7/_8 \times 3^1/_8''$. Signed with a monogram, bottom left. Private collection, Paris. C.C. 6

1894

Sketch for The Child Jesus Among the Doctors. Pen drawing. $6^1/_4 \times 5^1/_4''$. Page 64
Sketch for The Child Jesus Among the Doctors (fragment). Pen drawing. $27^1/_2 \times 11^3/_4''$. Page 65
First Notation for Coriolanus in the House of Tullius. Drawing tinted with gouache. $18^1/_2 \times 14^1/_2''$. Private collection, Paris. Page 62
Coriolanus in the House of Tullius. Oil. $18 \times 15''$. (Competition of painted sketches, February 6, 1894.) Ecole Nationale des Beaux-Arts, Paris. Page 63
The Child Jesus Among the Doctors. Oil. $64^3/_4 \times 51^1/_4''$. Signed lower right: Henri-Georges Rouault, and dated. Musée des Unterlinden, Colmar. Page 39
Study for The Child Jesus Among the Doctors. Pen drawing. $21^1/_4 \times 16^1/_4''$. Signed and dated lower center. Private collection, Paris. C.C. 4

1895

The Kiss of Judas. Charcoal. $16^1/_2 \times 12^3/_4''$. Private collection, Paris. Page 94
Self-Portrait. Charcoal and crayon. $28^3/_4 \times 21^1/_4''$. Private collection, Paris. Page 61
The Dead Christ Mourned by the Holy Women. Oil. $57^1/_2 \times 44^3/_4''$. (Competition for the Prix de Rome). Musée de Grenoble. Page 89
Stella Matutina. Oil. $106 \times 70^3/_4''$. Musée d'Avallon (Yonne). Page 66
Stella Vespertina. Oil. $106 \times 70^3/_4''$. Musée d'Avallon (Yonne). C.C. 13
Study. Drawing tinted with sepia. $21^1/_2 \times 13''$. Page 70

1897

The Return of the Prodigal Son. Charcoal and crayon. $11^3/_4 \times 11''$. Collection Dr. Pierre Collart, Paris. Page 69
Night Landscape (The Workyard). Watercolor and pastel. $24^3/_4 \times 33^1/_2''$. Signed and dated lower right center. Collection Mme. Henri Simon, Paris. Page 43

Night Landscape (The Good Samaritan). Watercolor and pastel. $26^1/_2 \times 37^1/_2''$. Page 91

1899

Christ and the Disciples at Emmaus. Charcoal. Private collection, New York. Page 72
Alexandre Rouault, the artist's father.
Pencil sketch. Page 18
Marie-Louise Rouault, née Champdavoine.
Pencil sketch. Page 18

1900

Nocturne (Landscape in Moonlight). Charcoal, pastel, and tempera. $11^1/_4 \times 9^1/_4''$. Private collection, Zurich. Page 90
Repast. Charcoal. $10^1/_2 \times 10^1/_2''$. The Tate Gallery, London. Page 68
Study of a Head. Drawing. $5^1/_2 \times 5^3/_4''$. Musée d'Art Moderne de la Ville de Paris, Girardin Bequest. Page 57
Face to Face. Colored brush drawing on canvas. $3^1/_4 \times 4''$. Collection M. and Mme. Marcel Poignard, Paris. Page 96
The Plain. Wash drawing. $6^3/_4 \times 7^1/_4''$. Signed and dated lower right. Private collection, Paris. Page 9
Landscape. Watercolor and pastel. $4 \times 6^3/_4''$. Signed and dated lower right. Private collection, Paris. C.C. 7
Landscape. Pastel. $5 \times 8''$. Private collection, Paris. C.C. 8
Portrait of Madame Paul Flat. Charcoal and pastel. Private collection. C.C. 14
The Nativity. Pen and brush. $17^1/_4 \times 12^1/_4''$. Private collection, Paris. Page 95
Christ and Disciples. Watercolor and pastel. $5^1/_2 \times 9^1/_2''$. Private collection, Paris. C.C. 12
Fisherman. Watercolor and pastel. $6^1/_4 \times 3^6/_8''$. Signed lower right. Collection Granoff, Paris. C.C. 15

1901

Daniel Defending Susanna. Oil. $16^1/_4 \times 13''$. Private collection, Paris. Page 67
The Promenade. Pastel and gouache. $9 \times 7''$. Collection M. and Mme. Marcel Poignard, Paris. Page 93
Judges. Colored brush drawing. $4^1/_4 \times 4''$. Private collection, Paris. Page 96
Paris (The Seine). Watercolor. $6^1/_2 \times 11''$. Signed and dated lower right. Private collection, Paris. C.C. 9
Landscape. Watercolor and pastel. Small size. Signed and dated lower right. Ex-collection Gruyer; Private collection. C.C. 10
Landscape. Watercolor and pastel. $8^3/_4 \times 6^1/_2''$. Signed lower right. Ex-collection Gruyer; Private collection. C.C. 11

Period 1902–1914

1902

Landscape. Oil and tempera. $6 \times 10''$. Private collection, Switzerland. Page 174
Circus Girl. Watercolor and pastel. $11^1/_4 \times 8''$. Private collection, Switzerland. Page 114

1903

Bathers. Watercolor. $17^1/_4 \times 13''$. Private collection, Paris. Page 128
Prostitutes. $9^3/_4 \times 9''$. Collection Mme. Hahnloser, Winterthur, Switzerland. Page 122

The Red Clown. Watercolor. $11 \times 9''$. Signed lower left. Ex-collection Girardin. C.C. 34
Clown with Dog. Watercolor and gouache. $6^1/_2 \times 7^1/_4''$. Signed and dated lower right. Collection Baron Boël, Belgium. C.C. 35
Clown with Drum. Watercolor, gouache, and pastel. $4^1/_4 \times 6''$. Signed upper right. Private collection, Switzerland. C.C. 36
Circus Act. Watercolor and pastel. $10 \times 12^3/_4''$. Signed center. Private collection. C.C. 46

1904

Ticket Sellers, Street Circus. Oil. $11^1/_2 \times 13^1/_2''$. Private collection, Paris. Page 116
Head of a Tragic Clown. Watercolor and pastel. $14^1/_2 \times 10^1/_2''$. Collection Baugerter, Montreux, Switzerland. Page 131
Duet. Oil. $8^3/_4 \times 6''$. Signed and dated lower right. Ex-collection Girardin; Musée d'Art Moderne de la Ville de Paris. C.C. 91
Landscape (Waterfall). $8^3/_4 \times 8''$. Signed and dated left center. Private collection. C.C. 55
The Wet Nurses. Watercolor and gouache. Signed and dated lower right. C.C. 139

1905

Clown and Child. Oil and tempera. $6^1/_2 \times 4^3/_4''$. Private collection, Winterthur, Switzerland. Page 132
Clown with Inkwell. Pastel, gouache, and India ink. $5 \times 5^1/_4''$. Collection M. and Mme. Marcel Poignard, Paris. Page 130
The Couple (The Loge). Gouache. $38 \times 30^3/_4''$. Collection Bührle, Zurich. Page 124
Olympia. Watercolor and pastel. $10^3/_4 \times 17''$. Private collection, Paris. Page 164
The Bridge. Watercolor and pastel. $10^3/_4 \times 14^1/_2''$. The Royal Museum of Fine Arts, Copenhagen. Page 136
Pitch-Ball Puppets (The Wedding of Nini-Patte-en-l'air). Watercolor. $20^1/_2 \times 26^1/_2''$. Private collection, Paris. Page 117
Monsieur et Madame Poulot. Watercolor and gouache. $27^1/_2 \times 20^1/_2''$. Collection Philippe Leclercq, Hem, France. Page 125
The Parade. Oil. $12^3/_4 \times 9^1/_2''$. Signed upper right. Private collection, Paris. Page 47
Drunken Woman. Watercolor and pastel. $27^3/_4 \times 21^1/_4''$. Signed lower right. Ex-collection Girardin; Musée d'Art Moderne de la Ville de Paris. Page 51
The Fallen Eve. Watercolor and pastel. $10 \times 8^1/_4''$. Signed lower center. Ex-collection Girardin; Musée d'Art Moderne de la Ville de Paris. Page 53
Circus (Pierrot, Punch, and Harlequin). Watercolor and pastel. $12^3/_4 \times 9^1/_2''$. Signed lower left. Ex-collection Girardin; Musée d'Art Moderne de la Ville de Paris. Page 75
Bal Tabarin (Dancing the Chahut). Watercolor and pastel. $27^3/_4 \times 21^1/_4''$. Signed lower left. Ex-collection Girardin; Musée d'Art Moderne de la Ville de Paris. Page 77
Versailles (The Fountain). Watercolor and pastel. $26^1/_2 \times 21''$. Signed lower right. Collection Philippe Leclercq, Hem, France. Page 79
Wrestler (The Parade). Watercolor, gouache, and pastel. $8^3/_4 \times 5''$. Signed and dated upper left. Ex-collection Girardin; Musée d'Art Moderne de la Ville de Paris. Page 55
Head of Christ. Oil. $45 \times 31''$. Signed upper left. Collection Walter P. Chrysler, Jr., New York. C.C. 21
Nude on a Blue Ground. Gouache. $9^1/_2 \times 8^3/_4''$. Signed upper left. Private collection, Winterthur, Switzerland. C.C. 22

Monsieur Loyal and Dancer. Watercolor and pastel. Signed and dated middle right. C.C. 44

Ticket Sellers, Traveling Circus. 11 × 13″. Signed and dated bottom center. Private collection, Switzerland. C.C. 53

Man Dressed Up. 7¹/₂ × 5¹/₄″. Signed upper right. Private collection. C.C. 92

Woman with a Hat. Watercolor. 8³/₄ × 6³/₄″. Signed and dated upper left. Private collection, Paris. C.C. 106

Mother and Child (The Clown's Wife). Oil and gouache. 6¹/₂ × 4³/₄″. Signed and dated lower left. Private collection, Winterthur, Switzerland. C.C. 107

Crossing the Bridge. Watercolor. 10 × 13¹/₄″. Signed lower right. Private collection, Solothurn, Switzerland. C.C. 61

Christ and Disciples (sketch). Pastel and ink. 6 × 5³/₄″. Signed lower right. Ex-collection Girardin; Musée d'Art Moderne de la Ville de Paris. C.C. 16

Sketch for *Monsieur et Madame Poulot.* Watercolor. 25¹/₂ × 18″. Signed and dated lower left. Private collection, Switzerland. C.C. 140

Prostitute, Back View. Watercolor. 26¹/₂ × 19³/₄″. Collection Lady Hulton, London. C.C. 23

Nude (sketch). Oil. 24 × 17¹/₂″. Signed upper right. Collection Philippe Leclercq, Hem, France. C.C. 70

1906

The Model. Watercolor. 11 × 9″. Page 118

Dancer Lacing Her Slipper. Watercolor, pastel, and gouache. 10 × 8¹/₂″. Private Collection, Switzerland. Page 113

Street-Fair Wrestlers. Watercolor and pencil. Private collection, U.S.A. Page 134

Prostitutes. Watercolor and pastel. 27¹/₂ × 21¹/₄″. Private collection, Basel. Page 120

Clown with Accordion (The Loge). Watercolor and pastel. 30³/₄ × 18″. Collection Mme. Henri Simon, Paris. Page 133

Equestrienne. Watercolor heightened with pastel. 26¹/₂ × 20″. Musée d'Art Moderne de la Ville de Paris, Girardin Bequest. Page 126

Parade. Watercolor and pastel. Page 135

Dancer. Watercolor and pastel. Page 123

Fete at the Edge of the Pool. Oil. 22 × 24″. Collection Netter, Paris. Page 137

Mother and Child (Madame Baignères and Her Son). Watercolor sketch. 8¹/₄ × 6³/₄″. Collection the Hon. and Mrs. John Hay Whitney, New York. Page 163

Prostitute. Watercolor, gouache, and pastel. 28 × 21³/₄″. Musée d'Art Moderne de la Ville de Paris, Girardin Bequest. Page 129

Prostitutes. Watercolor and pastel. 27¹/₂ × 19³/₄″. Page 121

Odalisque. 21¹/₄ × 24″. The Royal Museum of Fine Arts, Copenhagen. Page 138

The Salon (At the Theater). Watercolor. 28³/₄ × 21¹/₄″. Collection Baronne Lambert, Brussels. Page 127

Prostitute at Her Mirror. Watercolor. 28¹/₂ × 21³/₄″. Signed and dated upper left. Musée National d'Art Moderne, Paris. Page 83

At the Café. Watercolor and pastel. 15¹/₂ × 11¹/₂″. Signed upper right. Private collection. C.C. 24

Prostitute (With the Stove). Watercolor and pastel. 11 × 9″. Signed with monogram and dated, lower right. C.C. 26

Prostitute (With Two Figures). Watercolor and pastel. Signed with monogram and dated, lower left. The Royal Museum of Fine Arts, Copenhagen. C.C. 27

Prostitute Doing Her Hair. Watercolor and pastel. 11 × 8³/₄″.

Signed with monogram and dated, lower left. The Royal Museum of Fine Arts, Copenhagen. C.C. 28

Duet. Wash. Small size. Signed and dated lower right. C.C. 146

Nude (sketch). Watercolor. 11 × 8¹/₄″. Signed with monogram and dated, lower right. Private collection. C.C. 29

Trio. Oil. Signed lower left. C.C. 30

Nude with Arm Raised. Watercolor and pastel. 27³/₄ × 20¹/₂″. Signed with monogram and dated, upper right. C.C. 31

Punch. Oil and watercolor. 17¹/₂ × 13″. Collection Mme. Henri Simon, Paris. C.C. 37

Three Circus Performers. Watercolor. 14¹/₄ × 17³/₄″. Signed lower right. Museum of Art, Belgrade. C.C. 48

The Parade. Watercolor and pastel. 10¹/₄ × 8¹/₄″. Private collection. C.C. 47

Circus Performer. Watercolor and pastel. Signed and dated lower right. Private collection, U.S.A. C.C. 49

Women at the Theater. Watercolor. 7¹/₄ × 5¹/₄″. Signed and dated center left. Galerie Beyeler, Switzerland. C.C. 108

Woman with White Gloves. Oil. Signed upper right center. Private collection. C.C. 110

Faubourg (Street-Hawkers). Watercolor and gouache. 11¹/₄ × 9³/₄″. Signed and dated lower left. Private collection, Paris. C.C. 109

Nude with Arms Raised. C.C. 71

Nude with Arms Raised (sketch). Brush and oil. 21 × 13³/₄″. Signed lower right. Ex-collection Girardin; Musée d'Art Moderne de la Ville de Paris. C.C. 72

Nude. Oil wash. 11³/₄ × 10¹/₄″. Ex-collection Girardin; Musée d'Art Moderne de la Ville de Paris. C.C. 73

1907

Pitch-Ball Puppets (Puppets or *The Bride).* Oil 29¹/₂ × 41³/₄″. The Tate Gallery, London. Page 143

Parade. Watercolor and pastel. 25¹/₂ × 41¹/₄″. Collection Baugerter, Montreux, Switzerland. Page 142

Odalisque. Watercolor. 25¹/₄ × 38¹/₂″. Collection Baugerter, Montreux, Switzerland. Page 139

Conjurer. Oil and watercolor. 17¹/₄ × 13″. Collection Mme. Henri Simon, Paris. Page 161

Nude with Raised Arms. Watercolor and pastel. 12¹/₄ × 12″. Signed lower left. Ex-collection Girardin; Musée d'Art Moderne de la Ville de Paris. Page 85

Condemned Man. Oil. 41 × 29″. Signed and dated lower right. Private collection, Switzerland. Page 87

The Accused. Oil. 29¹/₄ × 41″. Signed and dated lower right. Ex-collection Girardin; Musée d'Art Moderne de la Ville de Paris. C.C. 85

Head of a Clown. Oil. 15¹/₂ × 12¹/₄″. Signed upper right. C.C. 38

Head of a Clown. Oil. 15¹/₂ × 12¹/₄″. Private collection, U.S.A. Page 144

Prostitutes. Oil and gouache. 39³/₄ × 25⁵/₈″. The Abrams Family Collection, New York. C.C. 25

Decorative Figures. Watercolor. 29¹/₄ × 41³/₈″. C.C. 80

1908

Woman's Profile. Private collection, U.S.A. Page 162

Judges. Oil. 29¹/₂ × 41″. The Royal Museum of Fine Arts, Copenhagen. Page 175

The Lecture. Oil. 12¹/₄ × 8″. Signed and dated upper right. Ex-collection Girardin; Musée d'Art Moderne de la Ville de Paris. Page 101

Prostitute. Oil and gouache. $10^1/_2 \times 7^3/_4''$. Signed lower right. Private collection, Winterthur, Switzerland. C.C. 33

The Court. Watercolor and gouache. $11^3/_4 \times 8''$. Signed lower right. Private collection, Winterthur, Switzerland. C.C. 86

Lawyer Pleading. Gouache. $9^3/_4 \times 6^1/_4''$. Signed upper left. Private collection, Winterthur, Switzerland. C.C. 87

Carried Away. Watercolor. $7^1/_2 \times 12^1/_4''$. Signed and dated lower right. Private collection, Paris. C.C. 89

The Judges. Oil. $30^1/_4 \times 22''$. Signed and dated upper right. Private collection, London. C.C. 88

The Little Clown. $10^1/_4 \times 8''$. C.C. 40

Bathers. Watercolor and pastel. $39^1/_2 \times 25^3/_4''$. Signed lower right. Private collection. C.C. 74

The Orator. Oil and gouache. $15^3/_4 \times 10^1/_2''$. Signed upper right. Private collection, Zurich. C.C. 95

Motorists. Ink and watercolor. $11^3/_4 \times 7^1/_4''$. Signed and dated lower left. Private collection, Paris. C.C. 93

The Model. Watercolor. $18^1/_2 \times 15^1/_8''$. Museum of Nantes, France. C.C. 81

Silhouette of a Woman with a Small Dog. Ink, watercolor, and pastel. $10^3/_4 \times 8^1/_4''$. Signed upper right. Private collection, Paris. C.C. 111

Woman Leaning on Her Elbows. Watercolor and pastel. $7^1/_4 \times 5^1/_2''$. Signed upper left. C.C. 112

Street Scene. Oil and gouache on cardboard. $16^1/_4 \times 9^1/_2''$. Signed lower left. Private collection, Winterthur, Switzerland. C.C. 141

Head of a Clown. Watercolor and oil. $23^3/_4 \times 18^1/_2''$. Dumbarton Oaks Research Library and Collection, Harvard University, Washington, D.C., C.C. 39

1909

The Barge. Watercolor and gouache. $23 \times 34^3/_4''$. Musée des Beaux-Arts, Grenoble. Page 105

Seated Nude. Watercolor. $10^3/_4 \times 8^1/_4''$. Signed upper left. Private collection, Winterthur, Switzerland. C.C. 75

Composition. Oil. Signed lower right. Private collection, Switzerland. C.C. 76

Motorist (At the Wheel). Watercolor. $10^3/_4 \times 13^1/_2''$. Signed and dated lower right. Inscribed: "To Dr. Bruyère, in cordial friendship". C.C. 94

Woman's Figure (bust) .Oil. $13^1/_4 \times 9^1/_2''$. Private collection, Paris. C.C. 113

Woman in a Feathered Hat. Ink and watercolor. $10^3/_4 \times 8^3/_4''$. Signed upper left. Private collection, Paris. C.C. 114

Woman and Blue Curtain. Ink and paint. Sight: $10^1/_4 \times 8^3/_4''$. Signed and dated lower right. Private collection, Paris. C.C. 115

Woman with Dog. Watercolor. $8^3/_4 \times 7''$. Signed and dated upper right. Private collection, Paris. C.C. 116

1910

Prostitutes (study). Oil. $36^1/_2 \times 25^1/_2''$. Collection Bangerter, Montreux, Switzerland. Page 119

Clown with Monkey. Oil paint and solvent (probably monotype). $22^1/_2 \times 15''$. Signed with monogram and dated lower left. C.C. 41

Two Profiles. Signed upper left. C.C. 97

The Flood. Watercolor. $9^1/_2 \times 12^1/_4''$. Signed and dated lower right. Private collection, Paris. C.C. 56

Parc de Versailles, the Staircase (The Terrace). Watercolor. $26^1/_2 \times 20^1/_2''$. Signed and dated lower left. Musée National d'Art Moderne, Paris. C.C. 62

Winter. Pastel and solvent. $7^1/_2 \times 12^1/_4''$. Signed lower right. Ex-

collection Girardin; Musée d'Art Moderne de la Ville de Paris. C.C. 63

Sick Woman. Oil and gouache. $11^1/_2 \times 15^3/_4''$. Signed and dated lower center. Private collection, Winterthur, Switzerland. C.C. 127

Still Life (sketch). Ex-collection Girardin. Page 184

"Stuck-up" Lady. Page 181

Bathers. Oil. Page 165

Seated Nude. Watercolor. $11^1/_2 \times 7''$. Private collection, Switzerland. Page 166

Mythological Composition. Oil and gouache. $23^1/_2 \times 18^1/_4''$. Private collection, Winterthur, Switzerland. Page 167

The Tribunal. Oil. $27^3/_4 \times 42^1/_4''$. Collection Mrs. Donald Stralem, New York. Page 109

Interior (Prostitutes in the Salon). Oil on cardboard. $18^1/_4 \times 26^3/_4''$. Private collection, Switzerland. C.C. 32

The Banquet. Oil and gouache. $17 \times 22^3/_4''$. Signed and dated upper right. Private collection, Berne. C.C. 96

1911

The Baptism of Christ. Watercolor and pastel. $24 \times 22''$. Musée d'Art Moderne de la Ville de Paris, Girardin Bequest. Page 169

Head of a Laborer (The Injured Man). Oil. $15^1/_4 \times 11''$. Collection Mr. and Mrs. Ralph F. Colin, New York. Page 168

Monsieur X. Oil. $31 \times 23''$. Albright Art Gallery, Buffalo. Page 141

Fugitives (Exodus). Pastel and gouache. $17^3/_4 \times 23^3/_4''$. Signed and dated lower right. Kunsthaus, Zurich. Page 149

The Jurist (The Lawyer). Oil. $15 \times 11''$. Signed and dated upper right. Private collection, Paris. C.C. 90

Tragic Clown. Oil wash. $14^3/_4 \times 10^1/_4''$. Signed and dated upper right. Private collection, Paris. C.C. 42

The White Pierrot. Watercolor and pastel. $29^1/_2 \times 24^3/_8''$. Signed and dated upper right. C.C. 45

Nudes (Decorative Figures). Watercolor and pastel. $17 \times 15^3/_4''$. Signed lower right. Private collection. C.C. 82

Arabesque. Watercolor and pastel. $17 \times 15^3/_4''$. Signed and dated lower right. Private collection. C.C. 84

The Financier. $7^1/_4 \times 10^1/_4''$. Signed and dated upper left. Private collection, U.S.A. C.C. 99

Landscape. Oil. $14^1/_4 \times 19^3/_4''$. Signed lower right. Private collection. C.C. 65

Faubourg of Toil and Suffering (Rue de la Solidarité). Paint and ink. $11 \times 10''$ (oval). Signed lower center. C.C. 134

The Poor Family (Exodus). Oil. $25^3/_4 \times 19^3/_4''$. Signed lower left. Musée de l'Annonciade, Saint-Tropez. C.C. 129

Landscape. Oil. $14^1/_8 \times 19^5/_8''$. Signed and dated lower right. Private collection, Paris. C.C. 60

1912

The Faubourg of Toil and Suffering. Tempera. $12^1/_2 \times 8''$. Collection Philippe Leclercq, Hem, France. Page 179

De Profundis. Brush drawing and watercolor. $8 \times 12^1/_2''$. Musée d'Art Moderne de la Ville de Paris, Girardin Bequest. Page 171

Christ Mocked. Tempera and pastel. $9^3/_4 \times 6^3/_4''$. Private collection, Paris. Page 177

Two Bathers. Oil. $26^1/_4 \times 43^3/_4''$. Signed lower left. Private collection. Switzerland. C.C. 78

Pedagogue. Pencil and gouache. $6 \times 8''$. Signed and dated lower left. Ex-collection Girardin; Musée d'Art Moderne de la Ville de Paris. C.C. 98

Motherhood (Run-Down Faubourg). Gouache heightened with pastel. $7^1/_4 \times 11^1/_4$". Signed upper right. Ex-collection Girardin; Musée d'Art Moderne de la Ville de Paris. C.C. 117

Leander. Gouache and crayon. $11^1/_4 \times 7^1/_2$". Signed and dated lower right. Ex-collection Girardin; Musée d'Art Moderne de la Ville de Paris. C.C. 136

Exodus. Pastel, watercolor, and ink. $5^3/_4 \times 11$". Signed lower left. Ex-collection Girardin; Musée d'Art Moderne de la Ville de Paris. C.C. 128

The Mother of the Family. Tempera. 15×10". Signed upper right. Private collection. C.C. 130

The Holy Countenance. Gouache. $22 \times 16^1/_2$". Collection Hahnloser, Winterthur, Switzerland. C.C. 18

Breton Boy. Gouache. $12^1/_2 \times 8^1/_4$". Signed lower right. Ex-collection Girardin; Musée d'Art Moderne de la Ville de Paris. C.C. 142

Homes of the Wretched. Gouache. Collection Hahnloser, Winterthur, Switzerland. Page 172

Village in the Snow. $6^1/_4 \times 12^1/_4$". Private collection, Winterthur, Switzerland. Page 173

African Landscape. Page 172

Winter Landscape. Gouache. $7^3/_4 \times 12^1/_4$". Collection Hahnloser, Winterthur, Switzerland. Page 173

Woman with Hat. Tempera. $11^3/_4 \times 7^1/_4$". Private collection, Paris. Page 180

Landscape. Gouache. Page 170

The Widow. Pencil and ink. $11^3/_4 \times 7$". Musée d'Art Moderne de la Ville de Paris, Girardin Bequest. Page 178

Landscape (The Barge). Gouache. $7^1/_2 \times 12^1/_4$". Ex-collection Girardin; Musée d'Art Moderne de la Ville de Paris. C.C. 64

Depressed Suburban Areas (Woman and Children). Gouache. Signed lower right. Ex-collection Girardin; Musée d'Art Moderne de la Ville de Paris. C.C. 132

Christ Mocked. Oil. $17^1/_2 \times 12^1/_4$". Ex-collection Girardin; Musée d'Art Moderne de la Ville de Paris. C.C. 17

1913

Rugged Rosa. $17^1/_4 \times 11^3/_4$". Private collection, Switzerland. Page 115

Landscape. Oil paint with petrol. $11^1/_2 \times 24^1/_2$". Signed lower right. Ex-collection Girardin; Musée d'Art Moderne de la Ville de Paris. Page 9

Wrestler. Oil and gouache. $40^1/_2 \times 28$". Signed and dated upper right. Private collection, U.S.A. C.C. 52

Lackey. Signed and dated upper left. Private collection. C.C. 100

Discussions. Tempera. Signed and dated upper right. Private collection. C.C. 120

Grotesque Figure in a Dressing Gown. Watercolor and gouache. $11^1/_2 \times 7^1/_2$". Signed and dated lower left. Ex-collection Girardin; Collection Frederick B. Serger, New York. C.C. 138

Landscape (House Behind Trees). Watercolor. $10 \times 12^3/_4$". Signed and dated lower right. Private collection. C.C. 57

The Little Port, with Figures. Watercolor and colored pencils. $8 \times 12^1/_4$". Signed and dated lower right. Private collection. C.C. 66

Versailles (sketch). Crayon and oil wash. $7^1/_2 \times 11^1/_2$". Signed and dated upper right. Ex-collection Girardin; Musée d'Art Moderne de la Ville de Paris. C.C. 67

Landscape (Winter). Watercolor. $8 \times 12^1/_4$". Signed and dated lower left. Private collection. C.C. 68

The Holy Countenance. Gouache. $28 \times 21^3/_4$". Signed lower right. Private collection, Zurich. C.C. 20

Men of Justice. Pencil, ink, and watercolor. $11^3/_4 \times 7^1/_2$". Musée d'Art Moderne de la Ville de Paris, Girardin Bequest. Page 176

Wrestler. Page 140

Christ Mocked. Oil. $28^3/_4 \times 23^3/_4$". Collection Miss Mary E. Johnston, U.S.A. Page 182

Tragic Clown. Oil. Private collection, U.S.A. Page 183

Little Pierrot. Pencil and oil wash. $12 \times 7^3/_4$". Signed lower right. Ex-collection Girardin; Musée d'Art Moderne de la Ville de Paris. C.C. 43

Acrobat. Watercolor. $15^1/_2 \times 11^3/_4$". Private collection, Winterthur, Switzerland. C.C. 50

Acrobat. Watercolor and ink. $15^1/_2 \times 12$". Signed lower right. Ex-collection Girardin; Musée d'Art Moderne de la Ville de Paris. C.C. 51

The Fop. Gouache heightened with pencil. $12^1/_4 \times 7^1/_4$". Signed lower right. Ex-collection Girardin; Musée d'Art Moderne de la Ville de Paris. C.C. 102

Madame X. Gouache. $12^1/_2 \times 8$". Ex-collection Girardin, Musée d'Art Moderne de la Ville de Paris. C.C. 118

La Belle Hélène (sketch). Gouache, brush and colored crayon. $12^1/_4 \times 7^1/_2$". Ex-collection Girardin; Musée d'Art Moderne de la Ville de Paris. C.C. 119

Father of the Family. Signed and dated upper right. C.C. 105

Landscape. Gouache. $7^1/_2 \times 12^1/_2$". Ex-collection Girardin; Collection Galerie Romanet. C.C. 58

The Hovel. Gouache, tempera, ink, and pencil. $12^1/_4 \times 7^1/_2$". Ex-collection Girardin; Musée d'Art Moderne de la Ville de Paris. C.C. 133

Christ on the Cross. Oil. $41^1/_2 \times 29^1/_2$". Private collection, Switzerland. C.C. 19

Trio. Pencil and gouache. $3^3/_4 \times 2^1/_2$". Signed lower right. Ex-collection Girardin; Musée d'Art Moderne de la Ville de Paris. C.C. 143

Verso of Trio: Breton, Back View (sketch). Brush drawing and pencil. $3^3/_4 \times 2^1/_2$". Ex-collection Girardin; Musée d'Art Moderne de la Ville de Paris. C.C. 144

1914

Workers (Interior). Tempera. Signed upper left. Private collection. C.C. 101

The Cook. Tempera. $12^3/_4 \times 8^1/_4$". Signed and dated upper left. Private collection, U.S.A. C.C. 121

Parisian Suburb (Beside the Seine). Chalks, ink, and tempera. $8 \times 12^1/_4$". Ex-collection Girardin; Musée d'Art Moderne de la Ville de Paris. C.C. 69

Punch. Private collection, Switzerland. C.C. 54

The Palace of Ubu. Gouache. $29^1/_2 \times 41^1/_2$". Private collection. C.C. 59

Nude with Necklace. Crayon and oil wash. $12^1/_4 \times 8$". Ex-collection Girardin; Musée d'Art Moderne de la Ville de Paris. C.C. 77

Nude (sketch). Oil wash. $12^1/_4 \times 8$". Ex-collection Girardin; Musée d'Art Moderne de la Ville de Paris. C.C. 79

Arabesque (sketch). Oil wash. $8 \times 12^1/_4$". Ex-collection Girardin; Musée d'Art Moderne de la Ville de Paris. C.C. 83

Invective (sketch). Oil wash. $11^1/_2 \times 6^3/_4$". Ex-collection Girardin; Musée d'Art Moderne de la Ville de Paris. C.C. 103

The Manager (Hector). Oil. Signed left center. Collection Philippe Leclercq, Hem, France. C.C. 104

Half-Caste Woman (sketch). Gouache and brush-drawing. $15^3/_4 \times 10^1/_2$". Ex-collection Girardin; Musée d'Art Moderne de la Ville de Paris. C.C. 122

Hortense (sketch). Brush-drawing. $11^3/_4 \times 7^1/_4''$. Ex-collection Girardin; Musée d'Art Modern de la Ville de Paris. C.C. 123

Madame Euphrasia (sketch). Gouache and brush-drawing. $12^3/_4 \times 8^1/_4''$. Ex-collection Girardin; Musée d'Art Moderne de la Ville de Paris. C.C. 124

Bust of a Woman. Oil. $10^3/_4 \times 7^1/_4''$. Private collection, Paris. C.C. 125

Woman in Profile. Tempera. $15 \times 8''$. Private collection, Paris. C.C. 126

The Zéphirin Family (sketch). Crayon and oil paint with petrol. $12^1/_2 \times 7^3/_4''$. Ex-collection Girardin; Musée d'Art Moderne de la Ville de Paris. C.C. 137

Mau-Mau (sketch). India ink brush drawing. $10^3/_4 \times 8''$. Ex-collection Girardin; Musée d'Art Moderne de la Ville de Paris. C.C. 165

Gypsy Woman (sketch). Crayon and brush drawing. $7^1/_2 \times 12^1/_2''$. Ex-collection Girardin; Musée d'Art Moderne de la Ville de Paris. C.C. 131

Faubourg of Toil and Suffering. Gouache. $12^1/_4 \times 7^3/_4''$. Signed and dated upper left. Ex-collection Girardin; Musée d'Art Moderne de la Ville de Paris. C.C. 135

Promenade. Oil on cardboard. $13^3/_4 \times 10''$. Signed lower left. Private collection, Winterthur, Switzerland. C.C. 145

Jean-Pierre. Oil wash. $12^1/_4 \times 8''$. Musée d'Art Moderne de la Ville de Paris. C.C. 147

Period 1915-1930

1915

The Reformer. $11^3/_4 \times 7''$. Musée d'Art Moderne de la Ville de Paris, Girardin Bequest. Page 220

Satisfied Man. Gouache. $11^1/_2 \times 7^1/_2''$. Signed upper left. Private collection, Winterthur, Switzerland. C.C. 166

Von X. Gouache, pencil, and ink. $11^3/_4 \times 7^1/_2''$. Signed lower left. Ex-collection Girardin; Musée d'Art Moderne de la Ville de Paris. C.C. 167

The Lovely Madame X. Tempera. $14^1/_4 \times 10''$. Signed upper right and lower left. Private collection, New York. C.C. 172

Monsieur Z. Small size. Signed and dated lower left. C.C. 171

Woman in a Green Dress. Tempera. $11^3/_4 \times 7^1/_4''$. Signed and dated lower left. Private collection, Paris. C.C. 173

Outcasts. Watercolor, heightened with gouache and ink. $7^1/_2 \times 12''$. Signed lower right. Ex-collection Girardin; Musée d'Art Moderne de la Ville de Paris. C.C. 194

Red Clown. Gouache. $11^1/_4 \times 7''$. Private collection, Winterthur, Switzerland. C.C. 154

Monk, Profile. Gouache. $18^1/_4 \times 13''$. Private collection, Berne. C.C. 168

1916

Grotesque. Colored inks, and brush drawing. $14^3/_4 \times 9^1/_2''$. Signed and dated lower center right. Private collection, Paris. C.C. 187

Grotesque. Brush drawing and colored inks. $14^1/_2 \times 9^1/_2''$. Signed lower right. Private collection, Paris. C.C. 188

Bestiary. Brush drawing and colored inks. $14^1/_2 \times 8^1/_4''$. Signed and dated lower right. Private collection, Paris. C.C. 193

Bestiary. Brush drawing and colored inks. $14^3/_4 \times 9^1/_2''$. Signed and dated lower right. Private collection, Paris. C.C. 195

1917

Portrait of the Painter Lebasque. Watercolor. $24 \times 19^3/_4''$. Signed with monogram and dated upper left. Collection Katia Granoff, Paris. Page 232

The Old Clown. Oil. $40 \times 29^3/_4''$. Signed and dated lower right. Collection Stavros Niarchos. Page 213

Clowning. Oil. Large size. Signed lower right. Private collection. C.C. 155

Bureaucrat. Brush drawing and watercolor. $11^3/_4 \times 6^3/_4''$. Signed and dated upper right. Private collection. C.C. 169

Grotesque. Colored inks, pastel, and gouache. $14^3/_4 \times 9^1/_2''$. Signed and dated lower right. Ex-collection Girardin; Musée d'Art Moderne de la Ville de Paris. C.C. 189

Grotesque. Colored inks and brush drawing. $15 \times 10''$. Signed lower left. Private collection, Paris. C.C. 190

Grotesque. Colored inks and brush drawing. $11^3/_4 \times 7^1/_2''$. Signed lower right. Private collection, Paris. C.C. 191

Nude. India ink. $15^1/_4 \times 9^1/_4''$. Signed lower right. Private collection, Winterthur, Switzerland. C.C. 196

Three Clowns. Oil. $41^1/_2 \times 29^1/_2''$. Signed lower right. Collection Joseph Pulitzer Jr., Saint Louis. C.C. 156

1918

Crucifixion. Oil. $41 \times 29''$. Signed lower right. Collection Henry P. McIlhenny, Philadelphia. C.C. 148

Vice Squad (for *Ubu*). Brush drawing. $13 \times 8^3/_4''$. Signed lower right. Ex-collection Girardin; Musée d'Art Moderne de la Ville de Paris. C.C. 163

For "Ubu". India ink. Signed and dated lower center. Private collection, Paris. C.C. 164

The Wandering Jew. India ink brush drawing. $11^1/_2 \times 7^1/_2''$. Signed lower right. Ex-collection Girardin; Musée d'Art Moderne de la Ville de Paris. C.C. 170

Arab. Gouache. $15 \times 10''$. Signed lower right. Private collection, Clarens, Switzerland. C.C. 198

1920

Pierrot. Oil. $39^1/_4 \times 28^1/_4''$. Stedelijk Museum, Amsterdam. Page 216

Christ in the Suburbs. $35^3/_4 \times 28^1/_4''$. Signed and dated left center. Collection Fukushima, Tokyo. Page 215

Lawyer Pleading. Gouache. $9^1/_2 \times 15^3/_4''$. Signed lower left. Private collection, Berne. C.C. 197

Christmas Landscape. Gouache. $19 \times 26^1/_2''$. Private collection, Switzerland. Page 153

Four Bathers. Oil. $29^1/_2 \times 39^3/_4''$. Signed lower left. Private collection, Switzerland. C.C. 199

1922

Miserere (No. 3): (*Jesus Spurned, Forever Flagellated*). Etching. $21^3/_4 \times 15^5/_8''$. Page 368

Miserere (No. 16): (*Lady of High Society Thinks She Can Take a Reserved Seat for Heaven*). Etching. $19^5/_8 \times 13^3/_4''$. Page 371

1923

Dancer. Oil. $16^1/_2 \times 11^3/_4''$. Signed and dated lower right. Private collection, Japan. C.C. 160

1924

Three Judges. Oil. $30 \times 41^1/_2''$. Private collection, Switzerland. Page 187

1925

Woman with Red Flower. Oil. $26^1/_2 \times 19^3/_4''$. Signed and dated lower right. Private collection, Switzerland. Page 217

Self-Portrait. Wash and lithograph crayon. $8^1/_4 \times 6^1/_2''$. Private collection, Paris. Page 209

The Workman's Apprentice (Self-Portrait). Oil. $26 \times 20^1/_2''$. Musée National d'Art Moderne, Paris. Page 199

Circus Women. Oil. Signed and dated lower left. Ex-collection Fukushima. Page 211

Pierrot. Oil. $25^1/_4 \times 18^1/_4''$. Signed lower left. Private collection, Switzerland. Page 191

Dancers with White Dog. Oil. $26^3/_4 \times 19^3/_4''$. Private collection, Switzerland. Page 189

Old Clown with White Dog. Oil. $28^3/_4 \times 19''$. Signed left center. Private collection, Switzerland. Page 195

Nude. Oil. $31^1/_2 \times 23^3/_4''$. Signed lower left. Collection Mr. and Mrs. A. A. Juvilier, New York. Page 157

Little Equestrienne. Oil. $10^1/_4 \times 9''$. Signed upper right. Collection Baugerter, Montreux, Switzerland. C.C. 161

Portrait of Ambroise Vollard.
Drawing in India ink. Page 25

1926

Ile-de-France Landscape. Oil. $8^3/_4 \times 15^3/_4''$. Signed and dated lower left. Private collection, Paris. Page 226

Judges (Danse Macabre, or Fleurs du Mal). Oil. Small size. Private collection, Japan. Page 218

Profile of a Clown. $22^1/_2 \times 15''$. Signed and dated lower left. Private collection, Japan. Page 212

Red-Nosed Clown. Oil. $29^1/_2 \times 20^1/_2''$. Signed lower left. Private collection, Japan. C.C. 157

Green-Nosed Clown. Oil. $26^1/_4 \times 19''$. Signed lower left. Private collection, Japan. C.C. 158

Portrait of a Woman. Oil. $28^1/_2 \times 20^1/_4''$. Private collection, Japan. C.C. 174

Miserere (No. 27): *(Sunt lacrymae rerum).* Etching. $22^5/_8 \times 16^1/_2''$. Page 369

Prostitute. Lithograph. $12^3/_4 \times 8^5/_8''$. Page 364

Buffoon. Lithograph. $13^3/_8 \times 8^5/_8''$. Page 362

Dancer. Oil. $15^3/_4 \times 11^3/_4''$. Private collection, Japan. C.C. 200

Portrait of Gustave Moreau. Lithograph from "Souvenirs Intimes." Page 21

Portrait of Huysmans. Lithograph from "Souvenirs Intimes," $9^5/_8 \times 6^{11}/_{16}''$. Page 23

Portrait of Léon Bloy. Lithograph from "Souvenirs Intimes," $9^7/_{16} \times 6^1/_2''$. Page 23

Portrait of André Suarès. Lithograph from "Souvenirs Intimes," $9^7/_{16} \times 6^7/_8''$. Page 23

1927

Circus Equestrienne. Oil. $28^1/_2 \times 21^1/_4''$. Signed upper right. Private collection, Japan. Page 219

Miserere (No. 47): *(De Profundis).* Etching. $16^7/_8 \times 23^3/_8''$. Page 372

Miserere (No. 8): *(Don't We All Wear Make-Up?).* Etching. $26 \times 16^3/_4''$. Page 370

Equestrienne. Lithograph. $11^7/_{16} \times 29''$. Page 361

Parade. Lithograph. $13 \times 8^5/_8''$. Page 365

1928

Les Réincarnations du Père Ubu. Etching. $11^5/_8 \times 7^{13}/_{16}''$. Page 367

Les Réincarnations du Père Ubu: Frontispiece. Etching. $11^5/_8 \times 7^5/_8''$. Page 366

1929

The Return of Ulysses. Pastel and India ink. $14^5/_8 \times 20^1/_2''$. Signed and dated lower right. C.C. 185

Two Heads in Profile. Pastel and gouache. $11 \times 8^3/_4''$. Signed and dated lower right. Private collection, Switzerland. Page 224

Composition: Two Women. $9^1/_4 \times 8^3/_4''$. Signed and dated upper right. Private collection, Switzerland. Page 225

The Road Is Long (Leftist Neighborhood). Watercolor and pastel. $18^3/_4 \times 13''$. Signed and dated lower left center. Private collection, Switzerland. Page 228

Trio (Mother and Children). Pastel and India ink. Signed and dated lower left. Page 223

Landscape (With Large Trees). Pastel. Signed and dated lower right. Page 222

Russian Ballet. Pastel. Signed lower left. Page 210

The Disciples at Emmaus. Oil. Small size. Private collection, Paris. C.C. 150

Clown's Head. Oil and gouache. $11 \times 9''$. Signed upper right. C.C. 159

Church in a Depressed Area. Pastel and gouache. Small size. Signed and dated lower center. Private collection. C.C. 178

Moving House. Pastel and gouache. Small size. Signed and dated lower left. Private collection. C.C. 180

The Old Wall Went On and On No. 1, Faubourg. Brush drawing, gouache, and pastel. Small size. Signed and dated lower right. Private collection. C.C. 179

Grotesque. Pastel and gouache. $11^1/_2 \times 8^3/_4''$. Signed lower right. Collection Bangerter, Montreux, Switzerland. C.C. 192

Portrait of Maria Lani. Brush drawing and pastel. $19^3/_4 \times 14^3/_4''$. Signed and dated lower right. Private collection, Paris. C.C. 175

Depressed Suburbs. Lithograph. $12^9/_{16} \times 8^5/_8''$. Page 363

1930

Faubourg. Pastel. Signed and dated lower right. Page 229

Cemetery. Pastel. $10^3/_4 \times 18^1/_2''$. Signed and dated lower right. Collection Philippe Leclercq, Hem, France. Page 227

Leftist Neighborhood (Depressed Suburban Area). Pastel. Signed and dated lower right. Page 231

Spanish Woman. Pastel. Signed and dated lower left. Collection Schempp, U.S.A. Page 214

Clowns. Pastel and gouache. $14 \times 18''$. Collection Mr. and Mrs. Richard L. Frank, San Francisco. Page 230

Satan. Brush drawing, gouache, and pastel. $9^1/_2 \times 7^3/_4''$. Signed and dated lower right. Private collection, U.S.A. C.C. 151

The Clown's Family. Gouache and pastel. Small size. Signed and dated lower right. Private collection. C.C. 162

The Fallen Eve (profile). Brush drawing, gouache, and pastel. $10^3/_4 \times 8^1/_4''$. Signed lower left. Private collection, U.S.A. C.C. 176

Tragedienne. Brush drawing, gouache, and pastel. Small size. Signed and dated lower left. C.C. 177

The Old Wall Went On and On No. 2, Faubourg. Brush drawing, gouache, and pastel. Small size. Signed and dated lower right. Private collection. C.C. 182

Prophet of Evil (Leftist Neighborhood). Gouache, and pastel. Small size. Signed and dated lower center. Private collection. C.C. 181

Graveyard. Brush drawing, gouache, and pastel. Small size. Signed lower left. Private collection. C.C. 183

Workers' Demands (Leftwing Neighborhood). Pastel. Signed and dated lower right. C.C. 186

Meeting. Brush drawing, gouache, and pastel. Small size. Signed and dated lower left. Collection Theodore Schempp, U.S.A. C.C.184

Christ Mocked. Pastel. C.C.152

To Pantin (The Funeral). Pastel. C.C.153

The Holy Countenance. Brush drawing, gouache, and pastel. Small size. Signed with monogram lower right. Private collection, Stockholm. C.C.202

Christ on the Cross. Brush drawing, gouache, and pastel. 14³/₄×13³/₄″. Private collection. C.C.149

Figure (study for *Miserere et Guerre*). 40×28³/₄″. Private collection, Paris. Page 221

Circus Trio. Oil. Large size. Signed upper right. The Phillips Collection, Washington, D.C., C.C.201

Period 1931-1939

1931

Gouache for *Les Réincarnations du Père Ubu.* 17×12³/₄″. Signed and dated lower right. Page 284

Head of a Man. Gouache. 15¹/₄×12¹/₄″. Signed and dated center right. Ex-collection Ambroise Vollard; Musée des Beaux-Arts, Basel. C.C.350

Grotesque. Gouache. 7¹/₄×8³/₄″. Signed lower right. Private collection. C.C.406

1932

Gouache for *Le Cirque de l'étoile Filante.* 4×8¹/₂″. Signed with monogram and dated upper right. Private collection. Page 276

Gouache for *Le Cirque de l'étoile Filante.* Signed and dated lower right. Private collection. Page 276

Dancer. Oil. Signed and dated lower center. Private collection. Page 262

The Injured Clown. Oil. 78³/₄×42¹/₄″. Private collection, Paris. Page 258

Dancer and Clown. Gouache. 7¹/₂×8³/₄″. Signed lower left. Ex-collection Ambroise Vollard; Collection Norbert Schimmel, New York. C.C.259

Composition for *Le Cirque de l'étoile Filante.* Gouache. Small size. Signed and dated upper right. Private collection, U.S.A. C.C.304

The Injured Clown. Oil. 78³/₄×47¹/₄″. Signed lower right. Private collection, Paris. C.C.311

Christ Mocked. Oil. 36×28¹/₂″. The Museum of Modern Art, New York. Page 201

The Little Family. Oil. 82×45³/₄″. Signed lower right. Private collection, Paris. Page 205

Reclining Skeleton. Gouache. 3¹/₂×8¹/₂″ (without border), 5¹/₄×11″ (with border). Signed lower right. Page 373

1933

Composition for *Le Cirque de l'étoile Filante.* 13¹/₂×9″. Signed and dated upper left. Private collection. Page 287

The Holy Countenance. Oil. 35³/₄×25¹/₂″. Signed and dated lower right. Musée National d'Art Moderne, Paris. Page 259

The Holy Countenance. Oil. 36×25³/₄″. Signed and dated lower right corner. Musée National d'Art Moderne, Paris, Gift of Mrs. Chester Dale. C.C.203

Man in a Green Coat. Gouache. 15¹/₂×11¹/₂″. Signed and dated upper right. Ex-collection Ambroise Vollard; Musée des Beaux-Arts, Basel. C.C.313

Queen of the Circus. Oil. Signed lower right. Private collection. C.C.374

Satan. Tapestry. 31¹/₂×19⁵/₈″. Tapestry executed in the ateliers of Madame Cuttoli. C.C.254

1934

The Wandering Jew. Gouache. 7¹/₂×8″. Signed and dated lower left. Private collection. Page 263

In the Press the Grape Was Trampled. Oil. 19×24″. Private collection, Paris. Page 265

1935

Christ on the Cross. Gouache. Collection Philippe Leclercq, Hem, France. C.C.211

1936

The Three Judges. Oil. 30³/₄×25¹/₄″. Signed lower right. Ex-collection Ambroise Vollard; The Tate Gallery, London. C.C.346

1937

Passion. Oil. Signed lower center. Page 260

Christ with Disciples. Oil. Small size. Signed lower right. Page 278

Nocturne. Oil. 5×9¹/₂″. Signed lower right. Page 279

Twilight. Oil. 40×28³/₄″. Signed lower right. Page 266

Christ and a Doctor. Oil. 19×12³/₄″. Signed lower left. Ex-collection Ambroise Vollard. Page 280

Pierrette. Oil. 8³/₄×6¹/₄″. Signed lower right. Page 283

Tramp. Oil. 9×7″. Signed lower center. Page 282

Interior. Oil. 24¹/₂×19″. Signed upper left. Page 271

Old Faubourg. Oil. 21¹/₂×27¹/₂″. Signed lower right. Page 267

Judge. Oil. 14¹/₂×9¹/₄″. Signed lower right. Page 261

Benito. Oil. 26¹/₂×21″. Signed lower left. Page 257

Nocturne (Danse Macabre). Oil. 18×13¹/₄″. Signed lower left. Page 270

The Old King. Oil. 30¹/₄×21¹/₄″. Signed lower right. Carnegie Institute, Pittsburgh. Page 237

The Holy Shroud. Oil. Small size. Signed lower right. Ex-collection Ambroise Vollard. C.C.204

The Holy Shroud. Oil. 41¹/₄×29³/₄″. Ex-collection Ambroise Vollard. C.C.205

Christ. Oil. Small size. Signed upper right. Ex-collection Ambroise Vollard. C.C.206

Landscape (The Passion). Oil. Small size. Signed lower left. Ex-collection Ambroise Vollard. C.C.212

Christ Mocked. Oil. 8³/₄×6¹/₄″. Signed lower right. Ex-collection Ambroise Vollard. C.C.213

Landscape (The Passion). Oil. Small size. Signed lower right. Ex-collection Ambroise Vollard. C.C.215

The Passion. Oil. Signed lower right. Ex-collection Ambroise Vollard. C.C.214

The Passion. Oil. 25¹/₂×18¹/₂″. Signed upper right. Ex-collection Ambroise Vollard; Collection Mr. and Mrs. A.A.Juvilier, New York. C.C.216

Christ and Doctor. Oil. Small size. Signed lower left. Ex-collection Ambroise Vollard. C.C.226

Christ and Fishermen. Oil. 12³/₄×16³/₄″. Signed lower left. Ex-collection Ambroise Vollard. C.C.227

Christ and Doctor. Oil. 19×12³/₄″. Signed upper right. Ex-collection Ambroise Vollard. C.C.228

Christ and Doctor. Oil. Small size. Signed upper right. Ex-collection Ambroise Vollard. C.C.229

Christ and Fishermen. Oil. Small size. Signed lower left. Ex-collection Ambroise Vollard. C.C. 230

Christ. Oil. Small size. Signed lower right. Ex-collection Ambroise Vollard. C.C. 231

Christ. Oil. $5^1/_4 \times 10''$. Signed lower center. Ex-collection Ambroise Vollard. C.C. 232.

Christ and Fishermen. Oil. $3^3/_4 \times 8''$. Signed lower right. Ex-collection Ambroise Vollard. C.C. 234

Christ and Disciple. Oil. Medium size. Signed lower right. Ex-collection Ambroise Vollard. C.C. 233

Christ and Poor Man. Oil. $24^1/_4 \times 19''$. Signed lower right. Ex-collection Ambroise Vollard. C.C. 235

Christ and Child. Oil. $41^1/_4 \times 29^1/_4''$. Signed lower right. Ex-collection Ambroise Vollard; Private collection. C.C. 237

Solitary Christ. Oil. $27^3/_4 \times 21^1/_2''$. Signed lower right. Ex-collection Ambroise Vollard. C.C. 236

Stella Matutina (The Passion). Oil. Signed lower right. Ex-collection Ambroise Vollard. C.C. 243

The Prince of Darkness. Oil. $23^3/_4 \times 18^1/_4''$. Signed upper left. Ex-collection Ambroise Vollard. C.C. 250

Satan. Oil. $20^1/_4 \times 15^3/_4''$. Signed lower left. Ex-collection Ambroise Vollard. C.C. 252

The Two Brothers. Oil. $11^3/_4 \times 8''$. Signed lower right. Ex-collection Ambroise Vollard. C.C. 260

Duet. Oil. $13^1/_2 \times 10''$. Signed lower left. Ex-collection Ambroise Vollard. C.C. 261

Male and Female Clowns. Oil. $4^1/_2 \times 8''$. Signed lower right. Ex-collection Ambroise Vollard. C.C. 262

Trio, Clowns. Oil. $6^1/_4 \times 7^1/_2''$. Signed upper right. Ex-collection Ambroise Vollard. C.C. 264

Street Circus. Oil. Small size. Signed lower right. Ex-collection Ambroise Vollard. C.C. 263

Clowns. Oil. Small size. Signed lower right. Ex-collection Ambroise Vollard. C.C. 265

Clowns. Oil Small size. Signed lower left. Ex-collection Ambroise Vollard. C.C. 266

Clowning. Oil. $41^1/_4 \times 29^3/_4''$. Ex-collection Ambroise Vollard. C.C. 267

Clown. Oil. $11 \times 17^3/_4''$. Ex-collection Ambroise Vollard. C.C. 269

English Clown. Oil. $25^3/_4 \times 17''$. Signed upper right. Ex-collection Ambroise Vollard; Collection Stavros Niarchos. C.C. 268

Punch. Oil. $18 \times 12^1/_4''$. Signed lower right. Ex-collection Ambroise Vollard. C.C. 270

Grotesque. Oil. $15^3/_4 \times 10^1/_4''$. Signed lower right. Ex-collection Ambroise Vollard; Private collection. C.C. 271

Clowns. Oil. Small size. Ex-collection Ambroise Vollard. C.C. 272

Trio. Oil. Small size. Signed upper right. Ex-collection Ambroise Vollard. C.C. 273

Pierrot Warrior. Oil. $8^1/_4 \times 6^3/_4''$. Signed center right. Ex-collection Ambroise Vollard. C.C. 274

Circus Girl. Oil. $3^1/_2 \times 3^1/_2''$. Signed upper right. Ex-collection Ambroise Vollard. C.C. 305

Equestrienne. Oil. $21^1/_4 \times 13^3/_4''$. Signed upper left. Ex-collection Ambroise Vollard. C.C. 306

The Dwarf. Oil. $27^1/_4 \times 19^3/_4''$. Signed lower right. Ex-collection Ambroise Vollard; Art Institute of Chicago. C.C. 308

Circus Girl. Oil. $23^1/_4 \times 15^1/_4''$. Signed upper right. Ex-collection Ambroise Vollard. C.C. 307

Street Circus: Parade. Oil. $11 \times 8^1/_2''$. Signed lower right. Ex-collection Ambroise Vollard. C.C. 309

Fleurs du Mal. Oil. $8^1/_4 \times 6''$. Signed lower right. Ex-collection Ambroise Vollard. C.C. 314

Fleurs du Mal. Oil. Small size. Signed lower right. Ex-collection Ambroise Vollard. C.C. 315

Autumn. Oil. $12 \times 8^1/_4''$. Signed lower right. Ex-collection Ambroise Vollard. C.C. 319

Bacchanal. Oil. $26^3/_4 \times 19''$. Signed lower left. Ex-collection Ambroise Vollard. C.C. 320

Legendary Landscape. Oil. Large size. Signed lower right. Ex-collection Ambroise Vollard; Collection Harris Jonas, New York. C.C. 322

Twilight. Oil. Small size. Signed lower right. Ex-collection Ambroise Vollard. C.C. 323

Twilight. Oil. Small size. Signed lower right. Ex-collection Ambroise Vollard. C.C. 324

Landscape (Twilight). Oil. $6^3/_4 \times 11''$. Signed lower right. Ex-collection Ambroise Vollard. C.C. 325

Christ and Fishermen. Oil. $26^3/_4 \times 50^1/_2''$. Signed lower right. Ex-collection Ambroise Vollard; Musée des Beaux-Arts de la Ville de Paris. C.C. 327

Sunset. Oil. $29^1/_4 \times 41^1/_2''$. Signed lower left. Ex-collection Ambroise Vollard; Worcester Art Museum (Loaned by Mrs. Aldus C. Higgins). C.C. 326

Judge. Oil. Medium size. Signed lower right. Ex-collection Ambroise Vollard. C.C. 348

The Provincial Tribunal. Oil. $42^1/_4 \times 28''$. Signed lower right. Ex-collection Ambroise Vollard; Private collection. C.C. 347

The Last Romantic. Oil. $26^1/_2 \times 19^1/_2''$. Signed lower right. Collection Dr. and Mrs. Harry Bakwin. C.C. 352

Antonio. Oil. $15^3/_4 \times 11''$. Signed lower right. Ex-collection Ambroise Vollard. C.C. 351

Butchers. Oil. $15^3/_4 \times 11''$. Signed lower right. Ex-collection Ambroise Vollard. C.C. 354

Father Ox. Oil. $8^1/_4 \times 5^1/_2''$. Signed lower right. Ex-collection Ambroise Vollard. C.C. 353

Soldier. Oil. Signed right. Ex-collection Ambroise Vollard; Private collection. C.C. 355

Profiles. Oil. $4^3/_4 \times 8''$. Signed lower right. Ex-collection Ambroise Vollard. C.C. 357

Chinaman. Oil. $41^1/_2 \times 29^1/_4''$. Signed lower left. Ex-collection Ambroise Vollard; Private collection. C.C. 356

Little Pageboy. Oil. $24^1/_2 \times 17^3/_4''$. Signed lower right. Ex-collection Ambroise Vollard. C.C. 358

Peasants. Oil. Medium size. Signed lower left. Ex-collection Ambroise Vollard. C.C. 359

Peasants. Oil. Medium size. Signed lower right. Ex-collection Ambroise Vollard. C.C. 360

Peasants. Oil. Medium size. Signed lower right. Ex-collection Ambroise Vollard. C.C. 361

Soldier. Oil. Small size. Signed lower right. Ex-collection Ambroise Vollard. C.C. 362

Face to Face. Oil. $12^1/_4 \times 8''$. Signed lower right. Ex-collection Ambroise Vollard. C.C. 376

Madame X. Oil. $8^3/_4 \times 6^3/_4''$. Signed lower left. Ex-collection Ambroise Vollard. C.C. 375

Carlotta. Oil. $15^3/_4 \times 12^1/_4''$. Signed lower right. Ex-collection Ambroise Vollard. C.C. 377

Italian Woman. Oil. $15^3/_4 \times 11^1/_2''$. Signed lower right. Ex-collection Ambroise Vollard. C.C. 379

Spanish Woman. Oil. Medium size. Signed upper right. Ex-collection Ambroise Vollard. C.C. 378

Spanish Woman. Oil. Small size. Signed lower right. Ex-collection Ambroise Vollard. C.C. 381

Little Country Girl. Oil. 10¼×14". Signed lower right. Ex-collection Ambroise Vollard. C.C. 380

Little Serving-Girl. Oil. 11¾×8". Signed lower right. Ex-collection Ambroise Vollard. C.C. 382

Marie. Oil. 20¼×13". Signed lower right. Ex-collection Ambroise Vollard; Private collection, Paris. C.C. 383

Walker-On. Oil. 14¾×10½". Signed lower left. Ex-collection Ambroise Vollard. C.C. 385

Old Arab. Oil. 11×8¼". Signed lower right. Ex-collection Ambroise Vollard. C.C. 390

Levantine Woman. Oil. 23¾×17". Signed lower right. Ex-collection Ambroise Vollard. C.C. 389

Moroccan Woman. Oil. 15½×11½". Signed lower right. Ex-collection Ambroise Vollard. C.C. 391

Flowers. Oil. 11¾×8". Signed lower right. Ex-collection Ambroise Vollard. C.C. 405

War. Oil. 15×11". Signed lower left. Ex-collection Ambroise Vollard. C.C. 407

In the Old Faubourg. Oil. 36¼×28½". Signed lower right. Page 273

Street Circus. Oil. Small size. Signed lower center. Page 286

Pierrot. Oil. 21¾×15¾". Signed lower left. Page 268

Pierrot. Oil. Medium size. Signed upper right. Page 269

1938

Frontispiece. Oil. Small size. Signed lower left. Page 277

Frontispiece for *Fleurs du Mal.* Oil. 5¼×10¼". Signed lower right. Page 277

Head of Christ (Passion). Oil. 41¼×29½". Cleveland Museum of Art, Gift of Hanna Fund. Page 281

Interior of a Church in Brittany. Oil. 42½×27¾". Signed lower right. Page 272

Old Faubourg. Oil. Large size. Signed lower right. Page 288

Peasant Woman. Oil. 40¾×29¼". Signed lower right. Page 275

The Passion. Oil. Small size. Signed lower right. Ex-collection Ambroise Vollard. C.C. 224

Christ Mocked. Oil. 26½×19¼". Signed lower right. Ex-collection Ambroise Vollard. C.C. 225

Christ and Lepers. Oil. 12¾×19¾". Signed lower right. Ex-collection Ambroise Vollard. C.C. 244

Darkness. Oil. 14¼×22". Signed lower right. Ex-collection Ambroise Vollard; Collection Philippe Leclercq, Hem, France. C.C. 251

Satan. Oil. 7½×6¾". Signed lower right. Ex-collection Ambroise Vollard. C.C. 253

The Bay of Departed Souls. Oil. 23×17½". Signed lower right. Private collection, Paris. C.C. 256

The Rising of the Dead. Oil. 8¾×6¾". Signed lower right. Ex-collection Ambroise Vollard. C.C. 258

De Profundis. Oil. 9×10". Signed lower right. Ex-collection Ambroise Vollard. C.C. 257

Harlequin. Oil. 18¼×12¾". Signed lower right. Ex-collection Ambroise Vollard. C.C. 294

Pierrot and Animal Trainer. Oil. 9½×10¼". Signed lower right. Ex-collection Ambroise Vollard. C.C. 296

Young Clown. Oil. 15¾×11½". Signed lower right. Ex-collection Ambroise Vollard. C.C. 295

Clown. Oil. 23×16¼". Signed lower right. Ex-collection Ambroise Vollard. C.C. 297

Cirque de l'étoile Filante. Oil. 28½×21". Signed lower right. Ex-

collection Ambroise Vollard; Collection Gottlieb, New York. C.C. 312

Ubu Awakening. Oil. 19×24½". Signed lower right. Ex-collection Ambroise Vollard. C.C. 317

Autumn. Oil. 40¼× about 26¾". Signed lower right. Ex-collection Ambroise Vollard; Private collection. C.C. 331

Stella Matutina. Oil. 6×10". Signed lower left. Ex-collection Ambroise Vollard. C.C. 333

Legendary Landscape (Christ and Fairground People). Oil. 26×40¼". Signed lower right. Ex-collection Ambroise Vollard; Private collection. C.C. 334

Stella Matutina. Oil. Medium size. Signed lower right. Ex-collection Ambroise Vollard. C.C. 336

Landscape (Legendary Landscape). Oil. 29¼×21½". Signed lower right. Ex-collection Ambroise Vollard. C.C. 335

Morning. Oil. 21½×27¾". Signed lower right. Ex-collection Ambroise Vollard. C.C. 337

Autumn. Oil. Medium size. Signed lower right. Ex-collection Ambroise Vollard. C.C. 338

Legendary Landscape. Oil. Large size. Signed lower right. Ex-collection Ambroise Vollard; Private collection. C.C. 339

Stella Matutina. Oil. 6×10". Signed lower right. Ex-collection Ambroise Vollard. C.C. 340

Stella Vespertina. Oil. 7¾×10¼". Signed lower right. Ex-collection Ambroise Vollard. C.C. 342

The Provincial Tribunal. Oil. 40×25¾". Signed lower right. Ex-collection Ambroise Vollard; Private collection. C.C. 349

Civil Servant Oil. 8¾×7". Signed lower right. Ex-collection Ambroise Vollard. C.C. 365

Diplomat. Oil. 12¼×8¾". Signed lower right. Ex-collection Ambroise Vollard; Musées Royaux des Beaux-Arts, Brussels. C.C. 366

Monsieur Louis. Oil. 15¾×11½". Signed lower right. Ex-collection Ambroise Vollard. C.C. 367

Peasants. Oil. 6×10". Signed lower right. Ex-collection Ambroise Vollard. C.C. 368

The Two Friends. Oil. 6¾×10¾". Signed lower right. Ex-collection Ambroise Vollard. C.C. 370

Gypsy. Oil. 15½×11½". Signed lower right. Ex-collection Ambroise Vollard. C.C. 369

Veronica. Oil. 15¾×10¾". Signed lower left. Ex-collection Ambroise Vollard. C.C. 386

Levantine Woman. Oil. 8¾×7". Signed lower right. Ex-collection Ambroise Vollard. C.C. 396

Levantine Man. Oil. 6×11½". Signed lower right. Ex-collection Ambroise Vollard. C.C. 398

Arab Noblemen. Oil. 7¼×10¾". Signed lower right. Ex-collection Ambroise Vollard. C.C. 397

Arabs. Oil. Small size. Signed lower left. Ex-collection Ambroise Vollard. C.C. 395

Faubourg of Toil and Suffering. Oil. 12¾×19¼". Signed lower right. Ex-collection Ambroise Vollard. C.C. 403

Project for a Fountain in Memory of Cézanne. Oil. 41½×29½". Signed lower right. Ex-collection Ambroise Vollard; Private collection. C.C. 408

Wild Animal. Oil. 10¾×16¼". Signed lower right. Ex-collection Ambroise Vollard. C.C. 409

Pierrot. Oil. 8×10¼". Signed lower right. Page 264

Pierrot. Oil. Small size. Signed lower right. Page 285

Head of Christ. Oil. 26½×19". Signed lower right. Private collection, Paris. Page 239

The Holy Shroud. Oil. Medium size. Ex-collection Ambroise Vollard; Private collection. C.C. 207

Christ. Oil. $27^1/_4 \times 21^3/_4''$. Signed lower right. Ex-collection Ambroise Vollard; Collection H.B., Brussels. C.C. 208

The Holy Shroud. Oil. Medium size. Signed lower right. Ex-collection Ambroise Vollard. C.C. 209

Christ. Oil. Small size. Signed lower right. Ex-collection Ambroise Vollard. C.C. 210

The Passion. Oil. Small size. Signed lower right. Ex-collection Ambroise Vollard. C.C. 217

The Passion. Oil. Small size. Signed lower right. Ex-collection Ambroise Vollard. C.C. 218

The Passion. Oil. Small size. Signed lower right. Ex-collection Ambroise Vollard. C.C. 219

The Passion. Oil. Small size. Signed lower right. Ex-collection Ambroise Vollard. C.C. 221

The Passion. Oil. Small size. Signed lower right. Ex-collection Ambroise Vollard. C.C. 220

The Passion. Oil. Small size. Signed lower right. Ex-collection Ambroise Vollard. C.C. 222

Christ and Disciples. Oil. Small size. Signed lower left. Ex-collection Ambroise Vollard. C.C. 241

Christ and Disciples. Oil. Medium size. Signed lower right. Ex-collection Ambroise Vollard. C.C. 239

Christ and Two Figures. Oil. $41^1/_2 \times 29^1/_2''$. Signed lower right. Ex-collection Ambroise Vollard; Private collection. C.C. 240

Christ and Doctors. Oil. Large size. Signed lower right. Ex-collection Ambroise Vollard; Collection Jacques Gelman, Mexico. C.C. 238

Christ in a Room with Three Figures. Oil. Signed lower right. Ex-collection Ambroise Vollard; Private collection. C.C. 242

Stella Matutina (The Passion). Oil. Signed lower right. Ex-collection Ambroise Vollard; Private collection. C.C. 243

The Flight into Egypt. Oil. $16^1/_4 \times 10^3/_4''$. Signed lower left. Musée des Beaux-Arts de la Ville de Paris. C.C. 245

Polycarp. Oil. $39^3/_4 \times 26^1/_2''$. Ex-collection Ambroise Vollard; Collection Mme. Hafter-Kottmann, Solothurn, Switzerland. C.C. 275

Pierrot. Oil. Small size. Signed lower right. Ex-collection Ambroise Vollard. C.C. 276

Pierrot. Oil. Small size. Signed lower right. Ex-collection Ambroise Vollard. C.C. 277

Pierrot. Oil. Small size. Signed lower right. Ex-collection Ambroise Vollard; Private collection. C.C. 278

Pierrot. Oil. Large size. Signed lower right. Ex-collection Ambroise Vollard. C.C. 279

Pierrot. Oil. Large size. Signed lower left. Ex-collection Ambroise Vollard. C.C. 280

Pierrot. Oil. Large size. Signed lower right. Ex-collection Ambroise Vollard. C.C. 281

Pierrot. Oil. Signed lower left. Ex-collection Ambroise Vollard. C.C. 282

Pierrot. Oil. Signed lower right. Ex-collection Ambroise Vollard. C.C. 283

Pierrot. Oil. Large size. Signed lower right. Ex-collection Ambroise Vollard. C.C. 284

Blue Pierrot. Oil. Medium size. Ex-collection Ambroise Vollard. C.C. 285

Pierrot. Oil. Signed lower right. Ex-collection Ambroise Vollard. C.C. 286

Pierrot. Oil. Signed lower right. Ex-collection Ambroise Vollard. C.C. 287

Pierrot. Oil. Medium size. Signed upper right. Ex-collection Ambroise Vollard. C.C. 288

Pierrot. Oil. Small size. Ex-collection Ambroise Vollard. C.C. 289

Pierrot. Oil. Medium size. Signed lower right. Ex-collection Ambroise Vollard. C.C. 291

Pierrot and Punch. Oil. Small size. Ex-collection Ambroise Vollard. C.C. 290

Pierrot. Oil. Small size. Signed lower right. Ex-collection Ambroise Vollard. C.C. 292

Pierrot. Oil. Large size. Signed lower right. Ex-collection Ambroise Vollard; Collection Mr. and Mrs. Nathan. Cummings, U.S.A. C.C. 293

Pierrot. Oil. $29^1/_4 \times 21^1/_4''$. Signed lower right. Musée des Beaux-Arts de la Ville de Paris. C.C. 298

Yellow Clown. Oil. $14^3/_4 \times 10^3/_4''$. Musée des Beaux-Arts de la Ville de Paris. C.C. 300

Grotesques (Circus). Oil. $21 \times 28^3/_4''$. Signed lower right. Ex-collection Ambroise Vollard; Collection Philippe Leclercq, Hem, France. C.C. 299

Circus Girl. Oil. Small size. Signed lower left. Ex-collection Ambroise Vollard. C.C. 310

Pierrot. Oil. Signed lower right. Ex-collection Ambroise Vollard C.C. 303

Twilight. Oil. $30 \times 22''$. Signed lower right. Collection Philippe Leclercq. Hem, France. C.C. 328

Twilight. Oil. Large size. Signed lower right. Ex-collection Ambroise Vollard; Private collection. C.C. 330

Nocturne. Oil. $27^5/_8 \times 21^5/_8''$. Signed lower right. Ex-collection Ambroise Vollard. C.C. 345

Autumn. Oil. Large size. Ex-collection Ambroise Vollard; Private collection. C.C. 329

Landscape. Oil. Small size. Signed lower right. Ex-collection Ambroise Vollard. C.C. 332

Soldiers. Oil. Small size. Signed lower right. Ex-collection Ambroise Vollard. C.C. 363

Soldiers. Oil. Small size. Signed lower right. Ex-collection Ambroise Vollard. C.C. 364

Spanish Woman. Oil. Small size. Signed upper left. Ex-collection Ambroise Vollard; Private collection. C.C. 384

Arabs. Oil. Small size. Signed lower right. Ex-collection Ambroise Vollard. C.C. 392

Arabs. Oil. Small size. Signed lower right. Ex-collection Ambroise Vollard. C.C. 394

Arabs. Oil. Small size. Signed lower left. Ex-collection Ambroise Vollard. C.C. 393

Old Faubourg. Oil. Signed lower right. Ex-collection Ambroise Vollard. C.C. 249

Old Faubourg. Oil. Medium size. Signed lower right. Ex-collection Ambroise Vollard; Private collection. C.C. 399

Old Faubourg. Oil. Medium size. Signed lower right. Ex-collection Ambroise Vollard. C.C. 401

Faubourg of Toil and Suffering. Oil. Signed lower right. Ex-collection Ambroise Vollard. C.C. 247

Old Faubourg. Oil. Medium size. Signed lower right. Ex-collection Ambroise Vollard. C.C. 400

Still Life. Oil. $32 \times 25^3/_4''$. Signed lower right. Musée de Valenciennes, France. C.C. 410

1939

Head of Christ. Oil. $21^5/_8 \times 17^3/_4''$. Signed lower right. Ex-collection Ambroise Vollard. C.C. 223

Crucifixion. Oil. $25^1/_2 \times 19^1/_4''$. Private collection, Paris. Page 274

Christ Mocked. Oil. $23^3/_4 \times 16^1/_2''$. Ex-collection Ambroise Vollard; The Abrams family collection, New York. Page 241

Christ and Sick Man. Oil. $22^1/_2 \times 17''$. Signed lower right. Collection Mme. Busvine, Pont-de-Larn, France. C.C. 246

Gilles. Oil. $26 \times 18^1/_2''$. Signed lower left. Ex-collection Ambroise Vollard; Collection Philippe Leclercq, Hem, France. C.C. 302

Père Ubu out for a Walk. Oil. $26^3/_4 \times 20^1/_2''$. Signed lower right. Collection G. B. Fischer, Germany. C.C. 316

Grotesque for "Ubu." Gouache. Signed lower center. Ex-collection Ambroise Vollard. C.C. 318

Nocturne. Oil. $19^3/_4 \times 26^3/_4''$. Signed lower right. Ex-collection Ambroise Vollard; Collection Philippe Leclercq, Hem, France. C.C. 344

Matutina. Oil. $28^3/_4 \times 21''$. Signed lower right. Ex-collection Ambroise Vollard; Collection Philippe Leclercq, Hem, France. C.C. 343

Monk. Oil. $25^3/_4 \times 19^3/_4''$. Signed lower right. Collection Evelyn Pumphrey, Santa Monica, California. C.C. 372

Head. Oil. C.C. 373

War (Two Soldiers). Oil. $22^1/_2 \times 16^1/_2''$. Signed lower right. Ex-collection Ambroise Vollard; Private collection, Geneva. C.C. 371

A Woman (for "Miserere"). Oil. Signed lower right. Ex-collection Ambroise Vollard; Private collection. C.C. 387

Pierrette. Oil. $24^1/_2 \times 18''$. Signed lower right. Ex-collection Ambroise Vollard; Musée des Beaux-Arts, Basel. C.C. 388

Old Faubourg of Toil and Suffering. Oil. $25 \times 19^1/_2''$. Signed lower right. Ex-collection Ambroise Vollard; Collection Mr. and Mrs. Werner E. Josten, New York. C.C. 402

Workers' Suburb. Oil. $20^1/_4 \times 15^3/_8''$. Signed lower right. Ex-collection Ambroise Vollard. C.C. 404

Russian Ballet. Oil. Signed lower right. Private collection, U.S.A. C.C. 411

In the Press, the Grape was Trodden (Miserere). Oil. $19^3/_4 \times 25^3/_4''$. Signed lower right. Ex-collection Ambroise Vollard; Private collection, U.S.A. C.C. 412

Biblical Landscape. Oil. $27^1/_4 \times 21^1/_4''$. Signed lower right. Ex-collection Girardin; Musée des Beaux-Arts de la Ville de Paris. C.C. 341

Equestrienne. Gouache. $18^1/_2 \times 15^1/_2''$. Private collection, Paris. Page 207

Acrobat. Oil. C.C. 413

Pierrot. Oil. $20^7/_8 \times 13^3/_4''$. Signed lower right. Collection Rothschild, Paris. C.C. 301

Decorative Figures. Pastel. Signed lower left. C.C. 321

The Bluebird. Brush drawing, oil and gouache. $23 \times 16^1/_2''$. Private collection, Paris. Page 235

Christ and Doctor. Oil. $10^3/_4 \times 10^3/_4''$. Signed lower right. Ex-collection Ambroise Vollard; Private collection. C.C. 248

Satan. Oil. Small size. Signed lower right. C.C. 255

Period 1940–1948

1941

Pierrot as Aristocrat. Oil. $44^1/_4 \times 28''$. Page 243

Kindly Bernard. Gouache. $12^1/_4 \times 9^1/_2''$. Signed lower right. Collection Tériade, France. C.C. 462

Black Pierrot. Gouache. $13 \times 8^1/_2''$. Signed upper right. Collection Tériade, France. C.C. 475

Two Stubborn Men. Gouache. $12^3/_4 \times 9^1/_2''$. Signed lower right. Collection Tériade, France. C.C. 463

White Pierrot. Gouache. $10^3/_4 \times 8^1/_2''$. Signed lower left. Collection Tériade, France. C.C. 464

Wastrel. Gouache. $12^3/_4 \times 9^1/_2''$. Signed lower left. Collection Tériade, France. C.C. 465

Little Pageboy in Red and Gold. Gouache. $12^1/_4 \times 10''$. Signed lower center right. Collection Tériade, France. C.C. 466

The Mocker. Gouache. $11^3/_4 \times 10^1/_4''$. Signed lower right. Collection Tériade, France. C.C. 467

Madame YXE. Gouache. $11 \times 8^3/_4''$. Signed lower left. Collection Tériade, France. C.C. 468

The Two Elders. Gouache. $11 \times 8^3/_4''$. Signed lower left. Collection Tériade, France. C.C. 469

Dancers. Gouache. $11 \times 9''$. Signed lower right. Collection Tériade, France. C.C. 470

Acrobat. Gouache. $10^3/_4 \times 8^3/_4''$. Signed lower right. Collection Tériade, France. C.C. 471

Wotthehell. Gouache. Signed lower center right. Collection Tériade, France. C.C. 472

Russalka. Gouache. Signed lower left. Collection Tériade, France. C.C. 473

Margot. Gouache. $12 \times 9^1/_2''$. Signed lower right. Collection Tériade, France. C.C. 474

1942

Christ Mocked. Oil. $41^1/_2 \times 29^3/_4''$. Museum of Art, Stuttgart. Page 307

Christ on the Cross. Oil. $25^1/_2 \times 20''$. Page 314

Thousand and One Nights. Oil. $22^3/_4 \times 17^1/_2''$. Page 325

The Flight into Egypt. Oil. Page 308

Pablo, the Spaniard. Oil. $16^1/_2 \times 11^1/_2''$. Private collection, Paris. Page 316

Winter. Oil. $13^3/_4 \times 17^1/_2''$. Page 312

Stella Vespertina (Landscape). Oil. $22 \times 17^1/_2''$. Signed lower left. Collection Galérie Louis Carré, Paris. C.C. 424

Christ and Fishermen. Oil. $23 \times 29^1/_2''$. Signed lower left. Collection Galérie Louis Carré, Paris. C.C. 423

Christ and Disciple. Oil. $11^1/_2 \times 15''$. Signed lower left. Collection Galérie Louis Carré, Paris. C.C. 425

Little Pierrot with Bouquet. Oil. $12^1/_4 \times 8^1/_4''$. Signed lower right. Collection Galérie Louis Carré, Paris. C.C. 441

Little Equestrienne. Oil. $21 \times 15^3/_4''$. Signed left center. Collection Galérie Louis Carré, Paris. C.C. 459

Circus. Oil. $26^3/_4 \times 20^1/_2''$. Signed lower left. Ex-collection Ambroise Vollard; Private collection, U.S.A. C.C. 460

Little Flower for a Tapestry. Oil. $14 \times 10''$. Signed lower left. Collection Galérie Louis Carré, Paris. C.C. 514

1943

Harlequin (Divertissement). Gouache. $11^1/_4 \times 9''$. Collection Tériade, France. Page 320

Passion. Oil. 41×29". Signed lower center. Ex-collection Ambroise Vollard; Collection Mr. and Mrs. Leigh B. Block, Chicago. Page 245

Reflective Pierrot. Oil. 29¹/₂×22". Signed center right. Collection Mr. and Mrs. Alex Hillman, New York. C.C. 442

Trio. Oil. 28¹/₂×22¹/₂". Signed lower left. Collection Philippe Leclercq, Hem, France. C.C. 443

Duet. Oil. 25³/₄×19³/₄". Signed lower right. Collection H.B., Brussels. C.C. 444

The Two Brothers. Oil. 29¹/₄×21". Signed lower right. Collection Galérie Louis Carré, Paris. C.C. 446

Pierrots. Oil. 23¹/₄×17³/₄". Signed lower left. Private collection, Paris. C.C. 445

1944

Biblical Landscape. Oil. Small size. Signed lower right. Private collection. C.C. 426

1945

Teresina (Agnes). Oil. 17¹/₂×12³/₄". Private collection. Page 317

Legendary Trio. Oil. 10³/₄×10¹/₂". Private collection. Page 313

Church Interior. Oil. 22×16¹/₂". Signed lower left. Private collection, Paris. C.C. 418

The Bridge. Oil. Small size. Signed lower left center. Private collection. C.C. 428

Pamphilius. Oil. 13×10¹/₄". Signed lower right. Private collection. C.C. 447

Fleurs du Mal (Figure Seen from the Front). Oil. 9×10¹/₄". Signed with monogram lower left. Ex-collection Ambroise Vollard; Private collection. C.C. 476

Fleurs du Mal (Figure Seen in Profile). Oil. 11×9¹/₄". Signed center toward right. Ex-collection Ambroise Vollard; Private collection. C.C. 477

Frontispiece for "Les Fleurs du Mal". Oil. 10×8". Signed lower left. Ex-collection Ambroise Vollard; Private collection. C.C. 478

De Profundis (Winter). Oil. 13×10". Signed lower left. Ex-collection Ambroise Vollard; Collection Mr. and Mrs. Nathan Cummings, U.S.A. C.C. 479

Oriental Woman (The Old Orient). Oil. 13¹/₄×12¹/₄". Signed lower left. Ex-collection Ambroise Vollard; Collection Mr. and Mrs. Nathan Cummings, U.S.A. C.C. 481

Autumn. Oil. 11¹/₂×7¹/₂". Signed lower right. Collection Norbert Schimmel, New York. C.C. 480

Christ and Disciples. Oil. 10¹/₂×16". Signed lower right. Ex-collection Ambroise Vollard; Private collection. C.C. 482

Jacob's Well. Oil. 12³/₄×20". Signed lower right. Ex-collection Ambroise Vollard; Collection Mr. and Mrs. Nathan Cummings, U.S.A. C.C. 484

Twilight. Oil. 8×16¹/₂". Collection B. Serger, New York. C.C. 485

Fugitive. Oil. 14³/₄×19". Signed lower right. Ex-collection Ambroise Vollard; Private collection. C.C. 486

Moonlight. Oil. 13¹/₂×16¹/₂". Signed lower right. Collection Norbert Schimmel, New York. C.C. 487

Neapolitan. Oil. 18¹/₄×12³/₄". Signed lower right. Private collection, Paris. C.C. 497

Bestiary. Oil. 10×10¹/₄". Signed lower left. Ex-collection Ambroise Vollard; Private collection. C.C. 528

Courtier. Oil. 10×6³/₄". Signed lower right. Ex-collection Ambroise Vollard; Private collection. C.C. 527

Bouquet with Fruit. Oil. 14×9¹/₂". Private collection. Page 324

Veronica. Oil. 19³/₄×14¹/₄". Signed lower right. Private collection, Paris. Page 249

Pierrot with Bouquet. Oil. 9¹/₂×7¹/₂". Signed lower right. C.C. 461

The Flight into Egypt. Oil. 24×18¹/₂". Signed lower right. Private collection, Paris. Page 251

Christian Spirit (Christ in the House of Martha and Mary). Oil. 18¹/₄×25³/₄". Signed lower right. Private collection, Paris. Page 253

Fragment for *The Child Jesus Among the Doctors*. Oil. 14³/₄×8¹/₄". Signed lower left. Private collection, Paris. C.C. 417

The Aristocrat. Oil. Medium size. Signed upper right. Private collection, Paris. C.C. 448

Clown. Oil. Medium size. Signed lower left. Private collection. C.C. 449

Nocturne. Oil. 8×9¹/₂". Signed lower right. Collection Philippe Leclercq, Hem, France. C.C. 483

Gay Dog. Oil. 12³/₄×8¹/₄". Private collection. C.C. 498

Saint Martha. Oil. 20¹/₄×13³/₄". Signed lower right. Private collection, Paris. C.C. 504

Profile. Oil. 11¹/₄×7¹/₄". Signed lower left. Private collection, France. C.C. 503

1946

Stella Vespertina. Oil. 19×13³/₄". Private collection, Paris. Page 311

De Profundis. Oil. 25³/₄×20¹/₄". Signed lower right. Musée National d'Art Moderne, Paris. C.C. 419

The Road. Oil. 7¹/₄×20¹/₂". Signed lower right. Private collection, Dublin. C.C. 427

Landscape with Big Trees. Oil. 27³/₄×12¹/₂". Signed lower right. Musée National d'Art Moderne, Paris. C.C. 430

Jim. Oil. Signed upper right. Private collection. C.C. 450

Graveyard. Oil. 10³/₄×10³/₄". Signed lower right. Private collection, France. C.C. 488

Dreamer. Oil. 13¹/₂×10¹/₂". Signed lower right. Musée National d'Art Moderne, Paris. C.C. 499

The Advocate Testu. Oil. 11×8". Signed lower right. Private collection, Paris. C.C. 500

Louisette. Oil. 11¹/₂×7¹/₄". Signed lower right. Private collection, Paris. C.C. 505

Decorative Flowers. Oil. 24¹/₂×21". Signed lower right. Musée National d'Art Moderne, Paris. C.C. 515

Decorative Flowers. Oil. Small size. Signed lower right. Private collection. C.C. 516

Decorative Flowers. Oil. 14¹/₂×10¹/₄". Private collection, Paris. Page 310

The Holy Countenance. Oil. 19³/₄×14¹/₄". Signed lower right. Private collection, Paris. Page 293

The Flight into Egypt. Oil. Signed lower right. Private collection, Dublin. C.C. 420

Bethany. Oil. Signed upper right. Private collection, France. C.C. 416

Nazareth. Oil. 14¹/₄×19³/₄". Signed lower right. Musée de Gand (Ghent), Belgium. C.C. 429

Little Pierrots. Oil. Signed lower right. Private collection, Paris. C.C. 451

Old Versailles. Oil. 7¹/₄×10³/₄". Signed lower right. Private collection, Japan. C.C. 489

Veteran (In Memory of H. Rupp). Oil. 17³/₄×8¹/₄". Signed lower right. Private collection, Paris. C.C. 501

Decorative Flowers. Oil. $12^3/_4 \times 8''$. Signed lower right. Private collection, Paris. C.C. 517

John Everyman. Oil. Small size. Signed lower right. Private collection, Paris. C.C. 521

Winter. Oil. $10^5/_8 \times 10^5/_8''$. Signed lower right. Private collection, France. C.C. 492

Winter. Oil and gouache. $15^3/_4 \times 12^1/_4''$. Signed lower left. Private collection, France. C.C. 522

Autumn. Oil. $19 \times 13^3/_4''$. Signed lower left. Private collection, Paris. C.C. 523

1947

The King of the Golden Isles. Oil. $19 \times 13''$. Private collection, U.S.A. Page 323

Harlequin. Oil. $15^1/_2 \times 14^1/_4''$. Private collection, Paris. Page 305

Carmencita. Oil. $19^3/_4 \times 12^1/_2''$. Private collection, Milan. Page 318

Teresina. Oil. $20 \times 13^3/_4''$. Private collection. Page 322

The Sibyl of Cumae. Oil. $20^1/_2 \times 14^3/_4''$. Signed lower right. Private collection, Paris. Page 297

The Redhead. Oil. $15^3/_4 \times 13''$ (or $18^1/_2 \times 13''$). Signed lower right. Private collection, Paris. C.C. 452

Judge. Oil. $12^3/_4 \times 8''$. Signed lower right. Private collection, Paris. C.C. 494

Judges. Oil. $12^1/_4 \times 9^1/_2''$. Signed lower right. C.C. 495

Judge. Oil. $4 \times 5^1/_2''$. Signed lower left. Ex-collection Theodore Schempp, U.S.A. C.C. 496

Decorative Flowers. Oil. $22^1/_2 \times 15^1/_2''$. Signed lower right. Private collection, France. C.C. 519

Decorative Flowers. Oil. $21^1/_4 \times 15^1/_2''$. Signed lower right. Private collection. C.C. 518

Decorative Flowers. Oil. $22 \times 15^3/_4''$. Signed lower right. Private collection, France. C.C. 520

Duet. Oil. Collection Norbert Schimmel, New York. Page 327

The Little Church. Oil. $19^1/_4 \times 12^3/_4''$. Signed lower right. Private collection, France. C.C. 421

On the Banks of the Jordan. Oil. $17^1/_2 \times 13^1/_2''$. Signed lower left. Musée de Dijon, France. C.C. 431

Biblical Landscape. Oil. $14^1/_4 \times 16^1/_4''$. Signed lower right. Private collection, France. C.C. 432

Biblical Landscape. Oil. $14 \times 19^3/_4''$. Signed lower right. Private collection, Paris. C.C. 433

Winter Twilight. Oil. $20^1/_4 \times 14^1/_4''$. Signed lower right. Private collection, Japan. C.C. 434

The Road. Oil. Signed lower right. Collection Ahrenberg, Stockholm. C.C. 439

Old Faubourg. Oil. $19^5/_8 \times 14^1/_8''$. Signed lower right. C.C. 526

Biblical Landscape. Oil. $20^1/_4 \times 14^1/_2''$. Signed lower left. Private collection, Paris. C.C. 435

Brothers' Duet. Oil. Medium size. Signed lower right. Collection Norbert Schimmel, New York. C.C. 453

Duet. Oil. $28 \times 21^3/_4''$. Signed lower right. Private collection, Paris. C.C. 454

Three-Quarter Portrait of a Woman. Oil. Signed lower right. Collection Morton G. Neumann, Chicago. C.C. 506

Monique. Oil. $20^1/_4 \times 14^1/_4''$. Signed lower right. Private collection. C.C. 507

Autumn. Oil. Signed lower right. Private collection, Paris. C.C. 440

Testu's Son. Oil. Medium size. Signed lower right. C.C. 529

1948

Head of a Clown. Oil. $26 \times 19''$. Museum of Fine Arts, Boston. Page 319

Autumn in Versailles. Oil. $28^1/_4 \times 22^1/_2''$. Private collection, Paris. Page 321

Biblical Landscape. Oil. Private collection, Switzerland. Page 309

Judges. Oil. $12 \times 9^1/_4''$. Private collection, France. Page 306

Bluebeard. Oil. $11^3/_4 \times 8^1/_4''$. Private collection, Japan. Page 328

Autumn (Nazareth). Oil. $26^3/_4 \times 41^1/_2''$. Signed lower right. Vatican Museum's. Page 301

De Profundis. Oil. $11^3/_4 \times 8^1/_4''$. Signed lower right. Private collection, Japan. C.C. 490

By the Waterside (Ile-de-France). Oil. $29^1/_2 \times 41^1/_2''$. Signed lower right. Kunsthaus, Zurich. C.C. 491

Exodus. Oil. $19^1/_4 \times 23^3/_4''$. Signed lower right. Private collection, Paris. C.C. 524

Dancers. Oil. $16^1/_2 \times 13''$. Collection Philippe Leclercq, Hem, France. Page 326

"Man is Wolf to Man". Oil. $18 \times 25^1/_2''$. Musée National d'Art Moderne, Paris. Page 315

The Passion. Oil. $23^3/_4 \times 17^1/_2''$. Signed lower right. Private collection, France. C.C. 414

Pax. Oil. $25^1/_4 \times 18''$. Signed lower right. Private collection, France. C.C. 415

Ecce Homo. Oil. $12^3/_4 \times 8''$. Signed lower right. Private collection. C.C. 422

The Sea of Galilee. Oil. $15^1/_2 \times 24''$. Signed lower right. Museum of Modern Art, Venice. C.C. 436

Suffer the Little Children to Come Unto Me. Oil. $21^1/_4 \times 27^1/_4''$. Signed lower right. Private collection, Paris. C.C. 437

Autumn (The Sea of Galilee). Oil. $28^1/_2 \times 20^1/_4''$. Signed lower right. Private collection, France. C.C. 438

Pierrot. Oil. $21^1/_4 \times 15''$. Signed center right. Private collection, Paris. C.C. 455

Pedro. Oil. $26 \times 17^3/_4''$. Signed lower right. Private collection. C.C. 456

Duet. Oil. $25^1/_4 \times 16^1/_2''$. Signed lower left. Private collection, Paris. C.C. 457

Patrice. Oil. $11^1/_2 \times 8''$. Signed lower right. Musée Toulouse-Lautrec, Albi. C.C. 502

Queen of the Circus. Oil. Signed lower right. Collection Morton G. Neumann, Chicago. C.C. 508

Head of Woman in Feathered Hat. Oil. Signed lower right. Private collection. C.C. 509

Theodora. Oil. Signed center right. Private collection. C.C. 510

Exodus (The Road Is Long). Oil. $25^3/_4 \times 19^3/_4''$. Signed lower right. Private collection, Paris. C.C. 525

Woman with a Hat. Oil. Collection Mr. and Mrs. Colin, U.S.A. Page 247

Head of a Woman. Oil. C.C. 513

In the Moonlight. Oil. Signed lower right. Collection Ahrenberg, Stockholm. C.C. 458

Winter Sun. Oil. $20^3/_8 \times 28^3/_4''$. Private collection, New York. C.C. 493

Carmencita. Oil. $21^1/_4 \times 14^5/_8''$. Signed lower center. Musée des Beaux-Arts, Lyons. C.C. 511

Queen of the Circus. Oil. Signed lower right. C.C. 512

Period 1949-1958

1949

Profile of Christ. The Benedictine Abbey at St. Benoît-du-lac, Canada. Page 329

The Passion. Oil. 34¹/₄×24¹/₂″. Signed lower right. C.C. 534

Biblical Landscape. Oil. 13×17³/₄″. Signed lower right. Private collection, Paris. Page 343

The Sacred Heart. Oil. 9¹/₂×5¹/₂″. Signed lower right. Vatican Library, Rome. C.C. 535

Joan of Arc. Oil. 19×26¹/₂″. Private collection, Paris. C.C. 533

Autumn. Oil. 21×28¹/₂″. Signed lower right. Private collection, Paris. C.C. 539

The Little Sorceress. Oil. 34³/₄×28¹/₂″. Signed lower left center. C.C. 557

1950

The Sea of Galilee. Oil. Private collection. Page 340

Crucifixion. Oil. 24³/₄×19¹/₄″. Signed lower right. Private collection, Paris. C.C. 536

Maternity (Faubourg of Toil and Suffering). 24³/₄×19¹/₄″. Collection Governor and Mrs. Nelson Rockefeller, New York. Page 339

1951

Joan of Arc. Oil. 11³/₄×9¹/₂″. Signed lower right. Private collection, Paris. Page 345

Old Street Circus. Oil. Small size. Private collection. Page 336

Duet. Oil. 15×10″. Private collection. Page 337

The Passion (Head of Christ). Oil. 13³/₄×11″. Signed lower right. Private collection, Paris. C.C. 530

1952

Seraphine (Old Traveling Circus). Oil. 14¹/₂×9¹/₂″. Private collection, France. Page 334

Christian Nocturne. Oil. 37¹/₄×25¹/₂″. Musée National d'Art Moderne, Paris. Page 332

End of Autumn (III). Oil. 44³/₄×29″. Private collection, France. Page 333

Moonlight. Oil. 18¹/₄×13″. Signed lower left. Private collection, Paris. Page 347

Onesimus. Oil. 15¹/₄×9¹/₄″. Signed lower right. Private collection, Paris. Page 349

Ecce Homo. Oil. 19³/₄×17³/₄″. Signed lower right. Private collection, Paris. C.C. 531

The Flight into Egypt. Oil. 14³/₄×13″. Signed lower right. Private collection, Paris. C.C. 538

Christian Spirit (Christ and Children). Oil. 27¹/₂×43¹/₄″. Signed lower right. Private collection, Paris. C.C. 537

Biblical Landscape with Two Trees. Oil. Large size. Signed bottom right. C.C. 546

Autumn Nocturne. Oil. 29¹/₂×38³/₄″. Signed center right. Collection Vincent Auriol, France. C.C. 540

End of Autumn (I). Oil. 29¹/₂×41¹/₂″. Signed lower right. Private collection, Paris. C.C. 541

End of Autumn (IV). Oil. 29¹/₄×41¹/₂″. Signed lower right. Col-lection Mr. and Mrs. Paul H. Sampliner, New York. C.C. 542

End of Autumn (V). Oil. 24³/₄×35¹/₂″. Signed lower right. Private collection, France. C.C. 543

Twilight. Oil. 23¹/₄×39¹/₂″. Signed lower right. Collection Carleton Smith, New York. C.C. 544

Magloire. Oil. 17¹/₂×11″. Signed lower center right. Private collection, Paris. C.C. 548

Clown. Oil. 15¹/₂×10″. Signed upper right. Private collection, U.S.A. C.C. 549

Little Louis (Old Street Circus). Oil. 15¹/₄×9³/₄″. Signed lower right. Private collection, Paris. C.C. 550

Dreamer. Oil. 22³/₄×15¹/₄″. Signed lower right. Collection Bergman, New York. C.C. 551

Mistigri. Oil. 15×9¹/₂″. Signed upper right. Private collection, Holland. C.C. 552

Kindly Bernard. Oil. 15³/₄×9¹/₂″. Signed upper right. Musée des Beaux-Arts, Brussels. C.C. 553

Yoko. Oil. 17¹/₂×12″. Signed upper right. Collection Bayeler, Switzerland. C.C. 558

Bitter-Sweet (Old Street Circus). Oil. 15×10″. Signed upper right. Private collection, France. C.C. 559

Snow-White. Oil. 22¹/₂×15³/₄″. Signed lower right. Private collection, Paris. C.C. 560

Rosine. Oil. Signed bottom right. Private collection, Paris, C.C. 561

Queen of the Circus. Oil. Signed upper right. C.C. 562

Profile. Oil. Signed lower right. C.C. 563

Levantine Woman. Oil. Signed lower right. C.C. 564

1953

Profile. Oil. 15¹/₄×10″. Collection Maurice Coutot, Paris. Page 335

Pierrotins. Oil. 9¹/₄×12¹/₂″. Private collection, Paris, Page 338

Biblical Landscape. Oil. Large size. Signed center right. Private collection, Japan. C.C. 545

Biblical Landscape with Tree Trunk. Oil. Medium size. Signed lower right. Private collection, Japan. C.C. 547

Pierrot. Oil. 20¹/₄×15″. Signed lower center right. Private collection, Paris. C.C. 554

Profile of a Clown (Old Street Circus). Oil. Signed bottom right. Private collection, England. CC. 556.

Pierrette. Oil. Private collection, France. Page 331

Decorative Flowers. Oil. 37×25¹/₄″. Signed lower right. Private collection, Paris. Page 353

1954

The Holy Countenance. Gouache. 15³/₄×12¹/₂″. Signed lower right. Private collection, Paris. C.C. 532

1956

Theodora. Oil. 24³/₄×17³/₄″. Private collection, Paris. Page 355

Sarah. Oil. 21³/₄×16¹/₂″. Private collection, Paris. Page 357

Clown. Oil. 16×11″. Private collection, Paris. C.C. 555

Profile. Oil. 24¹/₄×15³/₄″. Private collection, Paris. C.C. 565

Harlequin. Oil. 37×25¹/₄″. Private collection, Paris. Page 330

Bibliography

I. Books illustrated by Rouault with woodcuts, etchings, lithographs, or reproductions

Rouault, G., Souvenirs intimes, Paris, Frapier, 1926 (with 6 tipped-in lithographs).

Rouault, G., Paysages légendaires, Paris, Porteret, 1929 (with 6 tipped-in lithographs and 50 drawings, one lithograph in color for the first 12 copies).

Rouault, G., Petite banlieue, Paris, Editions des Quatre-Chemins, 1929 (with 6 lithographs and 100 reproductions, 2 hand-colored by the artist).

Arland, M., Les Carnets de Gilbert, Paris, Nouvelle Revue Française, 1931 (with one original lithograph and 5 color engravings).

Vollard, A., Les Réincarnations du Père Ubu, Paris, Vollard, 1932 (with 22 etchings and 104 wood-engravings).

Rouault, G., Le Cirque de l'étoile filante, Paris, Vollard, 1938; printer's date March 5, 1936 (with 17 etchings in color and 82 wood-engravings).

Suarès, A., Passion, Paris, Vollard, 1939 (with 17 etchings in color and 82 wood-engravings).

Rouault, G., Divertissement, Paris, Tériade, 1943 (with 15 color reproductions).

Rouault, G., Soliloques, Neuchâtel, Ides et Calendes, 1944 (with 8 color reproductions).

Rouault, G., Stella Vespertina, Paris, Drouin, 1947 (with 12 color reproductions).

Rouault, G., Miserere, Paris, Edition de l'Etoile Filante, 1948 (58 etchings).

II. Writings by the artist

"Trois Artistes: 'Noli me tangere' (Cézanne), 'La Toison d'Or' (Carrière), 'Le Grand Pan' (Rodin)," Mercure de France, February 16, 1910.

"Ingres Ressuscité," Mercure de France, December 10, 1912.

"Sur Forain," La Vie, 1913.

"L'Artiste," "Miserere," "Mère," Soirées de Paris, Nos. 26–27, July-August, 1914 (poems).

Extracts from writings in M. Puy, G. Rouault et son œuvre, Paris, Gallimard, 1920, pp. 15–16.

"Sur l'Ecole Française," L'Eclair, August 29, 1924.

Poems in Bulletin de la Vie Artistique, 1924, pp. 380–82, and 1925, pp. 127–30.

Prose and poetry in F. Fels, Propos d'artistes, Paris, La Renaissance du Livre, 1925, pp. 149–57 (reprinted with revisions and additional poems from Nouvelles Littéraires, Artistiques et Scientifiques, March 15, 1924).

"Deux Poèmes: Le Christ de l'Yser, Hommage au Solitaire," L'Amour de l'Art, November, 1925.

"Les Frontières Artistiques," in Les Appels de l'Orient, Paris, Emile-Paul Frères, 1925, pp. 177–82.

Letter-preface and two poems in G. Charensol, Georges Rouault, l'homme et l'œuvre, Paris, Editions des Quatre Chemins, 1926 (an extract reprinted in Art Vivant, February 15, 1926; the letter reprinted in Kunstblatt, August, 1927).

Souvenirs intimes, Paris, Frapier, 1926 (reminiscences of Moreau, Bloy, Cézanne, Baudelaire, Renoir, Daumier, Huysmans and Degas, with a preface by A. Suarès).

"Gustave Moreau," Le Correspondant, April 10, 1926.

"Déclaration sur le Musée Gustave Moreau," Beaux-Arts, October 16, 1926.

"Lettres de Georges Rouault a André Suarès," L'Art et les Artistes, April, 1926 (special number devoted to Moreau).

"A Feu Debureau," *Funambules*, December 1, 1926.

Miserere et Guerre, Paris, Vollard, 1927.

Poem-preface to J. Joëts, FLANDRE, Paris, Galerie d'Art du Montparnasse, 1927.

"A la Mémoire de Claude Monet," *L'Amour de l'Art*, No. 8, 1927 (poem).

"Claude Monet," *ibid*.

Poems in C. Terrasse, "Georges Rouault," *Art d'Aujourd'hui*, spring, 1928.

"Lettre de Georges Rouault," *Cahiers d'Art*, No. 3, 1928.

"Déclaration à Spectateur," *Spectateur*, June 18, 1928.

"Sur Huysmans," *Bulletin de la Société Huysmans*, No. 27, 1928.

Reply to a survey on "Quel est votre paysage préféré," *L'Intransigeant*, April 2, 1929.

Reply to a survey on "1830–1930," *L'Intransigeant*, November 23, 1929.

PAYSAGES LÉGENDAIRES, Paris, Porteret, 1929 (poems with illustrations).

"Pourquoi je me présente à l'Institut," *L'Intransigeant*, May 27, 1930.

Poem in C. Roger-Marx, "L'œuvre gravé de Georges Rouault," *Byblis*, Autumn, 1931.

"Sur André Derain," *Les Chroniques du Jour*, January, 1931.

"Evocations," *Les Chroniques du Jour*, April, 1931 (on Matisse).

"En Marge des doctrines," *Nouvelle Revue Française*, October, 1931.

"Rouault parle de son art," *Demain*, December 9, 1931.

"Poème," *L'Intransigeant*, February 8, 1932.

"La Conception de la beauté," *L'Intransigeant*, February 8, 1932.

"En Marge des doctrines," *L'Intransigeant*, November 15, 1932.

Reply to a survey on "Pouvez-vous dire quelle a été la rencontre capitale de votre vie," *Minotaure*, Nos. 3–4, 1933.

Reply to a survey on "L'Art d'aujourd'hui," *Cahiers d'Art*, No. 10, 1935.

Reply to a survey on "L'Art peut-il utiliser la photographie," *Revue de l'art ancien et moderne*, March 19, 1926.

Reply to a survey on "Le Métier," *Beaux-Arts*, October, 1936.

"Textes inédits," *Revue de Belles-Lettres*, Neuchâtel, 1936–1937.

"Soliloques" and "Notes sur la peinture," in C. Roulet, *Le peintre français Georges Rouault: textes inédits et notes d'etude*, Neuchâtel, Delachaux et Niestlé, 1937 (includes also a bibliographical note).

"Souvenirs sur Degas," *L'Intransigeant*, March 9, 1937.

Statements in D. Lord, "The Wisdom of Georges Rouault," *The Listener*, September 29, 1937.

"Climat pictural," *Renaissance*, October-December, 1937.

"Anciens et modernes," *Verve*, November, 1938.

LE CIRQUE DE L'ETOILE FILANTE, Paris, Vollard, 1938.

Preface to the catalogue of the exhibition of A. Girard, New York, Mrs. Cornelius J. Sullivan Galleries, 1938.

Excerpts from writings in R. Huyghe, LA PEINTURE FRANÇAISE: LES CONTEMPORAINS, Paris, Bibliothèque Française des Arts, 1939, pp. 26–27.

"Conceptions picturales," *Verve*, January-March, 1939.

"Visages réels ou imaginaires," *Verve*, July-October, 1939.

Facsimile of letter dated 1939 in catalogue, GEORGES ROUAULT: RETROSPECTIVE LOAN EXHIBITION, Boston, Institute of Modern Art, 1940.

"Visage de la France," *Verve*, September-November, 1940.

Excerpts from writings in "Georges Rouault," *Art in Australia*, June-August, 1941.

DIVERTISSEMENT, Paris, Tériade, 1943.

Article in *Le Point*, August-October, 1943.

Excerpts from writings in E. Hone, "Georges Rouault," *Liturgical Arts*, August, 1943 (reprinted from *Irish Ecclesiastical Record*, February, 1943).

"Souvenirs du jeune âge sont gravés dans mon cœur," *Le Point*, August-October, 1943.

Fascimile of letter to Vollard in U. E. Johnson, AMBROISE VOLLARD, EDITEUR, New York, Wittenborn, 1944.

Excerpts from writings with facsimile of handwriting in D. Théote, "Intimate Moments with Rouault: Three Wars," *Tricolor*, May, 1944.

SOLILOQUES, Neuchâtel, Ides et Calendes, 1944.

"Sur Léon Bloy," *Cahiers du Rhône*, 1944 (special number on Bloy).

"Notes Received from the Artist," in J. T. Soby, GEORGES ROUAULT, New York, Museum of Modern Art, 1945 (also includes brief extracts from poems).

"Existe-t-il un art expressioniste?," *Art Présent*, No. 1, 1945.

"Sur le métier de peintre," *Art Présent*, 1945.

"Opinions," *Le Point*, March, 1946.

"L'Essentiel, Peindre," *Spectateur*, June 18, 1946.

"Pensieri sull'Arte," *Lettere ed Arti* (Milan), July-August, 1946.

"Commentaire pictural," introduction to E. A. Jewell, GEORGES ROUAULT, Paris, Hyperion, 1947.

Preface to STELLA VESPERTINA, Paris, Drouin, 1947.

Preface to MISERERE, Paris, Edition de l'Etoile Filante, 1948.

"Message aux 'Nordiques Gantois,'" *La Métropole* (Antwerp), March 21, 1949.

"Sur l'art sacré," *La Croix*, May 11 and 12, 1952.

"Lettre à Edouard Schuré," *Le Goéland*, June, 1952.

"Avant-propos," *Kunsten-Idag*, No. 2, 1954 (special number on Rouault).

CORRESPONDANCE DE ROUAULT ET DE SUARÈS, Paris, Gallimard, 1960.

III. Writings on Rouault

(The following list does not mention texts on Gustave Moreau or texts dealing only indirectly with Georges Rouault which are referred to in the body of the book. We have limited ourselves strictly to writings devoted to the painter and his work. The literature on Rouault is so extensive that no claim is made here to completeness.)

1895–1896 (on the Salon des Champs-Elysées).

Serlat, R. *La Revue Encyclopédique*, April 15, 1895.

Fouquier, M. *Le XIXe Siècle*, May 6 and 14, 1895.

Javel, M. F. *L'Art français*, May 13, 1895.

Flat, P. *La Revue Bleue*, June 8, 1895.

Michel, A. *Le Journal des Débats*, June 10, 1895.

Roger-Marx, C. *Le Public*, May 1, 1896.

Roger-Marx, C. *La Revue Encyclopédique*, May 2, 1896.

Thiébault-Sisson. *Le Temps*, May 23, 1896.

Flat, P. *La Revue Bleue*, June 6, 1896.

Debay. *Demain*, June 11, 1896.

Carbo, P. *Le Progrès artistique*, June 18, 1896.
Geffroy, G. *La Vie artistique de 1897*, p. 328.

1897
L., E. *La Revue Blanche*, March 15 (on the Salon de la Rose Croix).
Anon. *Le Thyrse*, April (on the same).
Alexandre, A. *Le Figaro*, April 19 (on the Salon des Champs-Elysées).
Geffroy, G. *Le Journal*, April 19 (on the same).

1902
Bloy, L. Quatre ans de captivité à Cochons-sur-Marne, Vol. II, 1902–1904.

1903
Geffroy, G. *La Vie artistique*, Vol. VIII.

1904
Bloy, L. L'Invendable, 1904–1907, pp. 36, 60, 65, 69–71, 132, 288.

Reviews of the Salon d'Automne:
    Vauxcelles, L. *Gil Blas*, October 14.
    Valensol. *Petit Parisien*, October 14.
    Thiébault-Sisson. *Le Petit-Temps*, October 14.
    Alexandre, A. *Le Figaro*, October 14.
    Fouquier, M. *Le Journal*, October 14.
    Riotor, L. *Le Rappel*, October 15.
    Le Masque Rouge. *L'Action*, October 15.
    Faure, E. *Les Arts et la Vie*, November.
    Delaunay. *Le Journal de Caen*, December 20.

1905
Reviews of the Salon des Indépendants:
    Vauxcelles, L. *Gil Blas*, March 23.
    Anner. *L'Intransigeant*, March 28.
    Morice, C. *Mercure de France*, April 15.
Vauxcelles, L. *Gil Blas*, October 17 (on the Salon d'Automne).

1906
Anon. *Gil Blas*, February 2 (on the Galerie Berthe Weil exhibition).
Morice, C. *Mercure de France*, April 15 (on the Salon des Indépendants).
Le Senne, C. *La Revue Théâtrale*, April (on the same).

1907
Bloy, L. Le Vieux de la Montagne, 1907–1910, p. 197.
Anon. *L'Amitié de France*, May-June (on the Salon des Indépendants).
Vauxcelles, L. *Gil Blas*, September 30.
Apollinaire, G. *Je Dis Tout*, October 12–19.
Lestrange, R. de. *Le Tintamarre*, October 13.
Martineau, R. *Le Beffroy*, December.

1908
Anon. *New York Herald*, May 20 (on the Salon des Indépendants).
Reviews of the Salon d'Automne:
    Kahn, G. *Le Radical*, September 30.
    Roger-Marx, C. *Chronique des Arts*, October 10.
    Habert. *La Revue des Arts*, October 18.

1910
Favelle, J. Preface to the catalogue of the Rouault exhibition, Galerie Druet, Paris.
Reviews of the Galerie Druet exhibition:
    Schnerb, J. F. *Chronique des Arts*, February 26.
    S., A. *Paris-Journal*, March.
    Bender, S. *Courrier Français*, March 5.
    Rivière, J. *Nouvelle Revue Française*, April (reprinted in J. Rivière, *Etudes*, Paris, Nouvelle Revue Française, 1924, p. 52).
Puy, M. "Le Dernier état de la Peinture," *Le Feu* (reprinted in M. Puy, L'Effort des peintres modernes, Paris, 1933).

1911
La Palette, *Paris-Journal*, October 22 (on Rouault's ceramics).
Salmon, A. *Paris-Journal*, December 10 (on the same).
Vauxcelles, L. *Gil Blas*, December 15.

1912
Reviews of the Galerie Druet exhibition:
    Michaud, R. *Revue du Mois*, January 10.
    Kahn, G. *Mercure de France*, January 16.
    Allard, R. *Revue Indépendante*, January.
Apollinaire, G. *Paris-Journal*, July 5 (on the sketchbooks).
Salmon, A. La Jeune Peinture française, Paris, Société des Trente, A. Messein, pp. 30–32.

1913
Bloy, L. Au Seuil de l'Apocalypse, 1913–1915, pp. 119–299.

1914
Coquiot, G. Cubistes, Futuristes, Passéistes, Paris, Ollendorff, pp. 142 ff.

1915
Bloy, L. La Porte des Humbles, 1915–1917, pp. 71, 116, 190, 278, 286.

1916
Pinturicchio, *Carnet de la Semaine*, July 2.

1917
Vauxcelles, L. *Carnet des Artistes*, June 15.

1920
Puy, M. Georges Rouault et son œuvre, Paris, Gallimard.
Fry, R. Vision and Design, London, p. 159.
Salmon, A. *L'Art Vivant*, Paris, Crès, pp. 30–32.
Coquiot, G. Les Indépendants, Paris, Ollendorff, pp. 72 ff.
Galerie La Licorne, Paris. Catalogue of the Rouault exhibition.
Reviews of the Galerie La Licorne exhibition:
    Vauxcelles, L. *L'Amour de l'Art*, No. 1.
    Varenne, G. *Bonsoir*, November 16.
    René-Jean. *Comoedia*, November 20.
    Pellerin, J. *La Lanterne*, November 27.
    Salmon, A. *L'Europe Nouvelle*, November 28.
    Warnod, A. *L'Amour de l'Art*, November.
    Anon. *L'Humanité*, December 1.
    Anon. *L'Humanité*, December 15.

1921
Vauxcelles, L. *Excelsior*, July 28.

1923

Gordon, J. Modern French Painters, New York, Dodd Mead, pp. 89–90.

Lhote, A. *L'Amour de l'Art*, December (reprinted in A. Lhote, Parlons Peinture, Paris, Denoël et Steele, 1936, pp. 257–62).

Evenepoel, H. "Gustave Moreau et ses élèves," *Mercure de France* (letters, from 1894 to 1898).

1924

Carco, F. Le Nu dans la peinture moderne, Paris, Crès, pp. 134–36.

Coquiot, G. Des Peintres maudits, Paris, Delpeuch, pp. 101f.

Coquiot, G. Des Gloires déboulonnées, Paris, Delpeuch.

Lhote, A. *Cicerone*, February 1 (on Rouault's religious works).

Fels, F. *Nouvelles Littéraires*, March 15.

Galerie Druet, Paris. Catalogue of the Rouault exhibition.

Reviews of the Galerie Druet exhibition:
Vauxcelles, L. *L'Ere Nouvelle*, April 24.
René-Jean. *Comoedia*, April 27.
Warnod, A. *L'Avenir*, April 28.
Anon. *Journal des Débats*, April 28.
Chavance, R. *La Liberté*, April 29.
Trapenard, J. *Combat*, May 8.
George, W. *Bulletin de la Vie Artistique*, May 15.
Fry, R. *L'Amour de l'Art*, May.
Maritain, J. *Revue Universelle*, May 15 (partial reprint in *Cahiers d'Art*, No. 3, 1928; reprinted in expanded form in J. Maritain, Frontières de la poésie, Paris, L. Rouart, 1935, which was published in English as Art and Poetry, New York, Philosophical Library, 1943).
Anon. *Revue Mondiale*, September 1.
Vauxcelles, L. *Excelsior*, September 23.
Jaloux, E. *Nouvelles Littéraires*, October 17.
Charensol, G. *Paris-Journal*, November 14.
Guenne, J. *Nouvelles Littéraires*, November 15.
Coquiot, G. *Le 7e Jour*, December 25.

1925

Warnod, A. Les Berceaux de la jeune peinture, Montmartre-Montparnasse, Paris, Albin Michel, pp. 9, 175, 221.

Fels, F. Propos d'Artistes, Paris, Renaissance du Livre, pp. 149f.

Fry, R. Transformations, London, Chatto & Windus, pp. 24, 207ff. (American edition, New York, Brentano's, 1926).

Einstein, C. Die Kunst des 20. Jahrhunderts, Berlin, Propyläen, p. 50.

Lhote, A. *Cicerone*, February.

Anon. *L'Amour de l'Art*, February 2 (on the Buhler Collection).

Einstein, C. *Querschnitt*, March.

Anon. *Gazette du Franc*, March 6.

Salmon, A. *L'Amour de l'Art*, May (on the *Miserere*).

George, W. *L'Amour de l'Art*, pp. 271–76.

Anon. *Kunstblatt*, August.

Anon. *Art Vivant*, p. 128.

1926

Charensol, G. Georges Rouault, l'homme et l'œuvre, Paris, Editions des Quatre Chemins (including texts by Rouault reprinted in part in *Art Vivant*, February 15, 1926, and in *Kunstblatt*, August, 1927).

New Art Circle, New York. Etchings by Rouault Published

by Ambroise Vollard, Artlover Library, New York and Munich, J. B. Neumann's Bilderhefte (illustrations only).

Suarès, A. *L'Art et les Artistes*, April (letters from Suarès to Rouault, reprinted in G. Rouault, Souvenirs Intimes, Paris, 1926).

George, W. *The Arts*, June.

Pinturicchio. *Carnet de la Semaine*, November (on the sale of the Quinn Collection and the sketchbooks).

Vollard, A. Souvenirs d'un marchand de tableaux, Paris. Albin Michel (English edition, Recollections of a Picture Dealer, Boston, Little, Brown, 1936).

Bulliet, C. J. Apples and Madonnas, Chicago, Covici-Friede, pp. 152f.

Courthion, P. Panorama de la peinture française contemporaine, Paris, Simon Kra, pp. 123–31 (the same text appears in *Crapouillot*, July, 1927).

Scheffler, K. Geschichte der Europäischen Malerei vom Impressionismus bis zur Gegenwart, Berlin, Bruno Cassirer, p. 212.

B., P. *Gazette du Franc*, January 29.

Anon. *Bulletin de l'art française et japonais*, February 6.

Kállai, E. *Kunstblatt*, March.

Anon. *Bulletin de l'art français et japonais*, March.

Anon. *Cri de Paris*, June.

Anon. *Petit Parisien*, June 18.

1928

Bloy, L. *Cahiers d'Art*, No. 3 (with a letter from Rouault).

Maritain, J. *Cahiers d'Art*, No. 3.

Chabot, G. *Cahiers d'Art*, No. 3.

Daunay, R. *Le Nord Littéraire*, March 15.

Kospoth, B. J. *Paris Times*, May 20.

Terrasse, C. *Art d'Aujourd'hui*, Spring.

Silvestre, C. *Le Rouge et le Noir*, May–June.

Anon. *De Baasbode* (Rotterdam), July 11.

Chabot, G. *Revue d'Art* (Antwerp), September (reprinted as offprint in the series "Etudes d'art contemporain," with two lithographs of Rouault.)

Anon. *Liège-Echos*, December 7–13.

1929

Monsabert, Dom P. de. Le Monastère de Ligugé, Abbaye Saint-Martin de Ligugé.

Basler, A., and Kunstler, C. La Peinture indépendante en France, Vol. II: De Matisse à Segonzac, Paris, Crès, pp. 41f. (English translation, Modern French Painting: The Modernists from Matisse to de Segonzac, New York, W. F. Payson, 1931).

Raynal, M. *L'Intransigeant*, March 5.

Anon. *Journal des Débats*, March 12.

Anon. *New York Herald*, March 12.

George, W. *La Presse*, March 13.

Charensol, G. *Art Vivant*, March 15.

Sorgues, A. *La Voix*, March 17.

Anon. *Crapouillot*, April.

Charensol, G. *Ateliers*, June.

Malraux, A. *Formes*, December (translation with some changes in *American Arts Monthly*, September, 1936).

1930

Arts Club, Chicago. Catalogue of Rouault exhibition.

Cogniat, R. GEORGES ROUAULT, Paris, Crès.

Neumann, J. B. GEORGES ROUAULT, New York and Munich, Neumann & Franke (preface by W. Grohmann).

George, W. Preface to catalogue of Rouault exhibition, J. B. Neumann Graphisches Kabinett, Munich.

Museum of Modern Art. PAINTINGS IN PARIS FROM AMERICAN COLLECTIONS, ed. A. H. Barr, Jr., New York, Museum of Modern Art.

Flouquet, P.-L. *Le Monde*, March 1.

Brummer Gallery, New York. Catalogue of Rouault exhibition.

Reviews of the Brummer Gallery exhibition:

    Anon. *Art News*, April 5.

    Anon. *Evening Post*, April 5.

    McBride, H. *New York Sun*, April 5.

    Sweeney, J. J. *New York Times*, April 6.

    Anon. *New York Herald Tribune*, April 6.

    S., N. *New York American*, April 13.

    Anon. *Art Digest*, April 15.

    Watson, F. *The Arts*, April 16.

    Anon. *Town and Country*, April 15.

    Washburn-Freund, F. E. *Boston Herald*, April 20.

    Anon. *Arts*, April.

    Anon. *Parnassus*, April.

Klein, J. *Chicago Evening Post*, April 15.

Léon-Martin, L. *Art et Décoration*, April.

McBride, H. *Creative Art*, supplement, May.

Gauthier, M. *Art Vivant*, May 15 (bio-bibliographical notices on artists participating in the Art Vivant exhibition).

Cogniat, R. *Chroniques du Jour*, May.

Klein, J. *New Freeman*, May 24.

Reviews of the St. George's Gallery exhibition:

    Wilenski, R. H. *Apollo*, June.

    Anon. *Morning Post*, June 19.

    Earp, T. W. *New Statesman*, June 21.

    Anon. *Sunday Times*, June 22.

Cogniat, R. *Kunstblatt*, August (on avant garde theater design in France).

Basler, A. *Kunstblatt*, October.

Goodrich, L. *The Arts*, November (on the Neumann Gallery exhibition).

Anon. *Art Digest*, November 1 (on the same).

Anon. *Vient de Paraître*, December.

Poutermann, A. V. *Arts et Métiers Graphiques*, 1930–1931 (on Vollard).

Roger-Marx, C. *Plaisir de Bibliophile* (on the same).

1931

Blanche, J.-E. "Les Arts Plastiques" in LA TROISIÈME RÉPUBLIQUE, 1870 À NOS JOURS, Paris, Les Editions de France, p. 135.

Serouya, H. INITIATION À LA PEINTURE D'AUJOURD'HUI, Paris, La Renaissance du Livre, p. 139.

Vanderpyl, F. R. PEINTRES DE MON ÉPOQUE, Paris, Stock, pp. 141 f.

Demotte Gallery, New York. Catalogue of Rouault exhibition.

Flint, R. *Art News*, January 10 (on the Demotte Gallery exhibition).

George, W. *Formes*, March.

Dormoy, M. *Kunst und Künstler*, April.

Phillips, D. THE ARTIST SEES DIFFERENTLY, New York, Weyhe.

Arland, M. *Formes*, June.

Arland, M. *Nouvelle Revue Française*, July 1.

Rafols. *El Mati* (Spain), August 5.

Berthelot, P. *Beaux-Arts*, August 25 (on the Galerie des Quatre Chemins exhibition).

Lewisohn, S. A. *Creative Art*, September.

Roger-Marx, C. *Byblis*, Autumn (on Rouault's engravings).

Fierens, P. Preface to the catalogue of the Rouault exhibition, Galerie Schwarzenberg, Brussels.

C., H. *La Métropole* (Antwerp), November 1 (on the Brussels exhibition).

Périer, G.-D. *Liége-Echos*, November 5 (on the same).

Anon. *Demain* (New York), December 9 (special number: "Homage to Rouault").

1932

Zervos, C. *Cahiers d'Art*, Nos. 1–2 (on the illustrations for PÈRE UBU).

R. *Journal de Genéve*, March 9.

Anon. *Le Mois*, November.

1933

Puy, M. L'EFFORT DES PEINTRES MODERNES, Paris, A. Messein (first published as LE DERNIER ÉTAT DE LA PEINTURE, Paris, Le Feu, 1910).

Lhote, A. LA PEINTURE: LE COEUR ET L'ESPRIT, Paris, Denoël et Steele.

Weil, B. PAN DANS L'OEIL, Paris, Lipschutz.

Du Colombier, P. and Roland-Manuel. LES ARTS, Paris, Denoël et Steele.

Zahar, M. *Formes*, No. 31 (on PÈRE UBU).

Pach, W. *Parnassus*, January.

Anon. *Art News*, May 6 (on the Julien Levy Gallery exhibition).

Cogniat, R. *Beaux-Arts*, June 16 (on Rouault and Vollard).

Fierens, P. *L'Amour de l'Art*, June.

Pierre Matisse Gallery, New York. Catalogue of the Rouault exhibition.

Reviews of the Pierre Matisse Gallery exhibition:

    Anon. *Art News*, October 28.

    Anon. *Art Digest*, November 1.

    Anon. *Art Digest*, November 15 (includes digest of reviews of this exhibition).

Lewisohn, S. A. *Parnassus*, November (reprinted with some changes in S. A. Lewisohn, PAINTERS AND PERSONALITY, New York, Harper, 1937).

1934

Cheney, S. EXPRESSIONISM IN ART, New York, Liveright.

Benson, E. M. *Magazine of Art*, January (on the Pierre Matisse Gallery exhibition).

Cassou, J. *Marianne*, May 9.

Vanderpyl, F. R. *Petit Parisien*, June 14.

Fierens, P. *Journal des Débats*, June 20.

Lhote, A. *Nouvelle Revue Française*, August.

Lhote, A. *L'Intransigeant*, August 19.

Maritain, J. *Zivot* (Prague).

Vauxcelles, L. Catalogue of the exhibition of "Les Fauves," Beaux-Arts, Paris.

1935

Maritain, J. FRONTIÈRES DE LA POÉSIE ET AUTRES ESSAIS, Paris, L. Rouart, pp. 127 f. (English translation, ART AND POETRY, New York, Philosophical Library, 1943).

Fierens, P. "Georges Rouault" in R. Huyghe, HISTOIRE DE

L'ART CONTEMPORAIN: LA PEINTURE, Paris, Alcan, pp. 137f. (includes bibliography; reprinted from *Amour de l'Art*, June, 1933).
Grohmann, W. "Rouault" in ALLGEMEINES LEXIKON DER BILDENDEN KÜNSTLER, Leipzig, E. A. Seemann, Vol. XXIX, p. 106.
Vlaminck, M. DÉSOBÉIR, Paris, Corréa, pp. 126–28.
Ito, R. ROUAULT, Tokyo, Atelier Sha (in Japanese).
Vallon, Dr. *Art et Médecine*, May.
Rouzet, G. *Rex* (Brussels), June 1.
Lehmann, L. *Beaux-Arts*, August 9 (on the Fauves).
Dormoy, M. *Arts et Métiers Graphiques*, August 15.
Reviews of the Mayor Gallery exhibition:
    Blunt, A. *Spectator*, October 18.
    Bell, C. *New Statesman and Nation*, October 19.
    Clark, K. *Listener*, October 23.
Smith College Museum of Art, Northampton, Mass., Catalogue of Rouault exhibition.
McCausland, E. *Springfield Sunday Union and Republican* (Mass.), November 17 (on the Smith College exhibition).
H., P. E. *Art News*, November 23 (on the same).
Heitz, R. *La Vie en Alsace* (Strasbourg), November (on the Rouault painting in the Colmar museum).
Bignou Gallery, New York. Catalogue of the exhibition "Modern French Tapestries from the Collection of Mme. Paul Cuttoli."
Anon. *Fortune*, January (on the Bignou Gallery exhibition).
Vallon, Dr. *L'Avant-Garde* (Louvain), January 4.
Chabot, G. *L'Epoque* (Brussels), No. 4.
Reviews of the Galerie du Portique exhibition:
    Laprade, J. de. *Beaux-Arts*, February 14.
    Gros, G. J. *Paris-Midi*, February 21.
    Poulain, G. *Comoedia*, February 21.
    Chavance, R. *La Liberté*, February 22.
    Roger-Marx, C. *Le Jour*, February 22.
    G., R. *L'Intransigeant*, February 26.
    Fedgal, C. *La Semaine à Paris*, February 27.
    Salmon, A. *Gringoire*, March 6.
    Salmon, A. *Le Mois*, March.
Heitz, R. *Le Point*, May.
Roulet, C. *Revue de Belles-Lettres*, Neuchâtel, December.

1937
Escholier, R. LA PEINTURE FRANÇAISE DU XXe SIÈCLE, Paris, Floury, pp. 31 f.
Uckermann, P. d'. L'ART DANS LA VIE MODERNE, Paris, Flammarion, pp. 60–61, 75.
Roulet, C. LE PEINTRE FRANÇAIS GEORGES ROUAULT, Neuchâtel, Delachaux et Nietslé (offprint from *Revue de Belles-Lettres*, December, 1936).
Lewisohn, S. A. PAINTERS AND PERSONALITY, New York, Harper, pp. 112f.
Jacquinot, J. *Bulletin de la Société Huysmans*, No. 34 (on Huysmans, Rouault, and Bloy).
Blunt, A. *Spectator*, January 23 (on the Mayor Gallery exhibition).
Gillet, L. *Revue des Deux Mondes*, July 15.
Arland, M. *Nouvelle Revue Française*, August (on the exhibition "Maitres de l'Art Indépendant").
Lord, D. *Listener*, September 29.
Cogniat, R. *Le Point*, October.
George, W. *La Renaissance*, October–December (special issue devoted to Rouault, with a note by M. Dormoy).

Pierre Matisse Gallery, New York. Catalogue of the Rouault exhibition.
Reviews of the Pierre Matisse Gallery exhibition:
    Devree, H. *New York Times*, November 14.
    Anon. *Art Digest*, November 15.
    Davidson, M. *Art News*, November 20.
    McCausland, E. *Springfield Sunday Union and Republican* (Mass.), November 21.
    Breuning, M. *Parnassus*, December 4.

1938
Pach, W. QUEER THING, PAINTING, New York, Harper.
Zervos, C. HISTOIRE DE L'ART CONTEMPORAIN, Paris, Editions Cahiers d'Art, pp. 139–46.
Poutermann, J. G. *Arts et Métiers Graphiques*, No. 64 (on the publications of Vollard).
Kunsthalle, Basel. Catalogue of the exhibition "Vlaminck, Dufy, Rouault."
Reid and Lefevre Gallery, London. Catalogue of the exhibition "The Tragic Painters."
Leicester Galleries, London. Catalogue of the Rouault exhibition.
Anon. *London Studio*, September (on the Leicester Galleries exhibition).
Couturier, M. A. *Art Sacré*, September (on Rouault and the ecclesiastical public).
Wheeler, M. THE PRINTS OF GEORGES ROUAULT, New York, Museum of Modern Art; catalogue of the Museum of Modern Art exhibition.
Reviews of the Museum of Modern Art exhibition:
    Jewell, E. A. *New York Times*, October 1.
    Upton, M. *New York Sun*, October 1.
    Anon. *Art Digest*, October 1.
    McCausland, E. *Springfield Sunday Union and Republican* (Mass.), October 2.
    Anon. *Time*, October 3.
    Davidson, M. *Art News*, October 8.
Sweeney, J. J. *Parnassus*, November (on the Carnegie International exhibition).
Mellquist, J. *Commonweal*, December 23 (on Rouault as a Christian painter).

1939
Huyghe, R. LA PEINTURE FRANÇAISE: LES CONTEMPORAINS, Paris, Bibliothèque Française des Arts, pp. 26–27.
Terrasse, C. LA PEINTURE FRANÇAISE AU XXe SIÈCLE, Paris, Hyperion, p. 38 (English translation, FRENCH PAINTING IN THE XXth CENTURY, London and New York, Hyperion, 1939).
Richardson, E. P. THE WAY OF WESTERN ART, 1776–1914, Cambridge, Mass., Harvard University Press, pp. 178 f.
Museum of Modern Art. ART IN OUR TIME, New York.
Reviews of the Pierre Matisse Gallery exhibition:
    Davidson, M. *Art News*, February 11.
    Anon. *Art Digest*, February 15.
    Sweeney, J. J. *Parnassus*, April 21.
Clot, R.-J. *Prométhée*, April 6 (a comparison of "Saint Anne" of Leonardo da Vinci and "The Judge" of Rouault).
S., L. *Beaux-Arts*, May 3 (on the O. Petrides Gallery exhibition).
Bignou Gallery, New York. Catalogue of the Rouault exhibition.
Dormoy, M. *Arts et Métiers Graphiques*, May 15 (on the CIRQUE DE L'ETOILE FILANTE).

McGreevy, T. *London Studio*, June (on the Zwemmer Gallery exhibition).
Venturi, L. *Parnassus*, October.
Vauxcelles, L. *Beaux-Arts*, No. 343.

1940

Venturi, L. Georges Rouault, New York, Weyhe.
Venturi, L. Introduction to the catalogue of the Rouault retrospective loan exhibition, Institute of Modern Art, Boston (also Phillips Memorial Gallery, Washington, and Museum of Art, San Francisco).
Woolf, V. Roger Fry, London, p. 234.
Wilenski, R. H. Modern French Painters, New York, Reynal & Hitchcock.
Dalzell Hatfield Gallery. Catalogue of Rouault exhibition.
Buchholz Gallery, New York. Catalogue of Rouault exhibition.
Suarès, A. *Nouvelle Revue Française*, March (on Rouault and Vollard).
Reviews of the exhibitions at the Buchholz and Bignou Galleries:
  McBride, H. *New York Sun*, May 11.
  McCausland, E. *Parnassus*, May.
  Frankfurter, A. M. *Art News*, May 11.
  Anon. *Art Digest*, May 15 (two articles).
  Anon. *New Yorker*, May 18.
  Binsse, H. L. *America*, May 18.
Anon. *New Statesman and Nation*, August 10 (on the Redfern Gallery exhibition).
O'Connor, J. Jr. *Carnegie Magazine*, September (on the purchase of "The Old King").
Reviews of the Boston Institute of Modern Art exhibition:
  Frankfurter, A. M. *Art News*, November 9.
  Jewell, E. A. *New York Times*, November 10.
  Anon. *Art Digest*, November 15.
  Anon. *Art Digest*, December 1 (digest of criticism of this exhibition).

1941

Maritain, R. Les Grandes Amitiés (souvenirs), New York, Editions de la Maison Française, Vol. I, pp. 220–28 (English translation, We Have Been Friends Together, New York, Longmans, Green, 1942).
Cheney, S. The Story of Modern Art, New York, Viking Press, pp. 358–60, 484–86.
Lane, J. W. *Art News*, January 4.
Anon. *Art Digest*, January 15 (on the Pierre Matisse Gallery exhibition).
Frankfurter, A. M. *Art News*, January 18 (on the Chrysler Collection).
Anon. *Magazine of Art*, February (on the Phillips Memorial Gallery exhibition).
Smith, H. M. *Art News*, February 15–28.
O'Connor, J. *Carnegie Magazine*, March.
Marie Harrimann Gallery, New York. Catalogue of Rouault retrospective loan exhibition.
Reviews of Marie Harrimann Gallery exhibition:
  Genauer, E. *New York World Telegram*, April 12.
  Lane, J. W. *Art News*, April 15.
  Anon. *Art Digest*, April 15.
  Coates, R. M. *New Yorker*, April 26.
  McCausland, E. *Springfield Sunday Union and Republican* (Mass.), April 27.

Anon. *Art in Australia*, June–August.
Speaight, R. *Dublin Review*, July (reprinted in *Carnegie Magazine*, October).
Anon. *Magazine of Art*, No. 34 (on the Boston exhibition).
Maritain, R. *La Nouvelle Relève*, October.
Anon. *Art Digest*, November 1 (on the Guy E. Mayer Galleries exhibition).
Maritain, R. *Art News*, December 15–31.

1942

Georges-Michel, M. Peintres et sculpteurs que j'ai connus, New York, Brentano's, pp. 60–61.
Wheeler, M. 20th-Century Portraits, New York, Museum of Modern Art, pp. 16–17, 69, 81, 142.
Dorival, B. Preface to the catalogue of the Rouault exhibition, Galerie Louis Carré, Paris.
Mellquist, J. *Commonweal*, August 14 (on Rouault as "Prophet of Disaster").
Roulet, C. *Curieux*, October 9.

1943

Burgi, S. Jeu et sincérité dans l'art: Considérations psychologiques sur la peinture au xxe siècle, Neuchâtel, Baconnière, pp. 59–61.
Dorival, B. Les Etapes de la peinture française contemporaine, Paris, Gallimard, 1943–1946, 3 vols.
Leen, E. "A propos of Rouault," in Irish Art Handbook, pp. 21–28.
Lehmann, L., Laprade, J., Besson, G. Articles in *Le Point*, Nos. 26–27, August-October (special number on Rouault).
Hone, E. *Liturgical Arts*, August (reprinted from *Irish Ecclesiastical Record*, February).
Chadourne, P. *Présent*, November 8.
Christ, Y. *Echo des Etudiants de Montpellier*, December 4.

1944

Maritain, R. Les Grandes Amitiés, Vol. II, New York, pp. 37f.
Johnson, U. E. Ambroise Vollard, éditeur, New York, Wittenborn, pp. 27–31, 37–38, 137–50 (an appreciation and catalogue).
Anon. *Cahiers d'Art*, 1940–1944.
Roulet, C. Introduction to G. Rouault, Soliloques, Neuchâtel, Ides et Calendes.
Muller, E. *Labyrinthe* (Geneva), No. 2.
Bransten, E. H. *Pacific Art Review*, No. 3 (on the significance of the clown in paintings by Daumier, Picasso, and Rouault).
Venturi, L. "Georges Rouault," Gants du Ciel (Montreal), March.
Theote, D. *Tricolor*, May.
Carco, F. *Journal des Arts* (Zurich), September.
Jedlicka, G. *Das Werk*, November.
B., P. *Servir* (Lausanne), November 17.

1945

Georges-Michel, G. Chefs d'œuvres de peintres contemporains, New York, Editions de la Maison Française, pp. 120–22.
Jewell, E. A. Georges Rouault, New York, Hyperion.
Maritain, R. Adventures in Grace, New York, Longmans, Green, pp. 23–33 (excerpt in *Art News*, April 15).
Anon. "Rouault," in Current Biography, New York, H. W. Wilson, pp. 520–23.

San Lazzaro, G. di. CINQUANT'ANNI DI PITTURA MODERNA IN FRANCIA, Rome, Danesi, pp. 59–60.

Venturi, L. PAINTING AND PAINTERS, New York, Scribner, pp. 192–97.

Renaissance Society, Chicago. Catalogue of Rouault exhibition.

Delmas, G. *Magazine of Art*, March.

Soby, J. T. GEORGES ROUAULT, New York, Museum of Modern Art (catalogue of the Museum of Modern Art exhibition, with articles by C. O. Schniewind and G. Rouault; revised edition, 1947).

Reviews of the Museum of Modern Art exhibition:
Jewell, E. A. *New York Times*, April 8.
Maritain, R. *Art News*, April 15.
Breuning, M. *Art Digest*, April 15.
Crowninshield, F. *Vogue*, May.
Girard, A. *Ibid.*
Maritain, J. *Ibid.*
Girard, A. *Town and Country*, May.
Farber, M. *New Republic*, May 14.
Frankfurter, A. M. *Art News*, May 15.
Greenberg, C. *Nation*, May 19.
Kochnitzky, L. *View*, November.
Holme, B. *Studio*, December.

Diehl, G. *Confluences*, pp. 99–103.

Morel, Abbé M. *Cahiers d'Art Sacré*, No. 3.

Anon. *Norte*, December.

Estienne, C. *Terre des Hommes*, December 15.

Piérard, J. *Le National*, December 20.

Morel, Abbé M. *Gavroche*, December 20.

1946

Read, H. THE COAT OF MANY COLOURS, London, G. Routledge, pp. 308–10.

Reynolds, G. TWENTIETH-CENTURY DRAWINGS. London, Pleiades Books, pp. 11–12.

George, W. Preface to the catalogue of the Braque and Rouault exhibition, Tate Gallery, London.

James Vigeveno Galleries, Westwood, Calif. Catalogue of the Rouault exhibition.

Galerie St. Etienne, New York. Catalogue of Rouault exhibition.

Morel, Abbé M. Preface to the catalogue of the exhibition "Pour un art religieux," Galerie René Drouin, Paris.

Dormoy, M. Unpublished lecture on Vollard as publisher, delivered January 17 at the "Feuille Blanche."

Courthion, P. *Lettres Française*, February 15.

Anon. *Art Digest*, March (review of Galerie St. Etienne exhibition).

Parrot, J. *Le Livre et ses Amis*, April (on Vollard as publisher).

Morel, Abbé M. *Art et Industrie*, No. II.

Chéronnet, L. *Beaux-Arts*, April.

Elgar, F. *Carrefour*, April 13.

Brillant, M. *L'Epoque*, April 17.

Morel, Abbé M. *Arts*, April 19.

Cogniat, R. *Arts*, April 19.

George, W. *Opéra*, April 24.

Lassaigne, J. *La Bataille*, April 24.

Dorival, B. *Nouvelles Littéraires*, April 25.

Limbour, G. *Action*, April 26.

Du Colombier, P. *Paroles Françaises*, April 27.

T., J. *Heures Nouvelles*, April 30.

Gros, G.-J. *Le Monde*, April 30.

Marchand, J.-J. *Juin*, April 30.

Zahar, M. *L'Arche*, No. 16.

Gauthier, M. *Opéra*, May 1.

Champigneulle, B. *XXe Siècle*, May 1.

Mornac, J. *France d'abord*, May 1.

Barotte, R. *Quatre et Trois*, May 1.

Estienne, C. *Combat*, May 5.

Pichard, J. *La Croix*, May 5.

Lahonce, G. *Heures Nouvelles*, May 7.

Lacombe, A. *Le Paysage*, May 9.

Hugault, H. *La Nation*, May 15.

Anon. *Lettres Françaises*, May 15.

Anon. *Arts*, May 17.

Anon. *Figaro*, May 23.

Palie, A. *Combat*, May 23.

Anon. *Libération*, May 23.

Anon. *Libé-Soir*, May 23.

Poulain, E. *Résistance*, May 23.

Lemonnier, P. *Arts*, May 24.

A., M. *Paris*, May 31.

Reed, J. K. *Art Digest*, June (on the Kleemann Galleries exhibition).

Loucheim, A. B. *Art News*, June.

Anon. *Art News*, June (on the Tate Gallery exhibition).

Anon. *Le Monde*, June 8.

Frost, R. *Art News*, July.

Venturi, L. *Lettere ed Arti* (Milan), July-August.

Marchiori, G. *Emporium* (Bergamo), July.

Anon. *Le Monde*, July 4.

George, W. *Opéra*, July 17.

Anon. *Newsweek*, July 29.

George, W. *Résistance*, August 2 (on Rouault as a Christian artist).

R., P. R. *Cahiers d'Art Sacré*, August-September.

Anon. *Harper's Bazaar*, September.

Rousselot, J. *Magasin du Spectacle*, September-October.

Cassou, J. *Art News*, November.

Duchemin, J. L. *Le Livre et ses Amis*, November and December (on the lawsuit).

Coutot, M. *Arts*, December 13.

1947

Pierre Matisse Gallery, New York. Catalogue of Rouault exhibition.

Morel, Abbé M. Foreword to G. Rouault, STELLA VESPERTINA, Paris, Drouin.

Duchemin, J. L. *Le Livre et ses Amis*, January and February (continuation of series begun in 1946).

Mičko, H. *Pracé* (Prague), January 30 (on the Prague exhibition).

Anon. *Parallèle* 50, February 8 (on the same).

Arland, M. Preface to the catalogue of the Rouault exhibition, Galerie Odette des Garets, Paris.

Reviews of the Galerie Odette des Garets exhibition:
George, W. *Le Matin*, February 11.
J., R. *Le Monde*, February 11.
Bouret, J. *Ce Soir*, February 12.
Dess, P. M. *Aux Ecoutes*, February 14.
Descargues, P. *Arts*, February 14.
Roger-Marx, C. *Spectateur*, February 18.
Gros, G. J. *Une Semaine de Paris*, February 19.

Arland, M. *Soleils*, Vol. I, p. 40.

Anon. *Art News*, February (on Rouault's stained-glass).

Anon. *Gazette de Liège*, February 28 (on Rouault and Gromaire).

Arland, M. *Hommes et Mondes*, March (on Rouault and Kandinsky).

Anon. *Time*, March 3 (on the lawsuit).

Savary, L. *Tribune de Genève*, March 7.

Audin, J.-L. *Echo d'Oran* (Algeria), March 8.

Gibian, V. *America*, March 8.

Anon. *Littéraire*, March 15 (on Rouault, Waroquier, and Gromaire).

Nardy, C. *Bohême*, March.

On the lawsuit:

 Anon. *Figaro, Ce Matin, Parisien Libéré, Dépêche de Paris, Ordre, L'Aurore, Ce Soir, Le Pays, France Libre, Libération, L'Epoque, L'Aube*, March 20.

 Dorival, B. *Nouvelles Littéraires*, March 20.

 Descargues, P. *Arts*, March 21.

 Degand, L. *Lettres Française*, March 21.

 Vialatte, A. *Spectateur*, March 25.

 Dorival, B. *Bulletin des Musées de France*, Vol. XII, No. 5.

Van Eck, G. *Maandblad van Beeldenden Kunsten*, pp. 243–45.

Chastel, A. *Vie, Art, Cité* (Geneva), pp. 2–4.

Morel, Abbé M. *Études*, Vol. 283, pp. 188–91.

Coutot, M. *Arts de France*, Nos. 15–16 (on Rouault and Vollard).

Cogniat, M. *Vrai* (Brussels), December 14.

1948

Venturi, L. GEORGES ROUAULT, Paris, Skira.

Morel, Abbé M. Preface to the catalogue of the Rouault retrospective, Kunsthaus, Zurich.

Couturier, M. A. *L'Art Sacré*, pp. 109–10 (on the church at Assy).

George W. *Figaro Littéraire*, January 3 and 10.

Ivanof, A. *Il Messagero Veneto* (Venice), January 27.

Caso, P. *La Volonté* (Brussels), February 7.

Perocco, G. *Pomeriggio* (Bologna), April 30.

Apollonio, U. *Il Giornale di Trieste*, May 4.

Chevalier, D. *Arts*, May 28 (on the Zurich exhibition).

Barrat, R. *Témoignage Chrétien*, June 4.

Marchiori, G. *Il Mattino del Popolo* (Venice), July 20.

Hurethal, F. *Les Arts et la Vie*, August.

Anon. *Gazette du Palais*, September 11 and 13 (on the lawsuit).

Tappolet, W. *Du*, September.

San Lazzaro, G. di. *Il Giornale della Sera* (Rome), November 20.

On the exhibition of the *Miserere* at the Galerie Odette des Garets, Paris:

 Douaire, R. P. *Liturgical Art*, May.

 René-Jean. *Le Monde*, December 9.

 Moussinac, L. *Lettres Françaises*, December 9.

 Devoluy, J. *New York Herald Tribune*, December 17.

 Morel, Abbé M. *Vrai* (Brussels), December 28.

1949

Lehmann, L. Preface to the catalogue of the circulating exhibition of the *Miserere*, museums of Antwerp, La Louvière, Liège, Ghent, Rotterdam, Lille, Arras, Amiens, Besançon, Mulhouse.

Martin, K. Preface to the catalogue of the same exhibition, museums of Karlsruhe, Munich, Fribourg.

Courtney, J. *Bulletin of the Art Association* (Indianopolis), p. 194.

Roger-Marx, C. *La Gazette des Beaux-Arts*, Vol. 35, pp. 288–94.

Colleye, H. *La Métropole* (Antwerp), January 8.

Anon. *Esprit*, February (on the burning of Rouault's paintings).

Cogniat, R. *La Métropole*, February 2.

Borgeaud, G. *La Vie Intellectuelle*, March.

Arland, M. *Hommes et Mondes*, March.

Treich, L. *Le Soir* (Brussels), March 29.

Taillandier, Y. *Etudiantes*, April.

Lampe, J. *Wiener Tageszeitung* (Vienna), April 8.

Young, S. *Les Beaux-Arts* (Brussels), April 8.

Elgar, F. *Carrefour*, April 13.

Velle, M. *Le Drapeau Rouge* (Brussels), April 13.

Chabot, G. *Arts* (Brussels), June 9.

Reardon, E. J. *Catholic World*, October.

1950

Brion, M. GEORGES ROUAULT, Paris, Braun.

Mornand and Thomé. VINGT ARTISTES DU LIVRE.

Brest, J. R. Preface to the catalogue of the exhibition of the *Miserere*, Galeria Witcomb, Buenos Aires.

Régamey, R. P. Preface to the catalogue of the exhibition of French religious art, Rome, Florence, Milan.

Pernoud, R. *Art Sacré*, January.

Champigneulle, B. *Ecclesia*, April.

H. Ch. *L'Alsace*, May 13.

Roosval, J. *Dagens Nyheter Torsdagen* (Stockholm), June 15.

Maroni, M. *Corriere del Ticino*, September 2.

1951

Lassaigne, J. ROUAULT, Paris, Skira.

Cassou, J. Preface to the catalogue of the exhibition "Art Sacré," Musée National d'Art Moderne, Paris.

Dorival, B. Preface to the catalogue of the same exhibition, Eindhoven.

Arland, M. *Hommes et Mondes*, pp. 294–98.

Baucher, R. *Synthèses*, No. 56, pp. 218–25.

Reviews of the exhibition in Sweden:

 Berg, Y. *Dagens Nyheter*, January 25.

 Nasslund, G. *Stockholm Tidningen*, January 25.

 Palmgren, N. *Stockholm Tidningen*, January 25.

 Johansson, G. *Svenska Dagbladet*, January 31.

 Bredberg, G. *Svenska Morgenbladet*, February 7.

 Hjern, Kjell. *Konstrevy*, No. 2.

Montalais, J. de. *Samedi-Soir*, May 26.

Pichard, J. *La Croix*, August 26.

Dorival, B. *Les Musées de France*.

Thierry, R. *Ouest-France*, October 25.

Morel, Abbé M. *Études*, November (on the *Miserere*).

1952

Maulnier, T. Preface to the catalogue of the exhibition of the *Miserere*, Galerie Louis Carré, Paris.

Morris, W. Magazine of Art, Vol. 45, pp. 99–108 (on parallels between Rouault and Faulkner).

Dorival, B. *La Table Ronde*, No. 58, pp. 175–80.

Zervos, C. *Cahiers d'Art*, Vol. 27, pp. 101–104.

Ulatowski, J. *Preuves*, No. 21, pp. 58–59.

Cogniat, R. *Arts Plastiques*, No. 4, pp. 253–58.

Chastel, A. *Médecine de France*, No. 37.

Calmel, O. P. *La France Catholique*, January 11 (on the *Miserere*).

Elgar, F. *Carrefour*, March 5.

Salles, G. and Venturi, L. Prefaces to the catalogue of the Rouault exhibition, Palais des Beaux-Arts, Brussels, and Stedelijk Museum, Amsterdam.

Reviews of the Brussels and Amsterdam exhibitions:

Sosset, L.-L. *Beaux-Arts* (Brussels), March 21 (special issue devoted to Rouault).

Bernard, C. *La Nation Belge*, March 22.

Seaux, J. *Le Peuple* (Brussels), March 24.

Tellier, J.-L. *Vers l'Avenir* (Namur), March 26.

Sosset, L.-L. *Nouvelle Gazette de Bruxelles*, March 27.

Chabot, G. *La Croix du Nord* (Lille), March 30.

Colleye, H. *La Revue Générale* (Brussels).

Van Lier, H. *La Revue Nouvelle*, May 15.

Niehans, K. *De Telegraaf* (Amsterdam), May 17.

Wentinck, C. *Elsevier's Weekblad* (Amsterdam), May 17.

Engelman, J. *Vaterland*, May 21.

Kat, O. B. de. *Haarlem's Dagblad*, June 14.

Doelman, C. *De Groene Amsterdammer*, June 29.

Salles, G. and Venturi, L. Prefaces to the catalogue of the Rouault exhibition, Musée National d'Art Moderne, Paris.

Reviews of the Paris exhibition:

Chastel, A. *Le Monde*, July 9.

Besson, G. *Lettres Françaises*, July 11.

Roger-Marx, C. *Figaro Littéraire*, July 12.

Favre, L.-P. *Réforme*, July 19.

Falgairolle, A. de. *Le Provençal*, *July 20*.

Rollin, J. *Le Patriote de Saint-Etienne*, July 25.

Carney, P. *New York Herald Tribune*, July 26.

Delange, R. *Diario do Norte*, July 10 (on Rouault and Moreau).

Lake, C. *Christian Science Monitor*, August 23.

Brécy, R. *Aspects de la France*, September 19.

Schlocker, G. *Tages Anzeiger* (Zurich), September 19.

Bex, M. *Journal Musical Français*, September 25.

Gilles-Guilbert, C. *Correio da Manha* (Rio de Janeiro), October 4.

Dorival, B. *Figaro Littéraire*, October 13 (on Rouault and Bonhomme).

Chabot, G. *Beaux-Arts* (Brussels), November 7 (on Rouault as writer and poet).

Lerrant, J.-J. *Progres de Lyon*, November 7.

Champigneulle, B. *O Promeiro do Janeiro* (Porto), December 12.

1953

Maritain, J. Preface to the catalogue of the Rouault exhibition, Museum of Art, Cleveland; Museum of Modern Art, New York; County Museum, Los Angeles.

Arland, M. Preface to the catalogue of the Rouault exhibition, National Museum, Tokyo, and Museum, Osaka.

Pichard, J. *L'Art de l'Eglise*, No. 1 (special issue on Rouault).

Sciortino, G. *Fiera Letteraria* (Rome), March 8.

Bell, C. *Apollo*, October.

Mizue (Tokyo), November (special issue on Rouault).

Dorival, B. *Revue des Arts*, December.

Lansner, K. *Kenyon Review*, No. 3.

1954

Maritain, J. ROUAULT, New York, Abrams (with a note on Rouault's graphic art by W. S. Lieberman).

Finne, F. *Kunsten Idag*, No. 2, fasc. 28 (Oslo) (special issue with a foreword by Rouault).

Fels, F. *Arts*, Vol. V., Nos. 3–4.

Perocco, G. *Emposium*, Vol. 119, pp. 262–68.

Dorfles, G. *Letteratura*, Nos. 8–9, pp. 198–20.

Gengaro, M. L. *Humanitas*, Vol. IX.

Morel, Abbé M. Preface to the catalogue of the Rouault exhibition, Galleria d'Arte Moderna, Milan.

Reviews of the Milan exhibition:

Bernardi, M. *La Stampa*, April 22.

Borgese, L. *Corriere della Sera*, April 22.

Branz, S. *Il Gazzettino*, April 25.

Catania, F. *L'Ordine*, April 28.

Dragone, A. *Tutti*, May 2.

Carrieri, R. *Epoca*, May 2.

Baroni, C. *La Rocca*, May 15.

Gioseffi, D. *Il Giornale di Trieste*, May 26.

Baroni, C. *Il Popolo*, June 3.

Marussi, G. *Fiera Letteraria*, June 6.

Guzzi, V. *Il Tempo*, July 5.

Catania, F. *Corriere di Catania*, July 12.

1955

Dorival, B. CINQ ÉTUDES SUR GEORGES ROUAULT, Paris Editions universitaires.

Narkniss, M. Preface to the catalogue of the Rouault exhibition, Bezalel National Museum, Jerusalem.

H., J. C. *La Voix du Nord*, February 25.

Rothenstein, J. *Museums Journal*, March.

Smith, E. *Baltimore Museum News*, October.

1956

Dorival, B. GEORGES ROUAULT, Geneva, Éditions René Kister.

Coquet, D. J. Preface to the catalogue of the Rouault exhibition, Galerie Creuzevault, Paris.

Descargues, P. *Lettres Françaises*, May 24.

Cartier, J. A. *Jardin des Arts*, June.

Huyghe, R. Preface to the catalogue of the Rouault exhibition, Musée Toulouse-Lautrec, Albi.

Reviews of the Albi exhibition:

Poulain, G. *Dépêche du Midi*, July 11.

Desvoisins, J. *Dépêche du Midi*, July 22.

Poulain, G. *Lettres Françaises*, July 25.

Chastel, A. *Le Monde*, July 27.

Barotte, R. *Paris-Presse l'Intransigeant*, August 17.

Amunategui, F. *Dimanche-Matin*, October 14.

1957

Ferrarino, L. *Fiera Letteraria*, January 6.

Grenier, J. *L'Oeil*, April.

Y., V. *Arts*, June.

Dorival, B. *Informations Catholiques Internationales*, September 15.

Maritain, J. *Plastica* (Bogotá), October-December.

1958

Fukushima, S. GEORGES ROUAULT, Tokyo.

Aubert, J. *France-Amérique*, February 13.

Boatto, A. *Giornale del Mattino* (Florence), February 13.

France, J. M. *Het Parool* (Amsterdam), February 13.

Roger-Marx, C. *Ouest-France*, February 14.

Lerrant, J.-J. *Progrès de Lyon*, February 14.

Chastel, A. *Le Monde*, February 14.

Ganne, G. *L'Aurore*, February 14.

Martinie, A. H. *Le Parisien Libéré*, February 14.

Kiehl, R. *Dernières Nouvelles d'Alsace*, February 14.

Hermann, R. *La Croix*, February 14.

Colacicchi, G. *La Nazione*, February 14.

Cavalli, G. C. *Il Resto del Carlino* (Bologna), February 14.
Guzzi, V. *Il Tempo*, February 14.
Giannelli, D. *Il Popolo*, February 14.
Dragone, A. *Il Popolo Nuovo*, February 14.
Carluccio, L. *Gazzetta del Popolo*, February 14.
B., P. *Der Tag*, February 14.
Kinkel, H. *Stuttgarter Zeitung*, February 14.
Plünnecke, E. *Stuttgarter Nachrichten*, February 14.
Orth, R. *Bonner Rundschau*, February 14.
Darle, J. *L'Humanité*, February 14.
Rauschning, H. *Der Abend* (Berlin), February 14.
Anon. *The Times* (London), February 14.
Barotte, R. *Paris-Presse l'Intransigeant*, February 15.
T., C. *Il Giornale d'Italia*, February 15.
Hoff, C. *Der Tagesspiegel* (Berlin), February 15.
Tellier, J.-L. *Vers l'Avenir* (Namur), February 16.
Poulain, G. *La Dépêche du Midi*, February 16.
D., H. *New York Times*, February 16.
Barotte, R. *Le Provençal*, February 16.
Chabot, G. *La Métropole* (Antwerp), February 17.
Barotte, R. *Sud-Ouest*, February 18.
R., C. C. *Landeszeitung* (Lüneburg), February 18.
Jansen, E. *Neue Zeit* (Berlin), February 18.
Marc, A. *La Meuse* (Liège), February 19.
Elgar, F. *Carrefour*, February 19.
Courthion, P. *Arts*, February 19 (with articles by others in same issue).
Descargues, P. *Lettres Françaises*, February 20.
Fosca, F. *Tribune de Genève*, February 20.
Jansen, E. *Die Union*, February 20.
Chabrun, J.-F. *L'Express*, February 20.
S., P. E. *Aux Ecoutes*, February 21.
Guichard-Meili, J. *Témoignage Chrétien*, February 21.
Sosset, L. L. *Beaux-Arts* (Brussels), February 21.
Bessèges, A. *La France Catholique*, February 21.
Fumet, S. *Témoignage Chrétien*, February 21.
Aubertin, J. *Lumière*, February 22.
Ponente, N. *Attualitá*, February 22.
Ponente, N. *Il Punto*, February 22.
Venturi, L. *L'Espresso*, February 23.
Getlein, F. *Milwaukee Journal*, February 27.
Espezel, P. d'. *Aspects de la France*, February 28.
Rolin, B. *Beaux-Arts*, February 28.
Charensol, G. *Revue des Deux-Mondes*, March 1.
Kotula, A. *Zycie Literackie* (Cracow), March 2.
Turowicz, J. *Tygodnik Powszedni* (Cracow), March 2.
Morero, V. *La Voce del Popolo*, March 8.
Corosi, L. *Primeiro do Janeiro* (Porto), March 19.
Creuzeau, J.-M. *L'Homme Nouveau*, March 23.
Eeckhout, P. *Beaux-Arts* (Brussels), March 28.
Bracchi, L. *Corriere della Valtellina*, March 29.
Evere, J. *Slowo Powszechne* (Warsaw), March 30.
Fouchet, M.-P. *La Nef*, March.
Secrétan, J. *Gazette de Lausanne*, April 3.
Anon. *Kumamoto*, April 28.
Anon. *Minami Nippon*, April 28.
Anon. *Nishi Nippon Shi*, April 28.
Ganne, G. *Jardin des Arts*, April.
Morel, Abbé M. *Etudes*, April.
Anon. *Vogue*, April (with a photograph of Moreau's pupils).
Cabanne, P. *Lectures pour Tous*, April.

Barotte, R. *Le Provençal*, October 5 (on Rouault and Lehmann).
Venturi, L. *La Biennale di Venezia* (on Rouault and social revolt).

1959
Venturi, L. ROUAULT, Geneva, Skira.
Gauthier, R. *Nice-Matin*, January 25.
Coquelin, M. *Combat*, July 21.
McCue, G. *St. Louis Post Dispatch*, October 30.
Fumet, S. *La Croix*, October 30.

1960
Benesch, O., Dorival, B., and Vallery-Radot, J. Prefaces to the catalogue of the Rouault exhibition, The Albertina, Vienna.
Brun, Mgr. P. de. Poem in catalogue of the Rouault exhibition, The Dublin Building Centre, Dublin.
Dorival, B. Preface to the catalogue of the Rouault exhibition, Musée Cantini, Marseilles.
Guichard-Meili, J. *Témoignage Chrétien*, February 12.
D., M. *Gazetta Musical e de Todas* (Lisbon), March.
Muschik, J. *Neues Österreich*, March 6.
Koller, E. *Salzburger Nachrichten*, March 7.
Zettl, W. *Oberösterreichische Nachrichten*, March 10.
Real, A., *Diario de Noticias* (Lisbon), March 24.
Monteverdi, M. *L'Educatore italiano*, April 1.
W., J. *Irish Times*, May 5.
M., I. *Irish Independent*, May 20.
Cartier, J. A. *Combat*, June 6.
Barotte, R. *Le Provençal*, June 13 and 14.
Rouvier, C. *Le Provençal*, June 14.
Elgar, F. *Carrefour*, June 16.
Besson, G. *Lettres Françaises*, June 16.
Perruchot, H. *Le Méridional*, June 19.
Cingria, H. *Lettres Françaises*, June 23.
Cherpin, J. *Arts*, July 6.
Guichard-Meili, J. *Témoignage Chrétien*, July 15.
d'Yvoire, J. *Radio-Ciné-Télévision*, July 31.
Ashberg, J. *New York Herald*, August 17.
Toussaint, F. C. *France-Observateur*, August 24.
Marinelli, G. *La Voce Republica* (Rome), September 2.
Minarelli, L. *Il Piccolo Sera* (Trieste), September 8.
The New Yorker, November 5.
C. Z. O. *Pictures on Exhibit*, November.
Arland, M. *Plaisir de France*, December.
Arland, M. *Nouvelle Revue Française*, December.

1961
Roulet, C. ROUAULT, SOUVENIRS, La Bibliothèque des Arts Neuchâtel et Paris.
Crastre, V. *Les Cahiers du Sud*, No. 361, 161.
Zvěřina, F. *Státni nackladatelství Krásné literatury a umění* (Prague).
Chastel A. *Le Monde*, January 6.
Mauriac, C. *Le Figaro*, January 11.
George, W. *Combat*, January 30.
Petit, H. *Nouvelles Littéraires*, February 2.
G., C. *La Métropole* (Antwerp) February 4.
Cartier, J.-A. *Le Méridional* (Marseille), February 12.
Informations Catholiques Internationales, February.
Flory, E.-B. *La France Catholique*, March 3.
Francia, E. *Il Popolo* (Rome), March 4.
Boisdeffre, P. de. *Le Journal de Genève*, April 30.
Chabot, G. *Les Cahiers de la Biloque* (Ghent), May-June.

Chabot, G. *Beaux-Arts* (Brussels), September 22.
De Gentenaar (Ghent), September 25.
K., S. *Het Volk* (Ghent), September 25.
A., V. *Vooruit* (Ghent), September 25.
Cavens. *La Flandre Libérale*, September 25.
V., B. *La Métropole* (Ghent), September 26.
R., C. *La Voix du Nord*, September 26.
Colleye, H. *La Métropole* (Antwerp), September 30.

L., D. H. *La Libre Belgique*, October 4.
Caso. P. *Le Soir* (Brussels), October 8.
Le Figaro, November 7.
Malvaux, H. *Le Berry Républicain*, December 1.

1962
Yanagi, M. ROUAULT, Tokyo, Misuzu.
Traversi, G. *Visto* (Milan), January 1.

Exhibitions

1895 Paris, Salon des Champs-Elysées
1896 Paris, Salon des Champs-Elysées
1897 Paris, Salon des Champs-Elysées
       Paris, Salon de la Rose Croix (12 works)
1899 Paris, Salon des Champs-Elysées
1900 Paris, Salon des Champs-Elysées
1901 Paris, Salon des Champs-Elysées
1903 Paris, Salon d'Automne
1905 Paris, Salon des Indépendants
1906 Paris, Galerie Berthe Weil
1908 Paris, Salon d'Automne
1909 Paris, Salon des Indépendants
1910 Paris, Galerie Druet (first one-man show: 121 paintings, 8 drawings, 3 pieces of pottery executed by A. Metthey)
1911 Paris, Salon d'Automne
       Paris, Salon des Indépendants
       Paris, Galerie Druet (45 paintings, 58 pieces of pottery)
1912 Paris, Salon des Indépendants
       Paris, Galerie Druet
1920 Paris, Galerie La Licorne
1922 Paris, Galerie Barbazanges (pastels)
1924 Paris, Galerie Druet (88 paintings and 8 ceramics dating from 1897 to 1919)
1925 Berlin and Dusseldorf, Flechtheim Gallery
1926 Paris, Salon des Indépendants
       Paris, Galerie des Quatre Chemins
1927 Paris, Galerie Bing
1929 Paris, Galerie des Quatre Chemins (watercolors and gouaches)
1930 New York, Brummer Gallery
       Chicago, Arts Club
       London, St. George's Gallery
       Munich, Neumann Gallery
       Paris, Art Vivant
1931 Paris, Galerie des Quatre Chemins
       New York, Demotte Gallery
       Brussels, Galerie Schwarzenberg
       Geneva, Musée de l'Athenée

1933 New York, Pierre Matisse Gallery
       New York, Julien Levy Gallery
1934 Paris, Beaux-Arts, "Les Fauves"
1935 Northampton, Mass., Smith College Museum of Art
       London, Mayor Gallery
1936 Paris, Galerie Kaganovitch (Galerie du Portique)
       New York, Bignou Gallery, "Modern French Tapestries from the Collection of Mme. Paul Cuttoli"
1937 Paris, Musée du Petit-Palais, "Les Maîtres de l'Art Indépendant" (a separate room devoted to 42 works by Rouault)
       New York, Pierre Matisse Gallery
       London, Mayor Gallery
1938 Basel, Kunsthalle (with Vlaminck and Dufy)
       London, Alex Reid & Lefevre Ltd., "The Tragic Painters"
       London, Leicester Galleries
       Pittsburgh, Carnegie International Exhibition
       New York, Museum of Modern Art (graphic works)
       Paris, Galerie Zak
1939 New York, Bignou Gallery
       New York, Pierre Matisse Gallery
1939 London, Zwemmer Gallery
       Paris, Galerie O. Petrides
1940 Los Angeles, Dalzell Hatfield Gallery
       New York, Buchholz Gallery
       New York, Bignou Gallery
       London, Redfern Gallery
1940–1941 Boston, Institute of Modern Art,
       Washington, Phillips Memorial Gallery
       San Francisco, Museum of Art
1941 New York, Marie Harriman Gallery
       New York, Guy E. Mayer Galleries
1942 Paris, Galerie Louis Carré (10 paintings)
1945 New York, Museum of Modern Art (161 paintings, prints, stage designs, and tapestries)
       Chicago, Renaissance Society
1946 London, Tate Gallery, "Braque and Rouault" (14 paintings and 25 prints from the *Miserere*)

Paris, Galerie Drouin, "Pour un Art Religieux" (17 paintings, 30 prints)
Paris, Galerie Bing (with Modigliani, Soutine, and Utrillo)
New York, Galerie St. Etienne
New York, Kleemann Galleries
Westwood, Calif., James Vigeveno Galleries
1947 Prague, Gallery of the Intellectuals' Circle (10 paintings, 25 prints)
New York, Pierre Matisse Gallery
Paris, Galerie Odette des Garets
1948 Zurich, Kunsthaus (retrospective: 184 paintings, gouaches and watercolors; monotypes, lithographs and etchings)
Venice, Biennale (25 paintings)
Paris, Galerie Odette des Garets (showing of the entire *Miserere*)
1949–1950 Antwerp, La Louvière, Liège, Ghent, Rotterdam, Lille, Arras, Amiens, Besançon, Mulhouse, Karlsruhe, Munich, Fribourg (circulating exhibition of 26 paintings and prints from the *Miserere*)
1950 Buenos Aires, Galeria Witcomb (the *Miserere*)
Rome, Florence, Milan (exhibition of French religious art, including prints from the *Miserere*, paintings and enamels)
Paris, Galerie Marigny (15 early works)
1951 Stockholm, Gallery Samlaren, and Goteborg, Museum of Art (16 paintings and some prints)
Paris, Musée National d'Art Moderne, and Eindhoven, Museum of Modern Art, "Art Sacré" (with 22 paintings by Rouault)
Paris, Galerie de France (enamels of Ligugé)
1952 Brussels, Palais des Beaux-Arts, and Amsterdam, Stedelijk Museum (78 paintings and prints)
Paris, Galerie Louis Carré (second showing of the *Miserere*)
Paris, Musée National d'Art Moderne (104 paintings, prints, ceramics, stained-glass windows, enamels and tapestries)
1953 Cleveland, Museum of Art, and New York, Museum of Modern Art (67 paintings and prints); Los Angeles, County Museum (the same, with 90 paintings)
Tokyo, National Museum, and Osaka, Museum (85 paintings, prints)

1954 Milan, Galleria d'Arte Moderna (114 paintings, prints, ceramics, stained-glass windows, enamels and tapestries)
1955 Jerusalem, Bezalel National Museum (prints)
1956 Paris, Galerie Creuzevault (enamels and prints)
Albi, Musée Toulouse-Lautrec (47 paintings, watercolors, gouaches, drawings, pastels, prints from the *Miserere*)
1957 Rome, Galleria Odyssia (enamels)
Geneva, Museum, Print Room (paintings, etchings, lithographs)
1958 Delft, Gemeente Museum, "Modern Religious Art" (numerous works of Rouault)
Fribourg, Museum of Art and History (prints in black-and-white and in color)
Lausanne, Galerie Vallotton (prints)
Paris, Bibliothèque Nationale, "42nd Exhibition of the Society of Painters and Print-Makers: Homage to Rouault"
Paris, Galerie Le Garrec (lithographs)
Tokyo, "Homage to Rouault"
1960 Brest, Bibliothèque Municipale (etchings and lithographs)
Vienna, The Albertina (278 graphic works and drawings)
Dublin, The Dublin Building Centre (14 paintings and the *Miserere*)
Paris, Galerie Creuzevault (23 paintings and prints)
Marseilles, Musée Cantini
Assisi, "Pro Civitate Christiana" (paintings and prints)
Paris, Musée National d'Art Moderne, "Les Sources du XXe Siècle" (with 10 paintings by Rouault)
1961 Ghent, Musée des Beaux-Arts, "Hommage à Rouault" (76 works)
Los Angeles, County Museum (200 prints)
1961–1962 Tokyo and Kyoto (exhibition of French art in Japan, including 4 paintings, 2 washes, and 6 prints)
1962 Basel, Galerie Beyeler (47 works)

The exhibitions of the *Miserere* have been too numerous to permit listing all of them. They have followed one another continuously since 1948 in the United States, Canada, France, The Netherlands, Belgium, Germany, Austria, Italy, Spain, Portugal, Japan, Yugoslavia, Israel, etc.

Index

PHOTOGRAPHIC SOURCES

The black-and-white photographs reproduced in this book were generously supplied by Mlle. Isabelle Rouault. Some of them date from the first decades of this century, and others suffered the vicissitudes of wartime invasion. It seems pointless, therefore, to try to indicate in detail only the few sources that are known or still exist. We gratefully list the following sources of photographs, with the number of photographs from each source given in parentheses:

A.C.L., Brussels (1); The Rouault family archives, Paris (74); Archives photographiques des Musées Nationaux, Paris (1); Ina Banoy, Paris (2); André Barry, Paris (1); Bernheim Jeune, Paris (34); Berry-Hill Galleries, New York (1); Galerie Beyeler, Basel (1); Galerie Bing, Paris (2); Bonhétal, Paris (3); Brennwasser, New York (2); Rudolph Burckhardt, New York (2); Paul Bytebier, Brussels (19); André Caillet, Paris (5); Alfred Carlebach, London (1); Galerie Louis Carré, Paris (14); Catherineau, Lille (1); Cauvin, Paris (1); Yvonne Chevalier, Paris (275); Galerie Henri Creuzevault, Paris (4); Walter Dräyer, Zurich (41); Floyd Faxon, Los Angeles (1); Giraudon, Paris (10); Roger Hauert, Paris (3); Yves Hervochon, Paris (3); Florence Homolka (1); Hurault, Saint-Germain-en-Laye (11); Interfoto, Venice (2); Kunsthaus, Zurich (2); Laniepce, Paris (1); N. Mandel, Paris (1); Pierre Matisse Gallery, New York (1); André Mornay, New York (1); Musée d'Art et d'Histoire, Geneva (1); Musée d'Avalon (1); Museum of Modern Art, New York (1); National Gallery, London (1); O.E. Nelson, New York (2); Öffentliche Kunstsammlung, Basel (3); Papillon, Paris (4); Perls Galleries, New York (2); Piaget, Saint Louis (1); Poplin, New York (2); Galerie Romanet, Paris (3); Walter Rosenblum, New York (3); Maurice Routhier, Paris (1); San Francisco Museum of Art (1); Statens Museum for Kunst, Copenhagen (1); Stedelijk Museum, Amsterdam (1); Taylor & Dull, New York (1); Galerie Tooth, London (1); Marc Vaux, Paris (37); Vizzavona, Paris (11); Ambroise Vollard: The Rouault family archives, Paris (185); Wadsworth Atheneum, Hartford (1); Galerie Zak, Paris (3).